Asset Management and International Capital Markets

This innovative volume comprises a selection of original research articles offering a broad perspective on various dimensions of asset management in an international capital market environment. The topics covered include risk management and asset-pricing models for portfolio management, performance evaluation and performance measurement of equity mutual funds as well as the wide range of bond portfolio management issues.

Asset Management and International Capital Markets offers interesting new insights into state-of-the-art asset-pricing and asset management research with a focus on international issues. Each chapter makes a valuable contribution to current research and literature, and will be of significant importance to the practice of asset management.

This book is a compilation of articles originally published in *The European Journal of Finance.*

Wolfgang Bessler is Professor of Finance and Banking at the Justus-Liebig-University of Giessen, Germany. His research interests includes corporate finance, empirical capital market research, securities markets, and asset management. He is a member of the editorial board of *The European Journal of Finance* and associate editor of the *Journal of International Financial Markets, Institutions, and Money*, amongst others.

Wolfgang Drobetz holds the Chair for Corporate Finance and Ship Finance at the University of Hamburg, Germany. His research interests are corporate finance, asset-pricing, and asset management. He is a member of the editorial board of *The European Journal of Finance* and served as co-President of the European Financial Management Association (EFMA).

Chris Adcock is Professor of Financial Econometrics at the University of Sheffield, UK. His research interests are in portfolio selection and asset-pricing theory and the development of quantitative techniques for portfolio management. He has acted as an advisor to a number of international investment managers. He is founding Editor of *The European Journal of Finance* and has been an associate editor of several finance journals.

T0371732

Asset Management and International Capital Markets

Edited by
Wolfgang Bessler, Wolfgang Drobetz and Chris Adcock

Routledge
Taylor & Francis Group

LONDON AND NEW YORK

First published in paperback 2024

First published 2013
by Routledge
4 Park Square, Milton Park, Abingdon, Oxon OX14 4RN

and by Routledge
605 Third Avenue, New York, NY 10158

Routledge is an imprint of the Taylor & Francis Group, an informa business

© 2013, 2024 Taylor & Francis

This book is based on *The European Journal of Finance*, volume 15, issues 2, 3, 4, 5–6. The Publisher requests to those authors who may be citing this book to state, also, the bibliographical details of the special issue on which the book was based.

Publisher's Note
The publisher has gone to great lengths to ensure the quality of this reprint but points out that some imperfections in the original copies may be apparent.

British Library Cataloguing in Publication Data
A catalogue record for this book is available from the British Library

ISBN: 978-0-415-66187-4 (hbk)
ISBN: 978-1-03-292528-8 (pbk)
ISBN: 978-1-315-87278-0 (ebk)

DOI: 10.4324/9781315872780

Typeset in Times New Roman
by Taylor & Francis Books

Contents

Citation Information

The following chapters were originally published in *The European Journal of Finance*. When citing this material, please use the original issue information and page numbering for each article, as follows:

Chapter 1

From Markowitz to modern risk management
Gordon J. Alexander
The European Journal of Finance, volume 15, issues 5–6 (2009)
pp. 451–461

Chapter 2

Long-horizon consumption risk and the cross-section of returns: new tests and international evidence
Joachim Grammig, Andreas Schrimpf and Michael Schuppli
The European Journal of Finance, volume 15, issues 5–6 (2009)
pp. 511–532

Chapter 3

Performance measures and incentives: loading negative coskewness to outperform the CAPM
Alexandros Kostakis
The European Journal of Finance, volume 15, issues 5–6 (2009)
pp. 463–486

Chapter 4

Conditional performance evaluation for German equity mutual funds
Wolfgang Bessler, Wolfgang Drobetz and Heinz Zimmermann
The European Journal of Finance, volume 15, issue 3 (2009)
pp. 287–316

Chapter 5

Conditioning information in mutual fund performance evaluation: Portuguese evidence
Paulo Armada Leite and Maria Ceu Cortez
The European Journal of Finance, volume 15, issues 5–6 (2009)
pp. 585–605

Chapter 6

Performance and characteristics of mutual fund starts
Aymen Karoui and Iwan Meier
The European Journal of Finance, volume 15, issues 5–6 (2009)
pp. 487–509

Chapter 7

Individual home bias, portfolio churning and performance
Lars Nordén
The European Journal of Finance, volume 16, issue 4 (2010)
pp. 329–351

Chapter 8

Diversification benefits for bond portfolios
Wassim Dbouk and Lawrence Kryzanowski
The European Journal of Finance, volume 15, issues 5–6 (2009)
pp. 533–553

Chapter 9

*International bond diversification strategies: the impact
of currency, country, and credit risk*
Mats Hansson, Eva Liljeblom and Anders Löflund
The European Journal of Finance, volume 15, issues 5–6 (2009)
pp. 555–583

Chapter 10

*The performance of investment grade corporate bond funds:
evidence from the European market*
Leif Holger Dietze, Oliver Entrop and Marco Wilkens
The European Journal of Finance, volume 15, issue 2 (2009)
pp. 191–209

Introduction

Wolfgang Bessler, Wolfgang Drobetz and Chris Adcock

Asset Management and International Capital Markets contains a selection of original research articles that were first published in the *European Journal of Finance*. The majority of the articles are from a 2010 special issue of the Journal. The three additional articles were published in various issues of the Journal in 2009 and 2010. The objective of this book is to provide the reader with a broad perspective on different dimensions of asset management in an international capital market environment. The topics include risk management and asset-pricing models for portfolio management, performance evaluation and performance measurement of equity mutual funds as well as a wide range of bond portfolio management issues.

On May 29–30 2008, the conference 'Asset Management and International Capital Markets' took place in Frankfurt am Main in Germany. This conference was jointly organized by Wolfgang Bessler (Justus-Liebig-University, Giessen), Wolfgang Drobetz (University of Hamburg), and Jan Pieter Krahnen (Goethe University Frankfurt and CFS). The objective of this two-day conference was to bring together academics and members of the asset management industry to focus on state-of-the-art academic research in the areas of investment management and international capital markets. This special issue of the *European Journal of Finance* includes seven selected articles covering a wide spectrum of investment topics ranging from risk management, performance measurement, fund characteristics and consumption risk to fixed income portfolio management. The other papers were published in regular issues of the *European Journal of Finance* and are included to enhance the perspective of asset management topics covered in the book. All papers were subject to the rigorous refereeing process of this journal.

The first paper *'From Markowitz to modern risk management'* by Gordon Alexander extends and formalizes the ideas presented in the author's conference keynote speech. It starts with a review of the value-at-risk (VaR) concept as a measure of risk. It proceeds by focusing on the adequacy of a VaR measure and the impact on the investment outcomes of a portfolio manager who is subject to a VaR constraint. It turns out that a wide range of efficient low-risk portfolios can become infeasible under this constraint and that the manager might be forced to choose a portfolio with an unnecessarily high standard deviation. As a remedy, Alexander proposes the conditional value-at-risk (CVaR) as an alternative risk measure, which takes the shape of the return distribution below the VaR into account. The use of CVaR with properly chosen bounds avoids the perverse result that a riskier portfolio might be selected. Alexander also provides a brief review of current risk management systems in the banking industry and reveals that even the combination of the conventional VaR measure with commonly used stress tests cannot adequately determine minimum capital requirements because bank trading books usually contain short positions. Again, the CVaR measure is an important extension to the currently employed methodologies.

The second paper *'Long-horizon consumption risk and the cross-section of returns: New tests and international evidence'* by Joachim Grammig, Andreas Schrimpf, and Michael Schuppli addresses the question whether including long-run risk into the Consumption Capital Asset Pricing Model (CCAPM) helps to alleviate standard asset pricing puzzles. Equilibrium asset returns depend on investors' expectations about both short- and long-run changes in consumption growth. Therefore, the covariance of returns with contemporaneous consumption growth alone might understate the risk perceived by investors. The authors use German, British, and US data and extend the model of Parker and Julliard (2005). Their results indicate that this approach does not help to explain the cross-section of asset returns. However, including a proxy for long-run consumption risk reduces the estimated coefficient of relative risk aversion in the standard CRRA framework. Grammig, Schrimpf, and Schuppli conclude that more plausible parameter estimates rather than lower pricing errors can be regarded as the main achievement of the long-horizon CCAPM.

The third paper *'Performance measures and incentives: Loading negative coskewness to outperform the CAPM'* by Alexandros Kostakis examines strategies in the fund management industry in response to the adoption of simple performance measures. The starting point of his analysis is the notion that the use of conventional performance measures, such as the Sharpe ratio or Jensen's alpha, provide an incentive for fund managers to actively load on coskewness. Using a sample of UK equity unit trusts, Kostakis documents that managers indeed gamble with their investment strategies when simple performance benchmarks that are based only on the first two moments of the return distribution, are used. Indeed, there is evidence that coskewness risk is priced in the UK market and that most managers responded to these incentives by loading negative coskewness in order to capture a part of the corresponding premium. As an alternative performance measure the author suggests the intercept of the Harvey–Siddique two-factor asset-pricing model as more appropriate for prudent investors because it incorporates conditional skewness.

The fourth paper entitled *'Conditional performance evaluation for German equity mutual funds'* by Wolfgang Bessler, Wolfgang Drobetz and Heinz Zimmermann investigates the conditional performance of a sample of German equity mutual funds covering the period from 1994 to 2003 by using both the beta-pricing approach and the stochastic discount factor (SDF) framework. On average, mutual funds cannot generate large enough excess returns relative to their benchmark to cover their total expenses. Compared to unconditional alphas, fund performance sharply deteriorates when we measure conditional alphas. Given that stock returns are to some extent predictable based on publicly available information, conditional performance evaluation raises the benchmark for active fund managers because it gives them no credit for exploiting readily available information. Underperformance is more pronounced in the SDF framework than in beta-pricing models. The fund performance measures derived from alternative model specifications differ depending on the number of primitive assets taken to calibrate the SDF as well as the number of instrument variables used to scale assets and/or factors.

The fifth paper *'Conditioning information in mutual fund performance evaluation: Portuguese evidence'* by Paulo Leite and Maria Céu Cortez analyzes the unconditional and conditional performance of a sample of Portuguese mutual funds in a beta-pricing framework. They report evidence that mutual fund managers do not outperform the market, presenting negative or neutral performance. They also show the importance of incorporating conditioning information in performance evaluation models, as there is evidence of both time-varying betas and alphas related to the public information variables. It is also shown that the number of lags to be used in the stochastic detrending procedure is a critical choice, as it will impact the significance of the conditioning information. Finally, compared to the unconditional performance evaluation models, Leite and Cortez observe that the conditional models generally lead to a slight improvement of the performance estimates and of the explanatory power of the models.

The sixth paper *'Performance and characteristics of mutual fund starts'* by Aymen Karoui and Iwan Meier investigates the performance and the portfolio characteristics of newly launched US equity mutual funds. Compared with existing funds, these new funds initially generate a superior risk-adjusted performance. There is also evidence for short-term persistence among top-performing fund starts. At the same time, however, a large number of top-performing funds over the first 3 years drop directly to the bottom decile over the subsequent 3 years. This decline in performance cannot be explained by diseconomies of scale alone as these funds mature and grow in size. Karoui and Meier's results suggest that the initially favourable performance is to some extent attributable to the risk taking behaviour but are not the consequence of superior skills. Specifically, they document that fund starts exhibit higher ratios of unsystematic to total risk. Moreover, portfolios of new funds tend to be less diversified in terms of the number of stocks and their industry composition, and they are also invested in smaller and less liquid stocks.

The seventh paper by Lars Nordén entitled *'Individual home bias, portfolio churning and performance'* investigates the economic consequences of individual investors' home bias and portfolio churning in their personal pension accounts. The empirical analysis is carried out within a Heckman style two-stage framework to account for selection bias with respect to individuals' investment activity, and to allow for an endogenously determined home bias, portfolio churning, and performance. Results indicate that home bias leads to a lower risk-adjusted performance. Home-biased individuals' relatively inferior performance originates from insufficient risk-reduction due to a lack of international diversification. A higher degree of portfolio churning also deteriorates performance, despite the fact that churning is not associated with any direct transaction costs. However, home-biased individuals do not churn portfolios as often as individuals with a larger share of international asset holdings, which diminishes the negative effects of home bias on performance. Overconfidence is driven by a return-chasing behavior, where overconfident individuals favor international assets with high historical returns. Individuals with actual skill are more often men than women, are not tempted by high historical returns, and use international assets for the right reason – diversification.

The eighth paper *'Diversification benefits for bond portfolios'* by Wassim Dbouk and Lawrence Kryzanowski analyzes the diversification of bond portfolios. Differentiating the investment opportunity set by issuer type, credit rating, and time-to-maturity, the authors examine the minimum portfolio size required to capture significant diversification benefits. Their results indicate that these characteristics of bonds as well as the metric used to measure the marginal benefits of additional diversification determine the minimum portfolio size. In general, the marginal benefits of further diversification are optimized with portfolio sizes of 25 to 40 bonds. Nevertheless, in contrast to equity portfolios, the untapped benefits of full diversification are still large at these portfolio sizes. Dbouk and Kryzanowski hypothesize that this result may explain the empirical observation that bond funds, unlike equity funds, generally are value-neutral for unit holders based on gross returns and value-destroying based on net returns.

The ninth paper *'International bond diversification strategies: The impact of currency, country, and credit risk'* by Mats Hansson and Eva Liljeblom provides evidence on the diversification benefits of international investments in government bonds, emerging market debt and corporate bonds from the perspective of bond investors domiciled in different countries. In the spirit of De Roon, Nijman, and Werker (2001), they conduct mean–variance spanning and intersection tests that incorporate short-sale restrictions. The authors' empirical results indicate that government bonds of developed markets do not improve the risk-return spectrum, irrespective of whether currency risk is hedged or not. In contrast, currency hedged international corporate bonds and in particular emerging market debt, significantly shift the mean–variance frontier for a developed market investor and offer substantial diversification benefits even in the presence of short-sale constraints. From a practical perspective, it is interesting to observe that for the subset of developed markets' government bonds, the passive global benchmarks perform as well as the optimized portfolios.

The last paper *'The performance of investment grade corporate bond funds: evidence from the European market'* by Leif Holger Dietze, Oliver Entrop and Marco Wilkens examines the risk-adjusted performance of mutual bond funds offered in Germany which exclusively invest in the 'rather new' capital market segment of euro-denominated investment grade corporate bonds. The bond funds are evaluated employing a single-index model and several multi-index and asset-class factor models. In contrast to earlier studies dealing with (government) bond funds, the authors account for the specific risk and return characteristics of investment grade corporate bonds and use both rating-based indices and maturity-based indices, respectively, in their multi-factor models. In line with earlier studies they find evidence that corporate bond funds, on average, underperform the benchmark portfolios. Moreover, there is not a single fund exhibiting a significantly positive performance. These results are robust to the different models. Finally, Dietze, Entrop, and Wilkens examine the driving factors behind fund performance. They investigate the influence of several fund characteristics, particularly fund age, asset value under management, and management fee as well as the impact of investment style on the funds' risk-adjusted performance. They find indications that funds having lower exposure to BBB-rated bonds, older funds, and funds charging lower fees, attain a higher risk-adjusted performance.

This selection of papers on *'Asset management and international capital markets'* provides the reader with interesting new insights into state of-the-art asset-pricing and asset management research with a focus on international issues. All papers make valuable contributions to the literature and are of significant importance to the practice of asset management. We would like to thank Emily Ross of the publisher for her encouragement to produce this book and, as with the special issue itself, we express our gratitude to all the authors and referees.

We hope that you will enjoy reading these articles originally published in the *European Journal of Finance*.

From Markowitz to modern risk management

Gordon J. Alexander

Department of Finance, University of Minnesota, Minneapolis, MN 55455, USA

Nobel Laureate Harry Markowitz is often referred to as the 'founder of Modern portfolio theory' and deservedly so given his enormous influence on the money management industry.[1] However, it is my contention that he should also be referred to as the 'founder of Modern Risk Management' since his contributions to portfolio theory formed the basis for how risk is currently viewed and managed. More specifically, Markowitz argued that a portfolio of securities should be viewed through the lens of statistics where the probability distribution of its rate of return is evaluated in terms of its expected value and standard deviation. Since the ultimate selection of a portfolio involves the evaluation and management of risk as measured by standard deviation, it is clear that Markowitz's process of portfolio selection represents the birth of modern risk management whereby risk is quantified and controlled. In this paper, I will first, introduce *value-at-risk* as a measure of risk and how it relates to standard deviation, the risk measure at the heart of the model of Markowitz. Second, I will similarly introduce *conditional value-at-risk* (also known as *expected shortfall*) as a measure of risk and compare it with VaR. Third, I will briefly introduce *stress testing* as a supplemental means of controlling risk and will then present my conclusions.[2]

1. Value-at-risk

In 1989, the CEO of J.P. Morgan Bank ('Morgan', now JPMorgan Chase) asked for a daily 4:15 pm report that detailed the market risk of the bank's trading portfolio. Morgan subsequently ended up using value-at-risk (VaR) as a measure of market risk, and set up a subsidiary in 1994 known as RiskMetrics that not only educated the global marketplace about VaR but also freely provided data via a website to assist institutions in the estimation of their own VaR. In 1998, the success of RiskMetrics Group led to its spinoff by Morgan and listing on the New York Stock Exchange under the ticker *RMG*. VaR has subsequently risen to such a high level of prominence as a measure of risk that it is now 'widely used by corporate treasurers and fund managers as well as financial institutions' (Hull 2007, 195).

Just what is VaR? Hull (2007, 477) defines VaR as 'a loss that will not be exceeded at some specified confidence level'. Since the user must specify a confidence level t and a time horizon, a portfolio p's VaR, denoted VaR_p, can be stated more formally as:

$$\text{VaR}_p = zS_p - E_p, \tag{1}$$

where z denotes the $(1 - t)$ quantile of the portfolio's return distribution, and S_p and E_p denote the portfolio's standard deviation and expected return, respectively, as measured over the specified time horizon.[3] Hence, a hypothetical portfolio whose annual return is normally distributed with a mean of 10% and a standard deviation of 20% would have an annual VaR based on a 99% confidence level of

$$2.33 \times 20\% - 10\% = 36.6\%. \tag{2}$$

For example, if the portfolio has a current market value of €1,000,000,000, then it has a 1% chance of losing at least €366,000,000 by the end of the year.

When evaluating any portfolio on the basis of the mean and standard deviation of its return distribution, it is common to plot the location of the portfolio in a two-dimensional diagram as indicated by, for example, point p in Figure 1. However, it is also quite easy to indicate any portfolio's VaR in the diagram by rewriting Equation (1) as:

$$E_p = zS_p - \text{VaR}_p. \tag{3}$$

Note that this equation corresponds to a straight line with a slope of z and vertical intercept of $-\text{VaR}_p$. Thus, the VaR of our hypothetical portfolio can be found by extending a line with a slope of 2.33 toward the vertical axis and noting that the intercept occurs at the value of -36.6. Since $-36.6\% = -\text{VaR}_p$, it can be seen that the portfolio has a VaR of 36.6%.

According to the Markowitz model, an investor seeks to identify his or her optimal portfolio from the set of all possible portfolios that can be formed from an arbitrary set of n securities. The process of identifying the optimal portfolio involves identifying the *mean–variance boundary*. Specifically, a portfolio p belongs to the mean–variance boundary if and only if, for some expected return E^*, p solves the following problem:

$$\text{Minimize } V \tag{4}$$

$$\text{Subject to} : E'W = E^* \tag{5}$$

$$W'\mathbf{1} = 1, \tag{6}$$

where W is an $n \times 1$ vector of weights representing the proportion of the investor's wealth that is to be invested in each one of the n securities; $V = W'CW$ is the variance of the portfolio with weight vector W; C is the $n \times n$ variance-covariance matrix; E is an $n \times 1$ vector of the expected returns of the n securities; and $\mathbf{1}$ is an $n \times 1$ unit vector. Black (1972) and Merton (1972) have shown that the portfolios solving this minimization problem for varying values of E^* lie on a hyperbola in mean–standard deviation space. The upper half of this boundary, beginning with the *minimum variance portfolio* ('MVP') is known as the *mean–variance efficient frontier* (or simply 'efficient frontier'). The punch line of the Markowitz model is that an expected utility maximizing

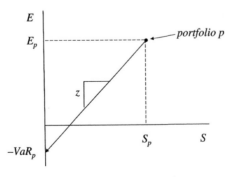

Figure 1. Representing a portfolio's VaR in mean–standard deviation space.

portfolio manager will select for investment a portfolio on the efficient frontier with the highest *certainty equivalent return* that is identified by the use of indifference curves.

Similarly, a portfolio p belongs to the *mean–VaR boundary* if and only if, for some expected return E^*, p solves the following problem:

$$\text{Minimize VaR} \tag{7}$$

$$\text{Subject to}: E'W = E^* \tag{8}$$

$$W'I = 1, \tag{9}$$

where VaR is defined in Equation (1). Note that the mean–variance and mean–VaR boundaries are identical since minimizing VaR is equivalent to minimizing V for a given level of expected return since z and E^* are constants in the context of objective function (7).

This observation leads to the following two theorems.

THEOREM 1 *If the minimum VaR portfolio ('MVaRP') exists, then it is mean–variance efficient.*

This can be seen in Figure 2 by noting what happens when lines with slope z are extended from points on the mean–variance boundary to the vertical axis, beginning with the point $p1$ corresponding to MVP. In particular, at first these lines have higher vertical intercepts but then starting at point MVaRP ($p2$) the lines have continually lower intercepts. Remembering what was shown in Figure 1, it follows that point MVaRP corresponds to the portfolio with minimum VaR.[4] Accordingly, the *mean–VaR efficient frontier* is the upper part of the mean–VaR boundary, beginning at MVaRP. Theorem 2 follows directly:

THEOREM 2 *MVP is mean–VaR inefficient for any $t < 1$.*

Figure 3 shows why this is so. Specifically, MVP has a lower expected return than MVaRP as shown in Figure 2. This observation means that there are portfolios that have both higher expected returns and lower VaRs than MVP. Hence, it follows that MVP is mean–VaR inefficient and that, accordingly, the mean–VaR efficient frontier is a proper subset of the mean–variance efficient frontier.

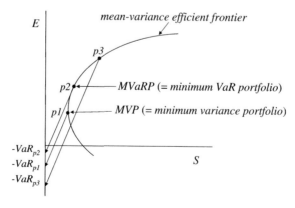

Figure 2. Comparing the minimum variance and minimum VaR portfolios.

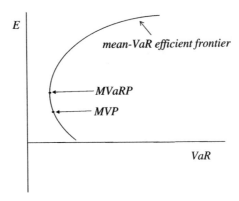

Figure 3. The mean–VaR efficient frontier.

What bearing do these observations have on the portfolio manager who uses the Markowitz mean–variance model for portfolio selection? Consider a situation at a bank such as JP Morgan Chase. To control the 'tail risk' of the bank's trading portfolio, it is reasonable to assume that the CEO has some notion of a maximum level of VaR that he or she believes is acceptable.[5] It follows that the portfolio manager must identify the *VaR-constrained mean–variance boundary*. Specifically, a portfolio p belongs to this boundary if and only if, for some expected return E^*, p solves the following problem:

$$\text{Minimize } V \tag{10}$$

$$\text{Subject to : } E'W = E^* \tag{11}$$

$$W'1 = 1 \tag{12}$$

$$zS - E^* \leq B, \tag{13}$$

where B is the maximum level of VaR that is acceptable to the CEO. Note that the last constraint can be rewritten as $E^* \geq zS - B$. Using different values of E^*, the constraint forces the portfolio manager to select a portfolio on or above a line in mean–standard deviation space with an intercept of B and a slope of z.

Figure 4 indicates what the CEO hopes will happen with this constraint. In this 'good' scenario, the CEO is preventing the portfolio manager from selecting a portfolio with a relatively high standard deviation since such portfolios, plotting below the constraint, are now infeasible. However, Figure 5 shows a possible 'bad' scenario. Here the CEO is also preventing the portfolio manager from selecting a portfolio with a relatively small standard deviation (such as MVP) as they are infeasible. Hence, it is possible that the portfolio manager might be forced to select a portfolio with a larger standard deviation than he or she would select if unconstrained.

At this point it is tempting to say 'so what?' Figure 6 shows why this is an undesirable outcome. Consider efficient portfolios S and L, where S has a relatively small expected return and standard deviation and L has a relatively large expected return and standard deviation. It follows that their cumulative probability distributions intersect at only one point. This point corresponds to a confidence level of t_i. Imagine that the CEO is using a confidence level of t, which means that the VaRs of S and L are equal to VaR$_S$ and VaR$_L$, respectively, where VaR$_S$ > VaR$_L$. While the portfolio manager would like to select S, he or she will be forced to select portfolio L when

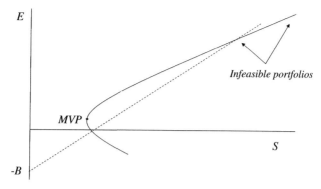

Figure 4. What the CEO hopes will happen with a VaR constraint.

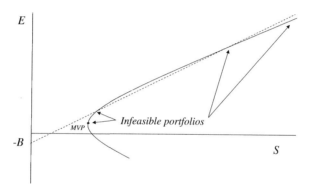

Figure 5. What can happen with a VaR constraint.

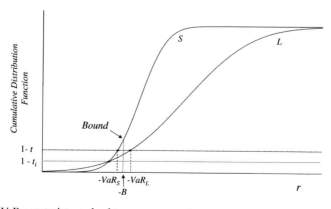

Figure 6. Using a VaR constraint can lead to a perverse outcome.

a bound of B is imposed where $\text{VaR}_S > B > \text{VaR}_L$. However, a visual inspection of the figure indicates that L has a higher probability of 'extremely bad outcomes', where 'extremely bad outcomes' are those that occur at a point below where the two distributions intersect. Thus, a VaR constraint can have the perverse effect of forcing the portfolio manager to select a portfolio with a higher probability of incurring an 'extremely bad outcome'. A remedy that has been proposed to ameliorate this problem is discussed next.

2. Conditional value-at-risk

The conditional value-at-risk (CVaR) of a portfolio is defined as its expected return, conditioned on the return being less than or equal to its VaR.[6] Using a 99% confidence level as an example, VaR involves measuring the upper end of the bottom 1% tail of the distribution, whereas CVaR measures the expected value of the 1% tail. More precisely, to calculate a portfolio's CVaR, one must first solve the following equation for k:

$$-\left[\int_{-\infty}^{-z} x\phi(x)\,\mathrm{d}x\right]\bigg/ (1-t) = k, \tag{14}$$

where $\phi(x)$ is the standard normal probability function. Having solved Equation (14) for k, portfolio p's CVaR is

$$\text{CVaR}_p = kS_p - E_p. \tag{15}$$

Note that $\text{CVaR}_p > \text{VaR}_p$ since $k > z$.[7]

Continuing with the earlier example involving a hypothetical portfolio whose annual return is normally distributed with a mean of 10% and a standard deviation of 20%, it can be determined from Equation (14) that based on a 99% confidence level, $k = 2.67$. Hence, the portfolio's annual CVaR is equal to $2.67 \times 20\% - 10\% = 43.4\%$. Accordingly, the portfolio with a current market value of €1,000,000,000 is expected to suffer a loss of €434,000,000 by the end of the year if a 'bad event' occurs, where a bad event is one that causes the portfolio to lose an amount equal to or greater than its VaR of €366,000,000.

Similar to VaR, it is quite easy to indicate a portfolio's CVaR in a mean–standard deviation diagram. Note that Equation (15) can be written as:

$$E_p = kS_p - \text{CVaR}_p. \tag{16}$$

Like Equation (3), this equation corresponds to a straight line with a slope of k and vertical intercept of $-\text{CVaR}_p$. As illustrated in Figure 7, our hypothetical portfolio's CVaR can be found by extending a line with a slope of 2.67 toward the vertical axis and noting that the intercept occurs at the value of -43.4. Since $-43.4\% = -\text{CVaR}_p$, it can be seen that the portfolio has a CVaR of 43.4%. Furthermore, since VaR and CVaR are found by extending lines from the point where the portfolio plots in the figure and that the line for CVaR has a slope greater than the slope of the line for VaR, the intercept for CVaR lies below the intercept for VaR.

Continuing with the VaR analogy, portfolio p belongs to the *mean–CVaR boundary* if and only if, for some expected return E^*, p solves the following problem:

$$\text{Minimize CVaR} \tag{17}$$

$$\text{Subject to}: \boldsymbol{E'W} = E^* \tag{18}$$

$$\boldsymbol{W'1} = 1, \tag{19}$$

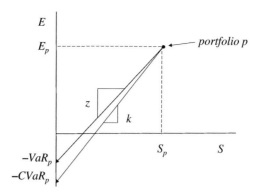

Figure 7. Representing a portfolio's CVaR in mean–standard deviation space.

where CVaR is defined in Equation (15). Furthermore, the mean–variance, mean–VaR, and mean–CVaR boundaries are identical since minimizing CVaR and VaR are equivalent to minimizing V for a given level of expected return. Theorem 3 follows.

THEOREM 3   *If the minimum CVaR portfolio ('MCVaRP') exists, then it is mean–variance efficient.*

This can be seen in Figure 8 by noting what happens when lines with slope k are extended from points on the mean–variance boundary to the vertical axis, beginning with the point $p1$ corresponding to MVP. As with VaR, at first these lines have higher vertical intercepts but then starting at point MCVaRP ($p2$) the lines have continually lower intercepts. Thus, point MCVaRP corresponds to the portfolio with minimum CVaR.[8] Accordingly, the *mean–CVaR efficient frontier* is the upper part of the mean–CVaR boundary, beginning at MCVaRP. Theorem 4 follows directly.

THEOREM 4   *MVP is mean–CVaR inefficient for any $t < 1$.*

Figure 9 shows that since MVP has a lower expected return that MCVaRP, it follows that MVP in *mean–CVaR* inefficient.

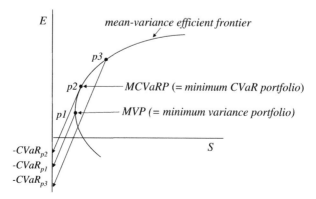

Figure 8. Comparing the minimum variance and minimum CVaR portfolios.

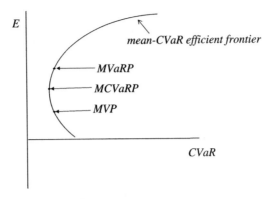

Figure 9. The mean–CVaR efficient frontier.

Note that the lines drawn in Figure 9 to determine the location of MCVaRP have a steeper slope (k) than the slope (z) of the lines drawn in Figure 3 to determine the location of MVaRP. This means that the expected return of MVaRP is greater than the expected return of MCVaRP. Theorem 5, illustrated in Figure 9, follows:

THEOREM 5 *MVaRP is mean–CVaR efficient for any $t < 1$.*

It follows that MCVaRP is mean–VaR inefficient since MCVaRP lies below MVaRP.

Similar to what was shown before with VaR, consider a portfolio manager at a bank who uses the Markowitz mean–variance model for portfolio selection but has a CEO who wishes to control the 'tail risk' of the bank's trading portfolio by setting a bound on the acceptable level of CVaR. It follows that the portfolio manager must identify the *CVaR-constrained mean–variance boundary.* Specifically, a portfolio p belongs to this boundary if and only if, for some expected return E^*, p solves the following problem:

$$\text{Minimize } V \tag{20}$$

$$\text{Subject to} : \boldsymbol{E'W} = E^* \tag{21}$$

$$\boldsymbol{W'1} = 1 \tag{22}$$

$$kS - E^* \le B. \tag{23}$$

Note that the last constraint can be rewritten as $E^* \ge kS - B$, indicating that the portfolio manager must select a portfolio on or above a line in mean–standard deviation space with an intercept of B and a slope of k, but now $k > z$.

Figure 10 expands upon Figure 5 to show that a 'good' scenario is still possible when the same bound B is used. As with a VaR constraint, the CVaR constraint prevents the portfolio manager from selecting a portfolio with a relatively high standard deviation since such portfolios, plotting below the constraint, are now infeasible. Note that the CVaR constraint is 'tighter' than the VaR constraint in the sense that some previously feasible high-risk portfolios are now infeasible if the same bound B is utilized for both constraints since the slope of the CVaR constraint (k) is steeper than the slope of the VaR constraint (z). However, when examining Figure 5 it is also straightforward to see that a 'bad' scenario is more acute with CVaR relative to VaR in that more low-risk portfolios are precluded from consideration given the steeper slope when the same bound

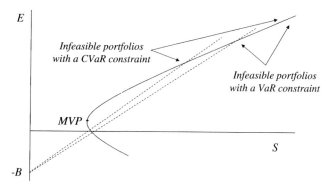

Figure 10. Comparing VaR and CVaR constraints with the same bound.

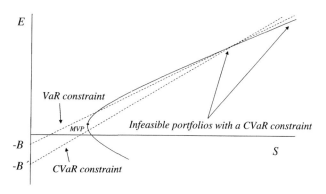

Figure 11. Comparing VaR and CVaR constraints with different bounds.

B is used. However, Figure 11 shows that it is possible to use a larger bound B' so that it precludes the same high-risk portfolios as the VaR constraint but does not preclude the low-risk portfolios from selection, unlike the VaR constraint.

3. Stress testing

A portfolio that passes stress testing and is thus permissible for selection is one whose returns under certain scenarios are equal to or greater than some bound. These scenarios can be historical ones, such as the crash in the US stock market in October 1987 and the terrorist attacks in New York City on 11 September 2001, or hypothetical ones, such as a major earthquake or a sudden large drop in the value of the US dollar.[9] Portfolios whose estimated return, conditioned on each scenario i happening, must constraints of the following form satisfy in order to be feasible:

$$W'R_i \geq T, \quad i = 1, 2, \ldots, m, \tag{24}$$

where R_i is an $n \times 1$ vector of estimated returns on the n securities conditioned on scenario i occurring and T is the bound; there are m scenarios.[10]

Note how a portfolio can have its 'tail risk' limited by using stress testing in conjunction with either VaR or CVaR by adding Equation (24) to the optimization problems given in

Equations (10)–(13) and (20)–(23), respectively. Furthermore, Bloomberg machines can be used to conduct stress tests of assorted historical events as well as calculate the VaR of a portfolio using several confidence levels.

4. Conclusion

Modern risk management has it roots in the mean–variance model of Markowitz, but focuses on the bottom tail of the return distribution in evaluating and controlling the risk of a portfolio. The most commonly used measure of tail risk, VaR, focuses on the upper end of the tail distribution in that it represents the return of the $(1 - t)$ quantile of the return distribution for a confidence level of t. However, it has been criticized by ignoring the shape of the tail distribution below this level. In response, CVaR has been advocated by, for example, Artzner et al. (1999), since it measures the expected value of the tail distribution. It can be viewed as the expected return of the portfolio, conditioned on a 'bad event' occurring. In this address, I show how VaR and CVaR of a portfolio can be represented in the mean–standard deviation diagram of Markowitz. I also show how the mean–variance, mean–VaR, and mean–CVaR boundaries are equivalent, but that the mean–VaR efficient frontier is a proper subset of the mean–CVaR efficient frontier, which in turn is a proper subset of the mean–variance efficient frontier.

Continuing, I show that portfolio managers who are limited to selecting a portfolio whose VaR does not exceed some bound could be forced to choose a portfolio that has not only a larger standard deviation but also a larger CVaR. Thus, a risk management system based on VaR could lead to the perverse result of a riskier portfolio being selected. However, the use of CVaR, with properly chosen bounds, avoids such a result.

International banks are currently required to use risk management systems based on VaR, with an amount of capital required for their trading portfolio being based on its magnitude. In addition, banks are required to have a rigorous stress testing system in place. This leaves open the question of whether a risk management system based on VaR and stress testing is as effective as one based on CVaR. In a recently completed working paper, Baptista, Yan, and I have used a simple model based on historical simulation to examine this question (see Alexander, Baptista, and Yan 2008). While the combination of VaR and stress testing seems to work well when short selling is not allowed, the combination can perform poorly when it is allowed. Since short selling is typically involved in trading portfolios, this raises serious concerns about the use of such risk management systems. When coupled with various implementation problems such as non-stationary distributions, increased liquidity problems during times of stress, acute estimation risk in modeling the tail distribution of a portfolio, and Black Swans ('unknown unknowns') of Taleb (2007), it is hardly surprising that Greenspan (2008) would comment that the current financial crisis 'will leave many casualties. Particularly hard hit will be much of today's financial risk-valuation system, significant parts of which failed under stress. … The problems, at least in the early stages of this crisis, were most pronounced among banks whose regulatory oversight has been elaborate for years'. While much work has been done to improve such systems, it is clear that much work remains to be done.

Acknowledgements

This paper is based on the Keynote Address given at the Asset Management and International Capital Markets Conference that was held in Frankfurt on 29 May 2008. The author is indebted to Alexandre M. Baptista for comments and many stimulating discussions on the topic.

Notes

1. Wikipedia, for example, makes such a reference to Markowitz: http://en.wikipedia.org/wiki/People_known_as_the_father_or_mother_of_something#Economics. Also see the press release announcing his being awarded the 1990 Alfred Nobel Memorial Prize in Economic Sciences: http://nobelprize.org/nobel_prizes/economics/laureates/1990/press.html.
2. My comments draw largely from Alexander and Baptista (2002, 2004, 2006). An excellent book on VaR, CVaR, and stress testing is Jorion (2007). Also see Crouhy, Galai, and Mark (2006) and Hull (2007).
3. Technically VaR is equal to $E_p - zS_p$. However, this typically produces a negative number. The desire to express VaR as a positive number results in Equation (1). It is also important to point out that Equation (1) and the subsequent analysis is based on the assumption that the portfolio's returns have a normal distribution (it is straightforward to show that similar results are obtained with a t-distribution).
4. Note that MVaRP might have an infinite expected return depending on the shape of the hyperbola and confidence level. I assume it has a finite expected return in all of my examples.
5. Motives for controlling the tail risk of the bank's trading portfolio are two-fold. First, it is a means of limiting the probability of default. Second, the bank's capital requirement is based in part on the VaR of its trading portfolio. For example, see Crouhy, Galai, and Mark (2006, 154–61) and the Basle Committee on Banking Supervision (2006), respectively. Also see Ball and Fang (2006) for a survey of the literature on VaR and bank regulation.
6. Due to the practice of expressing VaR and CVaR as positive numbers, technically $-$CVaR is the portfolio's expected return conditioned on the return being less than or equal to $-$VaR.
7. It is possible for a portfolio's VaR and CVaR to be equal when the lower mass of the probability density function is concentrated at the portfolio's VaR. That is, VaR = CVaR when the probability of observing a return less than the portfolio's VaR is zero. Since such distributions are highly unlikely, for expository purposes it is assumed that $CVaR_p > VaR_p$.
8. Note that MCVaRP might have an infinite expected return depending on the shape of the hyperbola and confidence level. I assume it has a finite expected return in all of my examples.
9. Banks are currently required to stress test their portfolios; see Basle Committee on Banking Supervision (2006) and Committee on the Global Financial System (2005).
10. The bounds can be of different values for the various scenarios; a constant bound is used here simply for expository purposes.

References

Alexander, G.J., and A.M. Baptista. 2002. Economic implications of using a mean-VaR model for portfolio selection: A comparison with mean-variance analysis. *Journal of Economic Dynamics and Control* 26: 1159–93.

Alexander, G.J., and A.M. Baptista. 2004. A comparison of VaR and CVaR constraints on portfolio selection with the mean-variance model. *Management Science* 50: 1261–73.

Alexander, G.J., and A.M. Baptista. 2006. Does the Basle Capital Accord reduce bank fragility? An assessment of the value-at-risk approach. *Journal of Monetary Economics* 53: 1631–60.

Alexander, G.J., A.M. Baptista, and S. Yan. 2008. Bank risk management with value-at-risk and stress testing: An alternative to conditional value-at-risk? Working Paper, Carlson School of Management, University of Minnesota, MN.

Artzner, P., F. Delbaen, J.-M. Eber, and D. Heath. 1999. Coherent measures of risk. *Mathematical Finance* 9: 203–28.

Ball, J., and V. Fang. 2006. A survey of value-at-risk and its role in the banking industry. *Journal of Financial Education* 32: 1–31.

Basle Committee on Banking Supervision. 2006. Basel II: International convergence of capital measurement and capital standards: A revised framework. http://www.bis.org/bcbs/.

Black, F. 1972. Capital market equilibrium with restricted borrowing. *Journal of Business* 45: 444–55.

Committee on the Global Financial System. 2005. Stress testing at major financial institutions: Survey results and practice. http://www.bis.org/cgfs/index.htm.

Crouhy, M., D. Galai, and R. Mark. 2006. *The essentials of risk management.* New York: McGraw-Hill.

Greenspan, A. 2008. We will never have a perfect model of risk. *Financial Times*, March 16. http://www.ft.com/cms/s/0/edbdbcf6-f360-11dc-b6bc-0000779fd2ac.html?nclick_check=1.

Hull, J.C. 2007. *Risk management and financial institutions.* Upper Saddle River, NJ: Pearson Prentice Hall.

Jorion, P. 2007. *Value at risk: The new benchmark for managing financial risk.* New York: McGraw-Hill.

Merton, R.C. 1972. An analytic derivation of the efficient portfolio frontier. *Journal of Financial and Quantitative Analysis* 7: 1851–72.

Taleb, N.N. 2007. *The Black Swan: The impact of the highly improbable.* New York: Random House.

Long-horizon consumption risk and the cross-section of returns: new tests and international evidence

Joachim Grammig[a], Andreas Schrimpf[b] and Michael Schuppli[c]

[a] Department of Economics, University of Tübingen, D-72074 Tübingen, Germany; [b] Centre for European Economic Research (ZEW, Mannheim), P.O. Box 10 34 43, D-68034 Mannheim, Germany; [c] Department of Economics, University of Münster, D-48143 Münster, Germany

This paper investigates whether measuring consumption risk over long horizons can improve the empirical performance of the consumption-based capital asset pricing model (CCAPM) for size and value premia in international stock markets (USA, UK, and Germany). In order to account for commonalities in size and book-to-market sorted portfolios, we also include industry portfolios in our set of test assets. Our results show that, contrary to the findings of Parker and Julliard [2005. Consumption risk and the cross-section of expected returns. *Journal of Political Economy* 113, no. 1: 185–222], the model falls short of providing an accurate description of the cross-section of returns under our modified empirical approach. At the same time, however, measuring consumption risk over longer horizons typically yields lower risk-aversion estimates. Thus, our results suggest that more plausible parameter estimates – as opposed to lower pricing errors – can be regarded as the main achievement of the long-horizon CCAPM.

1. Introduction

Understanding the behavior of asset prices and their relation to macroeconomic risks is one of the most fundamental issues in finance. As is well known, however, the consumption-based capital asset pricing model (CCAPM) as the traditional workhorse for studying this link has failed to explain a number of stylized facts in finance, such as the equity premium (Mehra and Prescott 1985), asset return volatility (Grossman and Shiller 1982), or value and size premia (Cochrane 1996; Lettau and Ludvigson 2001).[1] In this paper, we provide new evidence as to whether long-run consumption risk helps explain the cross-section of expected returns – especially value and size premia – in international stock markets. Our empirical approach follows Parker and Julliard (2005) in relating asset returns to consumption growth measured over longer horizons within a simple consumption-based framework with CRRA preferences.

We modify Parker and Julliard's empirical approach along two lines. First, we take into account recent criticism about the widespread use of size and book-to-market sorted portfolios in the empirical asset pricing literature (Phalippou 2007; Lewellen, Nagel, and Shanken 2007). In order to reduce the adverse effects of strong commonalities in size and book-to-market sorted portfolios, we follow the prescription of Lewellen, Nagel, and Shanken (2007) to include industry portfolios alongside with the conventionally used size and book-to-market portfolios. Second, we provide new international evidence by investigating the model's explanatory power for the cross-section of equity returns in the UK and Germany.

Our findings shed new light on the relative merits of the long-horizon (LH) CCAPM when it comes to explaining the cross-section of returns in international stock markets. First, we find that the model's ability to explain cross-sectional variation in returns is clearly limited when accounting for the common factor structure in size and book-to-market sorted portfolios. This result suggests that the good empirical performance on US test assets reported by Parker and Julliard (2005) may be overstated. Tests on size and book-to-market sorted portfolios from the UK and Germany corroborate the US evidence. Second, we find that measuring consumption risk over longer horizons typically yields lower risk-aversion estimates. Thus, our results suggest that more plausible parameter estimates – as opposed to a higher cross-sectional R^2 – can be viewed as the main achievement of the LH consumption-based approach.

The LH consumption-based approach is related to a growing body of theoretical literature on long-run consumption risk. Seminal work by Bansal and Yaron (2004) suggests that equilibrium asset returns depend on investors' expectations about both short- and long-run changes in consumption growth. Among other things, this result implies that the covariance of returns with contemporaneous consumption growth may understate the risk perceived by investors.[2] Even though the long-run risk framework has important implications for the explanation of risk premia and asset price fluctuations, previous empirical studies surveyed by Bansal (2007) have almost exclusively focussed on the US stock market. By estimating the model on UK and German portfolio returns, our paper explores the universality of the LH-CCAPM approach and, more generally, the role of long-run consumption risk in these markets.

This issue is particularly interesting since the countries considered in our study differ in several institutional respects. Banks play a central role in financial intermediation in Germany, whereas both the USA and the UK are known to have a market-based financial system (Allen and Gale 2001). There are also vast cross-country differences regarding the share of stocks in the net wealth position of households. Stock ownership is much more widespread in Anglo-Saxon countries where between one-third (UK) and half (USA) of all households directly or indirectly invest in equity. By contrast, only 17% of German households directly held stocks as of 1998, partly due to higher participation costs (Guiso, Haliassos, and Jappelli 2003). Among other things, households' stock holdings are crucially affected by a country's pension system. While many Americans and British rely on private mutual or pension funds for retirement saving (implying indirect stock ownership), Germans benefit from an extensive public pay-as-you-go pension system. As highlighted by Hamburg, Hoffmann, and Keller (2008), these factors may have an impact on households' consumption reaction to innovations in returns.[3]

Furthermore, some authors have argued that the well-known US 'equity premium puzzle' (i.e., the inability of the consumption-based approach to explain the high level of aggregate stock market returns compared with the T-Bill rate) may to some extent be due to extraordinarily high historical stock returns in the USA during the post-war period [See, e.g., the discussions in Cochrane (2007, 266) or Dimson, Marsh, and Staunton (2008)]. While the British stock market has performed equally well, the post WWII performance of German stocks has been lower. Hence, additional insights may be gained through a cross-country perspective.

The remainder of the text is structured as follows. Section 2 reviews the basic LH consumption risk approach and provides a discussion on the literature most closely related to our paper. Section 3 describes the empirical methods used for estimating and evaluating the different models. Section 4 presents the data and discusses empirical results. Finally, Section 5 concludes.

2. The LH consumption risk framework

2.1 *Parker and Julliard's approach*

This section briefly reviews the LH consumption-based asset pricing approach put forth by Parker and Julliard (2005). As a starting point, consider the traditional two-period consumption-based model. As is well known, the model implies Euler equations of the following form:

$$\mathbb{E}_t\left[\delta\frac{u'(C_{t+1})}{u'(C_t)}\ R^e_{t+1}\right] = 0, \tag{1}$$

where $u(\cdot)$ denotes current-period utility, δ the subjective time discount factor, and R^e_{t+1} the excess return on a risky asset. Empirical tests of consumption-based models are typically based on moment conditions implied by variants of Equation (1). Parker and Julliard (2005) use the model's first-order condition for the risk-free rate between points in time $t+1$ and $t+1+S$

$$u'(C_{t+1}) = \delta\mathbb{E}_{t+1}[R^f_{t+1,t+1+S}\ u'(C_{t+1+S})] \tag{2}$$

to substitute out period $t+1$ marginal utility in the above Euler equation. Assuming power utility and $\delta \approx 1$, Equation (1) can thus be rewritten as

$$\mathbb{E}_t[m^S_{t+1}\ R^e_{t+1}] = 0, \tag{3}$$

where $m^S_{t+1} = R^f_{t+1,t+1+S}((C_{t+1+S})/C_t)^{-\gamma}$ is the stochastic discount factor (SDF) and S denotes the horizon at which consumption growth is measured. As shown by Malloy, Moskowitz, and Vissing-Jørgensen (2008), a very similar SDF can be derived within the Epstein and Zin (1989) recursive utility framework of Hansen, Heaton, and Li (2008). Taking unconditional expectations and rearranging yield an expression for the expected excess return

$$\mathbb{E}[R^e_{i,t+1}] = -\frac{\mathrm{Cov}[m^S_{t+1}, R^e_{i,t+1}]}{\mathbb{E}[m^S_{t+1}]}, \tag{4}$$

which is similar to the case of the standard model except that the excess return now depends on its covariance with marginal utility growth over a longer time horizon. In other words, investors demand a higher risk premium on assets whose return is more positively correlated with consumption growth over a long horizon. Parker and Julliard (2005) refer to the covariance of an asset's excess return with the modified SDF as 'ultimate consumption risk'.

The model's asset pricing implications can be tested either by directly estimating the nonlinear specification given by Equation (3), or by using the representation given by Equation (4). Alternatively, the model can be estimated in its linearized form. Applying a first-order log-linear approximation of the SDF in the spirit of Lettau and Ludvigson (2001) yields

$$m^S_{t+1} = R^f_{t+1,t+1+S} - \gamma_S R^f_{t+1,t+1+S}\Delta c_{t+1+S}, \tag{5}$$

where $\Delta c_{t+1+S} = \ln(C_{t+1+S}/C_t)$ represents log consumption growth from t to $t+1+S$. Hence, the model using the linearized SDF in Equation (5) can be interpreted as a linear two-factor model. Furthermore, assuming the risk-free rate to be constant between t and $t+1+S$, the linear approximation reduces to a single factor model where the pricing kernel is a function of log consumption growth over long horizons.

2.2 *Related literature and further motivation*

An important aspect of the LH-CCAPM is that, in addition to retaining the parsimony of the power utility specification, it does not impair the basic assumptions of the consumption-based asset pricing framework. Yet, at the same time, the approach is consistent with various arguments why the covariance of an asset's return with contemporaneous consumption growth may understate its risk due to slow consumption adjustment. First, macroeconomic data on household consumption expenditure is difficult to obtain and survey-based quarterly statistics may not provide an accurate measure of consumption adjustment. Using LH consumption growth in empirical tests of the consumption-based framework may help to overcome the effect of measurement error in quarterly data.

Second, a wide range of factors not considered in the basic model, such as different sources of income, housing, and durable goods consumption, may enter the utility function. In this case, the utility function is nonseparable in that marginal utility with respect to one argument will always depend on the value of the other arguments. In addition, some of the consumption goods entering the utility function may involve a commitment (Chetty and Szeidl 2005). Obviously, the adjustment of durable goods and housing consumption requires households to incur considerable transaction costs. Moreover, many services such as telecommunications are typically subject to long-term contracts. These real-world features imply that aggregate consumption adjustment may be slow.

Third, due to market imperfections such as costs of gathering and processing information, agents' short-term behavior may deviate from utility-maximizing consumption smoothing. In the presence of such frictions, investors may not optimally adjust consumption or rebalance their portfolio if utility losses from nonoptimal behavior are small in magnitude (Cochrane 1989). Such 'near-rational' behavior appears plausible especially in the short run. Again, from an empirical point of view, the reaction of consumption to changes in aggregate wealth will probably not be reflected in quarterly observations, so that LH consumption growth provides a more exact measure of perceived consumption risk.

Furthermore, the CCAPM of Parker and Julliard (2005) is closely related to a growing body of literature suggesting that investors require a compensation for bearing long-run consumption risk in asset returns. Pioneering theoretical work by Bansal and Yaron (2004) models consumption and dividend growth as containing a small persistent predictable component. Therefore, current shocks to expected growth will affect expectations about consumption growth in both the short and long run. From a theoretical point of view, the proposed consumption and dividend process can be motivated by explicitly modeling a production economy as in Kaltenbrunner and Lochstoer (2007).[4] Bansal and Yaron (2004) show that in an economy with Epstein–Zin investor preferences, this additional source of risk helps to explain longstanding issues in finance such as the equity premium, low risk-free rates, high stock market volatility, and the predictive power of price–dividend ratios for LH stock returns. In addition, the long-run risk framework has strong implications for the cross-section of expected asset returns. If the representative agent is concerned about both short- and long-run consumption risk, she will require higher risk premia on assets that are correlated with long-run consumption growth. Modeling dividend and consumption growth as a vector autoregressive system, Bansal, Dittmar, and Lundblad (2005) determine the exposure of dividends to long-run consumption risk. They show that this exposure helps explain a large fraction of cross-sectional variation in returns across book-to-market, size, and momentum portfolios. Other recent papers documenting the relevance of long-run consumption risk for determining equilibrium asset returns include Bansal, Dittmar, and Kiku (2007), Hansen, Heaton, and Li (2008), Malloy, Moskowitz, and Vissing-Jørgensen (2008), and Colacito and Croce (2008).

In sum, a large body of evidence for the USA suggests that consumption growth measured over longer horizons may be an important risk factor explaining cross-sectional variation in returns. Indeed, Parker and Julliard (2005) show that the cross-sectional R^2 obtained when estimating the model on 25 US book-to-market and size portfolios increases with the horizon at which consumption growth is measured. Their nonlinear specification explains up to 44% of the cross-sectional variation in average excess returns for a horizon of 11 quarters. In this respect, the model's performance is similar to the conditional CCAPM of Lettau and Ludvigson (2001) and the Fama and French (1993) three-factor model. This finding suggests that long-run risk may help resolve the value premium puzzle.

Another prominent drawback of the canonical CCAPM with CRRA utility is that, given the observed risk premia, estimated coefficients of relative risk aversion are usually implausibly high (Hansen and Singleton 1983). This aspect is at the center of recent work by Rangvid (2008), who tests an international LH-CCAPM using world-consumption growth as a risk factor on excess aggregate stock market returns from 16 developed capital markets. The author shows that risk-aversion estimates for an internationally diversified investor decrease substantially to more plausible values if long-run consumption risk is taken into account. However, the beta-pricing version of the model has trouble explaining the cross-section of international stock index returns.

It is important to note that his empirical approach is based on the assumptions of an international representative investor, integrated financial markets, and purchasing power parity. This paper, in contrast, analyzes the ability of the LH-CCAPM to explain the individual cross-section of stock returns in three major stock markets. Besides requiring weaker assumptions, looking at only three countries enables us to use detailed consumption data that distinguish expenditure on nondurable goods and services from durable goods (rather than having to rely on measures of total consumption). Moreover, it allows us to pin down pricing errors for individual stock portfolios formed on characteristics such as size and book-to-market equity ratios, which are of particular interest in the empirical finance literature.

3. Empirical methodology

In this section we outline our empirical approach for exploring the performance of the LH consumption-based asset pricing framework. Moment restrictions necessary to estimate any model for the SDF by the generalized method of moments (GMM) can be derived from Euler equations similar to Equation (3). Nonetheless, we opt for the slightly different GMM estimation strategy employed by Parker and Julliard (2005), using moment conditions based on the expression for expected excess returns in Equation (4). There are three reasons for doing this: First, closely following Parker and Julliard's approach renders our empirical results comparable with theirs. Second, as we illustrate below, their approach allows us to empirically disentangle a model's ability to explain the equity premium from its cross-sectional explanatory power. Third, this approach provides an intuitive interpretation of our GMM estimation results: Using the moment restrictions in Equation (4) implies that the difference between empirical and theoretical moments can be interpreted as errors in expected returns, which in turn are proportional to pricing errors. These pricing errors will be directly comparable across models. More specifically, consider the vector of unconditional moment restrictions

$$\mathbb{E}[h(\Theta_{t+1}, \mu_S, \gamma_S, \alpha_S)] = 0, \tag{6}$$

where Θ_{t+1} represents the data (the vector of N test asset excess returns and consumption growth), whereas the model parameters are given as μ_S (mean of the SDF m_{t+1}^S) and γ_S (risk-aversion parameter of the representative agent). For the nonlinear model introduced in Section 2.1, the $(N + 1) \times 1$ empirical moment function $h(\cdot)$ is given by

$$h(\Theta_{t+1}, \mu_S, \gamma_S, \alpha_S) = \begin{bmatrix} R^e_{t+1} - \alpha_S \iota_N + \dfrac{(m^S_{t+1} - \mu_S)R^e_{t+1}}{\mu_S} \\ m^S_{t+1} - \mu_S \end{bmatrix}, \tag{7}$$

where R^e_{t+1} denotes the vector of N test asset excess returns, ι_N is an N-dimensional vector of ones, and the last moment condition is intended to identify the mean of the SDF. Following Parker and Julliard (2005) and Yogo (2006), we include an intercept parameter α_S in the moment function in Equation (7). When estimating a candidate model, this approach allows us to disentangle its predictive power for the overall level of stock returns compared with the risk-free rate (equity premium) from its cross-sectional fit across test assets. Since the point estimate for α_S will be expressed in units of expected returns, the parameter indicates the magnitude of a model's implied 'equity premium puzzle'. If the parameter is significant for a candidate model, this implies that this model has trouble explaining the excess returns of stocks over the risk-free rate.

We modify the estimation approach by Parker and Julliard (2005) in one important dimension. In a recent contribution, Lewellen, Nagel, and Shanken (2007) highlight statistical problems associated with the common use of size and book-to-market sorted portfolios in the empirical asset pricing literature. In particular, given the strong factor structure of these portfolios, Lewellen, Nagel, and Shanken (2007) point out that any model incorporating factors that are correlated with SMB and HML potentially produces a high cross-sectional R^2 when tested on these test assets. In order to avoid these problems, we expand the set of test assets to include industry portfolios along with the commonly used size and book-to-market sorted portfolios. This implies that our modified empirical approach provides a clearly tougher challenge for the candidate asset pricing models compared with Parker and Julliard (2005).

In addition to testing the nonlinear LH consumption-based model, we also compare the empirical performance of the linearized LH-CCAPM in Equation (5) with traditional factor models such as the CAPM and the Fama and French (1993) model. The moment function for the three candidate factor models differs slightly from the nonlinear model, reflecting the linear approximation of the SDF. Let f_{t+1} denote the vector of k factors, μ the vector of estimated factor means, and b the vector of coefficients measuring the marginal effect of the respective factors on the SDF. The $(N + k) \times 1$ moment function can then be written as

$$h(\Theta_{t+1}, \mu, b, \alpha) = \begin{bmatrix} R^e_{t+1} - \alpha_S \iota_N + R^e_{t+1}(f_{t+1} - \mu)'b \\ f_{t+1} - \mu \end{bmatrix}. \tag{8}$$

This moment function satisfies $N + k$ unconditional moment restrictions given by

$$\mathbb{E}[h(\Theta_{t+1}, \mu, b, \alpha)] = 0, \tag{9}$$

which can be used to estimate the parameters of the model by GMM. In this context, it is important to note that identification of the parameters of the linear model requires some normalization. Using demeaned factors in the moment function in Equation (8) achieves this, but it also implies that we have to correct standard errors for the fact that factor means are estimated along the way. Therefore, we use the augmented moment function in Equation (8), which imposes additional restrictions on the deviation of factors from their estimated means.[5]

In general, the GMM framework allows for various choices of the matrix determining the weights of individual moments in the objective function. As discussed in detail in Cochrane (2005, Chapter 11), the particular choice of weighting matrix affects both statistical properties and economic interpretation of the estimates. Even though second- or higher-stage GMM estimates based on the optimal weighting matrix of Hansen (1982) are efficient, they are difficult to interpret economically as they imply pricing some random combination of reweighted portfolios. Instead, relying on first-stage estimates with equal weights compromises efficiency while maintaining the economic interpretation of empirical tests. Therefore, our discussion of empirical results in Section 4 centers on first-stage GMM estimates.

As is customary in the literature on the evaluation of asset pricing models and anomalies, we also provide the cross-sectional R^2 as a measure of how well the particular model captures the variation of average returns across portfolios.[6] In order to take account of the methodological critique of the cross-sectional R^2 by Lewellen, Nagel, and Shanken (2007), we robustify our empirical approach by adding industry portfolios, and – most importantly – take the economic meaning of the point estimates seriously when evaluating the candidate asset pricing models.

In addition, we also report results from the 'test of overidentifying restrictions' based on iterated GMM estimation as a test of overall model fit. An alternative advocated by Hansen and Jagannathan (1997) is to use the inverse of the second moment matrix of returns as a first-stage weighting matrix. This approach allows us to compute the corresponding Hansen–Jagannathan (HJ) distance, which serves as an additional metric for model comparison.[7]

4. Empirical analysis

4.1 *Data*

This section provides a detailed overview of the data used in this paper. Data on personal consumption expenditure are available from national institutions in the respective country: the US Bureau of Economic Analysis (BEA), the UK Office for National Statistics (ONS), and the Federal Statistical Office (Destatis) in Germany. As is customary in the literature on consumption-based asset pricing, we use a measure of household's consumption of nondurable goods and services obtained from the official statistics.[8] We divide by quarterly population figures to express consumption in per capita terms. Finally, all consumption time-series are deflated by the respective consumer price index (CPI).

While data on different consumption categories (nondurables, durables, and services) are readily available at the quarterly frequency for both the USA and the UK, this is not the case for Germany. We, therefore, use detailed annual data on personal consumption expenditures for different items to construct the share of nondurables and services in total consumption per annum. In order to estimate quarterly per capita expenditure on nondurables and services, we assign the same share to all quarterly total expenditure observations within a given year. Another important aspect is the effect of Germany's reunification on consumption data. We correct for the negative outlier in the one-period (per capita) consumption growth rate due to the reunification using interpolation as in Stock and Watson (2003). Longer-horizon growth rates are then based on the corrected series. Our consumption data set covers the periods 1947:Q2–2004:Q3 for the USA, 1965:Q2–2003:Q4 for the UK, and 1974:Q2–2003:Q4 for Germany.

Our choice of test assets is mainly guided by two considerations. First, our aim is to analyze the ability of the LH-CCAPM to price the cross-section of stock returns in major financial markets outside the USA. Second, following the suggestions of Lewellen, Nagel, and Shanken (2007), we use a broad set of test assets including portfolios sorted on both book-to-market and size as well as industry. This choice is intended to avoid problems arising from strong commonalities in size and book-to-market sorted portfolios.

As is standard in the empirical finance literature, our set of test assets contains 25 US value and size portfolios introduced by Fama and French (1993). Similar portfolios capturing both size and value premia are constructed by Dimson, Nagel, and Quigley (2003) for the UK[9] and by Schrimpf, Schröder, and Stehle (2007) for Germany. The total number of listed stocks in the UK and Germany is much smaller than in the USA. Therefore, in both cases, stocks are sorted into only 16 portfolios in order to avoid potential biases in portfolio returns. For comparisons with traditional asset pricing models such as the CAPM and the Fama and French (1993) three-factor model, we obtain data on market returns, the excess return of small over big market capitalization firms (SMB), and the excess return of companies with high versus low book-to-market equity ratios (HML) from the same sources.

Returns on 10 US industry portfolios sorted according to SIC codes are available from Kenneth French's website.[10] In case of the UK, we use seven industry portfolios obtained from datastream which are available for the longest possible sample period matching the one of the other UK test assets. Our industry portfolios for the German stock market are obtained from the German Finance Database (Deutsche Finanzdatenbank) maintained at the University of Karlsruhe. The sample periods for test asset returns cover 1947:Q2–2001:Q4 for the USA, 1965:Q2–2001:Q1 for the UK, and 1974:Q2–2001:Q1 for Germany.[11] We compute excess returns on all portfolios using a country-specific proxy for the risk-free rate: for the USA and the UK, we use the 3-month T-bill rate. In the case of Germany, a 3-month money market rate from the time series database of Deutsche Bundesbank is used. Finally, we compute real returns on all risky and risk-free assets using the respective national CPI. We use these real returns in all of our empirical tests.[12]

4.2 *Empirical results: nonlinear model*

As pointed out in Section 3, we estimate the nonlinear LH-CCAPM for each of the three markets separately using the GMM. Our discussion of empirical results focuses on three aspects: a candidate model's ability to explain the equity premium ($\hat{\alpha}$), the plausibility of the estimated risk-aversion parameter ($\hat{\gamma}$), and its cross-sectional explanatory power as reflected by the cross-sectional R^2 and pricing error plots. In addition, we report results from J-tests based on iterated GMM estimates, the root mean squared error (RMSE) from first-stage GMM estimation, and the HJ-distance metric proposed by Hansen and Jagannathan (1997).

Our results for the USA, reported in Table 1, complement the evidence in Table 1 of Parker and Julliard (2005) and provide a reassessment of their findings.[13] It is important to keep in mind that we use an expanded set of test assets by adding 10 industry portfolios to the 25 Fama–French portfolios. As evinced by Table 1, the risk-aversion estimate for the standard CCAPM ($S = 0$) is rather large, mirroring previous results in the literature. It is worth noting, however, that the estimated RRA coefficient typically decreases to substantially lower values as we move from short- to long-term consumption risk. As is common in the empirical literature on consumption-based asset pricing models, standard errors are rather large, but it is worth noting that the precision of the estimates generally tends to increase with the horizon.[14] As the significant $\hat{\alpha}$ estimates show, a major limitation of the LH-CCAPM is the failure to explain the equity premium. In contrast to results reported by Parker and Julliard (2005), its magnitude hardly declines as the consumption growth horizon increases. Thus, the model leaves unexplained a substantial fraction of the excess return of stocks over the risk-free rate. The J-test rejects all short and LH specifications of the CCAPM.[15] Likewise, the consumption-based model is rejected by the test based on the HJ-distance for any horizon, but p-values are increasing as we extend the horizon. There is also slight

Table 1. Consumption risk and US stock returns – nonlinear LH-CCAPM.

Horizon	$\hat{\alpha}$ (standard error)	$\hat{\gamma}$ (standard error)	R^2	RMSE	HJ-distance (p-value)	J (p-value)
0	0.022	47.047	0.08	0.521	0.588	112.032
	(0.005)	(60.748)			(0.000)	(0.000)
1	0.019	29.839	0.09	0.518	0.586	106.706
	(0.005)	(29.742)			(0.001)	(0.000)
3	0.019	21.765	0.09	0.516	0.589	112.762
	(0.006)	(21.792)			(0.001)	(0.000)
5	0.018	20.357	0.11	0.512	0.586	109.375
	(0.005)	(18.600)			(0.005)	(0.000)
7	0.018	20.717	0.15	0.500	0.584	108.276
	(0.005)	(15.650)			(0.011)	(0.000)
9	0.020	20.512	0.18	0.491	0.584	110.046
	(0.004)	(12.487)			(0.014)	(0.000)
11	0.020	20.229	0.20	0.484	0.579	105.909
	(0.004)	(10.997)			(0.032)	(0.000)

Note: The reported values for $\hat{\alpha}$, $\hat{\gamma}$, R^2 and the RMSE are computed using equal weights across portfolios and large weight on the last moment (first-stage GMM with a prespecified weighting matrix). Standard errors are calculated using the procedure by Newey and West (1987) with $S + 1$ lags. The HJ-distance is based on first-stage GMM estimation using the weighting matrix proposed by Hansen and Jagannathan (1997) and p-values are obtained via simulation with 10,000 replications. The J-statistic is based on iterated GMM estimation. The sample period is 1947:Q2–2001:Q4 for returns and 1947:Q2–2004:Q3 for quarterly consumption.

evidence that the HJ-distance is lower in absolute terms for $S = 11$ compared with the standard CCAPM ($S = 0$).

Most importantly, however, the results presented in Table 1 suggest that the exclusive use of size and book-to-market portfolios [as in Parker and Julliard (2005)] overstates the empirical performance of the LH-CCAPM. If we include industry portfolios in our set of test assets, as advocated by Lewellen, Nagel, and Shanken (2007), we only find moderate improvements of the consumption-based asset pricing approach as the horizon of LH consumption risk increases. The estimated R^2 reaches a maximum of only 20% at a horizon of 11 quarters, which is half the value reported by Parker and Julliard (2005) for the same horizon. Therefore, the main empirical success of the LH-CCAPM seems to lie in more plausible estimates of the coefficient of relative risk aversion.

Next, we provide estimation results on the performance of the LH-CCAPM for the cross-section of returns in the UK and Germany, where previous literature on cross-sectional tests of consumption-based asset pricing models is rather scarce.[16] Estimation results for the UK reported in Table 2 largely confirm our findings for the USA. Even though the estimated coefficient of determination peaks at consumption growth horizons of three and seven quarters, the overall explanatory power of the LH-CCAPM remains comparably low. This is also evident from pricing errors summarized by the RMSE. In analogy to the R^2 measure, mispricing is least pronounced for medium horizons of three and seven quarters.[17] Moreover, the model cannot explain the overall level of UK stock returns. Nevertheless, the effect of LH risk on risk-aversion estimates is again remarkable. If we measure consumption growth over a time period of at least five quarters following the return, the estimated risk-aversion coefficient declines to values around five.

Table 3 summarizes the evidence on the empirical content of the LH-CCAPM framework for the German stock market. The results for the LH-CCAPM in Germany are quite in line with those

Table 2. Consumption risk and UK stock returns – nonlinear LH-CCAPM.

Horizon	$\hat{\alpha}$ (standard error)	$\hat{\gamma}$ (standard error)	R^2	RMSE	HJ-distance (p-value)	J (p-value)
0	0.025 (0.009)	14.787 (27.133)	0.09	0.671	0.505 (0.025)	48.102 (0.001)
1	0.024 (0.009)	3.685 (22.583)	0.01	0.700	0.501 (0.034)	45.177 (0.002)
3	0.021 (0.010)	15.012 (17.637)	0.14	0.654	0.500 (0.030)	49.357 (0.000)
5	0.023 (0.008)	5.651 (14.625)	0.05	0.686	0.498 (0.035)	47.964 (0.001)
7	0.021 (0.008)	8.950 (12.054)	0.13	0.656	0.497 (0.036)	48.309 (0.001)
9	0.023 (0.007)	4.517 (11.782)	0.07	0.680	0.499 (0.029)	47.405 (0.001)
11	0.022 (0.007)	5.036 (12.011)	0.09	0.671	0.496 (0.027)	47.800 (0.001)

Note: The reported values for $\hat{\alpha}$, $\hat{\gamma}$, R^2, and the RMSE are computed using equal weights across portfolios and large weight on the last moment (first-stage GMM with a prespecified weighting matrix). Standard errors are calculated using the procedure by Newey and West (1987) with $S + 1$ lags. The HJ-distance is based on first-stage GMM estimation using the weighting matrix proposed by Hansen and Jagannathan (1997) and p-values are obtained via simulation with 10,000 replications. The J-statistic is based on iterated GMM estimation. The sample period is 1965.Q2–2001.Q1 for returns and 1965:Q2–2003:Q4 for quarterly consumption.

Table 3. Consumption risk and German stock returns – nonlinear LH-CCAPM.

Horizon	$\hat{\alpha}$ (standard error)	$\hat{\gamma}$ (standard error)	R^2	RMSE	HJ-distance (p-value)	J (p-value)
0	0.015 (0.009)	61.927 (31.840)	0.09	0.730	0.544 (0.362)	61.121 (0.000)
1	0.013 (0.008)	59.990 (36.956)	0.16	0.701	0.545 (0.317)	43.436 (0.017)
3	0.013 (0.008)	27.586 (37.379)	0.05	0.744	0.545 (0.275)	97.116 (0.000)
5	0.013 (0.008)	11.850 (27.171)	0.05	0.745	0.552 (0.216)	44.760 (0.013)
7	0.010 (0.006)	17.963 (19.539)	0.12	0.718	0.554 (0.205)	46.184 (0.009)
9	0.012 (0.006)	11.482 (16.736)	0.09	0.726	0.551 (0.203)	45.088 (0.012)
11	0.007 (0.004)	19.987 (17.863)	0.22	0.675	0.552 (0.208)	46.216 (0.009)

Note: The reported values for $\hat{\alpha}$, $\hat{\gamma}$, R^2, and the RMSE are computed using equal weights across portfolios and large weight on the last moment (first-stage GMM with a prespecified weighting matrix). Standard errors are calculated using the procedure by Newey and West (1987) with $S + 1$ lags. The HJ-distance is based on first-stage GMM estimation using the weighting matrix proposed by Hansen and Jagannathan (1997) and p-values are obtained via simulation with 10,000 replications. The J-statistic is based on iterated GMM estimation. The sample period is 1974:Q2–2001:Q1 for returns and 1974:Q2–2003:Q4 for quarterly consumption.

for the US stock market discussed above. As evinced by the table, we find that the plausibility of parameter estimates varies with the consumption growth horizon. Risk-aversion estimates tend to decline to more plausible levels as we increase the time period over which consumption growth is measured, even though this decrease is not monotonous. At the same time, the estimated cross-sectional R^2 also varies with the horizon and reaches a maximum of 22% for $S = 11$. Comparing various CCAPM specifications in terms of average pricing errors (RMSE) for German stock portfolios leads to the same conclusion.

Interestingly, even the canonical consumption-based model does not imply an 'equity premium puzzle' for Germany. What is more, the relevant estimate $(\hat{\alpha})$ is further reduced if LH consumption risk is taken into account. Overall, the results for the UK and the German stock markets corroborate our earlier conclusion that, even though the ability of the LH-CCAPM to account for size and value premia is rather limited, the modified model helps to obtain more plausible risk-aversion parameter estimates.

4.3 Empirical results: linearized model

In order to facilitate comparison with traditional factor models for the SDF, we also estimate the linearized version of the LH-CCAPM. Tables 4–6 summarize estimation results assuming a constant risk-free rate, which implies a one-factor model where LH consumption growth serves as the single risk factor. In general, estimates are in accordance with those obtained for the nonlinear model.

As discussed in the previous subsection, when required to price a broader cross-section of assets, the LH risk CCAPM apparently has trouble explaining US excess returns (Table 4). Nevertheless, our results confirm those of Parker and Julliard (2005) in two other regards. First, the

Table 4. Consumption risk and US stock returns – linearized LH-CCAPM: GMM estimation.

Horizon	$\hat{\alpha}$ (standard error)	$\hat{b}$ (standard error)	$\gamma_S^{\text{implied}}$ (standard error)	R^2	RMSE	HJ-distance (p-value)	J (p-value)
0	0.020 (0.005)	75.573 (64.405)	54.076 (32.733)	0.12	0.508	0.474 (0.019)	120.940 (0.000)
1	0.020 (0.005)	30.132 (33.567)	22.896 (19.249)	0.08	0.520	0.565 (0.002)	108.800 (0.000)
3	0.019 (0.005)	20.887 (21.557)	14.499 (10.264)	0.09	0.517	0.587 (0.002)	113.112 (0.000)
5	0.019 (0.005)	18.211 (18.436)	11.544 (7.293)	0.09	0.517	0.583 (0.007)	109.064 (0.000)
7	0.018 (0.005)	19.611 (17.041)	10.716 (4.966)	0.13	0.506	0.582 (0.012)	108.482 (0.000)
9	0.019 (0.005)	21.438 (14.946)	10.038 (3.142)	0.17	0.494	0.583 (0.014)	110.078 (0.000)
11	0.019 (0.005)	22.500 (13.000)	9.236 (2.072)	0.21	0.482	0.578 (0.030)	107.345 (0.000)

Note: The reported values for $\hat{\alpha}$, $\hat{b}$, $\gamma_S^{\text{implied}}$, R^2, and the RMSE are computed using equal weights across portfolios (first-stage GMM with a prespecified weighting matrix). Standard errors are calculated using the procedure by Newey and West (1987) with $S + 1$ lags. The HJ-distance is based on first-stage GMM estimation using the weighting matrix proposed by Hansen and Jagannathan (1997) and p-values are obtained via simulation with 10,000 replications. The J-statistic is based on iterated GMM estimation. The risk-free rate is assumed to be constant. The sample period is 1947:Q2–2001:Q4 for returns and 1947:Q2–2004:Q3 for quarterly consumption.

Table 5. Consumption risk and UK stock returns – linearized LH-CCAPM: GMM estimation.

Horizon	$\hat{\alpha}$ (standard error)	$\hat{b}$ (standard error)	$\gamma_S^{\text{implied}}$ (standard error)	R^2	RMSE	HJ-distance (p-value)	J (p-value)
0	0.025 (0.009)	17.255 (34.993)	15.771 (29.159)	0.09	0.671	0.505 (0.028)	48.135 (0.001)
1	0.025 (0.009)	4.295 (23.865)	4.101 (21.753)	0.00	0.703	0.500 (0.038)	45.940 (0.001)
3	0.021 (0.010)	15.448 (19.431)	11.531 (10.654)	0.12	0.661	0.504 (0.027)	49.325 (0.000)
5	0.023 (0.009)	7.301 (15.406)	5.882 (9.920)	0.03	0.693	0.503 (0.031)	48.214 (0.001)
7	0.021 (0.009)	7.960 (12.344)	5.890 (6.660)	0.09	0.672	0.504 (0.032)	48.869 (0.001)
9	0.022 (0.008)	4.805 (12.396)	3.799 (7.701)	0.03	0.695	0.505 (0.029)	48.089 (0.001)
11	0.021 (0.008)	5.436 (11.685)	4.001 (6.275)	0.03	0.694	0.506 (0.026)	48.291 (0.001)

Note: The reported values for $\hat{\alpha}$, $\hat{b}$, $\gamma_S^{\text{implied}}$, R^2, and the RMSE are computed using equal weights across portfolios (first-stage GMM with a prespecified weighting matrix). Standard errors are calculated using the procedure by Newey and West (1987) with $S+1$ lags. The HJ-distance is based on first-stage GMM estimation using the weighting matrix proposed by Hansen and Jagannathan (1997) and p-values are obtained via simulation with 10,000 replications. The J-statistic is based on iterated GMM estimation. The risk-free rate is assumed to be constant. The sample period is 1965:Q2–2001:Q1 for returns and 1965:Q2–2003:Q4 for quarterly consumption.

Table 6. Consumption risk and German stock returns – linearized LH-CCAPM: GMM estimation.

Horizon	$\hat{\alpha}$ (standard error)	$\hat{b}$ (standard error)	$\gamma_S^{\text{implied}}$ (standard error)	R^2	RMSE	HJ-distance (p-value)	J (p-value)
0	0.014 (0.009)	24.194 (42.199)	21.639 (33.678)	0.01	0.758	0.534 (0.296)	45.299 (0.011)
1	0.015 (0.010)	76.771 (50.094)	44.036 (16.159)	0.16	0.701	0.527 (0.385)	44.223 (0.014)
3	0.013 (0.008)	21.763 (32.764)	15.372 (16.157)	0.02	0.757	0.544 (0.261)	41.935 (0.025)
5	0.013 (0.008)	15.934 (29.381)	10.996 (13.839)	0.03	0.754	0.551 (0.221)	42.565 (0.021)
7	0.010 (0.006)	19.573 (20.279)	11.373 (6.591)	0.09	0.730	0.556 (0.200)	46.847 (0.007)
9	0.012 (0.006)	13.894 (17.544)	8.527 (6.404)	0.05	0.743	0.555 (0.193)	45.917 (0.009)
11	0.006 (0.004)	22.898 (16.149)	10.290 (3.074)	0.20	0.683	0.555 (0.204)	46.934 (0.007)

Note: The reported values for $\hat{\alpha}$, $\hat{b}$, $\gamma_S^{\text{implied}}$, R^2, and the RMSE are computed using equal weights across portfolios (first-stage GMM with a prespecified weighting matrix). Standard errors are calculated using the procedure by Newey and West (1987) with $S+1$ lags. The HJ-distance is based on first-stage GMM estimation using the weighting matrix proposed by Hansen and Jagannathan (1997) and p-values are obtained via simulation with 10,000 replications. The J-statistic is based on iterated GMM estimation. The risk-free rate is assumed to be constant. The sample period is 1974:Q2–2001:Q1 for returns and 1974:Q2–2003:Q4 for quarterly consumption.

cross-sectional R^2 increases considerably for longer horizons. Second, GMM coefficient estimates suggest that the effect of consumption growth on the representative investor's SDF is estimated more precisely if consumption risk is measured over longer time periods. Moreover, the estimate of the risk-aversion coefficient declines to more economically plausible values as the horizon S increases.

The explanatory power of the linearized LH-CCAPM for the cross-section of returns seems clearly weaker when tested on UK stock portfolios. Similar to estimation results for the nonlinear specification, the coefficient of determination is highest for horizons of three (12%) and seven (9%) quarters. In addition, point estimates $\hat{b}$ suggest that the SDF is not systematically related to consumption risk, irrespective of the chosen horizon. Although implied risk-aversion estimates have high standard errors, they exhibit a considerable decline as we extend the horizon over which consumption risk is measured.

Results for the linearized version of the LH-CCAPM for the German stock market are provided in Table 6. As was the case for the nonlinear specification, the model has no problem explaining the overall level of stock returns. Taking LH risk into account improves the performance of the CCAPM in other respects. The empirical fit as measured by R^2 and RMSE is best for a consumption risk horizon of 11 quarters. Moreover, implied risk aversion appears to decrease with horizon (albeit in a nonmonotonous fashion). If consumption risk is measured over 11 quarters, the coefficient of relative risk aversion is estimated at a rather low value of 10 which is half the point estimate obtained for the conventional CCAPM. Moreover, the significance of $\hat{b}$, the parameter measuring the effect of consumption growth on the SDF, is far higher for $S = 11$ than for the canonical CCAPM.

Table 7. Traditional linear factor models and German, UK, and US stock returns – GMM estimation, size/book-to-market and industry portfolios.

Model	$\hat{\alpha}$ (standard error)	$\hat{b}_{m,e}$ (standard error)	$\hat{b}_{SMB}$ (standard error)	$\hat{b}_{HML}$ (standard error)	R^2	RMSE	HJ-distance (p-value)	J (p-value)
			A. USA					
Fama–French	0.017	1.356	0.693	4.017	0.56	0.361	0.568	94.449
	(0.007)	(1.748)	(1.715)	(1.598)			(0.001)	(0.000)
CAPM	0.025	−0.014			0.00	0.542	0.587	112.784
	(0.008)	(1.513)					(0.000)	(0.000)
			B. UK					
Fama–French	0.016	0.871	1.247	6.289	0.71	0.380	0.428	36.235
	(0.010)	(1.090)	(2.057)	(3.472)			(0.190)	(0.010)
CAPM	0.021	0.410			0.06	0.682	0.505	49.077
	(0.010)	(0.933)					(0.029)	(0.000)
			C. Germany					
Fama–French	−0.003	1.056	−4.731	3.342	0.70	0.419	0.515	35.499
	(0.007)	(2.078)	(3.611)	(2.529)			(0.332)	(0.065)
CAPM	−0.009	3.340			0.52	0.530	0.537	42.124
	(0.008)	(1.574)					(0.247)	(0.024)

Note: The reported values for $\hat{\alpha}$, $\hat{b}_{m,e}$, $\hat{b}_{SMB}$, $\hat{b}_{HML}$, R^2, and the RMSE are computed using equal weights across portfolios (first-stage GMM). The HJ-distance is based on first-stage GMM estimation using the weighting matrix proposed by Hansen and Jagannathan (1997), the J-statistic on iterated GMM estimation. The sample period is 1974:Q2–2001:Q1 for Germany, 1965:Q2–2001:Q1 for the UK, and 1947:Q2–2001:Q4 for the USA.

All together, inference for the linearized LH-CCAPM suggests that LH consumption risk helps improve the empirical performance of the consumption-based model in certain ways. Even though detailed empirical results differ across countries, some common patterns emerge. Most notably, measuring consumption risk over several quarters following the return helps to obtain much more plausible estimates of the representative investor's risk-aversion coefficient. This result is in accordance with recent evidence presented by Rangvid (2008).

4.4 *Comparison to traditional linear factor models and across sets of test assets*

Empirical results for the linearized CCAPM can be directly compared with those for the Fama and French (1993) three-factor model and the traditional CAPM, which are summarized in Table 7.

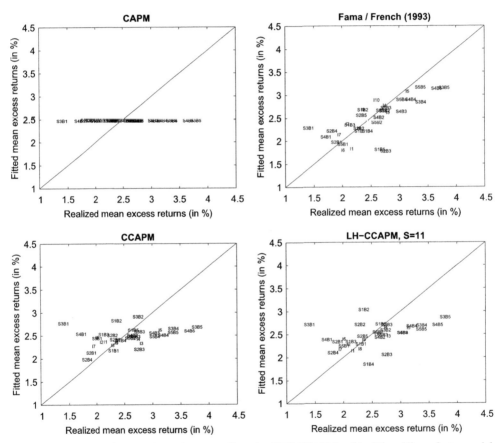

Figure 1. Pricing error plots for US stock returns – linearized LH-CCAPM and traditional linear factor models. Note: The figure compares realized mean excess returns on 25 value and size as well as 10 industry portfolios with those predicted by the CAPM, the Fama and French (1993) model, and the linearized LH-CCAPM (with constant risk-free rate) at different horizons. The portfolios are depicted in the following way: e.g., S1B1 refers to stocks in the smallest size and book-to-market Quintiles, while S5B5 refers to stocks in the largest size and book-to-market Quintiles; industry portfolios are depicted as I plus the corresponding industry number running from 1 to 10. Fitted excess returns are based on first-stage GMM estimation with identity weighting matrix. The sample period is 1947:Q2–2001:Q4.

Estimates for 35 US portfolios in Panel A are in line with previous evidence in the literature [e.g., Fama and French (1993) or Lettau and Ludvigson (2001)]: while the Fama–French three-factor model explains more than 50% of cross-sectional variation in returns, the standard CAPM performs extremely poorly. Accordingly, as shown in Figure 1, portfolio excess returns predicted by the CAPM appear to be almost unrelated to realized average excess returns. In contrast, fitted excess returns for the Fama–French model and, to a lesser extent, the LH-CCAPM line up more closely to the 45° line. At the same time, estimation results in Table 7 also indicate that, with the exception of HML, none of the proposed Fama–French factors seem to significantly affect the SDF of the representative US investor. A closer examination of the relative magnitude of mispricing across size and value portfolios in Figure 2 reveals that these are remarkably similar for both consumption-based models. In other words, accounting for long-run risk does not help to better explain returns on portfolios that are already poorly priced by the canonical model.

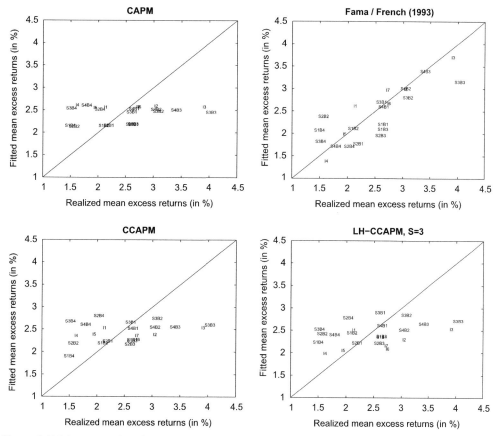

Figure 2. Pricing error plots for UK stock returns – linearized LH-CCAPM and traditional linear factor models. Note: The figure compares realized mean excess returns on 16 value and size as well as seven industry portfolios with those predicted by the CAPM, the Fama and French (1993) model, and the linearized LH-CCAPM (with constant risk-free rate) at different horizons. The portfolios are depicted in the following way: e.g., S1B1 refers to stocks in the smallest size and book-to-market Quartiles, while S4B4 refers to stocks in the largest size and book-to-market Quartiles; industry portfolios are depicted as I plus the corresponding industry number running from one to seven. Fitted excess returns are based on first-stage GMM estimation with identity weighting matrix. The sample period is 1965:Q2–2001:Q1.

As illustrated in Figure 2, this conclusion also holds for the UK. The empirical fit of the canonical and the modified CCAPM are relatively similar both in terms of pricing errors on individual portfolios as well as regarding the magnitude of average mispricing (average distance to the 45° line). This result is consistent with parameter estimates reported in Tables 5 and 7. By contrast, the high explanatory power of the Fama and French (1993) model typically found for the USA is even higher for the cross-section of UK stock returns. First-stage GMM estimates reveal that the model explains as much as 71% of cross-sectional variation in returns, compared with only 6% for the CAPM and 9% for the canonical CCAPM ($S = 0$). However, coefficients measuring the marginal impact of the respective financial risk factors on the SDF reported in Table 7 are not significantly different from zero.

In the case of Germany (Panel C), the cross-sectional R^2 obtained for the long-run risk model – up to about 20% at 11 quarters – is clearly qualified by the high explanatory power of the ad

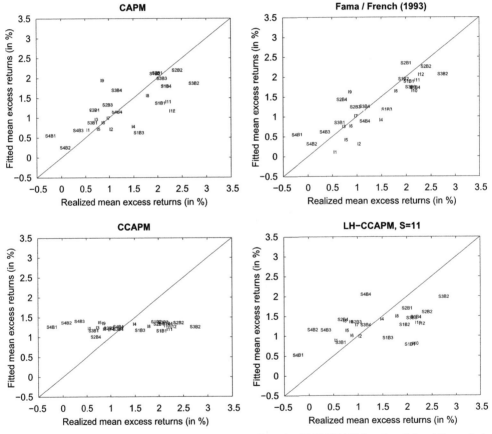

Figure 3. Pricing error plots for German stock returns – linearized LH-CCAPM and traditional linear factor models. Note: The figure compares realized mean excess returns on 16 value and size as well as 12 industry portfolios with those predicted by the CAPM, the Fama and French (1993) model, and the linearized LH-CCAPM (with constant risk-free rate) at different horizons. The portfolios are depicted in the following way: e.g., S1B1 refers to stocks in the smallest size and book-to-market Quartiles, while S4B4 refers to stocks in the largest size and book-to-market Quartiles; industry portfolios are depicted as I plus the corresponding industry number running from 1 to 12. Fitted excess returns are based on first-stage GMM estimation with identity weighting matrix. The sample period is 1974:Q2–2001:Q1.

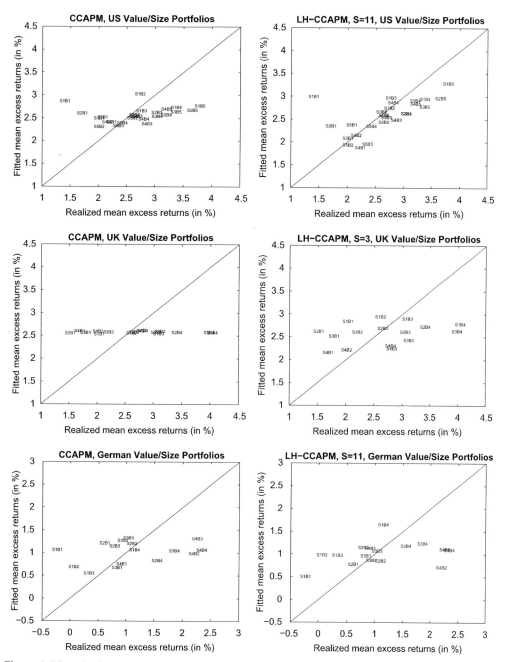

Figure 4. Linearized consumption-based models: pricing error plots for value and size portfolios. Note: The figure compares realized mean excess returns with those predicted by the standard CCAPM ($S = 0$) and the linearized LH-CCAPM (with constant risk-free rate and $S = 11$), estimated on value and size portfolios. The portfolios are depicted in the following way: e.g., S1B1 refers to stocks in the smallest size and book-to-market Quartiles, while S4B4 (S5B5) refers to stocks in the largest size and book-to-market Quartiles. Fitted excess returns are based on first-stage GMM estimation with identity weighting matrix.

hoc factor model of Fama and French (1993) (70%) and the CAPM (52%). Actually, the CAPM performs surprisingly well when tested on a cross-section of 28 industry, value, and size portfolios, as reflected by significant $\hat{b}$ estimates and the smallest HJ-distance of all candidate models.[18] Nevertheless, the three-factor model performs even better in that it provides an explanation for the overall level of returns relative to the risk-free rate and is not rejected by the test of overidentifying restrictions at the 5% significance level. Comparing all three models in terms of their explanatory power for German stock returns, the long-run consumption risk model does not provide any advantage over the two traditional linear models based on financial factors. Pricing error plots in Figure 3 confirm this conclusion as the magnitude of pricing errors is considerably lower for the three-factor model of Fama and French (1993). Interestingly, both short and LH-CCAPM generate the highest pricing errors on exactly the same portfolios, which are German small growth stocks (S1B1) and transportation companies (I10).

Summing up, the empirical success of long-run consumption risk compared with the canonical CCAPM in terms of cross-sectional explanatory power is qualified by the astonishingly good performance of the three-factor model.[19] At the same time, our results for the UK and the USA confirm the bad performance of the CAPM typically found in empirical model comparisons. Surprisingly, we find that this model explains as much as 52% of cross-sectional variation in returns across German portfolios. In any case, measuring risk in stock returns as their covariance with long-run consumption growth leads to some improvements over the canonical CCAPM in terms of overall empirical fit. In particular, while moving from short- (Canonical CCAPM) to long-term consumption risk (LH-CCAPM) may help to reduce pricing errors on *average*, the relative mispricing across *individual assets* (especially value and size portfolios) is strikingly similar for both consumption-based models. Overall, value and size premia still remain a major challenge for the LH-CCAPM.[20]

Finally, we investigate to what extent our conclusions regarding the relative cross-sectional fit of the candidate consumption-based models are driven by the inclusion of industry portfolios in our set of test assets. For each country, we estimate the short and LH-CCAPM on value and size portfolios only. Figure 4 gives a visual summary of the empirical results. The two upper plots reproduce the remarkable increase in explanatory power for the LH approach vis-á-vis the canonical model found by Parker and Julliard (2005) for US Fama–French portfolios. A comparison with plots for the larger set of test assets (Figure 1) illustrates the negative effect of including industry portfolios in the case of the USA. However, this adverse effect does not appear to be uniform across countries and models. Comparing pricing error plots for the UK and Germany, we find that the cross-sectional explanatory power of the traditional model appears to be lower (higher) when tested on UK (German) value and size portfolios only. While the inclusion of industry portfolios clearly weakens the empirical performance of the LH model in the USA, this conclusion does not hold for the two European markets.

5. Conclusion

Recent work by Parker and Julliard (2005) suggests that measuring consumption growth over several quarters following the return substantially improves the explanatory power of the consumption-based asset pricing paradigm. Their modified empirical setup addresses the issue of measurement error in quarterly consumption and is robust to various arguments as to why consumption expenditure may be slow to adjust to innovations in aggregate wealth. Besides, their model is closely related to the literature on long-run consumption risk, as it implies expressions for expected returns that are similar to the testable implications of long-run risk models with recursive utility such as Hansen, Heaton, and Li (2008).

Our work contributes to the literature on long-run consumption risks in three respects: First, by expanding the set of test assets to include industry portfolios, we take into account recent criticism regarding the widespread use of value and size portfolios as test assets (Phalippou, 2007; Lewellen, Nagel, and Shanken 2007). Under our modified empirical approach, we find that LH consumption risk falls short of providing a complete account of the cross-section of expected returns. In this way, our findings suggest that the LH consumption-based approach does not resolve the famous 'value premium puzzle'.

Second, evaluating the proposed CCAPM separately for three countries enables us to compare results across capital markets. In this sense, our findings provide additional out-of-sample evidence and address potential data-snooping concerns. Empirical results for Germany and the UK indicate that measuring consumption risk over longer horizons indeed helps increase the empirical performance of the CCAPM, albeit at modest levels. For both markets, estimated coefficients of determination remain below those obtained for the factor model of Fama and French (1993).

Third, our analysis confirms the evidence of Parker and Julliard (2005), who find that point estimates of the investor's risk-aversion parameter vary with the time interval over which consumption growth is measured. In line with evidence reported by Rangvid (2008), we find that accounting for LH consumption risk typically delivers more sensible estimates. This is true for all three equity markets considered in this study.

Summing up, accounting for LH consumption risk within the CCAPM framework indeed seems to improve the model's cross-sectional explanatory power in certain ways. On the one hand, the model still falls short of providing an accurate description of size and value premia. On the other hand, the estimated risk aversion of an investor who is concerned about long-run consumption risk is much lower and therefore more plausible compared with the standard model. In this sense, LH consumption risk appears to be a more accurate measure of macroeconomic risk factors in stock returns than contemporaneous consumption growth.

Acknowledgements

The authors are indebted to Martin Bohl, Bernard Dumas, Halit Gonenc, Christian Salm, Stephan Siegel, Tao Wu, two anonymous referees, and audiences at the 43rd meeting of the Euro Working Group on Financial Modelling (London), 15th annual meeting of the German Finance Association (Münster), 6th International Meeting of the French Finance Association (Paris), 11th Symposium on Finance, Banking, and Insurance (Karlsruhe), the Tübingen-Konstanz empirical finance seminar as well as seminar participants at University of Münster, University of Tübingen, and ZEW Mannheim for useful comments and suggestions. We also thank Kenneth French and Stefan Nagel for making portfolio data available on their websites.

Notes

1. The consumption-based asset pricing model has its roots in the original articles by Rubinstein (1976), Lucas (1978), and Breeden (1979).
2. Research on the long-run implications of the consumption-based asset pricing framework has constituted a rather prominent field in recent literature (Jagannathan and Wang 2007; Bansal, Dittmar, and Kiku 2007; Hansen, Heaton, and Li 2008; Rangvid 2008). More detailed information on how our paper is related to the extant literature is provided in Section 2.2.
3. Several authors focus on consumption and investment decisions of stockholders versus nonstockholders. In particular, a recent contribution by Malloy, Moskowitz, and Vissing-Jørgensen (2008) studies the long-run consumption risk of US stockholders. A detailed study using microlevel consumption data for all three countries under consideration is beyond the scope of this paper.

4. The existence of a persistent component in consumption and dividends is empirically confirmed by Bansal, Kiku, and Yaron (2007).

5. For a detailed discussion of this issue see Cochrane (2005, Chapter 13) and Yogo (2006, Appendix C).

6. The computation of the cross-sectional R^2 in the GMM framework follows the extant literature (e.g., Lettau and Ludvigson 2001; Parker and Julliard 2005): $R^2 = 1 - \text{Var}_c(\bar{R}_i^e - \hat{R}_i^e)/\text{Var}_c(\bar{R}_i^e)$, where Var_c denotes a cross-sectional variance, $\bar{R}_i^e$ is the time series average of the excess return on asset i, and $\hat{R}_i^e$ is the fitted mean excess return for asset i implied by the model.

7. For computational details and the simulations for the model test based on the HJ-distance, the reader is referred to the Appendix in Parker and Julliard (2005).

8. Additional estimations (not shown) confirm that our main conclusions are largely unaffected if total consumption expenditure is used instead of nondurables and services consumption.

9. Returns on the 16 portfolios as well as Market, HML and SMB factors can be downloaded from Stefan Nagel's webpage: http://faculty-gsb.stanford.edu/nagel

10. http://mba.tuck.dartmouth.edu/pages/faculty/ken.french/

11. Notice that the overall sample period, however, is longer due to the LH consumption growth (up to S) aligned to the returns: USA (2004:Q3), UK (2003:Q4), GER (2003:Q4).

12. CPI data for the USA, the UK, and Germany are available from the BEA, the IMF International Financial Statistics, and the OECD Economic Outlook, respectively.

13. In order to render our results comparable across countries, we limit the horizon at which long-run consumption risk is measured to 11 quarters.

14. The overlap of observations of long-run consumption growth induces serial correlation, which must be accounted for when conducting inference in case of the LH-CCAPM. Our estimate of the covariance matrix of GMM estimates is computed by the procedure of Newey and West (1987) with $S + 1$ lags.

15. This is a common finding in the empirical asset pricing literature: even the best performing models such as the Fama–French three-factor model are often rejected by formal statistical tests [e.g., Lettau and Ludvigson 2001].

16. An exception is the work of Gao and Huang (2004), who use UK value and size portfolios, whereas other papers such as Hyde and Sherif (2005a, 2005b) for the UK and Lund and Engsted (1996) for Germany estimate consumption-based models separately for each industry sector or market index.

17. We discuss pricing errors on individual portfolios in more detail below.

18. This result is remarkable given the poor performance of the standard CAPM documented in the paper by Schrimpf, Schröder, and Stehle (2007), which is based on an evaluation of the model on monthly data.

19. A major disadvantage of Fama and French's three-factor model is that there is still no full agreement in the literature about what the true risks underlying SMB and HML actually are. See, e.g., Petkova (2006) for a risk-based explanation in an empirical implementation of an ICAPM in the spirit of Merton (1973).

20. However, models using macroeconomic factors will always be at a disadvantage to models using financial factors (Cochrane 2007, 7) due to a less precise measurement of macroeconomic variables. Moreover, these models allow for a more structural analysis of the economic determinants of risk premia, which typically cannot be delivered by models using merely financial factors.

References

Allen, F., and D. Gale. 2001. *Comparing financial systems*. Cambridge, MA: MIT Press.

Bansal, R. 2007. Long-run risk and financial markets. NBER Working Paper 13196, National Bureau of Economic Research.

Bansal, R., R. Dittmar, and D. Kiku. 2007. Cointegration and consumption risks in asset returns. *Review of Financial Studies* 22, no. 3: 1343–75.

Bansal, R., R.F. Dittmar, and C.T. Lundblad. 2005. Consumption, dividends, and the cross section of equity returns. *Journal of Finance* 60, no. 4: 1639–72.

Bansal, R., D. Kiku, and A. Yaron. 2007. Risks for the long run: Estimation and inference. Working Paper, University of Pennsylvania.

Bansal, R., and A. Yaron. 2004. Risks for the long run: A potential resolution of asset pricing puzzles. *Journal of Finance* 59, no. 4: 1481–509.

Breeden, D.T. 1979. An intertemporal asset pricing model with stochastic consumption and investment opportunities. *Journal of Financial Economics* 7: 265–96.

Chetty, R., and A. Szeidl. 2005. Consumption commitments: Neoclassical foundations for habit formation. Working Paper, University of California, Berkeley.

Cochrane, J.H. 1989. The sensitivity of tests of the intertemporal allocation of consumption to near-rational alternatives. *American Economic Review* 79, no. 3: 319–37.

Cochrane, J.H. 1996. A cross-sectional test of an investment-based asset pricing model. *Journal of Political Economy* 104, no. 3: 572–621.

Cochrane, J.H. 2005. *Asset pricing*. Princeton, NJ: Princeton Univ. Press.

Cochrane, J.H. 2007. Financial markets and the real economy. In *Handbook of the equity risk premium*, ed. R. Mehra, 237–325. Amsterdam: Elsevier.

Colacito, R., and M.M. Croce. 2008. Risks for the long run and the real exchange rate. Discussion Paper, UNC.

Dimson, E., P. Marsh, and M. Staunton. 2008. The worldwide equity premium puzzle: A smaller puzzle. In *Handbook of the equity risk premium*, ed. R. Mehra. Amsterdam: Elsevier.

Dimson, E., S. Nagel, and G. Quigley. 2003. Capturing the value premium in the United Kingdom. *Financial Analysts Journal* 59, no. 6: 35–45.

Epstein, L., and S. Zin. 1989. Substitution, risk aversion, and the temporal behavior of consumption growth and asset returns I: A theoretical framework. *Econometrica* 57: 937–69.

Fama, E.F., and K.R. French. 1993. Common risk factors in the returns on stocks and bonds. *Journal of Financial Economics* 33: 3–56.

Gao, P., and K.X. Huang. 2004. Aggregate consumption–wealth ratio and the cross-section of stock returns: Some international evidence. Working Paper RWP 04-07, Federal Reserve Bank of Kansas City, Kansas City, MO.

Grossman, S.J., and R.J. Shiller. 1982. The determinants of the variability of stock market prices. *American Economic Review* 71: 222–7.

Guiso, L., M. Haliassos, and T. Jappelli. 2003. Household stockholding in Europe: Where do we stand and where do we go? *Economic Policy* 123–70.

Hamburg, B., M. Hoffmann, and J. Keller. 2008. Consumption, wealth and business cycles in Germany. *Empirical Economics* 34: 451–76.

Hansen, L.P. 1982. Large sample properties of generalized method of moments estimators. *Econometrica* 50, no. 4: 1029–54.

Hansen, L.P., J.C. Heaton, and N. Li. 2008. Consumption strikes back? Measuring long-run risk. *Journal of Political Economy* 116, no. 2: 260–302.

Hansen, L.P., and R. Jagannathan. 1997. Assessing specification errors in stochastic discount factor models. *Journal of Finance* 52, no. 2: 557–90.

Hansen, L.P., and K.J. Singleton. 1983. Stochastic consumption, risk aversion, and the temporal behavior of asset returns. *Journal of Political Economy* 91: 249–65.

Hyde, S., and M. Sherif. 2005a. Consumption asset pricing models: Evidence from the UK. *The Manchester School* 73, no. 3: 343–63.

Hyde, S., and M. Sherif. 2005b. Don't break the habit: Structural stability tests of consumption asset pricing models in the UK. *Applied Economics Letters* 12: 289–96.

Jagannathan, R., and Y. Wang. 2007. Lazy investors, discretionary consumption, and the cross-section of stock returns. *Journal of Finance* 62, no. 4: 1623–61.

Kaltenbrunner, G., and L.A. Lochstoer. 2007. Long-run risk through consumption smoothing. Working Paper, London Business School.

Lettau, M., and S. Ludvigson. 2001. Resurrecting the (C)CAPM: A cross-sectional test when risk premia are time-varying. *Journal of Political Economy* 109: 1238–87.

Lewellen, J., S. Nagel, and J. Shanken. 2007. A skeptical appraisal of asset-pricing tests. Working Paper, Stanford.

Lucas, Robert E. J. 1978. Asset prices in an exchange economy. *Econometrica* 46, no. 6: 1429–45.

Lund, J., and T. Engsted. 1996. GMM and present value tests of the C-CAPM: Evidence from the Danish, German, Swedish and UK stock markets. *Journal of International Money and Finance* 15, no. 4: 497–521.

Malloy, C.J., T.J. Moskowitz, and A. Vissing-Jørgensen. 2008. Long-run stockholder consumption risk and asset returns. Working Paper, Northwestern University.

Mehra, R., and E. Prescott. 1985. The equity premium: A puzzle. *Journal of Monetary Economics* 15: 145–61.

Merton, R.C. (1973). An intertemporal capital asset pricing model. *Econometrica* 41, no. 5: 867–87.

Newey, W.K., and K.D. West. 1987. A simple, positive semi-definite, heteroskedasticity and autocorrelation consistent covariance matrix. *Econometrica* 55, no. 3: 703–8.

Parker, J. A., and C. Julliard. 2005. Consumption risk and the cross section of expected returns. *Journal of Political Economy* 113, no. 1: 185–222.

Petkova, R.G. 2006. Do the Fama–French factors proxy for innovations in predictive variables? *Journal of Finance*, 61, no. 2: 581–612.

Phalippou, L. 2007. Can risk-based theories explain the value premium? *Review of Finance* 11: 143–66.

Rangvid, J. 2008. The long-run world consumption risk of international stock markets. Working Paper, Copenhagen Business School.

Rubinstein, M. 1976. The valuation of uncertain income streams and the pricing of options. *Bell Journal of Economics* 7: 407–25.

Schrimpf, A., M. Schröder, and R. Stehle. 2007. Cross-sectional tests of conditional asset pricing models: Evidence from the German stock market. *European Financial Management* 13, no. 5: 880–907.

Stock, J.H., and M.W. Watson. 2003. Forecasting output and inflation: The role of asset prices. *Journal of Economic Literature* 151: 788–829.

Yogo, M. 2006. A consumption-based explanation of expected stock returns. *Journal of Finance* 61, no. 2: 539–80.

Performance measures and incentives: loading negative coskewness to outperform the CAPM

Alexandros Kostakis

Department of Economics, University of Glasgow, Adam Smith Building, G12 8RT, Glasgow, UK

This study examines the incentives in fund management due to the adoption of specific performance measures. A mean–variance measure such as Jensen's alpha incentivizes fund managers to load negative coskewness risk. This risk is shown to be priced in the UK stock market during the period January 1991–December 2005, bearing a premium of 2.09% p.a. Hence, a new performance measure, the intercept of the Harvey–Siddique two-factor asset pricing model is proposed to be more appropriate for prudent investors. Using this model, the performance of UK equity unit trusts is examined for the same period. Though most of the managers significantly underperformed their benchmark, they correctly responded to their incentives, loading negative coskewness and reaping part of the corresponding premium.

1. Introduction

The most important development in financial markets during the last decades is their domination by institutional investors. The Office of National Statistics reports that the individual ownership of the companies listed in the London Stock Exchange (LSE) has decreased from 54% in 1963 to just 12.8% in 2006. One of the most successful investment vehicles is the unit trust.[1] According to the Investment Company Institute (ICI), 1903 unit trusts with a British domicile were managing $786 billion in December 2006.[2]

The outstanding success of mutual funds is due to the fact that they provide access to professional management and a highly diversified portfolio even for investors with low initial capital. In a world of perfect competition and symmetric information, investing in actively managed mutual funds would be an optimal solution. However, the delegated nature of fund management creates a series of problems related to asymmetric information. One of these is the problem of the *ex post state verification*, i.e. the problem of fairly evaluating the investment outcome. To resolve this problem, it is necessary to have an objective way to select and compensate managers.

Measuring investment performance has attracted a lot of attention in the literature and various measures have been suggested, according to which managers should be classified and rewarded. The most commonly used measures are the Sharpe ratio, Treynor ratio and Jensen's alpha, intercept of the Capital Asset Pricing Model (CAPM). The literature on US mutual funds using these measures is voluminous, dating back to Treynor (1965) and Sharpe (1966). For UK funds, these measures have been employed for performance evaluation purposes inter alia by Blake and Timmermann (1998), Quigley and Sinquefield (2000) as well as Thomas and Tonks (2001).

All these measures have their roots in the static mean–variance world of Markowitz (1952). Consequently, there are a series of inherent problems in these measures, since they neglect the intertemporal risk premia priced in capital markets (see the seminal work of Merton 1973; and the recent study of Campbell and Vuolteenaho 2004) as well as the risk premia arising due to higher co-moments (Kraus and Litzenberger 1976; Harvey and Siddique 2000). In particular, the present study examines the impact of coskewness on performance measurement. Coskewness measures the symmetry of an asset returns' distribution in relation to the market returns' distribution. This is an important concept because negative coskewness essentially represents a higher probability of extreme negative returns in the risky asset over market returns.

Severe criticism to the CAPM assumptions comes from the utility theory too. The assumption of quadratic preferences is clearly rejected, since it implies increasing absolute risk aversion. A desirable property of a utility function is that agents are averse to negative skewness, and have a preference for payoffs exhibiting positive skewness. This behaviour is termed prudence (Kimball 1990). Furthermore, experimental evidence indicates that there is an asymmetrically higher impact on utility by losses in comparison to gains, leading to utility frameworks such as the prospect theory (Kahneman and Tversky 1979) or disappointment aversion (Gul 1991). These value functions imply that agents are even more averse to negative skewness.

Nevertheless, aversion to negative skewness is a crucial feature that has been relatively neglected in asset pricing. Notable exceptions are the studies of Harvey and Siddique (2000), Dittmar (2002) and Smith (2007) for the US market as well as Hung et al. (2004) for the UK market. The latter study exploits the Huang–Litzenberger stochastic discount factor (SDF) approach to examine whether a coskewness or a cokurtosis risk factor is priced in the LSE. In particular, the squared and the cubic excess market returns have been added as additional regressors to a Fama–French asset pricing model. The results of this study do not lead to unambiguous results with respect to whether higher comoments risk premia are priced.

The recent performance evaluation literature uses Carhart's alpha, the intercept of the Carhart (1997) regression that extends the CAPM by adding the size, value and momentum strategies as risk factors. The literature on US mutual funds is vast. The studies of Bollen and Busse (2004), Chen et al. (2004) and Kosowski et al. (2006) provide recent examples. Cuthbertson et al. (2007) provide an excellent survey of the literature. With respect to the UK, multi-factor models have been used by Tonks (2005) for the performance evaluation of pension funds as well as by Otten and Bams (2002), Fletcher and Forbes (2002) and Cuthbertson et al. (2008) for the evaluation of equity trusts. These studies provide overwhelming evidence that the majority of the funds exhibit negative managerial ability.

There are two major problems with this measure: First, there is no robust, universally accepted theoretical reason why these strategies should be considered as risk factors. As a result, we run into the problem of characterizing randomly fluctuating returns as risk factors. Secondly, this measure attributes returns to specific strategies, not their fundamental source of risk. Consequently, there will always be the incentive for fund managers to construct alternative strategies that outperform this measure too. For instance, there are a series of studies suggesting that portfolios of stocks sorted on the basis of their liquidity may yield positive Carhart alphas, giving rise to an illiquidity risk factor (Pastor and Stambaugh 2003).

In this study, we review the assumptions on which the most commonly used performance measures are based, and examine the incentives that these measures generate. Fund managers try to distinguish themselves from their peers on the basis of these measures, and they respond to this incentive by adopting investment strategies that generate excess returns and help them outperform. We also propose an appropriate performance measure for risk-averse and prudent investors that is based on the sound economic theory, and we evaluate the performance of UK equity unit trusts according to this measure.

In particular, the Harvey and Siddique (2000) asset pricing model, which adds a zero-cost negative coskewness strategy as an extra factor to the CAPM, is proposed to be the most appropriate one for a prudent investor. This model takes into account the risk premia formed in capital markets due to the participants' aversion to negative skewness.[3] The intercept of this model, which we term as the *Harvey–Siddique alpha*, is employed as a measure to evaluate the performance of UK equity unit trusts during the period January 1991–December 2005. To the best of our knowledge, the only study that has explicitly used the Harvey–Siddique model for performance evaluation purposes is Moreno and Rodriguez (2005) for the case of Spanish funds. A series of other performance evaluation studies have incorporated the concept of skewness into their analysis. For instance, Fletcher and Forbes (2004) use the Huang–Litzenberger SDF approach for the evaluation of UK equity unit trusts, while Ding and Shawky (2007) employ this framework for the evaluation of hedge funds.

In order to perform our analysis, the returns of a zero-cost coskewness spread portfolio have been calculated for the UK, showing that the average monthly return of this strategy was 2.09% p.a. over the period January 1991–December 2005. Previewing our results, the median unit trust investing in the FTSE All-Share universe had a Harvey–Siddique alpha of −2.36% p.a., while the corresponding median Jensen alpha was −1.77% p.a. and the median Carhart alpha was −2.32% p.a. With respect to the managers' incentives, it is shown that almost all of the examined trusts had a positive loading on the negative coskewness spread strategy. Most interestingly, the trusts with the highest Jensen alphas were those with the highest loadings on the negative coskewness factor. We also provide evidence that the nonnormality of the trusts' performance distribution can be partly attributed to heterogeneous risk-taking, with the coskewness strategy being a main source of this heterogeneity.

An implication of our findings is that prudent investors should employ the *Harvey–Siddique alpha* in order to neutralize the incentive of trust managers to load coskewness risk. For these investors, most of the UK unit trusts exhibited a significantly negative managerial ability. However, managers were very successful in reaping the negative coskewness premium priced in the market, boosting their returns and correctly responding to their incentives, since they have been evaluated according to mean–variance measures that regard this premium to be a 'free lunch'.

The rest of the article is organized as follows: Section 2 discusses the relationship between skewness, preferences and asset pricing. Section 3 reviews the most commonly used performance measures, discussing the incentives they generate, and Section 4 provides the details of the data and the related methodological issues. Section 5 discusses the results of unit trust performance evaluation, and Section 6 examines their robustness, while Section 7 concludes.

2. Why is negative coskewness risk priced in the markets?

2.1 Skewness and preferences

It is expected that a risk-averse and prudent investor has a preference over a positively skewed payoff distribution and an aversion towards a negatively skewed one. There is significant evidence in the markets supporting this argument. The popular portfolio insurance products are protecting investors against downside risk. Moreover, modern risk management mainly deals with the avoidance of extreme negative returns. The most characteristic example is the measurement of Value-at-Risk.

Furthermore, option-implied distributions, especially after the October 1987 crash, are typically negatively skewed. In particular, deep out-of-the-money puts, which are popular instruments for portfolio insurance, have quite high prices relative to the ones implied by the Black and Scholes (1973) model. As a result, the implied volatility-strike price graph exhibits a 'smirk', in contrast to the constant volatility assumption of Black and Scholes. This feature of option prices has been termed *crashophobia* (Jackwerth 2004). On the other hand, the preference for positive skewness is evident in lotteries. Agents are willing to participate in lotteries with positively skewed payoffs (Golec and Tamarkin 1998), even though these have negative expected values, i.e. they are unfair games. It is worth mentioning that the participation in such unfair games increases as positive skewness increases (e.g. jackpots in lotteries). A similar explanation has been suggested by Tufano (2008) for the success of UK premium bonds.

The impact of skewness is often examined using the power utility function that treats symmetrically utility gains and losses caused by a wealth change of the same magnitude. Actually, this is also a property of the mean–variance analysis. Despite this assumption, there is significant experimental evidence that agents are mainly averse to losses, not just to volatility. The prospect theory of Kahneman and Tverksy (1979) as well as the disappointment-aversion framework of Gul (1991) imply that investors maintain an asymmetric attitude towards losses as compared with gains. In general, this class of value functions captures the feature of first-order risk aversion (Segal and Spivak 1990) and implies that investors are even more averse to negative skewness in comparison to power utility agents.

There are a number of regulatory and psychological issues related to loss aversion. Moreover, pension funds and insurance companies usually face legal obligations to pay out fixed or quasi-fixed amounts. The same holds true for households with liabilities over mortgages, loan installments or fees. Habit formation is another example of anchoring one's preferences around a reference point and being reluctant to accept any wealth level below that point. This mixture of obligations and preferences make pension funds, insurance companies and individuals extremely averse to negative movements in asset prices.

2.2 *Coskewness in asset pricing*

The central problem in asset pricing is to find a valid SDF, M, for future payoffs. Formally, the SDF is assumed to be positive (Harrison and Kreps 1979), it is unique under complete markets and satisfies the following relationship:

$$P_t = E_t[M_{t+s}X_{t+s}] \tag{1}$$

where P_t is the price of an asset at time t, and X_{t+s} denotes the asset's payoff at time $t+s$.

In a one-period ahead framework, $R_{t+1}^G = X_{t+1}/P_t \equiv 1 + R_{t+1}$ is employed to re-write Equation (1) as

$$1 = E_t\left[M_{t+1}R_{t+1}^G\right]. \tag{2}$$

It is straightforward to derive the following relationships (Smith and Wickens 2002), which relate the SDF, the gross return of a risky asset, R_{t+1}, as well as that of a risk-free asset, r_t^f:

$$1 = E_t(M_{t+1})\left(1 + r_t^f\right) \Rightarrow E_t(M_{t+1}) = \frac{1}{1 + r_t^f} \tag{3}$$

and

$$E_t\left(R_{t+1}^G\right) = \frac{1 - \text{Cov}\left(M_{t+1}, R_{t+1}^G\right)}{E_t(M_{t+1})} \qquad (4)$$

Combining these two equations, we get a central result in the asset pricing theory:

$$E_t(R_{t+1}) - r_t^f = -\left(1 + r_t^f\right)\text{Cov}(M_{t+1}, R_{t+1}) \qquad (5)$$

This equation implies that the expected excess return of a risky asset depends on the covariance of the SDF with this risky return.

Harvey and Siddique (2000) use the marginal rate of substitution $U'(W_{t+1})/U'(W_t)$ as a SDF to show the implications of this specification. Taking a first-order Taylor series expansion of $U'(W_{t+1})$ around W_t, we get the standard CAPM analysis. However, there is no particular reason why the truncation of the Taylor series expansion should occur at the first order. If the truncation takes place at the second order, then

$$U'(W_{t+1}) \simeq U'(W_t) + U''(W_t)(W_{t+1} - W_t) + \frac{U'''(W_t)(W_{t+1} - W_t)^2}{2!} \Rightarrow$$

$$\frac{U'(W_{t+1})}{U'(W_t)} \simeq 1 + \frac{U''(W_t)W_t}{U'(W_t)}R_{m,t+1} + \frac{U'''(W_t)W_t^2}{2U'(W_t)}R_{m,t+1}^2$$

$$= 1 - \gamma R_{m,t+1} + \frac{U'''(W_t)W_t}{2U''(W_t)}\frac{U''(W_t)W_t}{U'(W_t)}R_{m,t+1}^2$$

$$= 1 - \gamma R_{m,t+1} + \frac{1}{2}\gamma\eta R_{m,t+1}^2 \qquad (6)$$

where we have used the simple budget constraint $W_{t+1} = W_t(1 + R_{m,t+1})$ with R_m being the market return, the definition of the Arrow–Pratt measure of relative risk aversion, $\gamma \equiv -U''(W_t)W_t/U'(W_t)$ and the coefficient of relative prudence $\eta \equiv -U'''(W_t)W_t/U''(W_t)$, as defined by Kimball (1990). Furthermore, defining $\tilde{b} \equiv U''(W_t)W_t/U'(W_t) = -\gamma$ and $\tilde{c} \equiv U'''(W_t)W_t^2/2U'(W_t) = 1/2\gamma\eta$, the SDF implied by Equation (6) can now be written as:

$$M_{t+1} = 1 + \tilde{b}R_{m,t+1} + \tilde{c}R_{m,t+1}^2 \qquad (7)$$

This is not a linear SDF, since the squared market returns are involved. Recalling the fundamental asset pricing Equation (5) of the SDF approach, the expected excess return of an asset now depends on the covariance of this asset's returns not only with the market return but also with the squared market return. This is exactly what coskewness measures. In the case of a prudent and risk-averse investor, we have that $\eta > 0 \Rightarrow \tilde{c} > 0$, so the fundamental equation of asset pricing (5) can be written as:

$$E_t(R_{t+1}) - r_t^f = -\left(1 + r_t^f\right)\tilde{b}\text{Cov}(R_{m,t+1}, R_{t+1}) - \left(1 + r_t^f\right)\tilde{c}\text{Cov}(R_{m,t+1}^2, R_{t+1}) \qquad (8)$$

Therefore, for a given level of $\text{Cov}(R_{m,t+1}, R_{t+1})$, we have two cases with respect to $\text{Cov}(R_{m,t+1}^2, R_{t+1})$. On the one hand, if $\text{Cov}(R_{m,t+1}^2, R_{t+1}) > 0$, then $E_t(R_{t+1}) - r_t^f$ is now lower in comparison to the case of $\tilde{c} = 0$. This implies that if the risky asset's returns are positively coskewed with the market returns, then this asset will bear a lower risk premium. On the other hand, if $\text{Cov}(R_{m,t+1}^2, R_{t+1}) < 0$, then $E_t(R_{t+1}) - r_t^f$ is now higher. In other words, a prudent investor seeks an extra risk premium in order to hold an asset, the returns of which are character-ized by negative coskewness. Therefore, if financial markets are populated by prudent investors, expected returns should be higher for assets exhibiting negative coskewness. This is a key result in our analysis, predicting the existence of a negative coskewness premium.

3. Performance measures and incentives in fund management

3.1 *Raw returns*

Since the work of Markowitz (1952), it has been understood that there exists a direct positive relationship between risk and returns. However, managers and funds are still often ranked accord-ing to their raw returns. The new breed of funds, appearing as 'absolute return' seeking funds, reflects the lack of understanding of the link between risk and return. Using raw returns as a performance measure essentially means that the investor is indifferent to risk, i.e. his utility is not decreasing in volatility/risk, and risk premia are thought to be 'free lunches'. If a manager is evaluated according to raw returns, he will be incentivized to undertake the highest possible level of risk.

3.2 *Sharpe ratio*

Most of the performance studies have been evaluating investment strategies according to their risk-adjusted returns. One of the most commonly used measures of risk-adjusted performance is the Sharpe ratio due to Sharpe (1966):

$$SR = \frac{E(R_p) - r^f}{\sigma_p} \qquad (9)$$

where $E(R_p)$ is the average fund's return over a specific period; r^f, the risk-free rate; and σ_p, the standard deviation of the fund's returns in the same period. Using this measure, fund managers do not have the incentive to invest in more volatile assets, since higher volatility essentially penalizes their excess returns.

The Sharpe ratio is a purely mean–variance measure, neglecting higher moments. Nevertheless, these higher moments bear risk premia in a market with prudent investors, as previously discussed. Consequently, the rational response of the fund manager is to invest in assets that exhibit negative skewness in order to reap the corresponding risk premium and be classified as a 'winner'.

There are a series of examples documenting the existence of these strategies. Investing in emerging countries' bonds as well as noninvestment grade bonds is a straightforward case. These bonds have a higher probability of default in comparison with investment grade bonds. As a result, their returns are more negatively skewed and they provide higher yields. If a manager matches bonds with the same volatility but with different degrees of skewness, he will achieve a higher Sharpe ratio until the default occurs.

Goetzmann et al. (2007) analyse methods of maximizing a portfolio's Sharpe ratio using deriva-tives. Shorting different fractions of out-of-the-money puts and calls creates a negatively skewed distribution of returns and leads to the maximum Sharpe ratio. Their example also shows that hedge funds and other investment vehicles that use derivative assets can manipulate their Sharpe ratio. Leland (1999) provides an example of a dynamic strategy of cash and stocks as well as static strategies using options that generate negative skewness and outperform in terms of the Sharpe ratio. Finally, Adcock (2005) shows how to exploit skewness in order to construct a hedge fund that has superior mean–variance performance. Given this evidence, such funds should not be evaluated by mean–variance measures.

The inappropriateness of the Sharpe ratio for skewed returns is also mentioned in Ziemba (2005), who suggests a modification of the Sharpe ratio to emphasize the importance of the downside risk. The symmetric downside-risk Sharpe ratio (DSR) is given by

$$\text{DSR} = \frac{E(R_p) - r^f}{\sqrt{2(\sigma_-^2)}} \tag{10}$$

with

$$\sigma_-^2 = [1/(T-1)] \sum_{t=1}^{T} (R_{p,t} - E(R_p))_-^2, \tag{11}$$

and the returns used are only those below the average $E(R_p)$. Essentially, this measure adjusts the excess returns by using the semi-variance instead of variance.

3.3 *Jensen alpha and Treynor ratio*

Within the CAPM framework, Jensen (1968) introduced the intercept of the following regression as a measure for the fund manager's ability:

$$r_{p,t} = \alpha_{\text{Jensen}} + \beta_p r_{m,t} + \epsilon_t \tag{12}$$

where $r_{p,t}$ stands for the excess returns of the trust; $r_{m,t}$, the excess return of a suitable market index; and β_p, the fund's CAPM beta. The intercept (α_{Jensen}) shows whether the manager has added any value over and above the return justified by the risk he had undertaken. The concept of risk here is summarized in the CAPM beta. Closely related is the measure proposed by Treynor (1965):

$$\text{TR} = \frac{E(R_p) - r^f}{\beta_p} \tag{13}$$

Following the spirit of the Sharpe ratio, the Treynor ratio adjusts excess returns for the corresponding CAPM beta risk (β_p).

As it has been discussed, the CAPM is a static mean–variance measure, neglecting all other sources of risk, in particular those arising due to the higher moments and the stochastic evolution of the underlying risk factors affecting the asset returns. Consequently, if evaluated according to the CAPM, managers are incentivized to employ strategies that load intertemporal and higher comoments risks in their portfolios. It is known that fund managers construct strategies that exploit patterns such as the size, value and momentum 'anomalies' in order to add value to their portfolios. Temporary success of these strategies generates a positive Jensen alpha classifying the manager as a Winner. These strategies are supposed to have zero CAPM beta risk, but they are not necessarily riskless.

3.4 *Carhart alpha*

The basic doctrine of the financial theory is that 'free lunches', in the spirit of Harrison and Kreps (1979), should be ruled out.[4] Furthermore, since the Fama–French (1993) and momentum (Jegadeesh and Titman 1993) strategies are very simple to construct and implement, their returns cannot be regarded as genuinely added value. Reflecting these arguments, Carhart (1997) suggested the intercept of the four-factor model:

$$r_{p,t} = \alpha_{\text{Carhart}} + \beta_p r_{m,t} + \beta_1 \text{SMB}_t + \beta_2 \text{HML}_t + \beta_3 \text{MOM}_t + \epsilon_t \tag{14}$$

i.e. the *Carhart alpha,* as a performance measure.

The Carhart regression (14) essentially attributes the fund's returns generated by the size (SMB), value (HML) and momentum (MOM) strategies to the corresponding risk factors. The intercept of this regression (α_{Carhart}) reveals the value that the manager has added to his portfolio above what the beta risk could justify and these known strategies could generate. The most important feature of this measure is that it neutralizes the incentive to adopt these strategies, since they are recognized as risk factors.

Despite the significance of this contribution, the Carhart measure has two main disadvantages. First, managers would still try to find patterns in stock returns in order to outperform on the basis of this measure too. Even though the Carhart model reduces the possible opportunities, there exist other such strategies that generate abnormal returns within this model (see e.g. the illiquidity risk factor in Pastor and Stambaugh 2003). The need for a more general measure capturing all these types of risks is obvious. Secondly, there is no robust theory explaining why the size, value and momentum strategies are characterized as risk factors. Hence, this model may misinterpret randomly fluctuating returns for risk factors, penalizing genuinely added value. Consequently, a measure based on the sound economic theory is needed.

3.5 *Harvey–Siddique alpha*

Given the theoretical motivation of Section 2, it is argued that a prudent investor should evaluate his investments according to the following model:

$$r_{p,t} = \alpha_{\text{HS}} + \beta_p r_{m,t} + c(S^- - S^+)_t + \varepsilon_t \tag{15}$$

where $(S^- - S^+)$ stands for the returns of the negative coskewness spread strategy, defined in the next section. The intercept of this model, (a_{HS}), termed as the *Harvey–Siddique alpha,* will give us the value added by the manager over and above the covariance and negative coskewness risks.

As Harvey and Siddique (2000, p. 1276) point out, this asset pricing model has two main advantages over a model that includes the squared market returns as a factor (e.g. as in Kraus and Litzenberger 1976): First, the measure of standardized coskewness is constructed by residuals, so it is by construction independent of the market return and, secondly, β_p in Equation (15) is similar to the standard CAPM beta. Moreover, standardized coskewness is unit free and analogous to a factor loading. Apart from the parsimony in comparison with the Carhart (1997) measure, the Harvey–Siddique alpha is also more general since it captures the excess returns from every possible strategy that loads negative skewness to the portfolio, and it is based on an asset pricing model built within a rigorous utility theory framework.

4. Data and methodology

We follow the methodology of Harvey and Siddique (2000) to construct the zero-cost negative coskewness portfolio ($S^- - S^+$). Using 60 monthly excess returns $r_{i,t}$, we regress the market model for each individual stock i

$$r_{i,t} = \alpha_i + \beta_i r_{m,t} + \varepsilon_{i,t} \qquad (16)$$

extracting the residuals $\varepsilon_{i,t}$, which are by definition orthogonal to the excess market returns $r_{m,t}$. Therefore, these residuals are net of the systematic risk as this is measured by the covariance of the stock returns with the market returns. However, they still incorporate the coskewness risk. Therefore, we can get a measure of the standardized coskewness of each stock's returns with the market returns. This is given by:

$$\beta_{i,\text{SKD}} = \frac{E[\varepsilon_{i,t}\varepsilon_{m,t}^2]}{\sqrt{E[\varepsilon_{i,t}^2]E[\varepsilon_{m,t}^2]}} \qquad (17)$$

where $\varepsilon_{i,t}$ is the residual previously extracted from the market model for stock i at time t; and $\varepsilon_{m,t}$, the deviation of the excess market return at time t from the average excess market return in the examined period.[5]

Ranking the stocks according to this coskewness measure, we form a value-weighted portfolio of the 30% stocks with the most positively coskewed returns (S^+), while the 30% stocks with the most negatively coskewed returns form another portfolio (S^-). The next step is to find the returns of these portfolios on the 61st month. The spread of these two portfolios' returns ($S^- - S^+$) will yield the return generated by the self-financing strategy of buying the stocks with the most negatively coskewed returns and selling short the stocks with the most positively coskewed returns.

To construct the coskewness measure, β_{SKD}, we employ data for monthly returns and market values of all stocks being listed in the FTSE All Share Index during the period 1986–2005 with at least 61 observations. The number of stocks utilized to create the coskewness portfolios varied from 413 (with market value of £339,404 million) in December 1991 to 581 in January 2004 (with market value of £1,045,331 million). The risk-free rate is given by the interbank monthly rate, and the market returns are the returns of the FTSE All Share Index. The source for the data and the FTSE All Share Index listings is Thomson Datastream and Worldscope, respectively.

The coskewness portfolios' returns are constructed for the period January 1991–December 2005. Table 1 presents the average returns of the zero-cost coskewness spread portfolio ($S^- - S^+$) and the market excess returns for various periods. A striking feature of the zero-cost portfolio is that it yielded, on average, a return of 2.09% p.a., over the period 1991–2005, having a very low standard deviation. Figure 1 shows these returns along with the excess market returns. The subperiod analysis showed that the negative coskewness risk was more highly priced in the last subperiod, i.e. January 2001–December 2005.

Following Cuthbertson et al. (2008), we proxy the size strategy returns (SMB) as the difference between the monthly returns of the Hoare Govett Small Cap and the FTSE 100 indices and the value strategy returns (HML) as the spread between the monthly returns of the MSCI UK Growth and the MSCI UK Value indices. The returns of the momentum strategy (MOM) were calculated by ranking all available stocks at time t according to their returns between the months $t - 12$ and $t - 1$. The top 30% (value-weighted) of these stocks were classified as Winners and the bottom 30% as Losers. The spread of their monthly returns at $t + 1$ is taken as the momentum strategy return. The portfolios were rebalanced on a monthly basis.

Table 1 indicates that the size and value strategies yielded positive returns mainly during the subperiod January 2001–December 2005. Estimating the measures of standardized coskewness of these strategies for the period January 2001–December 2005, these were $\beta_{\text{SKD}}^{\text{SMB}} = -0.257$ for the SMB strategy and $\beta_{\text{SKD}}^{\text{HML}} = -0.107$ for the HML strategy. The MOM strategy yielded

Table 1. Excess market, size, value, momentum and coskewness returns.

	Excess market (%)	$(S^- - S^+)$ strategy (%)	Size strategy (%)	Value strategy (%)	Momentum strategy(%)
Panel A: Total period 1991–2005					
Average monthly returns	0.42	0.174	0.175	0.18	0.169
Standard deviation	4.01	0.96	3.65	2.81	1.39
Panel B: Subperiod 1991–1995					
Average monthly returns	0.73	0.021	−0.08	0.09	0.15
Standard deviation	4.09	0.62	3.63	2.14	0.74
Panel C: Subperiod 1996–2000					
Average monthly returns	0.63	0.21	−0.001	0.001	0.09
Standard deviation	3.71	1.07	4.01	3.52	1.64
Panel D: Subperiod 2001–2005					
Average monthly returns	−0.09	0.28	0.61	0.44	0.26
Standard deviation	4.21	1.11	3.31	2.61	1.62

Note: This table presents the average monthly returns and the corresponding standard deviation of the coskewness, the size, the value and the momentum strategy along with the excess market returns. Panel A presents the results for the total period January 1991–December 2005; Panel B, the corresponding results for the subperiod January 1991–December 1995; Panel C, the subperiod January 1996–December 2000; and Panel D, the subperiod January 2001–December 2005.

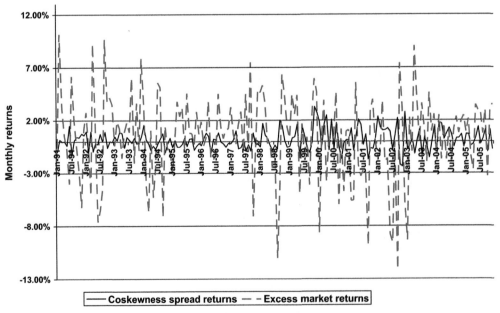

Figure 1. Excess market returns and coskewness strategy returns.
Notes: This figure shows the monthly excess returns of the FTSE All Share Index (dashed line) and the monthly returns of the zero-cost coskewness spread strategy (solid line), as defined in Section 4, during the period January 1991–December 2005.

Table 2. Unit trusts' descriptive statistics.

Periods	Number of trusts ≥ 60 observations	Trusts' average excess returns (p.a.)	Average Sharpe ratio	Average downside Sharpe ratio
Panel A: Trusts' returns and Sharpe ratios				
1991–1995	150	4.61	−0.089	−0.051
1996–2000	197	−5.76	−0.116	−0.065
2001–2005	265	−2.01	−0.04	−0.022
1991–2005	273	−2.93	−0.039	−0.024

	Average Jensen alpha (p.a.) (%)	Average Carhart alpha (p.a.) (%)	Average Harvey–Siddique alpha (p.a.) (%)
Panel B: Trusts' Jensen, Carhart and Harvey–Siddique alphas			
1991–1995	−3.65	−3.37	−3.81
1996–2000	−1.30	−1.57	−1.91
2001–2005	−0.98	−2.68	−2.33
1991–2005	−1.23	−1.97	−2.12

Note: Panel A presents the number of trusts with more than 60 observations, their average annualized excess returns as well as the average Sharpe ratios and downside Sharpe ratios during the whole sample period period, January 1991–December 2005, and the subperiods January 1991–December 1995, Janurary 1996–December 2000 and January 2001–December 2005. Panel B reports the average annualized Jensen, Carhart and Harvey–Siddique alphas of the trusts for the same periods

a positive average return throughout the examined period, but this was even higher during the last subperiod. The measure of standardized coskewness had a value of $\beta_{SKD}^{MOM} = -0.08$ for the whole period and $\beta_{SKD}^{MOM} = -0.43$ for the last subperiod. Hence, all these strategies had negatively coskewed returns, especially when they yielded high average returns. As a result, a trust manager who followed these strategies was loading negative skewness to his portfolio, extracting the corresponding premium.

For the UK unit trusts, the Lipper fund database is used to acquire Net Asset Values (NAV) on a monthly basis.[6] We select the unit trusts that are marked for sale in the UK, and they have domicile either in the UK or overseas. The performance evaluation study refers to unit trusts that have the FTSE All Share Index as their fund manager benchmark in the Lipper database, justifying the use of the returns of this index as a proxy for market returns. To alleviate the problem of survivorship bias, the database we utilize also includes unit trusts that have ceased operations before 2005. To have a meaningful performance study, only trusts with more than 61 observations of NAVs were employed. This selection leaves us with 273 unit trusts having more than 60 monthly returns for the period January 1991–December 2005. The minimum number of trusts in our final data set is 150 in 1991, and the maximum number is 273 in 2004. Table 2 provides the number of trusts for the examined subperiods as well as their average excess returns.

5. Unit trusts' performance

5.1 *Average returns and Sharpe ratios*

The average excess returns earned by the equity trusts are given in Panel A of Table 2. An interesting observation is that the trusts exhibited consistently lower returns in comparison with the excess returns of the FTSE All Share Index in the whole sample period as well as in the three examined subperiods. The high fees they charged is regarded to be the main reason why this under-performance is observed.[7] Non-stock holdings could provide another explanation, but the lack of holdings data does not allow us to test it formally. However, the results of the CAPM analysis showed that the average beta of the trusts was 0.93, providing some evidence for this argument.

Panel A of Table 2 also provides the average Sharpe ratios of the trusts for the period January 1991–December 2005. For the calculation of this average, the individual Sharpe ratio of each trust with more than 60 monthly returns was first calculated. It should be reminded that during bear market phases, Sharpe ratios can take negative values. The purpose of calculating this ratio is to compare it with the DSR that replaces the variance of the monthly returns with their semi-variance. The average DSRs are also reported in Panel A of Table 2. The most important finding is that the average DSR is much lower, in absolute value, in comparison with the average Sharpe ratio for each of the examined subperiods as well as the whole sample period. The explanation for this finding is that twice the returns' semi-variance was much higher than their variance; consequently, the excess returns were much more severely penalized under the DSR measure.

The previous result is consistent for all of the individual trusts and shows that the trusts' returns were negatively skewed indeed. This is an interesting finding for prudent investors who are averse to negative skewness as well as for loss averse investors who are even more averse to this feature. It also shows that if the DSR replaces the Sharpe ratio as a performance measure, the managers will be incentivized to avoid large negative returns, meeting the preferences of their clients.

5.2 *Jensen alpha*

Focussing now on measures based on asset pricing models, the first measure to employ is Jensen's alpha, given by the intercept of regression (12). Over the period January 1991–December 2005, the median trust had a Jensen alpha of −1.77% p.a. Figure 2 shows the distribution of the estimated Jensen alphas for all the trusts during this period. It is evident that the majority of the trusts have negative alphas, but their distribution is positively skewed. This finding implies that there are a few trusts who have quite high positive alphas. Having ranked the trusts according to their alphas, Table 3 shows the corresponding values for various percentiles of the distribution. The upper 25% of the trusts had a positive alpha, though very few of these estimates were statistically significant. On the other hand, the bottom 45% of the trusts exhibited alphas of less than −2% p.a.. These results are in accordance with the previous literature, as this is reviewed in Cuthbertson et al. (2007).

The common practice of ranking trusts according to their alpha point estimates could be misleading, since the standard error of the estimate is not taken into account. It has been suggested by Kosowski et al. (2006) that ranking trusts according to their *t*-statistics is more appropriate, since this adjusts the point estimate for its in-sample variability (standard error). Table 4 presents such a ranking, using the corresponding *t*-values.[8] Using a 95% confidence interval for the *t*-statistic, only 5% of the trusts exhibited significantly positive managerial ability. On the other hand, more than 30% of the trusts exhibited significantly negative managerial ability.

An immediate conclusion from the shape of the alphas' distribution is that according to this static, mean–variance measure, managerial ability existed, but only for a very small portion of the trust managers. Furthermore, even the quadratic investors who chose the bottom 30% trusts would

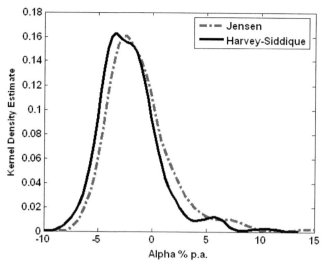

Figure 2. Jensen and Harvey–Siddique alphas.
Note: This figure shows the distribution of the trusts' Jensen alpha estimates (dash-dotted line) and the distribution of the trusts' Harvey–Siddique alpha estimates (solid line) during the period January 1991–December 2005. This distribution as well as the distributions in the following figures were smoothed using a Kernel density estimator. We employed a Gaussian kernel function and the corresponding optimal bandwith (Silverman 1986).

Table 3. Alpha rankings, total period 1991–2005.

	Top	1%	5%	10%	30%	median	70%	90%	95%	99%	Bottom
Jensen alpha (%)	15.51	9.05	4.57	2.31	−0.37	−1.77	−2.96	−4.32	−4.89	−6.08	−15.67
t-stat	1.97	1.96	2.31	1.35	−0.27	−0.97	−3.59	−3.38	−2.62	−3.89	−3.97
p-value	0.03	0.03	0.01	0.09	0.37	0.25	<0.01	<0.01	0.01	<0.01	<0.01
Carhart alpha (%)	13.68	4.92	3.01	1.08	−1	−2.32	−3.37	−4.66	−5.48	−7.15	−16.49
t-stat	1.98	3.2	0.98	0.51	−2.64	−1.56	−3.88	−4.25	−2.42	−2.57	−4.23
p-value	0.03	<0.01	0.25	0.35	0.01	0.13	<0.01	<0.01	0.01	0.01	<0.01
H–S alpha (%)	11.20	6.45	2.87	0.88	−1.20	−2.36	−3.69	−4.97	−5.68	−6.94	−17.07
t-stat	1.43	1.84	1.01	0.49	−0.88	−2.34	−3.53	−3.61	−2.37	−4.27	−4.28
p-value	0.14	0.08	0.21	0.35	0.29	0.01	<0.01	<0.01	0.01	<0.01	<0.01
boots. p-value	0.06	0.03	0.14	0.31	0.18	0.01	<0.01	<0.01	<0.01	<0.01	<0.01

Note: This table presents the rankings of the trusts over the whole sample period, January 1991–December 2005, based on the estimates of the annualized Jensen, Carhart and Harvey–Siddique (H–S) alphas. In particular, the annualized alpha estimates for various percentiles of the trusts' rankings are reported along with their corresponding t-statistics and p-values. Reported t-values use Newey–West (1987) heteroskedasticity and autocorrelation consistent standard errors. The last line of the Table reports the corresponding p-values for the Harvey–Siddique alpha of each fund, as they are derived from the bootstrap methodology discussed in Section 6.2.

have been significantly better off if they had invested in a low-cost index fund. Since we deal with net returns, high expenses and management fees could well be a reason for the significant underperformance of many trusts. The nonnormality of the alphas' distribution[9] can be explained in two ways: either managers exhibited heterogeneous abilities, with a few of them being highly skilful or these managers adopted heterogeneous risk-taking strategies. The next subsections investigate further these hypotheses.

Table 4. *t*-Statistics rankings, total period, 1991–2005.

	Top	1%	5%	10%	30%	Median	70%	90%	95%	99%	Bottom
t-Jensen alpha	2.81	2.61	1.91	0.85	−0.18	−1.14	−2.05	−3.59	−4.18	−4.80	−6.96
Jensen alpha (%)	13.71	6.99	6.05	1.73	−0.40	−1.32	−3.24	−5.21	−3.28	−6.07	−3.25
p-value	<0.01	0.01	0.07	0.27	0.39	0.21	0.05	<0.01	<0.01	<0.01	<0.01
t-Carhart alpha	3.20	1.98	1.38	0.64	−0.65	−1.55	−2.47	−4.03	−4.39	−4.97	−7.14
Carhart alpha (%)	4.92	13.6	1.45	1.57	−1.17	−3.64	−1.87	−4.45	−3.45	−5.96	−3.35
p-value	<0.01	0.03	0.16	0.33	0.33	0.08	<0.01	<0.01	<0.01	<0.01	<0.01
t-H–S alpha	2.20	1.98	1.31	0.40	−0.71	−1.54	−2.60	−3.90	−4.58	−5.33	−6.70
H–S alpha (%)	5.85	9.55	6.12	1.41	−1.45	−1.55	−4.17	−4.82	−4.46	−4.70	−3.21
p-value	0.01	0.03	0.09	0.37	0.25	0.08	0.01	<0.01	<0.01	<0.01	<0.01

Note: This table presents the rankings of the trusts over the whole sample period, January 1991– December 2005, based on the *t*-statistics of the Jensen, Carhart and Harvey–Siddique alphas. In particular, the *t*-statistics for various percentiles of the trusts' rankings are reported along with their corresponding annualized alphas and *p*-values. Reported *t*-values use Newey–West (1987) heteroskedasticity and autocorrelation consistent standard errors.

5.3 Carhart alpha

This subsection evaluates the trusts by using the intercept of the Carhart asset pricing model in Equation (14) as a performance measure. The rankings of the trusts according to their Carhart alphas, along with the corresponding *t*-statistics and *p*-values are given in Table 3, while Table 4 provides the rankings according to the *t*-values of the Carhart alpha point estimates. In comparison to Jensen's alpha, the main conclusion is that the achieved performance is now much lower for every percentile of the trusts' distribution. Figure 3 plots the distribution of the trusts' Carhart alphas.

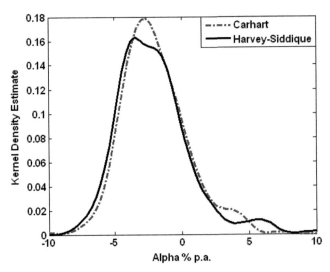

Figure 3. Carhart and Harvey–Siddique alphas.
Note: This figure shows the distribution of the trusts' Carhart alpha estimates (dash-dotted line) and the distribution of the trusts' Harvey–Siddique alpha estimates (solid line) during the period January 1991–December 2005.

In particular, the median trust's Carhart alpha was -2.32% p.a. over the period January 1991–December 2005. Therefore, it is argued that attributing the returns of the size, momentum and value strategies to the corresponding risk factors, as the Carhart regression does, significantly diminishes the performance of the trust managers. Interestingly, there were only very few funds that exhibited a positive and statistically significant alpha over this period. This result points to the argument that, if an investor considers the documented 'anomalies' as risk factors, he would be much better off by investing in a low-cost index fund rather than the median UK equity unit trust. Nevertheless, the relative ranking of the funds according to their Carhart alphas is similar to their corresponding ranking according to their Jensen alphas. Formally, the Spearman's correlation coefficient of these two rankings is $\rho = 0.916$.[10]

With respect to managerial incentives, Figure 4 depicts the loadings of the trusts' returns on the size, value and momentum factors over the whole sample period. It is interesting to observe that the managers mainly followed size strategies. There is no evidence for a unanimous adoption of value and momentum strategies, since the estimates of the corresponding loadings are evenly distributed around zero for the examined trusts. In particular, while 199 of the trusts had a significantly (at the 5% level) positive loading on the size strategy, only 48 of them had a significantly positive loading on the momentum strategy, and just 11 of them on the value strategy. These findings are in line with Cuthbertson et al. (2008) and in contrast to the stylized facts of the US literature (Carhart 1997), i.e. that the managers consistently follow value and momentum strategies.

The explanation for this finding lies in the fact that these strategies yielded highly volatile returns, which were not consistently positive throughout our sample period. Consequently, we would not expect managers to stick to specific strategies, especially when these are not performing well. This is a fundamental issue demonstrating the main disadvantage of the Carhart model, that is to assume that managers follow specific strategies even though these do not persistently yield positive returns, and do not rigorously represent any specific risk factor. This is also an important issue when comparing asset pricing models on the basis of a selection criterion. In particular, we

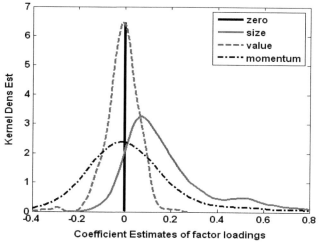

Figure 4. Size, value and momentum factor loadings.
Note: This figure plots the densities of the estimated loadings on the size ($\hat{\beta}_1$, solid curve), value ($\hat{\beta}_2$, dashed curve) and momentum ($\hat{\beta}_3$, dash-dotted curve) strategies for each trust, derived from the Carhart regression (14) for the period January 1991–December 2005. The vertical line corresponds to a zero coefficient.

employ the Schwartz information criterion (SIC), that captures the trade off between obtaining the better fit model and using the fewest possible regressors.[11] Our regression analysis shows that on the basis of this criterion, for the 38% of the funds the CAPM should be preferred. The reason is that for these funds, the enhancement of the explanatory power in the Carhart model is not sufficient to justify the use of three additional regressors. Therefore, the parsimony of the asset pricing model is a highly desirable property.

5.4 *Harvey–Siddique alpha*

This subsection presents the results of the unit trusts' evaluation using the Harvey–Siddique asset pricing model given in Equation (15). Interestingly, the examined trusts had a median Harvey–Siddique alpha of −2.36% p.a. This is much lower than the median Jensen alpha. Figure 2 plots the distribution of the Harvey–Siddique alphas along with the distribution of the Jensen alphas. It is evident that the whole distribution is shifted to the left, as we switch from the Jensen alpha to the Harvey–Siddique alpha. The main explanation for this difference is that trust managers followed coskewness strategies, earning positive returns that were regarded as 'abnormal returns' according to the CAPM. If a manager had genuinely added value to his portfolio, without adding negative skewness, then there should be no difference between the results derived by these two measures.

To verify this conjecture, it is interesting to note that 263 out of the total 273 trusts had a positive loading (coefficient $\hat{c}$) on the coskewness factor, and this positive loading was statistically significant at the 5% level for 175 funds during the examined period. Figure 5 plots the density

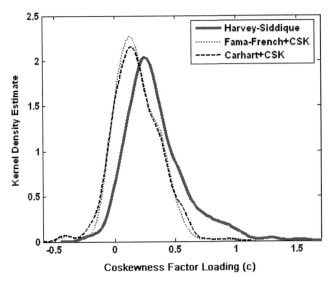

Figure 5. Coskewness factor loadings.
Note: This figure plots the densities of the estimated factor loadings ($\hat{c}$) on the coskewness strategy from three asset pricing models. The solid curve shows the density of the estimated factor loadings ($\hat{c}$) from the Harvey–Siddique regression (15) for each trust. The dotted curve shows the corresponding density of the estimated coskewness factor loadings derived from the augmented Fama–French model, given in Equation (19). The dashed curve shows the density of the estimated coskewness factor loadings derived from the augmented Carhart model, which is defined in Equation (20). The estimates of these loadings refer to the period January 1991–December 2005.

of the loadings on the coskewness strategy (solid line), showing that more than 90% of the trusts had a positive coefficient estimate, and more than the 50% of the trusts had a coefficient point estimate of more than 0.25. This finding confirms that the majority of the funds were employing strategies that essentially loaded negative skewness, without this implying that they consciously followed the specific negative coskewness spread strategy $(S^- - S^+)$, as defined in Equation (15).[12] The Spearman correlation coefficient for the rankings of the trusts according to their Jensen and Harvey–Siddique alphas is found to be $\rho = 0.969$.

Ranking the trusts according to their Harvey–Siddique alphas, Table 3 reports their estimates for various percentiles of this distribution. It is striking to observe that only the 16% of the trusts had positive alphas. On the other hand, the 55% of the funds had an alpha of less than -2% p.a.. Ranking the trusts according to the t-values of these alphas in Table 4, the results are equivalent. Only three funds had significantly positive alphas at the 5% level, while 41% of the trusts had significantly negative alpha estimates. With respect to the distribution of the alphas, this is now closer to normality, being less positively skewed in comparison with the Jensen alphas' distribution.[13]

Interestingly, the two trusts with the highest Jensen alphas (15.5% and 13.71% p.a. correspondingly), which account for the extreme positive tail of the distribution, are the trusts with the 2nd and 8th (out of 273) highest loadings of the coskewness risk factor (with coefficient point estimates of $\hat{c} = 1.53$ and $\hat{c} = 0.98$ correspondingly). Hence, the conjecture of heterogeneous risk-taking we previously made is supported by the results and part of this heterogeneity is due to the negative coskewness risk. With respect to the explanatory power of the Harvey–Siddique model, we found that this should be preferred to the CAPM on the basis of the SIC for all of the trusts we examined. The enhancement in the explanatory power through the addition of the coskewness risk factor comes at the minimum possible cost, i.e. only one extra regressor, leading to lower values of SIC for each trust. As a result, the parsimony of the Harvey–Siddique model is verified to be a highly attractive characteristic for the sample of trusts we examine.

There are two main conclusions from these results: The first is that prudent investors, who are averse to negative skewness and should use the Harvey–Siddique alpha to evaluate their trust managers, would have been better off by investing in a low-cost index fund, as compared with more than 80% of the available trusts over the period January 1991–December 2005.[14] The second conclusion is that managers were very successful in reaping the negative coskewness premium, presenting it as 'added value'- higher Jensen alpha. Figure 6 presents in a scatterplot the estimate of the Jensen alpha for each trust versus the estimate of the negative coskewness strategy loading $(\hat{c})$, demonstrating this positive relationship. The Pearson correlation coefficient of these two variables is 0.45. More formally, regressing the Jensen alpha point estimates on the coskewness factor loadings, we get the following result (t-values are given in the parentheses):

$$\hat{\alpha}_{\text{Jensen}} = \underset{(-11.8)}{-0.0318} + \underset{(9.32)}{0.0593} \; \hat{c} \quad R^2 = 24.3\%$$

The regression results show that a large part of the variation in the Jensen alphas can be explained by the trusts' coskewness factor loadings alone. This relationship is strongly significant. This finding confirms the argument that the trusts with the highest Jensen alphas were on average those that loaded most of the negative coskewness risk. In other words, it can be argued that unit trusts would have been useful investment vehicles for agents with quadratic preferences that regard the coskewness premium as a 'free lunch', but not for prudent investors.

Comparing the results derived from the Harvey–Siddique models with the corresponding results derived from the Carhart model, we find that for 63% of the examined trusts the Harvey–Siddique

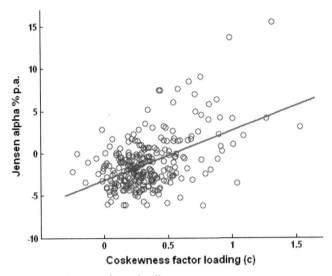

Figure 6. Jensen alphas and coskewness factor loadings.
Note: This figure presents the scatterplot of the Jensen alpha estimates from regression (12) versus the coefficient estimates ($\hat{c}$) on the coskewness strategy from regression (15) for each trust for the period January 1991–December 2005. It also plots the fitted values from a standard least-squares regression involving these variables.

model should be preferred on the basis of the SIC. Again, the parsimony of this model is a highly attractive feature. The distribution of the Harvey–Siddique alphas is very similar to the distribution of the Carhart alphas, as this can be seen from Figure 3. This result provides support for the argument that the coskewness factor may partly capture the information contained in the Carhart regressors. Finally, the Spearman correlation coefficient between the trusts' rankings according to the Carhart and Harvey–Siddique alphas is $\rho = 0.9362$.

6. Robustness

6.1 *Adding the coskewness factor to the Fama–French and Carhart models*

In this subsection, we examine whether the previous results are modified if we take the Fama–French or the Carhart model as the benchmark, and augment it by adding the negative coskewness factor ($S^- - S^+$). This approach has been taken by Hung et al. (2004) in an asset pricing context and by Ding and Shawky (2007) in a performance evaluation context. In particular, we examine if the addition of the coskewness factor affects the conclusions with respect to trusts' managerial ability, whether the evidence for the loading of the negative coskewness risk is robust to the inclusion of other risk factors, as well as whether the augmented models exhibit superior explanatory power.

As it has been previously discussed, the Fama–French model adds to the CAPM a size and a value risk factor. Consequently, the Fama–French alpha (α_{FF}) is the intercept of the following regression model:

$$r_{p,t} = \alpha_{FF} + \beta_p r_{m,t} + \beta_1 \text{SMB}_t + \beta_2 \text{HML}_t + \epsilon_t \tag{18}$$

Employing this asset pricing model for the 273 trusts of our sample during the period January 1991–December 2005, we estimate their Fama–French alphas. Figure 7 exhibits the distribution

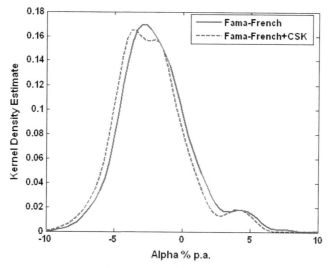

Figure 7. Fama–French and Fama–French augmented alphas.
Note: This figure shows the distribution of the trusts' estimated alphas derived from the Fama–French asset pricing model, which is given in Equation (18) (solid curve) as well as the corresponding distribution of the alphas derived from the augmented Fama–French model, which is given in Equation (19) (dashed curve). These alpha estimates of the trusts refer to the period January 1991–December 2005.

of these trusts' alphas. This is very similar to the distribution of the Carhart alphas illustrated in Figure 3. The magnitude of the Fama–French alphas is also similar to the Carhart ones. In particular, the median trust has a Fama–French alpha of -2.19% p.a. It is interesting to note that 220 of these trusts had a negative Fama–French alpha point estimate, and for 113 of them this point estimate is significantly negative at the 5% level. The Spearman rank correlation coefficient between the Fama–French and the Carhart measures is extremely high, equal to $\rho = 0.979$.

Adding the negative coskewness factor to the Fama–French model, the augmented regression to be estimated is given by:

$$r_{p,t} = \alpha_{\text{FF+CSK}} + \beta_p r_{m,t} + \beta_1 \text{SMB}_t + \beta_2 \text{HML}_t + c(S^- - S^+)_t + \epsilon_t \tag{19}$$

The intercept of this model, $\alpha_{\text{FF+CSK}}$, shows the value that the manager added to the portfolio once the returns generated by the size, value and coskewness strategies have been attributed to the corresponding risk factors. We estimate this augmented model, and the distribution of the corresponding alphas is plotted in Figure 7. The inclusion of the coskewness factor shifts the whole distribution of the Fama–French alphas to the left. The median trust had an augmented Fama–French alpha of -2.57% p.a. The estimated alpha was negative for 231 of the trusts, while this estimate was significantly negative at the 5% level for 123 of these trusts. With respect to the trusts' rankings according to these two measures, their Spearman correlation coefficient is equal to $\rho = 0.974$.

The dotted curve in Figure 5 illustrates the density of the estimated coskewness factor loadings ($\hat{c}$) derived from regression (19). The magnitude of these loadings is slightly reduced relative to the Harvey–Siddique model, but they are still predominantly positive. In particular, 234 out of the total 273 trusts had a positive loading on the coskewness factor, and for 101 of these trusts this loading was significantly positive at the 5% level. The explanation we put forward for this finding is that the value and size factors partly capture the negative coskewness risk. Nevertheless, the fact that the estimated coskewness loadings do not evaporate in the presence of these factors leads to the conclusion that the coskewness factor we have employed in this study carries important information for the trusts' returns.

On the basis of the SIC, the augmented Fama–French model should be preferred to its standard version for 32% of the examined trusts. This is an important result if we take into account the fact that the SIC heavily penalizes the inclusion of an additional regressor. To stress the importance of the coskewness factor, it should be noted that comparing the standard Fama–French model with the Harvey–Siddique one on the basis of the SIC, the latter is preferred for 66% of the trusts. The explanatory power of the Harvey–Siddique model coupled with its attractive parsimony make it the preferred one.

We repeat the previous analysis, adding now the negative coskewness factor to the Carhart model which is given in Equation (14). Hence, the augmented Carhart model is now given by

$$r_{p,t} = \alpha_{\text{Carhart+CSK}} + \beta_p r_{m,t} + \beta_1 \text{SMB}_t + \beta_2 \text{HML}_t + \beta_3 \text{MOM}_t + c(S^- - S^+)_t + \epsilon_t \quad (20)$$

The intercept of this model, $\alpha_{\text{Carhart+CSK}}$, shows the value the manager added to the portfolio once the returns generated by the size, value, momentum and coskewness strategies have been attributed to the corresponding risk factors. The estimated alphas are very similar to the ones derived by the augmented Fama–French model, to the extent that the two distributions are not distinguishable. The median trust has an augmented Carhart alpha of -2.52% p.a. For 232 of the trusts, the estimated alpha was negative, while this estimated value was significantly negative for 124 trusts. The ranking of the trusts based on the augmented Carhart model is very similar to the ranking based on its standard version. The corresponding Spearman rank correlation coefficient is equal to $\rho = 0.979$.

The estimated loadings on the coskewness factor ($\hat{c}$) are very similar to the ones derived by the augmented Fama–French model. Their distribution is illustrated by the dashed curve in Figure 5. Even though their magnitude is slightly reduced with respect to the Harvey–Siddique model, they are still positive for 229 of the examined trusts. Moreover, for 106 of these trusts the coskewness factor loading was significantly positive at the 5% level. Therefore, the argument that the trusts' managers loaded negative coskewness to their portfolios during the examined period holds true even when we include the commonly used value, size and momentum risk factors.

Comparing the Carhart model with its augmented version on the basis of the SIC, the Carhart model is preferred for the 65% of the trusts. These results provide further support for the argument that the Carhart factors mimic the coskewness factor to some extent. In other words, the addition of the coskewness factor to the Carhart model is not expected to immensely enhance the explanatory power of the augmented model. Nevertheless, the finding that the inclusion of the coskewness factor leads to a lower SIC value for the rest 35% of the trusts' acts as a warning for the fitness of the Carhart model. The information contained in the negative coskewness factor is of great importance for the appropriate performance attribution of a large number of funds.

6.2 *Bootstrap analysis*

The previous analysis relied on t-statistics to examine the significance of the performance measures' point estimates. This is a valid procedure under the Gauss–Markov assumption of normality for the regressions' residuals. Nevertheless, the nonnormality of the alphas' distribution and the evidence of heterogeneous risk-taking may cast doubts on the validity of the normality assumption, especially for the trusts at the tails of the alphas' distribution. If the residuals are not normally distributed, then the t-statistics may lead to spurious results, and the extreme alpha estimates may be due to sampling variability, i.e. luck. Employing the Jarque–Bera test, the assumption of normality in residuals is violated for the majority of the funds for each asset pricing model considered. In order to examine the impact of sampling variability on the results discussed in the previous sections, this subsection employs a simple bootstrap methodology at the individual fund level.[15]

In particular, we employ the following bootstrap procedure, accordingly adjusted for the Harvey–Siddique asset pricing model. Extracting the time series of residuals $\{\hat{\epsilon}_{i,t}, t = T_{i0}, \ldots, T_{i1}\}$ for each trust i from the regression

$$r_t = \hat{\alpha}_{HS} + \hat{\beta}r_{m,t} + \hat{c}(S^- - S^+)_t + \hat{\epsilon}_t, \tag{21}$$

we draw a sample with replacement for each of these trusts and create a pseudo-time series of resampled residuals $\{\hat{\epsilon}_{i,t_\varepsilon}^{b^l}, t_\varepsilon = s_{T_{i0}}^{b^l}, \ldots, s_{T_{i1}}^{b^l}\}$, where b^l is an index for the bootstrap number, and where each of the time series indices $s_{T_{i0}}^{b^l}, \ldots, s_{T_{i1}}^{b^l}$ are drawn randomly from $[T_{i0}, \ldots, T_{i1}]$.

Using this pseudo-time series of resampled residuals, we construct for each trust, i, a time-series of monthly excess returns $r_{t_\varepsilon}^{b^l}$ for each bootstrapped sample b^l, employing the already estimated set of coefficients $\{\hat{\alpha}_{HS}, \hat{\beta}, \hat{c}\}$

$$r_{t_\varepsilon}^{b^l} = \hat{\alpha}_{HS} + \hat{\beta}r_{m,t} + \hat{c}(S^- - S^+)_t + \hat{\epsilon}_{t_\varepsilon}^{b^l} \tag{22}$$

for $t = T_{i0}, \ldots, T_{i1}$ and $t_\varepsilon = s_{T_{i0}}^{b^l}, \ldots, s_{T_{i1}}^{b^l}$. We subsequently use these pseudo-returns to re-estimate regression (15) for each bootstrap sample b^l, and we get an alpha estimate $\{\hat{\alpha}_{HS}^{b^l}\}$. Repeating the previous steps 1000 times, we have a set of 1000 alpha estimates for each fund i, having bootstrapped its residuals. This distribution of bootstrapped alphas can help us to derive confidence intervals for the point estimate without imposing any parametric assumption on the fund's residuals. In doing so, we can derive more robust conclusions with respect to the statistical significance of the estimated Harvey–Siddique alphas. In particular, the last line of Table 3 reports the corresponding p-values derived by the bootstrap methodology. The results show that the conclusions regarding the significance of the estimated Harvey–Siddique alphas do not get modified if we use the bootstrapped residuals.

We have also compared the bootstrapped alphas' distributions for a series of funds with the ones derived under the conventional regression analysis. The results, not reported due to space limitations but available upon request, show that the inference under the bootstrap methodology is not considerably different from the standard approach. Most importantly, the derived bootstrapped alphas' distributions are relatively symmetric; this is a quite interesting result, in light of the skewed bootstrapped alphas' distributions derived in Kosowski et al. (2006). The explanation we put forward is that the inclusion of a coskewness factor may considerably contribute to the symmetry of the residuals' distribution, since it attributes highly skewed returns to the corresponding risk factor, unlike other models that would regard them as residuals. The nonnormality in the regressions' residuals under the Harvey–Siddique model is mainly due to their excess kurtosis.

7. Conclusion

Higher moments in asset returns is a relatively neglected issue in the investment performance evaluation literature. This issue becomes even more important, if one takes into account the experimental evidence that large negative returns affect utility asymmetrically more than positive returns do. Consequently, a prudent investor should not use mean–variance measures to evaluate his investments, because they neglect his actual preferences and regard the negative coskewness premium as a 'free lunch'.

In the case of delegated asset management, this issue is very crucial, since the fund manager, if evaluated through mean–variance measures, will falsely interpret that the fund shareholder has no preferences over skewness, and he will be incentivized to follow tactical asset allocation strategies that load this type of risk, in order to reap the corresponding premium. Clearly, this situation generates a mismatch between objectives and outcomes, leading to erroneous conclusions with respect to the *ex post state verification* of the investment performance.

The limitations of the static, mean–variance measures motivate the adoption of a performance measure that adjusts for the negative coskewness risk, documented to be priced in the UK stock market. The Harvey–Siddique two-factor asset pricing model is qualified to be appropriate for a prudent investor, and it has a sound theoretical basis, unlike the Carhart asset pricing model. The intercept of this model, which we term as the *Harvey–Siddique alpha*, will reveal the genuine outperformance for such an investor, resolving the *ex post verification problem*.

This measure was employed for the evaluation of the UK equity unit trusts that had the FTSE All Share Index as their benchmark for the period January 1991–December 2005. The vast majority of the trusts exhibited a negative Harvey–Siddique alpha, significantly under-performing their benchmark. Actually, the median under-performance of the trusts (-2.32%) for prudent investors was of greater magnitude than the current average expense ratio they charge (*circa* 1.5%).

Interestingly, most of the trusts loaded negative coskewness to their portfolios, capturing part of the corresponding premium and correctly responding to their incentives, since they are currently being evaluated through mean–variance measures. This finding shows how a prudent investor would misinterpret this premium for genuinely added value, if he was using such a measure too. Hence, the call for the shift of interest from outperforming to matching investors' preferences and objectives becomes even more important, reflecting the advice of Charles Ellis (2005, p. 115) not to play 'the Loser's Game of trying to beat the market – a game that almost every investor will eventually lose'.

Acknowledgements

ESRC support through grant PTA-030-2005-00017 is gratefully acknowledged. The author would like to thank Adrian Jarvis of Morley Fund Management for the help with the data and his insightful comments. The author would also like to thank the participants of the FMA 2007 Doctoral Tutorial (Barcelona), CRETE 2007 (Naxos), EFA 2007 Doctoral Tutorial (Ljubljana), CFS Conference on Asset Management and International Capital Markets 2008 (Frankfurt), FMA Europe 2008 (Prague) as well as Keith Cuthbertson, Tom Flavin, Jonathan Fletcher, Chrisostomos Florackis, Mark Freeman, Campbell Harvey, Yvan Lengwiler (CFS discussant), Dirk Nitzsche, Alessandro Sbuelz (EFA discussant), Akhtar Siddique, Peter Spencer, Hany Shawky (FMA 2008 discussant), Dick Sweeney (FMA 2007 discussant) and Mike Wickens for their helpful suggestions.

Notes

1. The term 'unit trust' corresponds to the most commonly used term 'open-end mutual fund'. Henceforth, the two terms will be interchangeably used.
2. See the 2007 ICI Fact Book for further details.
3. Adcock (2007) stresses the importance of taking skewness into account when measuring portfolio performance.
4. Accepting 'free lunches' would be equivalent to discarding asset allocation. If there exist strategies that add value to portfolios without undertaking any further risk, then the optimal portfolio choice collapses to an infinite demand schedule for these strategies.
5. Following Harvey and Siddique (2000), we work with monthly returns. Coskewness factor returns could have been calculated on a weekly basis, extracting more information from higher-frequency data. Nevertheless, the funds' NAVs are available at a monthly frequency, and hence the factor returns should correspond to this frequency too. Moreover, in case weekly returns were calculated, the corresponding portfolios should have been rebalanced on a weekly basis,

making the issue of transaction costs even more crucial. We would like to thank an anonymous referee for raising this issue.

6. It should be noted that the NAV is calculated after the deduction of management fees and other expenses.
7. Khorana et al. (2009) claim that the equity trusts marked for sale in the UK had an average total expense ratio of 1.42% p.a. in 2002. The corresponding total shareholer cost was 2.48%.
8. In this study, reported t-values use Newey–West (1987) heteroskedasticity, and autocorrelation consistent standard errors.
9. The Kolmogorov–Smirnov test was employed to formally test the hypothesis of normality for the standardized alphas. The hypothesis of normality was rejected at levels even lower than 1%.
10. The Spearman's rank correlation coefficient is given by $\rho = 1 - \dfrac{6 \sum d_i^2}{n(n^2 - 1)}$, with $d_i = x_i - y_i$, where x_i and y_i are correspondingly the rankings of fund i according to the measures under examination, and n the number of funds.
11. Formally, the Schwartz Information Criterion (SIC) takes the value $\text{SIC} = n \ln(\text{RSS}/n) + (k + 1)\ln(n)$, where n is the number of observations; RSS, the sum of squared residuals; and k, the number of explanatory variables in the model. This expression is an increasing function of RSS and k. The model with the lower value of SIC is preferred.
12. Fund management practice shows that managers try to find and exploit patterns in stock returns in order to generate portfolios that beat the measures according to which they are evaluated. Therefore, a negative coskewness strategy does not necessarily mean that the manager consciously picks stocks with this characteristic, but that the strategies he implements actually mimic this statistical characteristic.
13. The null hypothesis of normality is marginally rejected at the 5% level using the Kolmogorov–Smirnov test.
14. We have evaluated the performance of unit trusts using the various measures for three distinct subperiods. The subperiod analysis verifies the robustness of the reported results. The median Harvey–Siddique alpha was lower than the median Carhart alpha and Jensen alpha for each of the subperiods. Moreover, the majority of the trusts loaded negative coskewness risk in each subperiod. This effect was more pronounced during the last subperiod, January 2001–December 2005, when the coskewness premium was at its highest level. The results are not reported due to space considerations and are available upon request.
15. Kosowski et al. (2006) suggest a novel cross-sectional bootstrap methodology to distinguish 'skill' from 'luck' in US mutual funds. Cuthbertson et al. (2008) also employ this novel bootstrap methodology to evaluate UK unit trusts for a series of commonly used performance measures. In contrast, our study employs a simpler, fund-by-fund bootstrap approach.

References

Adcock, C.J. 2005. Exploiting skewness to build an optimal hedge fund with a currency overlay. *European Journal of Finance* 11: 445–62.

Adcock, C.J. 2007. Measuring portfolio performance using a modified measure of risk. *Journal of Asset Management* 7: 388–403.

Black, F., and M. Scholes. 1973. The pricing of options and corporate liabilities. *Journal of Political Economy* 81: 637–54.

Blake, D., and A. Timmermann. 1998. Mutual fund performance: Evidence from the UK. *European Finance Review* 2: 57–77.

Bollen, N.P.B., and J.A. Busse. 2004. Short-term persistence in mutual fund performance. *Review of Financial Studies* 18: 569–697.

Campbell, J.Y., and T. Vuolteenaho. 2004. Bad beta, good beta. *American Economic Review* 94: 1249–75.

Carhart, M. 1997. On persistence in mutual fund performance. *Journal of Finance* 52: 57–82.

Chen, J., H. Hong, M. Huang, and J. Kubik. 2004. Does fund size erode mutual fund performance? The role of liquidity and organization. *American Economic Review* 94: 1276–302.

Cuthbertson, K., D. Nitzsche, and N. O' Sullivan. 2007. Mutual fund performance, Working Paper, Cass Business School.

Cuthbertson, K., D. Nitzsche, and N. O'Sullivan. 2008. Mutual fund performance: Skill or luck? *Journal of Empirical Finance* 15: 613–34.

Ding, B., and H.A. Shawky. 2007. The performance of hedge fund strategies and the asymmetry of return distributions. *European Financial Management* 13: 309–31.

Dittmar, R.F. 2002. Nonlinear pricing kernels, kurtosis preference, and evidence from the cross section of equity returns. *Journal of Finance* 57: 369–402.

Ellis, C.D. 2005. Investing success in two easy lessons. in *Bold thinking on investment management*, ed. R.N. Sullivan, Charloteville: CFA Institute.

Fama, E.F., and K.R. French. 1993. Common risk factors in the returns on stocks and bonds. *Journal of Financial Economics* 33: 3–56.

Fletcher, J., and D. Forbes. 2002. An exploration of the persistence of UK unit trusts performance. *Journal of Empirical Finance* 9: 475–93.

Fletcher, J., and D. Forbes. 2004. Performance evaluation of UK unit trusts within the stochastic discount factor framework. *Journal of Financial Research* 27: 289–306.

Goetzmann, W., J. Ingersoll, M. Spiegel, and I. Welch. 2007. Portfolio performance manipulation and manipulation-proof performance measures. *Review of Financial Studies* 20: 1503–46.

Golec, J., and M. Tamarkin. 1998. Bettors love skewness, not risk at the horse track. *Journal of Political Economy* 106: 205–25.

Gul, F. 1991. A theory of disappointment aversion. *Econometrica* 59: 667–86.

Harrison, M., and D. Kreps. 1979. Martingales and arbitrage in multiperiod security markets. *Journal of Economic Theory* 20: 381–408.

Harvey, C., and A. Siddique. 2000. Conditional skewness in asset pricing tests. *Journal of Finance* 55: 1263–95.

Hung, D.C., M. Shackleton, and X. Xu. 2004. CAPM, higher co-moment and factor models of UK stock returns. *Journal of Business Finance and Accounting* 31: 87–112.

Jackwerth, J.C. 2004. *Option-implied risk-neutral distributions and risk aversion.* Charlotteville: Research Foundation of AIMR.

Jegadeesh, N., and S. Titman. 1993. Returns to buying winners and selling losers: Implications for stock market efficiency. *Journal of Finance* 48: 65–91.

Jensen, M.C. 1968. The performance of mutual funds in the period 1945–1964. *Journal of Finance* 23: 389–416.

Kahneman, D., and A. Tverksy. 1979. Prospect theory: An analysis of decision under risk. *Econometrica* 47: 263–91.

Khorana, A., H. Servaes, and P. Tufano. 2009. Mutual fund fees around the world. *Review of Financial Studies* (forthcoming).

Kimball, M.S. 1990. Precautionary saving in the small and the large. *Econometrica* 58: 53–73.

Kosowski, R., A. Timmermann, R. Wermers, and H. White. 2006. Can mutual fund 'stars' really pick stocks? New evidence from a bootstrap analysis. *Journal of Finance* 56: 2551–95.

Kraus, A., and R. Litzenberger. 1976. Skewness preference and the valuation of risk assets. *Journal of Finance* 31: 1085–100.

Leland, H.E. 1999. Beyond mean–variance: Risk and performance measurement in a nonsymmetrical world. *Financial Analysts Journal* 27–36.

Markowitz, H.M. 1952. Portfolio selection. *Journal of Finance* 7: 77–91.

Merton, R.C. 1973. An intertemporal capital asset pricing model. *Econometrica* 41: 867–87.

Moreno, D., and R. Rodriguez. 2005. Performance evaluation considering the coskewness: A stochastic discount framework. *Managerial Finance* 32: 375–92.

Newey, W.K., and K.D. West. 1987. A simple, positive semi-definite, heteroskedasticity and autocorrelation consistent covariance matrix. *Econometrica* 55: 703–8.

Otten, R., and D. Bams. 2002. European mutual fund performance. *European Financial Management* 8: 75–101.

Pastor, L., and R.F. Stambaugh. 2003. Liquidity risk and expected stock returns. *Journal of Political Economy* 111: 642–85.

Quigley, G., and Sinquefield. 2000. Performance of UK Equity unit trusts. *Journal of Asset Management* 1: 72–92.

Segal, U., and A. Spivak. 1990. First order versus second order risk aversion. *Journal of Economic Theory* 51: 111–25.

Sharpe, W.F. 1966. Mutual fund performance. *Journal of Business* 39: 119–38.

Silverman, B.W. 1986. *Density estimation for statistics and data analysis.* London: Chapman and Hall.

Smith, D.R. 2007. Conditional coskewness and asset pricing. *Journal of Empirical Finance* 14: 91–119.

Smith, P.N., and M.R. Wickens. 2002. Asset pricing with observable stochastic discount factors. *Journal of Economic Surveys* 16: 397–446.

Thomas, A., and I. Tonks. 2001. Equity performance of segregated pension funds in the UK. *Journal of Asset Management* 1: 321–43.

Tonks, I. 2005. Performance persistence of pension fund managers. *Journal of Business* 78: 1917–42.

Treynor, J. 1965. How to rate management of investment funds. *Harvard Business Review* 43: 63–75.

Tufano, P. 2008. Saving whilst gambling: An empirical analysis of UK premium bonds. *American Economic Review* 98: 321–6.

Ziemba, W. 2005. The symmetric downside-risk Sharpe ratio. *Journal of Portfolio Management* 108–122.

Conditional performance evaluation for German equity mutual funds

Wolfgang Bessler[a], Wolfgang Drobetz[b] and Heinz Zimmermann[c]

[a] Center for Finance and Banking, Justus-Liebig-University Giessen, Licher Strasse 74, 35394 Giessen, Germany;
[b] Institute of Finance, University of Hamburg, Von-Melle-Park 5, 20146 Hamburg, Germany;
[c] Department of Finance, University of Basel, Petersgraben 51, 4003 Basel, Switzerland

We investigate the conditional performance of a sample of German equity mutual funds over the period from 1994 to 2003 using both the beta-pricing approach and the stochastic discount factor (SDF) framework. On average, mutual funds cannot generate excess returns relative to their benchmark that are large enough to cover their total expenses. Compared to unconditional alphas, fund performance sharply deteriorates when we measure conditional alphas. Given that stock returns are to some extent predictable based on publicly available information, conditional performance evaluation raises the benchmark for active fund managers because it gives them no credit for exploiting readily available information. Underperformance is more pronounced in the SDF framework than in beta-pricing models. The fund performance measures derived from alternative model specifications differ depending on the number of primitive assets taken to calibrate the SDF as well as the number of instrument variables used to scale assets and/or factors.

1. Introduction

The public interest in the German equity mutual fund industry has grown rapidly during the last decade. While total mutual fund holdings in Germany amounted to €128.9 billion in 1990, this number sharply increased to €1'003.0 billion by the end of 2003 (BVI 2005).[1] Equity funds (including balanced funds) account for 54% of total mutual fund holdings (Maurer 2004). This increasing interest in equity investments might be explained by the commonly held belief that they should play a major role in the development of the German pension system, which is shifting away from pure defined benefit plans towards a system which puts more emphasis on private pension savings. Nevertheless, as measured by international standards, the German mutual fund industry is still fairly small. By the end of the year 2000, the capital invested in mutual funds in the United States amounted to €27'570 per capita, while the corresponding figure in Germany was only €5'154 (BVI 2005). Krahnen, Schmid, and Theissen (2006) and Theissen (2004) argue that the minor importance of mutual funds in Germany is a side effect of its bank-based system and its comparatively small stock market. The largest mutual fund companies are bank subsidiaries, and most of their retail business is done over the bank-counter. Banks are inclined to sell their own funds and advise their customers in this direction. As a result, the industry is characterized by a restrictive distribution network, where the savings banks, the credit-cooperatives, and the large universal banks account for about 80% of all managed assets (Maurer 2004).

Given the increasing importance of the German mutual fund industry, performance measurement has also become a crucial issue from an investor's perspective. Unconditional measures of performance compare the average return on an asset with an appropriate benchmark designed to control for the asset's average risk. The returns and betas are measured as averages over the evaluation period. These averages are taken unconditionally, that is, no other information than past returns are used in the performance evaluation. In contrast, conditional performance measures relate to changes in the state of the economy and explicitly account for time-variation in expected returns. They include information on the correlation structure between a fund's beta and expected market returns.

If expected returns and risks vary over time, an unconditional approach to performance measurement will be unreliable. Jensen (1972) notes that the time-variation in risks and risk premiums will be confused with average performance. However, early empirical studies interpret the variation in mutual fund risks and risk premiums as reflecting superior information or market timing. More recently, Ferson and Schadt (1996) suggest that any benchmark should not ascribe superior performance to a managed portfolio strategy that can be replicated using publicly available information. This notion is based on the observation that the returns and risks of stocks and bonds are at least partly predictable (Cochrane 1999; Schwert 2002). If predictability reflects changing return expectations (Ferson and Harvey 1991, 1993; Ferson and Korajczyk 1995), valid performance measures must incorporate this time-variation. In fact, conditional versions of asset pricing models better explain the cross-sectional variation in expected returns (Cochrane 1996; Jagannathan and Wang 1996).

Using the traditional beta-pricing framework, our results indicate that – compared to unconditional models – fund performance substantially deteriorates when we measure conditional alphas both in single-index and multi-factor models. Based on the full set of our information variables, the mean conditional alpha for general funds is -0.130% per month, or about -1.5% per year. In comparison, taking a simple average for all funds over the 1997 to 2003 period, the mean total expense ratio is only 1.06%. Accordingly, adding back management fees, German equity mutual funds underperform on a before fee basis. Given that stock returns are partly predictable using publicly available information, the part of fund performance which is attributable to time-variation in expected returns should be deducted from total performance.

In performance evaluation tests based on stochastic discount factor (SDF) models, underperformance is even more pronounced and can even be as low as -4% per year. Conditional analysis raises the benchmark for active managers because it gives them no credit for using readily available information, and this makes it more likely for funds to show no abnormal performance. The pronounced level shift in fund performance when switching from the beta-pricing approach to the SDF framework (even in unconditional models) can be attributed to the fact that more 'complicated' SDF models and a larger number of primitive assets lead to stronger pricing conditions.

The remainder of this article is structured as follows. In Section 2 we introduce conditional performance evaluation techniques using both the beta-pricing approach and the SDF framework. Section 3 describes the mutual fund data, and Section 4 presents our empirical results. Section 5 provides a summary and concludes.

2. Conditional performance measurement

This section introduces the main ideas behind conditional performance evaluation. We start with the traditional beta-pricing approach in Section 2.1 and proceed with the SDF framework in Section 2.2.

2.1 *Conditional performance evaluation in a beta-pricing framework*

Ferson and Schadt (1996) modify Jensen's alpha to incorporate conditional information, as represented by a set of information variables. Their model involves time-varying betas and exploits the (unconditional) correlation between these conditional betas and public information variables. Time-variation in betas of managed portfolios may come from three different sources. First, the betas of portfolio assets may change over time. Second, the weights of a passive investment strategy vary as relative values change. And third, a manager can actively adjust the portfolio weights by deviating from a buy-and-hold strategy. To capture the combined effect of these factors on the risk exposures, we start with the following specification:

$$r_{P,\,t+1} = \beta_P(Z_t)r_{B,\,t+1} + \varepsilon_{P,\,t+1}, \tag{1a}$$

$$E[\varepsilon_{P,\,t+1} \mid Z_t] = 0, \tag{1b}$$

$$E[\varepsilon_{P,\,t+1}r_{B,\,t+1} \mid Z_t] = 0, \tag{1c}$$

where $r_{P,\,t+1}$ and $r_{B,\,t+1}$ in Equation (1a) are the time $t+1$ excess returns on the fund portfolio P and the benchmark portfolio B, respectively. Z_t is a vector of information variables that proxy for the full set of information available at time t, and $\beta_P(Z_t)$ denotes the time t conditional market betas of the excess return on portfolio P. Unobserved returns, labeled $\varepsilon_{P,\,t+1}$, are assumed iid with mean zero, constant variance, and zero cross-sectional correlation. Equation (1b) assumes semi-strong market efficiency (i.e. the informational content of the Z_t variables is fully exploited in the regression), and Equation (1c) implies that $\beta_P(Z_t)$ are conditional regression coefficients. Any unbiased forecast of the difference between the portfolio return and the product of the portfolio beta and the excess return on the market portfolio which is different from zero is based on information that is more informative than Z_t. In empirical tests, a functional form of $\beta_P(Z_t)$ is required to estimate the model. Following Shanken (1990), Ferson and Schadt (1996), and Silva, Ceu Cortez, and Armada (2003), we assume a linear form for the changing conditional beta of a managed portfolio:

$$\beta_{P,t+1} = \beta_P(Z_t) = \beta_{0P} + B'_P z_t, \tag{2}$$

where $z_t = Z_t - E(Z)$ is the normalized vector of deviations of the information variables from their unconditional means, and B_P is a coefficient vector with the same dimension as Z_t. The coefficient β_{0P} can be interpreted as the 'average beta', that is, the beta when all instrument variables are equal to their means. The elements of B_P measure the sensitivity of the conditional beta to deviations of the information variables from their means.

If the linear model in Equation (2) holds exact, empirical tests of the return generating process that results from combining Equations (1) and (2) imply running an ordinary least squares (OLS) (rather than a weighted least squares, WLS) regression of a managed portfolio's excess returns upon the market factor and the product of the market factor with lagged information (Admati and Ross 1985; Ferson and Schadt 1996):

$$r_{P,t+1} = \alpha_P + \delta_{1P}r_{B,t+1} + \delta'_{2P}(z_t r_{B,t+1}) + \varepsilon_{P,t+1}. \tag{3}$$

Taking expected values of Equation (3) reveals that the model implies $\alpha_P = 0$, $\delta_{1P} = b_{0P}$, and $\delta_{2P} = B_P$.[2] The products of the future benchmark return and the predetermined information variables capture the covariance between the conditional beta and the conditional expected market return (given z_t). These interaction terms serve as a control for common movements in a fund's conditional beta and the conditional expected benchmark return. The conditional alpha, α_P, is measured net of the effects of these risk dynamics. An unconditional alpha contains a bias due to the common variation in betas and expected market returns, and the covariance between beta and future market returns could falsely be interpreted as the result of a manager's superior performance (Grinblatt and Titman 1989). The model in Equation (3) assumes that managers do not possess superior information, and the null hypothesis of no abnormal performance allows for a covariance between beta and the future market returns.

Jagannathan and Wang (1996) demonstrate that the conditional capital asset pricing model can be interpreted as an unconditional model for average expected returns with more than one beta. This interpretation is also suitable for the model in Equation (3), where $(\delta_{1P}, \delta_{2P})$ is a vector of regression coefficients or betas on the multiple factors, which are defined as $(r_{B,t+1}, z_t r_{B,t+1})$. The benchmark return is the first factor and the product of the benchmark return and the lagged information variables are the additional factors. The latter can be interpreted as the returns on dynamic trading strategies, which hold z_t units of the market index, financed by borrowing or selling z_t units in treasury bills. Hansen and Jagannathan (1991) and Cochrane (1996) argue that scaled returns can be interpreted as the payoffs of actively managed portfolios.

2.2 *Conditional performance evaluation in an SDF framework*

2.2.1 *Admissible performance measures*
Chen and Knez (1996) start from the Euler-equation and define a fund's conditional alpha for a given SDF, labeled as m_{t+1}, as follows:

$$\alpha_{Pt} \equiv E(m_{t+1}R_{P,t+1} \mid Z_t) - 1, \tag{4}$$

where we denote α_{Pt} as the SDF alpha, and $R_{P,t+1}$ is the gross return of the fund at time $t + 1$. The performance of the fund measures the difference between the expected risk adjusted gross return of the fund (conditional on Z_t) and its price, which is 1. If the performance is positive (negative), this implies that the fund offers a higher (lower) risk-adjusted excess return than expected, indicating superior (inferior) performance.[3] However, the theoretical results in Chen and Knez (1996) point to several measurement problems with SDF alphas. Unless a manager's fund lies in the payoff space generated by the primitive assets, any performance measure is possible.[4] As a minimum requirement for performance measurement tests to deliver meaningful results, Farnsworth et al. (2002) require that if a given SDF prices a set of N primitive assets, then α_{Pt} in Equation (4) must be zero, provided that the fund forms a portfolio of these primitive assets (at no costs) and that the portfolio strategy uses only public information available at time t. In this case, we have $R_{P,t+1} = x(Z_t)'R_{t+1}$, where R_{t+1} is a vector of primitive asset returns, and $x(Z_t)$ is a vector of portfolio weights depending on a set of information variables. Letting 1 be a scalar or a vector, depending on the context, the corresponding α_{Pt} is an admissible performance measure, assigning zero performance to an uninformed manager's portfolio:[5]

$$
\begin{aligned}
\alpha_{Pt} &= [E(m_{t+1}x(Z_t)'R_{t+1} \mid Z_t)] - 1 \\
&= x(Z_t)'[E(m_{t+1}R_{t+1} \mid Z_t)] - 1 \\
&= x(Z_t)'1 - 1 = 0.
\end{aligned}
\tag{5}
$$

The SDF alpha in Equation (4) will only produce valid inferences if the candidate SDF satisfies the Euler-equation for a set of N primitive assets. Therefore, we proceed as in Farnsworth et al. (2002) and simultaneously estimate the parameters of the candidate SDFs and the SDF alpha using the following system of equations:

$$u1_t = (m_{t+1}R_{t+1} - 1) \otimes Z_t \quad u2_t = \alpha_P - m_{t+1}R_{P,t+1} + 1, \tag{6}$$

where $u1_t$ denotes the vector of pricing errors relating to the primitive assets, whose gross returns are collected in the vector R_{t+1}, and $u2_t$ is the pricing error of the fund with gross return $R_{P,t+1}$. "$\otimes$" is the Kronecker product, multiplying every deviation from the Euler-equation with the entire vector of information variables, Z_t. Accordingly, the first part of the system of equations (where the size depends on the number of primitive assets) defines a set of orthogonality conditions involving the pricing error and the information variables. The last equation incorporates the parameter α_P, which is the mean of the conditional SDF alpha, defined in Equation (4). Under the null hypothesis of no abnormal fund performance, α_P should be equal to zero.[6] The sample moment condition is $g = T^{-1} \sum_t (u1_t', u2_t')'$, allowing to simultaneously estimate the parameters of the SDF model and the fund's alpha using Hansen's (1982) Generalized Method of Moments (GMM). In the simplest specification, where the vector of information variables, Z_t, only contains a constant, α_P measures an unconditional SDF alpha.

The Euler-equation implies that the mean of the SDF should be equal to the inverse of the gross return on a risk-free security, hence, $E(m_{t+1}) = 1/E(R_{f,t+1})$. This condition can be imposed by including a proxy for the risk-free security into the set of primitive assets. Dahlquist and Söderlind (1999) and Farnsworth et al. (2002) demonstrate that failure to impose this restriction on the SDF can result in the estimation of a valid discount factor which implies a mean-variance tangency portfolio lying off the efficient frontier. Therefore, in addition to our set of primitive assets, we include a moment condition for the risk-free security to impose the mean restriction on the SDF.

A problem in the GMM estimation procedure is that the number of moment conditions grows exponentially if many funds are evaluated simultaneously. Therefore, we estimate the system of equations in (6) separately for each fund in our sample. Farnsworth et al. (2002) prove that this procedure is not restrictive, and estimating the system of equations for one fund at a time is equivalent to estimating a system with many funds simultaneously. The estimates of α_P for any subset of funds are invariant to the presence of another subset of funds in the system.

2.2.2 Modeling the SDF

The SDF alpha in the system of equations in (6) depends on the specification of the SDF, and the latter is not unique unless financial markets are complete. This indeterminacy implies that different models of the SDF can measure fund performance differently. We employ the following three broad model classes: (i) linear factor model SDFs, (ii) primitive-efficient SDFs, and (iii) Bakshi-Chen SDFs. This choice of SDF models is comprehensive. The first model class incorporates standard asset pricing models (e.g. the capital asset pricing model), and the second and third models guarantee pricing given a set of primitive asset returns and absence of arbitrage, respectively.

Linear factor model SDFs: Linear factor models are models where m_{t+1} is linear in prespecified factors. They can capture many different asset pricing models, including the capital asset pricing model, the three-factor model of Fama and French (1993), and a capital asset pricing model with higher moments (Dittmar 2003). In the most general form, they start with:

$$m_{t+1} = a(Z_t) + b(Z_t)F_{t+1}, \tag{7}$$

where F_{t+1} denotes the vector of (gross) returns at time $t + 1$ on traded or non-traded factors. As before, Z_t is a vector of predetermined information variables with dimension $L \times 1$, where L denotes the number of information variables plus a constant. In the unconditional case, Z_t reduces to the constant and, hence, the weight parameters a and b are time-constant.

Ferson and Jagannathan (1996) demonstrate that any multiple-beta model can be expressed in the Euler-equation form with a particular specification of the SDF. We test both the capital asset pricing model and the Fama and French (1993) three-factor model specification of the SDF. In the unconditional version of the capital asset pricing model the SDF is given as (Dybvig and Ingersoll 1982):

$$m_{t+1} = a + bR_{M,t+1},$$ (8)

where $R_{M,t+1}$ is the gross market return. The SDF for the Fama and French (1993) three-factor model is specified as follows:

$$m_{t+1} = a + b_1 R_{M,t+1} + b_2 HML_{t+1} + b_3 SMB_{t+1},$$ (9)

where HML_{t+1} and SMB_{t+1} are the gross returns on the high minus low book-to-market and small minus big (measured in terms of market capitalization) style portfolios, respectively. Plugging Equations (8) and (9) into the Euler-equation and estimating the system of equations in (6) for the set of primitive assets plus the risk-free security identifies the parameters a and b.

Hansen and Richard (1987) argue that conditional factor models are not directly testable because the econometrician cannot observe an agent's information set. However, given a set of predetermined information variables, Cochrane (1996, 2001) suggests that conditional factor models can be tested by scaling factors. Conditional factor pricing models allow that the parameters are time-varying, and again the simplest approach is to assume linearity. With a single factor and a single information variable (plus a constant), denoted by Z_t, we have:

$$\begin{aligned} m_{t+1} &= a(Z_t) + b(Z_t)F_{t+1} \\ &= a_0 + a_1 Z_t + (b_0 + b_1 Z_t)F_{t+1} \\ &= a_0 + a_1 Z_t + b_0 F_{t+1} + b_1(Z_t F_{t+1}). \end{aligned}$$ (10)

Therefore, instead of a one-factor model with time-varying coefficients, we now have a three-factor model $(Z_t, F_{t+1}, Z_t F_{t+1})$ with fixed coefficients (plus a constant). Linearity is convenient, but not restrictive (Bekaert and Liu 2004; Ferson and Siegel 2001). Cochrane (1996) suggests that one can simply add scaled factors and estimate the *unconditional* moments of the model as if conditioning information did not exist. With K factors and L information variables (including a constant) there are $L \times (K+1)$ parameters to estimate in Equation (10). To identify the parameters, the number of primitive assets (N) must suffice $N \geq K+1$.

Primitive-efficient SDFs: Hansen and Jagannathan (1991) show that the projection of an SDF, m_{t+1}, on the vector of primitive asset returns, R_{t+1}, yields:

$$m_{t+1}^{PE} = 1' E(R_{t+1} R_{t+1}' \mid Z_t)^{-1} R_{t+1}.$$ (11)

The SDF in Equation (11), m_{t+1}^{PE}, is usually called a primitive-efficient SDF because it is a linear function of the returns on the primitive assets, where $1' E(R_{t+1} R_{t+1}')^{-1}$ provides the portfolio weights. It is admissible and prices a given set of primitive assets by construction. We follow Chen and Knez (1996), Dahlquist and Söderlind (1999), and Farnsworth et al. (2002) and assume that the weight vector is a linear function of the information variables in the Z_t vector. Specifically, we have:

$$m_{t+1}^{PE} = Z_t' M R_{t+1},$$ (12)

where M denotes the parameters of the model, with dimensions depending on the specification. In the unconditional case with only a constant variable, the SDF is simply a linear combination of the primitive assets. Multiplying the primitive asset returns by lagged information variables expands the payoff space and results in 'dynamic strategies' (Cochrane 2001). This procedure results in scaled factor models that can be estimated using GMM as if the model was unconditional. With N primitive assets and L instrument variables (including a constant), there are $N \times L$ weight parameters to estimate and $N \times L$ orthogonality conditions, implying that the system of equations is exactly identified.

Bakshi-Chen SDFs: The existence of a strictly positive SDF is equivalent to a no-arbitrage condition. Chen and Knez (1996) and Dahlquist and Söderlind (1999) impose positivity by cutting off the specification of the SDF at zero. An alternative (ad hoc) approach to ensure that risk premiums are positive is to work with exponential functions.[7] Bakshi and Chen (1998) propose a model in which the SDF is the exponential of a linear function of the logarithmic returns on the primitive assets:

$$m_{t+1}^{BC} = \exp\left[Z_t' C \ln(R_{t+1})\right], \tag{13}$$

where C denotes the parameters of the model, with dimensions depending on the specification. The model in Equation (13) is similar to the primitive efficient model, but in this case the SDF is a nonlinear function of the primitive asset returns and is forced to take on only positive values. Again, with $N \times L$ coefficients and $N \times L$ orthogonality conditions, the system is exactly identified.

3. Data

Fund data: In this study we analyze the database of the Bundesverband Investment und Asset Management (BVI). Membership in the BVI is mandatory for all German mutual fund companies, institutional fund companies, and asset management companies. Accordingly, the database contains all funds of its 74 members starting as early as 1950. We exclude funds that invest in foreign stock markets and restrict our sample to domestic equity funds in order to avoid problems of dealing with currency risk (Paape 2003). The funds are divided into regular equity mutual funds, small- and mid-cap funds, and growth funds. The sample contains monthly data on 98 general funds, 12 small- or mid-cap funds, and 6 growth funds, resulting in a total of 116 funds over the period from January 1980 to December 2003.[8] For comparison, Griese and Kempf (2003) also investigated equity mutual funds with an investment objective in German stocks. Their data are from Micropal and contain a slightly larger number of 123 funds (including foreign funds). Bams and Otten (2002) analyze European equity mutual funds and include only 57 German funds (including index funds) in their sample. Fund classifications are taken from Hoppenstedt, and the investment objectives were double-checked by examining the fund fact sheets available from the websites of the fund management companies. We use a reduced sample of 50 selected funds for which we have a full return history over the period from January 1994 to December 2003 (120 months). This smaller sample consists of 47 general funds and 3 small- and mid-cap funds.

We collect the mutual fund net asset values measured on a monthly basis from the BVI database and compute simple fund returns, assuming that total distributions (i.e. dividends and capital gain distributions, if any) were reinvested in the fund at the beginning of the following month. Accordingly, the returns are net of management fees and expenses but disregard load charges and exit fees (if any).

Benchmark returns: To alleviate the benchmark problem (Grinblatt and Titman 1994; Roll 1978; Roll and Ross 1994) we use a variety of benchmark indexes. Many funds in our sample explicitly use the DAX blue-chip index as their benchmark. The DAX only consists of 30 blue-chip stocks and, hence, it may not capture the total investment opportunity set available to fund managers. To check the robustness of our results, we also use the MSCI Germany Total Return Index and the Datastream Germany Total Return Index (with dividends reinvested) as benchmark portfolios. Moreover, the Karlsruher Kapitalmarktdatenbank provides the DAFOX index, which represents a broad value-weighted market proxy of all stocks traded in the premier market segment ('Amtlicher Handel') of the Frankfurt Stock Exchange. The coefficients of correlation between the returns on the DAFOX index and the other indexes are all above 0.97.

To test the Fama and French (1993) three-factor model, we use *SMB* and *HML* as additional style portfolios to capture the size effect (Banz 1981) and the value effect (Fama and French 1992; Lakonishok, Shleifer, and Vishny 1994), respectively. The *SMB* factor is proxied by the monthly return difference between the return on the SMAX index and the DAX 30 index.[9] The *HML* factor is constructed using the data published on the website of Kenneth French. We use the market-to-book ratio as the defining criterion and compute monthly return differences between the value portfolio (low market-to-book ratio) and the growth portfolio (high market-to-book ratio).

Primitive assets: In an SDF framework, a set of reference assets is needed to determine the coefficients of the SDF. The parameters are estimated using the GMM such that the SDF model produces a 'small' pricing error. In theory, all assets available should be included in the estimation. However, similar to the problem that only a proxy for the true market portfolio can be used in securities market analysis, only a subset of all available assets can be employed. The decision of which assets to include is guided by the type of assets in which the funds invest, that is, the choice of primitive assets should reflect a fund manager's investment universe. In addition to the risk-free security, our set of primitive assets is represented by the 10 German sector indexes according to the Datastream classification.[10] Table 1 provides summary statistics of these sector indexes over the sample period from January 1994 to December 2003. The *R*-square denotes the explanatory power of predictive regressions of the sector index returns on lagged values of three information variables.

Information variables: We work with a set of public information variables that previous studies used for predicting stock returns and risk over time. The instrument variables are (i) the lagged dividend yield of the Datastream Germany Total Return Index, (ii) the lagged level of the one-month interest rate for Euro deposits (German Mark deposits before 1 January 2002) on the Eurocurrency market, and (iii) the lagged slope of the term structure. The time *t* dividend yield is computed as the average value of dividends paid over the last 12 months on the (value-weighted) Datastream index, divided by the index value at time *t*. Following Lewellen (2004), we use the natural log of the dividend yield rather than the raw series because it has better time-series properties. The term spread is calculated as the difference between the yield on long-term government bonds (with maturity of at least 10 years) and the three-month interest rate for Euro (German Mark) deposits on the Eurocurrency market.

For conditional performance measurement models to produce meaningful results, a necessary condition is that the information variables possess predictive power. The econometric method used in most prediction studies is an OLS regression of stock returns on lags of the predictor variables. Based on conventional critical values for the *t*-test, several studies concluded that there is evidence for predictability. However, recent studies argue that the apparent stock return predictability based on standard *t*-tests might be spurious (Amihud and Hurvich 2004; Campbell and Yogo 2006; Lewellen 2004; Stambaugh 1999; Torous, Valkanov, and Yan 2004). In particular, a problem arises if a predictor variable is highly persistent and its innovations are strongly correlated with returns.[11]

In Panel A of Table 2 the excess returns on our four benchmark indexes are regressed on the lagged predictor variables separately one at a time using OLS. We report conventional *t*-statistics and *t*-statistics that are adjusted for regressor persistence following Amihud and Hurvich (2004). The results reveal that the dividend yield does not have predictive power, which could be explained by the fact that our sample contains the 1990s, a decade during which several studies claimed that the dividend yield lost its forecasting abilities (Goyal and Welch 2003; Rey 2004). In contrast, both

Table 1. Summary statistics of primitive assets.

	Sector 1	Sector 2	Sector 3	Sector 4	Sector 5	Sector 5	Sector 7	Sector 8	Sector 9	Sector 10
Mean	0.0324	0.0087	0.0079	0.0082	0.0092	0.0081	0.0069	0.0096	0.0103	0.0046
Maximum	0.5135	0.2349	0.1638	0.1949	0.1750	0.1194	0.1739	0.3832	0.1075	0.2682
Minimum	−0.3936	−0.1646	−0.1638	−0.1930	−0.2579	−0.1377	−0.2213	−0.3183	−0.0533	−0.2744
Standard deviation	0.1425	0.0743	0.0662	0.0673	0.0790	0.0458	0.0675	0.1086	0.0303	0.0741
JB test statistic	6.9247	3.9532	1.1102	2.1235	6.0573	8.7276	1.3090	16.5177	17.3392	51.0554
p-value	0.0314	0.1385	0.5740	0.3459	0.0484	0.0127	0.5197	0.0003	0.0002	0.0000
R^2	0.0420	0.0674	0.0293	0.0581	0.0184	0.0104	0.0314	0.0458	0.0074	0.0485
Adjusted R^2	0.0172	0.0433	0.0042	0.0338	−0.0070	−0.0152	0.0063	0.0211	−0.0183	0.0239

Note: This table reports the summary statistics of the primitive assets that are used to estimate the parameters of the SDF model in performance measurement tests within the Euler-equation framework. We use the 10 sector indexes (on a total return basis) according to the Datastream classification as the set of primitive assets (in addition to the risk-free security to fix the mean of the SDF). The sample period runs from January 1994 to December 2003 (120 monthly return observations). Mean values are in percentages per month. The R^2 denotes the explanatory power of predictive regressions of the sector index returns upon lagged values of three information variables.

the short-term interest rate and the term spread exhibit strong predictive power. A conventional t-test indicates statistical significance of the coefficients on the lagged predictor variables at the 5% level. With highly persistent regressors, these results might overstate the true predictive power of our information variables. However, the bias-adjusted t-statistics based on the method proposed by Amihud and Hurvich (2004) indicate that the prediction power of the short-term interest rate

Table 2. Regressions of stock market excess returns on lagged information variables.

	MSCI Germany	Datastream Germany	DAX 30	DAFOX
Panel A: Single-predictor regressions				
Log dividend yield				
Coefficient	0.023	0.022	0.024	0.011
t-statistic	0.789	0.872	0.789	0.504
Amihud-Hurvich t-statistic	0.739	0.825	0.727	0.478
R^2	0.005	0.006	0.005	0.002
Short-term interest rate				
Coefficient	−0.174	−0.170	−0.177	−0.151
t-statistic	−2.074**	−2.300**	−2.033**	−2.169**
Amihud-Hurvich t-statistic	−2.000**	−2.202**	−1.917*	−2.087**
R^2	0.035	0.042	0.033	0.038
Term spread				
Coefficient	0.019	0.018	0.020	0.014
t-statistic	2.250**	2.444**	2.309**	2.071**
Amihud-Hurvich t-statistic	2.036**	2.212**	2.076**	1.855*
R^2	0.041	0.048	0.043	0.035
Panel B: Multi-predictor regressions				
Log dividend yield				
Coefficient	−0.006	−0.005	−0.006	−0.012
t-statistic	−0.180	−0.180	−0.187	−0.418
Short-term interest rate				
Coefficient	−0.130**	−0.126**	−0.129**	−0.122**
t-statistic	−2.347	−2.576	−2.239	−2.470
Term spread				
Coefficient	0.015**	0.014**	0.017**	0.012*
t-statistic	2.215	2.230	2.195	1.937
Adjusted R^2	0.034	0.046	0.035	0.033
Wald test (χ^2-statistic)	18.710	21.271	18.052	19.059
	(0.000)	(0.000)	(0.000)	(0.000)

Note: This table reports the estimation results of predictive regressions of excess benchmark returns on the information variables in single- and multi-predictor specifications. The information variables are (i) the lagged log dividend yield on the Datastream Germany Total Return Index, (ii) the lagged level of the one-month interest rate for Euro deposits (German Mark deposits before 1 January 2000) on the Eurocurrency market, and (iii) the lagged slope of the term structure, computed as the difference between the yield on long-term government bonds (with maturity of at least 10 years) and the three-month interest rate for Euro (German Mark) deposits on the Eurocurrency market. The sample period is from January 1994 to December 2003 (120 months). For each regression specification the estimated coefficients and the standard t-statistics are reported. In addition, for the single-predictor specifications in panel A we provide the bias-adjusted t-statistic following the method proposed by Amihud and Hurvich (2004). The multi-predictor regressions in panel B apply Hansen's (1982) Generalized Method of Moments (GMM), using a heteroskedasticity and autocorrelation consistent covariance matrix as the weighting matrix and a constant and all three lagged information variables to specify the orthogonality conditions. The χ^2-statistic tests the null hypothesis that the coefficients of all three information variables are jointly equal zero. ***, **, *denote statistical significance at the 1%, 5%, 10% level, respectively.

and the term spread is robust. The coefficients are generally estimated at the 5% significance level; only in two cases significance is reduced to the 10% level.

The results of multi-predictor regressions where all three information variables are used simultaneously to model expected returns are shown in Panel B of Table 2. We use the GMM to estimate the multi-predictor regressions, using a heteroskedasticity and autocorrelation consistent covariance matrix as the weighting matrix and a constant plus all three lagged information variables as instruments to specify the orthogonality conditions. Our estimation results reveal that the single-predictor results in panel A are robust in the multivariate case. A Wald test rejects the null hypothesis that all three information variables are jointly equal to zero. Overall, we interpret these regression results as evidence that our predictor variables are appropriate to model the time-variation in expected returns.

4. Empirical results

In this section, we present the empirical results. Section 4.1 starts with the results of the traditional beta-pricing approach, and Section 4.2 proceeds with the results of the SDF framework. Section 4.3 compares the results from both models and provides possible explanations for the differences in the levels of abnormal returns.

4.1 *Results from the beta-pricing framework*

4.1.1 Measuring conditional alphas and betas

We start with the results for an unconditional model and use the Datastream Germany Total Return Index as the market proxy in the single-index model. For the small- and medium-cap funds in the single-index model we use the DAFOX as the market proxy. In the Fama and French (1993) three-factor models we generally employ the DAFOX as the market proxy. The results are shown in Table 3. The mean abnormal return in the single-index model for the subsample of general funds is −0.045% per month, or about 55 basis points per year. The negative alpha in the three-factor model is even −0.217% per month, or −2.6% per year. In contrast, small- and mid-cap funds slightly outperform the multi-factor benchmark. However, the absolute values are low, and given the sample size, this latter result should not be overemphasized.

Tables 4 and 5 show the results of conditional performance evaluation models in the standard beta-pricing setup. We start by testing conditional versions of the single-index model and use each information variable separately one at a time in Table 4 and all three information variables simultaneously in Table 5. All information variables are demeaned. In general, we observe that the distribution of conditional alphas shifts to the left, that is, fund performance becomes worse when we control for public information. Depending on the information variable, the mean conditional alpha in Table 4 for the subsample of general funds varies between −0.052% and −0.111% per month. Using all information variables, the average estimated alpha in Table 5 is −0.130% per month, or roughly −1.5% per year. The null hypothesis that all interaction terms corresponding to the three instrument variables are jointly equal to zero can be rejected for 36 funds, that is, almost three-quarters of our sample.

Our analysis is based on mutual fund returns net of costs, that is, management fees were already deducted from the funds' returns. Taking the −1.5% annual underperformance as the benchmark and adding back the average total expense ratio of 1.06% over the 1997 to 2003 period, we find that funds underperform by approximately 45 basis points *before* fees. This indicates that, on average, active fund management cannot add value. However, our results are less pronounced

Table 3. Measures of performance using unconditional models.

	Unconditional CAPM					Fama-French three-factor model								
	α_P	$t(\alpha_P)$	β_P	$t(\beta_P)$	R^2	α_P	$t(\alpha_P)$	β_{1P}	$t(\beta_{1P})$	β_{2P}	$t(\beta_{2P})$	β_{3P}	$t(\beta_{3P})$	R^2
Panel A: Mean values of individual fund regressions														
General	−0.045	−0.286	1.037	32.32	0.894	−0.217	−1.329	1.030	23.13	−0.008	0.283	−0.078	−2.080	0.889
Small- and mid-cap	0.008	0.005	0.851	14.82	0.694	0.293	0.999	1.062	17.12	−0.207	−3.170	0.329	4.141	0.769
All funds	−0.042	−0.269	1.026	31.27	0.882	−0.187	−1.189	1.032	22.77	−0.020	0.076	−0.053	−1.707	0.882
Panel B: Median values of individual fund regressions														
General	−0.061	−0.358	1.066	33.37	0.931	−0.261	−1.517	1.045	23.58	0.021	0.788	−0.111	−2.393	0.926
Small- and mid-cap	0.081	0.271	0.848	13.94	0.702	0.377	1.264	1.078	17.43	−0.186	−3.254	0.357	4.980	0.768
All funds	−0.058	−0.354	1.060	32.48	0.930	−0.243	−1.487	1.049	23.42	0.004	0.130	−0.101	−2.266	0.923
Panel C: Results for equally-weighted portfolios														
General	−0.045	−0.391	1.037	52.37	0.963	−0.217	−1.557	1.030	31.88	−0.008	−0.317	−0.077	−2.273	0.948
Small- and mid-cap	0.008	0.003	0.851	17.76	0.740	0.293	1.182	1.062	20.03	−0.207	−3.406	0.329	−3.406	0.816
All funds	−0.034	−0.303	1.025	53.42	0.963	−0.186	−1.329	1.032	31.92	−0.020	−0.743	0.053	−1.538	0.947

Note: This table shows the results from unconditional CAPM tests based on the following regression model (market model):

$$r_{P,t+1} = \alpha_P + \beta_P r_{B,t+1} + \varepsilon_{P,t+1},$$

where $r_{P,t+1}$ is the excess return on a fund and $r_{B,t+1}$ is the excess return on the benchmark index. Benchmark indexes are the Datastream Germany Total Return Index for general funds, and the DAFOX for small- and mid-cap funds. The sample period is from January 1994 to December 2003, and the full return history (120 months) is available for 47 general funds and 3 small- and mid-cap funds (50 surviving funds). The Fama-French (1993) three-factor model is specified as follows:

$$r_{P,t+1} = \alpha_P + \beta_{1P} r_{B,t+1} + \beta_{2P} HML_{t+1} + \beta_{3P} SMB_{t+1} + \varepsilon_{P,t+1},$$

where the DAFOX is used as the market proxy for all funds irrespective of the segment they belong to. HML is the return on a portfolio of high book-to-market stocks minus low book-to-market stocks, and SMB is the return difference between the DAX 30 and the SDAX indexes. Alphas are expressed in percentages per month. All t-ratios are adjusted for heteroscedasticity using the White (1980) covariance matrix.

than those in Bams and Otten (2002), who document that the average fund in their sample of German funds underperforms before fees by -1.32% per year on a conditional basis.

To double-check our results, we run the regressions using all four alternative benchmark indexes as market proxies. In results not shown here, we compute the rank correlations of the conditional versions of Jensen's alpha for the specification that uses all three instrument variables. Our results are robust to the choice of the benchmark index, and with one exception the rank correlations are above 0.99.

Table 4. Measures of performance using the conditional CAPM (1).

	α_P	$t(\alpha_P)$	δ_{1P}	$t(\delta_{1P})$	δ_{2P}	$t(\delta_{2P})$	# sign.	R^2
Panel A: Information variable = Term spread								
Mean values of individual fund regressions:								
General	−0.102	−0.786	1.047	34.059	0.052	1.278	25	0.896
Small- and mid-cap	0.090	0.232	0.838	14.117	−0.091	−1.019	0	0.697
All funds	−0.091	−0.725	1.035	32.862	0.044	1.140	25	0.884
Median values of individual fund regressions:								
General	−0.137	−0.882	1.080	34.730	0.077	1.604	25	0.935
Small- and mid-cap	0.126	0.375	0.831	12.317	−0.109	−1.189	0	0.703
All funds	−0.106	−0.777	1.071	34.003	0.066	1.497	25	0.932
Results for equally weighted portfolios:								
General	−0.102	−0.947	1.047	57.013	0.052	1.843		0.864
Small- and mid-cap	0.090	0.281	0.838	17.740	−0.078	−1.169		0.740
All funds	−0.084	−0.751	1.033	57.080	0.046	1.618		0.964
Panel B: Information variable = Short-term interest rate								
Mean values of individual fund regressions:								
General	−0.111	−0.831	1.026	34.049	−0.738	−1.757	29	0.898
Small- and mid-cap	0.075	0.179	0.870	15.129	0.879	1.088	1	0.699
All funds	−0.100	−0.771	1.016	32.914	−0.641	−1.587	30	0.886
Median values of individual fund regressions:								
General	−0.115	−0.717	1.053	35.270	−0.913	−2.257	29	0.938
Small- and mid-cap	0.150	0.385	0.851	13.622	0.566	0.546	1	0.714
All funds	−0.111	−0.682	1.045	34.377	−0.793	−2.166	30	0.937
Results for equally weighted portfolios:								
General	−0.111	−1.114	1.026	60.864	−0.739	−3.020		0.965
Small- and mid-cap	0.075	0.231	0.870	17.666	0.879	1.350		0.745
All funds	−0.095	−0.910	1.014	60.546	−0.671	−2.798		0.965
Panel C: Information variable = Log dividend yield								
Mean values of individual fund regressions:								
General	−0.052	−0.391	1.034	32.733	3.323	0.921	23	0.900
Small- and mid-cap	0.015	0.014	0.860	14.394	−7.785	−0.805	1	0.701
All funds	−0.048	−0.367	1.023	31.633	2.657	0.817	24	0.888
Median values of individual fund regressions:								
General	−0.067	−0.444	1.057	33.557	4.633	0.976	23	0.937
Small- and mid-cap	0.101	0.277	0.844	13.902	−2.548	−0.225	1	0.722
All funds	−0.059	−0.425	1.049	33.158	4.305	0.855	24	0.935

(Continued)

Table 4. Continued.

	α_P	$t(\alpha_P)$	δ_{1P}	$t(\delta_{1P})$	δ_{2P}	$t(\delta_{2P})$	# sign.	R^2
Results for equally weighted portfolios:								
General	−0.052	−0.515	1.034	53.117	3.324	1.102		0.963
Small- and mid-cap	0.015	0.046	0.860	16.644	−7.785	−1.122		0.740
All funds	−0.044	−0.380	1.021	54.195	2.603	0.847		0.963

Note: This table shows the results from conditional CAPM tests, where each predetermined information variable is used separately one at a time in the following regression model:

$$r_{P,t+1} = \alpha_P + \delta_{1P} r_{B,t+1} + \delta_{2P}(z_t r_{B,t+1}) + \varepsilon_{P,t+1},$$

where $r_{P,t+1}$ is the excess return on a fund, $r_{B,t+1}$ is the excess return on the benchmark index, and z_t denotes a predetermined (lagged) information variable. Benchmark indexes are the Datastream Germany Total Return Index for general funds, and the DAFOX for small- and mid-cap funds. As the predetermined information variables we use the term-spread (panel A), the short-term interest rate (panel B), and the log dividend yield (panel C) separately one at a time. The sample period is from January 1994 to December 2003, and the full return history (120 months) is available for 47 general funds and 3 small- and mid-cap funds (50 surviving funds). R^2 denotes the adjusted R-squares of the regressions, and #sign denotes the number of funds with a significant coefficient (δ_{2P}) on the interaction term including the lagged information variable (at the 10% level of statistical significance). Alphas are expressed in percentages per month. All t-ratios are adjusted for heteroscedasticity using the White (1980) covariance matrix.

Overall, compared to an unconditional assessment of mutual fund performance on the basis of Jensen's alpha, our results suggest that the performance of our sample of general funds appears even more unfavorable in a conditional framework. These findings are consistent with those in Dahlquist, Engström, and Söderlind (2000) for Swedish funds, but they are in contrast with the original evidence in Ferson and Schadt (1996) for US mutual funds and Silva, Ceu Cortez, and Armada (2003) for European bond funds. The latter two studies reveal a tendency for better performance when predetermined information variables are incorporated into the analysis. In two follow-up studies with larger samples, Christopherson, Ferson, and Glassman (1998) and Ferson and Qian (2004) do not report any significant effect on the distribution of alphas.

To confirm our interpretation, we compute the term $B'_P Cov[z_t, r_{B,t+1}]$ and find that it is a positive 0.000859 for the average general fund. This finding implies that the correlation of fund betas with the expected market return that is attributable to the predetermined information variables tends to be positive, indicating that fund managers tend to increase their market betas when expected returns are high conditional on public information and/or reduce their market betas when expected returns are low.[12] Traditional performance measurement studies in an unconditional setting and, in particular, timing models interpret the covariance between beta and future market returns solely as a result of a portfolio manager's superior (private) performance. In contrast, the conditional setup assumes that markets are semi-strong efficient. Fund managers do *not* have superior information but rather exploit public information. To come up with a fair performance measure, the part of the ex post abnormal return that is attributable to time-variation in expected returns based on public information and changing betas must be excluded. As suggested by Chen and Knez (1996), using public information-based dynamic portfolios as performance references leads to 'tougher' performance yardsticks.

4.1.2 Cross-sectional distribution of mutual fund alphas

To explore the shift in alphas when switching from an unconditional to a conditional framework in greater detail, we look at the entire distribution of abnormal returns. Table 6 shows the cross-sectional distribution of t-statistics for individual fund alphas. Following Ferson and Qian (2004),

Table 5. Measures of performance using the conditional CAPM (2).

	α_P	$t(\alpha_P)$	δ_{1P}	$t(\delta_{1P})$	$\delta_{TS,P}$	$t(\delta_{TS,P})$	$\delta_{SR,P}$	$t(\delta_{SR,P})$	$\delta_{DY,P}$	$t(\delta_{DY,P})$	R^2	pval(F)
Panel A: Mean values of individual fund regressions												
General	−0.130	−1.002	1.032	40.511	0.025	0.790	−0.636	−1.540	0.491	0.309	0.904	0.084 [35]
Small- and mid-cap	0.111	0.288	0.858	14.281	−0.066	−0.771	0.508	0.669	−5.012	−0.413	0.705	0.423 [1]
All funds	−0.116	−0.924	1.021	38.937	0.019	0.697	−0.567	−1.407	0.160	0.266	0.892	0.104 [36]
Panel B: Median values of individual fund regressions												
General	−0.131	−1.074	1.047	41.457	0.044	1.078	−0.635	−1.841	1.118	0.304	0.943	0.010
Small- and mid-cap	0.169	0.494	0.826	14.026	−0.104	−1.163	0.294	0.301	−0.186	−0.015	0.726	0.584
All funds	−0.129	−1.034	1.043	40.563	0.041	0.990	−0.619	−1.769	1.011	0.289	0.939	0.011
Panel C: Results for equally weighted portfolios												
General	−0.130	−1.228	1.032	72.646	0.025	1.026	−0.637	−2.749	0.488	0.201	0.964	0.019
Small- and mid-cap	0.111	0.340	0.858	16.157	−0.066	−0.870	0.508	0.822	−5.012	−0.641	0.738	0.383
All funds	−0.111	−0.997	1.019	70.227	0.020	0.828	−0.603	−2.635	−0.047	−0.018	0.964	0.042

Note: This table shows the results from conditional CAPM tests, where all predetermined information variables are used simultaneously in the following regression model:

$$r_{P,t+1} = \alpha_P + \delta_{1P} r_{B,t+1} + \delta'_{1P} \left(z_t r_{B,t+1} \right) + \delta'_{2P} \left(z_t r_{B,t+1} \right) + \varepsilon_{P,t+1},$$

where $r_{P,t+1}$ is the excess return on a fund, $r_{B,t+1}$ is the excess return on the benchmark index, and z_t denotes the vector of predetermined (lagged) information variables. Benchmark indexes are the Datastream Germany Total Return Index for general funds and the DAFOX for small- and mid-cap funds. As predetermined information variables we use the term-spread (*TS*), the short-term interest rate (*SR*), and the log dividend yield (*DY*) simultaneously. The sample period is from January 1994 to December 2003, and the full return history (120 months) is available for 47 general funds and 3 small- and mid-cap funds (50 surviving funds). R^2 are the adjusted R-squares of the regressions, and pval(*F*) denotes the probability value of the *F*-test for the null hypothesis that all coefficients on the interaction terms including the predetermined variables (collected in the vector δ_{2P}) are simultaneously equal to zero. The figures in brackets in the last column denote the number of funds for which the null hypothesis is rejected. Alphas are expressed in percentages per month. All *t*-statistics are adjusted for heteroscedasticity using the White (1980) covariance matrix.

Table 6. Cross-sectional distribution of t-statistics for individual fund alphas.

	(1) Null	(2) Uncond. model	(3) Term spread	(4) Short-term rate	(5) Dividend yield	(6) All information variables	(7) Uncond. model	(8) All information variables
		Single-index model					Three-factor model	
Minimum t-statistic		−1.9087	−2.6894	−2.8722	−2.5358	−2.9042	−2.9799	−2.3682
Bonferroni p-value (−)		1.4676	0.2051	0.1210	0.3135	0.1104	0.0877	0.4909
$t < -2.326$	0.25	0	4	4	1	5	6	1
$-2.326 < t < -1.960$	1.00	0	0	1	2	0	6	2
$-1.960 < t < -1.645$	1.25	3	5	3	2	12	9	8
$-1.645 < t < 0$	22.50	28	27	32	30	23	22	29
$0 < t < 1.645$	22.50	18	13	9	14	9	7	10
$1.645 < t < 1.960$	1.25	0	0	0	0	0	0	0
$1.960 < t < 2.326$	1.00	1	1	1	0	1	0	0
$t > 2.326$	0.25	1	0	0	1	0	0	0
Maximum t-statistic		2.6711	2.2885	2.1881	2.8804	2.0984	1.2873	1.5583
Bonferroni p-value (+)		0.2154	0.5976	0.7663	0.1181	0.9514	5.0129	3.0521

Note: This table shows the cross-sectional distribution of heteroscedasticity-consistent t-statistics for the estimated alphas using different model specifications. For the single-index model in column (2), the unconditional alphas are the intercepts in regressions of fund excess returns on the excess returns on the Datastream Germany Total Return Index and the DAFOX for the subsamples of general funds and small- and mid-cap funds. The conditional (lagged) information variables in columns (3)–(6) are the intercepts in regressions of fund excess returns on the benchmark index and the product of the index with the vector of predetermined (lagged) information variables. The unconditional alphas in the Fama and French (1993) three-factor model in column (7) are the intercepts in the regressions of fund excess returns on the DAFOX and the HML and SMB long-short portfolios. The conditional alphas in the three-factor model are the intercepts that result when fund excess returns are regressed on the factors and the products of the factors with the vector of predetermined (lagged) information variables. The entries in the middle block of the table indicate the number of funds for which the t-statistics for alpha falls within the range of critical values of a standard normal distribution. The Bonferroni p-value is the maximum or minimum one-tailed p-value from the distribution of t-statistics across all funds multiplied by the number of funds. As predetermined information variables we use the term-spread, the short-term interest rate, and the log dividend yield simultaneously. The sample period is from January 1994 to December 2003, and the full return history (120 months) is available for 47 general funds and 3 small- and mid-cap funds (50 surviving funds).

we summarize the results by presenting the fractions of the t-statistics that lie between standard critical values for a normal distribution, which is the asymptotic distribution for the t-values. Column (1) shows the fractions that would be expected under the null hypothesis of no abnormal performance if the normal distribution provides a good approximation for the t-values. Using the minimum and maximum t-statistic for each model, we test the hypothesis that all alphas are jointly equal to zero using the Bonferroni p-value. This is a one-tailed test of the null hypothesis that all alphas are zero against the alternative that at least one alpha is positive (Bonferroni p-value (+)) or negative (Bonferroni p-value (−)).

Similar to Ferson and Schadt (1996) and Ferson and Qian (2004), we find in column (2) of Table 6 that the distribution of the unconditional alphas is centered slightly to the left of the distribution under the null hypothesis. There are 28 funds with insignificantly negative alphas and t-statistics between 0 and −1.645, whereas three funds exhibit negative alphas that are even statistically significant (with t-values below −1.645). There is one fund with a significantly positive alpha (with a t-value above 2.326). Nevertheless, none of the extreme t-statistics are significant based on the Bonferroni test, although unconditional performance measures suggest a negative performance, on average. Consistent with the regression results for the Fama and French (1993) three-factor model in Table 3, column (7) of Table 6 indicates that the cross-sectional distribution of t-statistics shifts even further to the left, that is, there are more extreme negative alphas for individual funds. For example, there are six funds with t-values below −2.326, and the Bonferroni p-value rejects the null hypothesis that all alphas are zero against the alternative that at least one is negative at the 10% level.[13]

Overall, for the unconditional models we observe that funds have more negative than positive alphas. Of the significant alphas (with absolute t-statistics larger than 1.645), all are negative, with only one exception for the single-index model. A binomial test rejects the null hypothesis that 50% of the alphas are positive. The corresponding t-statistics are −1.697 for the one-factor model and −4.808 in the three-factor model. Although this result indicates poor performance from an investor's perspective, a caveat is that it is difficult to know where the distribution of the alphas should be centered under the hypothesis of no abnormal performance. On the one hand, Sharpe (1991) and Malkiel (2003) argue that transaction costs are deducted from the funds' returns but not from the benchmark returns and, hence, the alphas of fund returns should be centered to the left of zero. On the other hand, our sample of funds selected for the conditional analysis suffers from a survivorship bias, which shifts the distribution of alphas to the right.

Looking at the distribution of t-statistics for the conditional performance model when all three information variables are used in column (6), the distribution becomes even more skewed to the left. Most important, 40 funds exhibit negative alphas, and there are 5 funds with t-values below −2.0. We cannot reject the null hypothesis that all fund alphas are jointly equal to zero against the alternative of superior performance, but the minimum t-statistic is close to being significantly negative when considering a 10% confidence level (with p-value = 0.1104). A binomial test again rejects the null hypothesis that 50% of the alphas are positive; the corresponding t-statistic is −4.243.

4.2 Results from the SDF framework

4.2.1 Specification tests for SDF models

We start with several specification tests for the different SDF models. To provide a benchmark, the first line in Table 7 shows the results from a constant discount factor model in which the SDF is assumed to be fixed over time and equal to the inverse of the sample mean of the gross one-month interest rate. A constant SDF model can be motivated by risk neutrality, where the marginal rate of substitution of a risk-neutral investor (with time-additive, state independent utility) is constant over time. The average monthly interest rate is 0.309% and, hence, the inverse of the one-month gross return is 0.997 $[= 1/(1 + 0.00309)]$. As shown in the first line of Table 7, the estimated value of the constant SDF is 0.996, which is very close to the inverse of the sample mean of the gross 1-month interest rate. Panels A and B of Table 7 show the results of the different SDF models.[14] All means of the fitted values of our SDF models are slightly below 1.00, indicating that these models are effective in fixing at least the mean of the 'true' SDF. Similar to Farnsworth et al. (2002), the standard deviation increases as the SDF model becomes more 'complicated', that is, as we move from a one-factor model to multi-factor models and, even more pronounced, from unconditional to conditional models. This result can be explained by referring to Hansen and Jagannathan's (1991) volatility bounds for admissible SDFs and the underlying projection argument. The minimum variance of an admissible SDF increases as the number of primitive assets increases. Conditional SDF models can be tested by adding scaled factors and simply estimating the unconditional moments of this extended model (Cochrane 2001). New 'assets' (interpreted as dynamic trading strategies) are added to the model by scaling the factors and/or the primitive

Table 7. Stochastic discount factor models.

	$E(m)$	$SD(m)$	$\rho_1(m)$	Minimum	Maximum	# $(m < 0)$
Constant discount factor	0.9961	0.0000	0.0000	0.9963	0.9961	0
Panel A: Unconditional SDF models						
SDF-CAPM	0.9965	0.0784	0.015	0.7922	1.2763	0
SDF-Bakshi-Chen	0.9970	0.4007	−0.071	0.2893	2.1600	0
SDF-Fama-French	0.9905	0.4745	0.055	−0.7183	2.1711	3
SDF-primitive-efficient	0.9969	0.3883	−0.062	−0.1113	1.8680	1
Panel B: Conditional SDF models						
SDF-CAPM	0.9910	0.3112	−0.146	−0.1860	1.8866	1
SDF-Bakshi-Chen	0.9970	0.8410	−0.057	0.0012	5.6034	0
SDF-Fama-French	0.9800	0.7361	−0.153	−0.9771	2.8601	13
SDF-primitive-efficient	0.9969	0.6953	0.043	−0.7683	2.5521	10

Note: This table shows the results from specification tests for the different SDF models, denoted as m_{t+1}, using the following system of equations:

$$u1_t = (m_{t+1} R_{t+1} - 1) \otimes Z_t$$

where $u1_t$ denotes the vector of pricing errors relating to the N primitive assets, whose gross returns are collected in the vector R_{t+1}, and Z_t is the vector of predetermined information variables. The parameters of the SDFs are estimated using Hansen's (1982) GMM, minimizing a quadratic form of the pricing errors. The standard errors of the estimated coefficients are corrected for the effects of heteroscedasticity using the White (1980) methodology. $E(m)$ is the sample mean, $SD(m)$ is the sample standard deviation, and $\rho_1(m)$ is the first-order autocorrelation of the estimated SDF (fitted values). The primitive assets are the 10 sector portfolios according to the Datastream classification and the risk-free security. In linear models of the SDF (SDF-CAPM and SDF-Fama-French) the Datastream Germany Total Return Index is used as the market proxy. The predetermined information variables are the term-spread, the short-term interest rate, and the log dividend yield. To avoid an explosive number of orthogonality conditions, the results for the conditional specifications of both the SDF-Bakshi-Chen model and the SDF-primitive-efficient model are based on the short-term interest rate as the only information variable in the estimation. In contrast, for the SDF-CAPM and the SDF-Fama-French models we use the full set of information variables to scale factors. The sample period is from January 1994 to December 2003, and the full return history (120 months) is available for 47 general funds and 3 small- and mid-cap funds (50 surviving funds).

assets by the lagged information variables. One would therefore expect that the standard deviation of the estimated SDF is higher in conditional models compared to unconditional models.

A second observation is that the number of negative values in the time series of estimated SDFs is small in most specifications, as indicated by the last column of Table 7. The Euler-equation suggests that a negative value of the SDF implies that it assigns positive prices to negative payoffs at some point in time. As the standard deviation of the estimated SDF increases, the number of instances where the estimated SDF takes on a negative value increases. The value of a highly volatile SDF is ambiguous. On the one hand, more volatility is necessary to explain the historical equity premium (Mehra and Prescott 1985), or equivalently, to suffice the Hansen and Jagannathan (1991) volatility bound. On the other hand, a more volatile discount factor does not necessarily exhibit better pricing properties, and more volatility may imply lower power to detect abnormal performance.

Following Farnsworth et al. (2002), we also explore the dynamic performance of the different SDF models. In frictionless markets a transformation of the equilibrium price process follows a martingale with respect to the information set that market participants use to form expectations. Specifically, the discounted gross return, $m_{t+1} R_{t+1}$, should not be predictable based on lagged information variables, collected in Z_t (Cochrane 2001; Zimmermann 1998). To test this prediction, we compute the pricing errors, $m_{t+1} R_{t+1} - 1 \equiv u1$, for each equation in our system and regress them on the vector of lagged information variables, Z_t.[15] The predicted pricing errors should not be significantly different from zero using any information available at time t. The model implies that the regression coefficients should be zero. Even if there was predictability in a return, R_{t+1}, using lagged information variables, Z_t, it should be removed when R_{t+1} is multiplied by the 'correct' m_{t+1}. A related requirement is that the standard deviation of the fitted pricing errors of each equation should be small if the model captures the predictable variation in expected stock returns (Ferson and Harvey 1993; Ferson and Korajczyk 1995; Kirby 1998).

Table 8 shows the standard deviation of the fitted pricing errors in the different SDF models for each primitive asset. The constant discount factor model can serve as a benchmark model because it cannot explain any of the predictability. As an example, take the returns of sector 1. The monthly standard deviation of the fitted values for this sector is 2.91%, as shown in the first line of Table 8. With a constant SDF, this approach is equivalent to a regression of the gross returns on sector 1 multiplied by the estimated constant m minus 1 on the lagged information variables. In comparison, the standard deviation of the monthly raw return on sector 1 is 14.25%, as shown in Table 1. Because an R-square measures the percentage of variance explained, the R-square in a regression of the returns on sector 1 on the lagged information variables is roughly 4.2% [$=(0.02908/0.1425)^2$]. This value is exactly equal to the (unadjusted) R-square shown at the bottom of Table 1 for the predictive regression involving sector 1 and the three information variables.

Panel A in Table 8 presents the results for the unconditional SDF models. These models are unconditional in the sense that they do not exploit the predictive power of the information variables for raw returns, R_{t+1}. However, the SDF, m_{t+1}, is time-varying and the product $m_{t+1} R_{t+1}$ potentially follows a martingale. Similar to Farnsworth et al. (2002), none of the models can explain the predictable variation in sector returns better than the constant SDF model. The SDF-CAPM model explains a reasonable fraction of the predictability, implying that the standard deviations of the fitted values are relatively small. The other three models cannot capture the time-variation in expected returns. In many cases, the standard deviations of the fitted pricing errors are even larger than the standard deviations of the sectors' raw returns. This result implies that the product

Table 8. Dynamic performance of SDF models.

	Sector 1	Sector 2	Sector 3	Sector 4	Sector 5	Sector 6	Sector 7	Sector 8	Sector 9	Sector 10	Risk-free
Constant discount factor	2.908%	1.920%	1.128%	1.616%	1.067%	0.466%	1.192%	2.314%	0.259%	1.626%	0.076%
Panel A: Unconditional SDF models											
SDF-CAPM	2.647%	1.874%	0.949%	0.451%	1.074%	1.768%	0.917%	0.490%	2.031%	0.812%	2.060%
SDF-Fama-French	8.775%	10.083%	9.751%	9.239%	9.516%	11.163%	10.003%	8.317%	11.262%	9.587%	11.276%
SDF-primitive-efficient	8.384%	7.275%	8.464%	8.833%	8.336%	7.711%	9.086%	9.723%	7.900%	9.107%	7.727%
SDF-Bakshi-Chen	6.171%	5.965%	7.087%	7.366%	6.894%	6.488%	7.681%	8.165%	6.808%	7.689%	6.632%
Panel B: Conditional SDF models											
SDF-CAPM	1.806%	1.725%	1.191%	1.272%	1.451%	1.242%	1.435%	1.661%	1.367%	1.026%	1.120%
SDF-Fama-French	3.041%	3.397%	3.592%	3.773%	3.577%	3.542%	3.456%	3.668%	3.999%	4.254%	3.642%
SDF-primitive-efficient	0.000%	0.000%	0.000%	0.000%	0.000%	0.000%	0.000%	0.000%	0.000%	0.000%	0.000%
SDF-Bakshi-Chen	0.000%	0.000%	0.000%	0.000%	0.000%	0.000%	0.000%	0.000%	0.000%	0.000%	0.000%

Note: This table shows the standard deviations of the fitted pricing errors from the following system of equations:

$$u1_t = (m_{t+1} R_{t+1} - 1) \otimes Z_t$$

where $u1_t$ denotes the vector of pricing errors relating to the N primitive assets, whose gross returns are collected in the vector R_{t+1}, m_{t+1} is the SDF, and Z_t is the vector of predetermined information variables. The fitted pricing errors are the fitted values of regressions of $u1_t$ on Z_t using different models of the SDF, and the entries in the table show the corresponding standard deviations for all primitive assets. The parameters of the SDFs are estimated using Hansen's (1982) GMM, minimizing a quadratic form of the pricing errors. The standard deviations of the estimated coefficients are corrected for the effects of heteroscedasticity using the White (1980) methodology. The primitive assets are the 10 sector portfolios according to the Datastream classification and the risk-free security. In linear models of the SDF (SDF-CAPM and SDF-Fama-French) the Datastream Germany Total Return Index is used as the market proxy. The predetermined information variables are the term-spread, the short-term interest rate, and the log dividend yield. To avoid an explosive number of orthogonality conditions, the results for the conditional specifications of both the SDF-Bakshi-Chen model and the SDF-primitive-efficient model are based on the short-term interest as the only information variable in the estimation. In contrast, for the SDF-CAPM and the SDF-Fama-French models we use the full set of information variables to scale factors. The sample period is from January 1994 to December 2003, and the full return history (120 months) is available for 47 general funds and 3 small- and mid-cap funds (50 surviving funds).

of $m_{t+1}R_{t+1} - 1$ has even larger regression coefficients upon Z_t than R_{t+1}, indicating particularly poor pricing performance.

Panel B of Table 9 presents the results for the conditional SDF models. The conditional SDF-primitive-efficient and the conditional SDF-Bakshi-Chen models produce standard deviations of the fitted pricing errors that are virtually zero. In general, we observe that the conditional models perform better than the unconditional ones. This finding can be explained by the nature of the GMM estimation procedure. Conditional models exploit the lagged instrument variables to form a set of orthogonality conditions, and the parameters are estimated to make the expected product of the pricing errors and the lagged instrument variables as close to zero as possible in the sample.[16]

4.2.2 Using SDF alphas to measure mutual fund performance

Table 9 presents the cross-sectional distribution of individual fund alphas for the different SDF models. To characterize the distribution of SDF alphas, we report the mean and the median alphas, the alphas of the bottom 3 and bottom 10 funds, and the alphas of the top 3 and top 10 funds. We also show the SDF alpha when the system of equations in (6) is estimated using an equally weighted portfolio of all funds. Moreover, the table shows the Bonferroni p-values for the null hypothesis that all alphas are jointly zero.

In the unconditional SDF-CAPM model, the average estimated underperformance is 0.149% per month, or roughly 1.79% per year. The same result is obtained for an equally weighted portfolio of all funds. The average expense ratio was 1.06%, indicating that the average fund strongly underperforms already under the simplest SDF model, even after adding back total expense ratios. The performance of the top 3 and bottom 3 funds indicates strong negative skewness of the distribution of individual fund alphas. This shape of the distribution does not strongly depend on the SDF-model.

Table 10 shows the rank correlations between the estimated alphas. In many cases, the correlations are quite high, indicating that the relative performance of individual funds is quite robust to alternative specifications of the SDF. Rank correlations range between 0.72 and 0.95 for the unconditional models in Panel A, and between 0.64 and 0.91 for the conditional models in Panel B. The lowest rank correlations generally involve the SDF-Fama-French model, which tends to be the poorest performing model (see Tables 7 and 8). In results not presented here, we also compute the rank correlations between unconditional and conditional versions of each model. These rank correlations range between 0.72 (for the SDF-Fama-French models) and 0.94 (for the SDF-CAPM models). Overall, we conclude that the relative performance measured for the individual funds is reasonably correlated across different SDF models. Nevertheless, compared to the unconditional SDF-CAPM model, the mean of the distribution generally shifts to the left in all other models of the SDF. This finding is in contrast to the results by Farnsworth et al. (2002) and Fletcher and Forbes (2004), who report similar performance measures across different SDF models. For example, in Panel A of Table 9 the average alpha for the unconditional SDF-primitive-efficient model is -0.177% per month, or about -2.10% per year. The mean SDF alpha for the SDF-Fama-French three-factor model sharply deteriorates to -0.304% per month, or -3.65% per year. This large negative performance is confirmed when an equally weighted portfolio of funds is used instead of estimating the system of equations separately for each fund and reporting the average SDF alpha. However, given the poor time-series properties of the estimated SDF for this model (see Tables 7 and 8), this result should not be overemphasized.

As expected, the results in Panel B of Table 9 suggest that compared to an unconditional assessment the conditional performance of our funds appears even more unfavorably (with an exception of the SDF-Bakshi-Chen model). The average conditional SDF alphas sharply decrease to values

Table 9. Measures of performance using the SDF framework.

	Bonferroni p-value (−)	Bottom 3	Bottom 10	Mean	EW-Portf.	Median	Top 10	Top 3	Bonferroni p-value (+)
Panel A: Unconditional SDF models									
SDF-CAPM	0.005	−0.448	−0.322	−0.149	−0.149	−0.179	0.007	0.112	0.942
SDF-Fama-French	0.094	−0.838	−0.476	−0.304	−0.304	−0.275	−0.059	0.089	0.935
SDF-primitive-efficient	0.136	−0.414	−0.348	−0.177	−0.192	−0.205	−0.031	0.297	1.528
SDF-Bakshi-Chen	0.068	−0.456	−0.399	−0.238	−0.210	−0.256	−0.103	0.073	1.354
Panel B: Conditional SDF models									
SDF-CAPM	0.000	−0.528	−0.478	−0.340	−0.360	−0.343	−0.207	−0.018	2.788
SDF-Fama-French	0.000	−0.924	−0.537	−0.330	−0.320	−0.280	−0.108	0.043	0.000
SDF-primitive-efficient	0.007	−0.692	−0.347	−0.234	−0.272	−0.223	−0.042	0.023	6.965
SDF-Bakshi-Chen	0.001	−0.519	−0.407	−0.243	−0.290	−0.221	−0.076	0.006	5.703

Note: This table shows the distribution of mutual fund SDF alphas for different models of the SDF, m_{t+1}, from estimations of the following system of equations:

$$u1_t = (m_{t+1} R_{t+1} - 1) \otimes Z_t$$

$$u2_t = \alpha_P - m_{t+1} R_{P,t+1} + 1,$$

where $u1_t$ denotes the vector of pricing errors relating to the N primitive assets, whose gross returns are collected in the vector R_{t+1}, $u2_t$ is the pricing error of the fund with gross return $R_{P,t+1}$, m_{t+1} is the SDF; and Z_t is the vector of predetermined information variables. α_P is the SDF alpha, depending on the model of the SDF. All parameters are estimated using Hansen's (1982) GMM, minimizing a quadratic form of the pricing errors. The standard errors of the estimated coefficients are corrected for the effects of heteroscedasticity using the White (1980) methodology. The primitive assets are the 10 sector portfolios according to the Datastream classification and the risk-free security. In linear models of the SDF (SDF-CAPM and SDF-Fama-French) the Datastream Germany Total Return Index is used as the market proxy. The predetermined information variables are the term-spread, the short-term interest rate, and the log dividend yield. To avoid an explosive number of orthogonality conditions, the results for the conditional specifications of both the SDF-Bakshi-Chen model and the SDF-primitive-efficient model are based on the short-term interest as the only information variable in the estimation. In contrast, for the SDF-CAPM and the SDF-Fama-French models we use the full set of information variables to scale factors. The Bonferroni *p*-value is the maximum or minimum one-tailed *p*-value from the distribution of *t*-statistics across all funds multiplied by the number of funds. The sample period is from January 1994 to December 2003, and the full return history (120 months) is available for 47 general funds and 3 small- and mid-cap funds (50 surviving funds).

Table 10. Rank correlations of SDF alphas.

	SDF-CAPM	SDF-Fama-French	SDF-primitive efficient	SDF-Bakshi-Chen
Panel A: Unconditional model specifications				
SDF-CAPM	1			
SDF-Fama-French	0.7279	1		
SDF-primitive-efficient	0.9476	0.7940	1	
SDF-Bakshi-Chen	0.8553	0.7219	0.9405	1
Panel B: Conditional model specifications				
SDF-CAPM	1			
SDF-Fama-French	0.6415	1		
SDF-primitive efficient	0.6791	0.6623	1	
SDF-Bakshi-Chen	0.7203	0.7540	0.9102	1

Note: This table contains the Spearman rank correlations of the estimated SDF alphas for the sample of 50 selected funds using different specifications for the SDF. The SDF alphas are estimated from the system of equations in (6) using Hansen's (1982) GMM. The sample period is from January 1994 to December 2003.

between -0.234% and -0.340% per month, which implies a large underperformance between -2.80% and -4.00% per annum, depending on the model for the SDF. As discussed in Section 4.1.1 above, using public information-based dynamic portfolios as the reference leads to 'tougher' performance yardsticks. Another more technical explanation for our findings is that a more 'complicated' SDF leads to more restrictive pricing conditions. In a conditional setup, the SDF becomes more complicated in the sense that scaled returns (interpreted as the returns on dynamic trading strategies) and/or scaled factors are added. As shown by Hansen and Jagannathan (1991), imposing additional assets implies that the volatility bound for SDFs shifts upward and entails stronger pricing restrictions, that is, the minimum variance of admissible SDFs increases. A ray from the origin to the minimum point of the volatility bound has the interpretation of a Sharpe ratio (De Santis 1995; Drobetz 2003). Conditional models specify a stronger benchmark, explaining why fund performance looks particularly poor when the tests incorporate conditioning information.

The distribution of our estimated SDF alphas is again negatively skewed, and this property is reflected in the Bonferroni p-values. With only one exception (the conditional SDF-Fama-French model), we cannot reject the null hypothesis that all conditional SDF alphas are jointly equal to zero against the alternative hypothesis that there is at least one significantly positive alpha (Bonferroni p-value $(+)$). In contrast, in most instances we can reject the null hypothesis that all SDF alphas are jointly equal to zero against the alternative hypothesis that there is at least one significantly negative alpha (Bonferroni p-value $(-)$).[17]

4.3 *Comparing the results from beta-pricing models and SDF models*

In this section, we compare the estimated SDF alphas with the traditional Jensen's alphas. A general observation is that the performance of our German equity mutual funds looks much worse in the Euler-equation framework than in the traditional beta-pricing setup. For example, the average unconditional Jensen's alpha in Table 3 is -0.042% per month, or roughly 0.50% per annum, whereas the average unconditional alpha in the SDF-CAPM specification in Table 9 is -0.149% per month, or roughly -1.79% per year. The corresponding conditional performance measures are -0.116% (Table 5) and -0.340% (Table 9) per month, or about -1.39% and -4.00% per year, respectively.

A crucial question that arises is whether elegance and generality of the SDF framework comes at the cost of estimation efficiency for risk premiums and testing power for model specifications. Kan and Zhou (1999) compare the SDF methodology using the GMM with maximum likelihood estimates of the static linear capital asset pricing model. Their results seem to suggest that the SDF methodology performs much worse than the beta-pricing approach in specification tests. They explain this result by noting that the Euler-equation is merely a restriction on part of the first and second moments between asset returns and factors. However, without a fully specified model of asset returns this implies ignoring many other first and second moments, thereby producing large estimation errors in the factor risk premiums.

However, this conclusion might be premature for two reasons. First, the specification tests in Tables 7 and 8 indicate that, except for the SDF-Fama-French model, our SDF models behave reasonably well. Second, Jagannathan and Wang (2002) document that Kan and Zhou's (1999) results are based on false assumptions. Specifically, they ignore the fact that the risk premium parameters in the two methods are not identical (albeit strictly related) and directly compare the asymptotic variances of the two estimators. Jagannathan and Wang (2002) present a more appropriate test setup that explicitly incorporates the transformation between the risk parameters in the two methods and conclude that the SDF methodology is asymptotically as efficient as the beta-pricing method. Specification tests of asset pricing models based on the two methods are also equally powerful.

To gain some preliminary insight, we estimate the direct counterpart of a static Jensen's alpha in the SDF framework and label this performance measure 'SDF Jensen's alpha'. Specifically, instead of using the full set of primitive assets in the system of equations in (6), we estimate the SDF-CAPM model by merely requiring that the SDF prices the benchmark index and the risk-free security.[18] Following Dybvig and Ingersoll (1982), the SDF is assumed to be a linear function of the market index, which is represented by the Datastream Germany Total Return Index. In this simple setup the system to be estimated consists of only three equations. Since the SDF is a linear combination of the market index, the first equation formulates the pricing restriction on the index itself as a primitive asset, and the second equation contains the pricing restriction on the risk-free security. The third equation involves the pricing restriction on the specific fund to be evaluated and the corresponding SDF Jensen's alpha.

A graphical comparison of the results is depicted in Panel A of Figure 1. The figure displays alternative performance measures for all 50 funds in our sample: (i) the traditional Jensen's alpha, (ii) the SDF Jensen's alpha, and (iii) the SDF alpha from the SDF-CAPM model. The means of all series match the values reported in the tables above. Specifically, the mean Jensen's alpha in our sample is −0.042% per month (Table 3), and the mean SDF-CAPM alpha is −0.149% per month (Table 9). Most important, the mean SDF Jensen's alpha is −0.042% per month, which is identical to its direct and more common counterpart in the beta-pricing formulation. In fact, as can be inferred from Figure 1, the corresponding two lines with individual alphas exactly coincide. From this finding we conclude that the empirical results from the SDF methodology and the beta-pricing method are inherently related with each other, as suggested by asset pricing theory. In addition, the SDF-CAPM alphas are highly correlated with the Jensen's alphas; the rank correlation is 0.91. Nevertheless, there is a notable level shift, which is responsible for our previous finding that funds tend to look worse in an SDF framework.

Panel B of Figure 1 presents the same results in the conditional setup, where all three information variables are used to account for the time-variation in expected returns. The average conditional SDF Jensen's alpha is −0.063% per month, or −0.76% per annum, which makes funds look better in this case compared to the Ferson and Schadt (1996) framework, for which we report a

Panel A: Unconditional performance measures (50 funds)

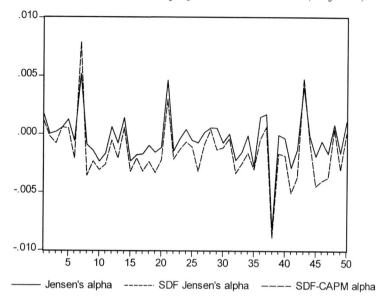

Panel B: Conditional performance measures (50 funds)

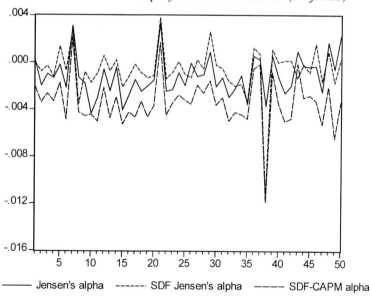

Figure 1. Beta-pricing models versus stochastic discount factor (SDF) models.

Note: This figure displays alternative performance measures from tests in the beta-pricing framework and the SDF methodology for our reduced sample of 50 funds: (i) the traditional Jensen's alpha, (ii) the SDF Jensen's alpha, and (iii) the SDF alpha from the SDF-CAPM model. The sample period is from January 1994 to December 2003, and the full return history (120 months) is available for 47 general funds and 3 small- and mid-cap funds (50 surviving funds). The units are in percentages per month.

mean conditional alpha of −0.116% per month, or −1.39% per year (Table 5). However, the average conditional SDF Jensen's alpha is still slightly lower than its average unconditional analogue, which supports our general notion that funds look worse under conditional performance measures. Similar to the unconditional setup in Panel A, the figure in Panel B reveals that the conditional alpha of the SDF-CAPM model assigns the lowest performance to our funds, with a mean alpha of −0.340% per month (Table 9). As can be expected from a mere visual inspection, the rank correlations between the performance measures are again high; they range between 0.66 (for Jensen's alpha and the SDF Jensen's alpha) and 0.81 (for Jensen's alpha and the SDF-CAPM alpha).

Overall, we find that the SDF methodology and the beta-pricing method deliver closely related performance measures in empirical tests, as suggested by asset pricing theory. We cannot conclude that either one approach leads to grossly misleading performance evaluation results. Nevertheless, our analysis suggests that the level of underperformance depends on the model specification and the estimation technique. One immediate source of the differences in our results is the choice of the primitive assets. With a larger set of primitive assets, the number of equations in the system to be estimated increases, thereby imposing additional moment restrictions that affect the parameter estimates (Bekaert and Liu 2004; Hansen and Jagannathan 1991). This is mechanically true, although our 10 sector portfolios are merely subindexes of the market index. Additional restrictions always imply a stronger benchmark, leading to a lower estimated fund performance.

5. Conclusions

In this article, we address two important issues that have influenced the recent performance measurement literature. First, we discuss how to extend the classical unconditional securities market line analysis to incorporate conditioning information and to compute conditional Jensen's alphas. This strand of the literature has been inspired by the influential studies by Ferson and Schadt (1996) and Christopherson, Ferson, and Glassman (1998). Second, given the deficiencies of securities market line analysis and following the general trend in the recent asset pricing literature, we switch the focus from the classical beta-pricing framework to the more general SDF framework. This development is based on previous work by Chen and Knez (1996) and Farnsworth et al. (2002).

We investigate the performance of a sample of German equity mutual funds. Our general finding is that mutual funds, on average, hardly produce returns that are large enough to cover their expenses. This conclusion has been drawn from a variety of model specifications and is robust to many different benchmarks. We start by measuring fund performance in the classical unconditional beta-pricing framework. Based on Jensen's alpha as a performance measure, mutual funds slightly underperform. Funds look worse, when we apply the three-factor model of Fama and French (1993) as the benchmark. Fund performance substantially deteriorates when we measure conditional alphas both in single-index and multi-factor models. For example, based on the full set of information variables, the mean conditional alpha for our sample of general funds is estimated to be −0.130% per month, or about −1.5% per year. In comparison, taking a simple average for all funds over the 1997 to 2003 period, the mean total expense ratio was only 1.06%. Accordingly, if we add back management fees, German mutual equity funds underperform on a before fee basis. Using a conditional three-factor model, fund performance tends to look even worse. These results should not come as a surprise: Given that stock returns are partly predictable using publicly available information, the part of fund performance that is attributable to time-variation in expected returns should be deducted. Accordingly, conditional analysis raises the performance yardstick for active managers because it gives them no credit for exploiting readily available information.

We then proceed to performance measurement in the Euler-equation framework and test different (unconditional and conditional) specifications of the SDF. The result that funds underperform before costs is much more pronounced, even in the unconditional SDF models. Underperformance after fees can even be as low as 4% per year. To the best of our knowledge, our article is the first that directly compares the results from performance measurement tests in the beta-pricing setup and the SDF framework. We document that both methods are in fact inherently related, as suggested by asset pricing theory, and that the relative performance of the funds in our sample (i.e. their rankings within the sample) is highly correlated across models. However, there is a pronounced level shift when switching from the beta-pricing to the SDF framework, which can be attributed to the fact that more 'complicated' SDF models and a larger number of primitive assets (which are required to estimate the parameters of the SDF models) lead to stronger pricing restrictions. This explanation is a direct result from Hansen and Jagannathan's (1991) analysis on volatility bounds for admissible SDFs.

Acknowledgements

We thank two anonymous referees, Chris Adcock (the editor), Yakov Amihud, Alexander Kempf, Peter Kugler, and the participants of the European Financial Management Association Meeting (EFMA) 2007 in Vienna and the German Finance Association Meeting (DGF) 2007 in Dresden for valuable comments.

Notes

1. The numbers include both retail funds and institutional funds. Institutional funds account for more than 50% of these figures.
2. Bansal and Harvey (1996) suggest a similar approach, using a nonparametric benchmark. Adcock et al. (2007) show that evidence for time variation in beta using the model in (3) is equivalent to non-normality in the unconditional distribution of asset returns.
3. For the link to performance measures in a beta-pricing framework see Söderlind (1999).
4. This result ultimately rests upon Hansen and Jagannathan's (1991) projection argument for the (infinite) set of admissible SDFs.
5. See Farnsworth et al. (2002, p. 476). However, this is only a minimum requirement and cannot solve the more general measurement problems described in Chen and Knez (1996).
6. Farnsworth et al. (2002) use this system of equations to estimate the performance of US mutual funds, and Fletcher and Forbes (2004) apply the same framework to assess the performance of UK unit trusts. Chen and Knez (1996) and Dahlquist and Söderlind (1999) use a different methodology to estimate fund performance in an SDF framework that is directly based on the minimum value of the quadratic form in the GMM estimation and the related J-statistic.
7. See Boudoukh et al. (2007), De Santis and Gerard (1997, 1998), Harvey (2001), and Ostdiek (1998).
8. Following Malkiel's (1995) approach, we find a survivorship bias of 45 basis points if only surviving funds were used. The annual attrition rate was 2–3% per year.
9. The SMAX index used to be the small- and medium-cap index provided by Deutsche Börse AG. Deutsche Börse AG changed its index classification scheme as of 2004, and the SMAX index has been continued as a small-cap index of 50 small stocks in the prime segment, denoted as SDAX.
10. See Chen and Knez (1996). In contrast, Farnsworth et al. (2002) use a broad market index and a set of style portfolios, and Fletcher and Forbes (2004) use size portfolios as primitive assets.
11. All sample autocorrelations of our information variables at the first lag are above 0.9, indicating strong persistence and possibly non-stationarity. The null hypothesis of a unit root cannot be rejected for all three series using both Augmented Dickey-Fuller and Phillips-Perron tests. In contrast, the results of the KPSS-test (Kwiatkowski et al., 1992) are inconclusive, and we assume that all three series are not sufficiently informative to determine whether they are stationary or integrated.
12. In contrast, for our sample of small- and mid-cap funds we find opposite results. They indicate that fund managers tend to reduce their market betas when public information implies relatively high expected market returns, and vice versa. Fund performance tends to look worse in a conditional framework. Ferson and Warther (1996) also report that the performance of some funds switches from negative to positive and suggest a new money-flow hypothesis.

13. See Kosowski et al. (2006) for a discussion of non-normality in the distribution of the t-ratios.
14. Using all information variables simultaneously leads to an explosive number of orthogonality conditions. Therefore, the results in Panel B of Table 7 for the conditional specifications of both the SDF-Bakshi-Chen model and the SDF-primitive-efficient model are based on the short-term interest as the only information variable in the GMM estimation. In contrast, for the SDF-CAPM and the SDF-Fama-French models we use the full set of information variables to scale factors.
15. This procedure is similar to the widely used Sargan-test (Sargan, 1958) of over-identifying restrictions. See also Davidson and MacKinnon (2004).
16. The conditional SFD-Fama-French model, however, performs worse than the constant SDF model in explaining predictable return variation. This finding confirms previous results by Kirby (1998).
17. In contrast to Farnsworth et al. (2002), Jagannathan and Wang (2002) suggest omitting the risk-free security from the set of primitive assets. In results not reported here, we find that our findings do not change qualitatively. However, the models grossly overestimate the risk-free rate, that is, if the risk-free security is not used as a primitive asset, these models are not able to correctly fix the mean of the stochastic discount factor.
18. To be consistent with the beta pricing framework, we omit the information variables as individual 'factors' to compute the SDF Jensen's alphas.

References

Adcock, C., M. Ceu Cortez, M. Rocha Armada, and F. Silva. 2007. A model for time varying betas. Working Paper, University of Sheffield and University of Minho.

Admati, A., and S. Ross. 1985. Measuring investment performance in a rational expectations equilibrium model. *Journal of Business* 58: 1–26.

Amihud, Y., and C. Hurvich. 2004. Predictive regressions: A reduced-bias estimation method. *Journal of Financial and Quantitative Analysis* 39: 813–41.

Bakshi, G., and Z. Chen. 1998. Asset pricing without consumption or market portfolio data. Working Paper, College Park, University of Maryland.

Bams, D., and R. Otten. 2002. European mutual fund performance. *European Financial Management* 8: 75–101.

Bansal, R., and C. Harvey. 1996. Performance evaluation in the presence of dynamic trading strategies. Working Paper, Duke University.

Banz, R. 1981. The relationship between return and market value of common stock. *Journal of Financial Economics* 9: 3–18.

Bekaert, G., and J. Liu. 2004. Conditioning information and variance bounds on pricing kernels. *Review of Financial Studies* 17: 339–78.

Boudoukh, J., R. Michaely, M. Richardson, and M. Roberts. 2007. On the importance of measuring payout yield: Implications for empirical asset pricing, *Journal of Finance* 62: 877–915.

BVI (Bundesverband Investment und Asset Management). 2005. Aktuelle Fragen der Altersvorsorge mit Investmentfonds. http://www.bvi.de.

Campbell, J., and M. Yogo. 2006. Efficient tests of stock return predictability. *Journal of Financial Economics* 81: 27–60.

Chen, Z., and P. Knez. 1996. Portfolio performance measurement: Theory and applications. *Review of Financial Studies* 9: 511–55.

Christopherson, J., W. Ferson, and D. Glassman. 1998. Conditioning manager alphas on economic information: Another look at the persistence of performance. *Review of Financial Studies* 11: 111–42.

Cochrane, J., 1996. A cross-sectional test of an investment-based asset pricing model. *Journal of Political Economy* 104: 572–621.

Cochrane, J., 1999. New facts in finance. *Economic Perspectives*, 36–58.

Cochrane, J., 2001. *Asset pricing*. New Jersey: Princeton University Press.

Dahlquist, M., S. Engström, and P. Söderlind. 2000. Performance and characteristics of Swedish mutual fund. *Journal of Financial and Quantitative Analysis* 35: 409–23.

Dahlquist, M., and P. Söderlind. 1999. Evaluating portfolio performance with stochastic discount factors. *Journal of Business* 72: 347–84.

Davidson, R., and J. MacKinnon. 2004. *Econometric theory and methods*. New York: Oxford University Press.

De Santis, G. 1995. Volatility bounds for stochastic discount factors: Tests and implications from international financial markets. Working Paper, University of Southern California.

De Santis, G., and B. Gerard. 1997. International asset pricing and portfolio diversification with time-varying risk. *Journal of Finance* 52: 1881–912.

De Santis, G., and B. Gerard. 1998. How big is the premium for currency risk? *Journal of Financial Economics* 49: 375–412.

Dittmar, R. 2003. Nonlinear pricing kernels, kurtosis preferences, and evidence from the cross-section of asset returns. *Journal of Finance* 62: 369–403.

Drobetz, W. 2003. Volatility bounds for stochastic discount factors on global stock markets. *Journal of Applied Social Science Study* (Schmollers Jahrbuch) 123: 1–30.

Dybvig, P., and J. Ingersoll. 1982. Mean-variance theory in complete markets. *Journal of Business* 55: 233–52.

Fama, E., and K. French. 1992. The cross-section of expected stock returns. *Journal of Finance* 47: 427–65.

Fama, E., and K. French. 1993. Common risk factors in the returns on bonds and stocks. *Journal of Financial Economics* 33: 3–53.

Farnsworth, H., W. Ferson, D. Jackson, and S. Todd. 2002. Performance evaluation with stochastic discount factors. *Journal of Business* 75: 473–504.

Ferson, W., and C. Harvey. 1991. The variation of economic risk premiums. *Journal of Political Economy* 99: 385–415.

Ferson, W., and C. Harvey. 1993. The risk und predictability of international equity returns. *Review of Financial Studies* 6: 527–66.

Ferson, W., and R. Jagannathan. 1996. Econometric evaluation of asset pricing models. In *Handbook of Statistics 14: statistical methods in finance*, eds G. Maddala and C. Rao, 1–30. Amsterdam: Elsevier.

Ferson, W., and R. Korajczyk. 1995. Do arbitrage pricing models explain the predictability of stock return? *Journal of Business* 68: 309–49.

Ferson, W., and M. Qian. 2004. Conditional performance evaluation: Revisited. Working Paper, Boston College.

Ferson, W., and R. Schadt. 1996. Measuring fund strategy and performance in changing economic conditions. *Journal of Finance* 51: 425–61.

Ferson, W., and A.F. Siegel. 2001. The efficient use of conditioning information in portfolios, *Journal of Finance* 56: 967–982.

Ferson, W., and V. Warther. 1996. Evaluating fund performance in a dynamic market. *Financial Analysts Journal* 52: 20–28.

Fletcher, J., and D. Forbes. 2004. Performance evaluation of UK unit trusts within the stochastic discount factor framework. *Journal of Financial Research* 27: 289–306.

Goyal, A., and I. Welch. 2003. Predicting the equity premium with dividend ratios. *Management Science* 49: 639–54.

Griese, K., and A. Kempf. 2003. Lohnt aktives Fondsmanagement aus Anlegersicht? Ein Vergleich von Anlagestrategien in aktiv und passiv verwalteten Aktienfonds, *Zeitschrift für Betriebswirtschaft* 73: 201–224.

Grinblatt, M., and S. Titman. 1989. Portfolio performance evaluation: Old issues and new insights. *Review of Financial Studies* 2: 393–421.

Grinblatt, M., and S. Titman. 1994. A study of monthly mutual fund returns and performance evaluation techniques, *Journal of Financial and Quantitative Analysis* 29: 419–444.

Hansen, L. 1982. Large sample properties of generalized method of moments estimators. *Econometrica* 50: 1029–54.

Hansen, L., and R. Jagannathan. 1991. Implications of security market data for models of dynamic economies. *Journal of Political Economy* 99: 225–62.

Hansen, L., and S. Richard. 1987. The role of conditioning information in deducing testable restrictions implied by dynamic asset pricing models. *Econometrica* 55: 587–613.

Harvey, C. 2001. The specification if conditional expectations. *Journal of Empirical Finance* 8: 573–638.

Jagannathan, R., and Z. Wang. 1996. The conditional CAPM and the cross-section of expected returns. *Journal of Finance* 51: 3–53.

Jagannathan, R., and Z. Wang. 2002. Empirical evaluation of asset pricing models, A comparison of SDF and beta methods. *Journal of Finance* 57: 2337–67.

Jensen, M. 1972. Optimal utilization of market forecasts and the evaluation of investment performance. In *Mathematical methods in investment and finance*, eds G. Szego and K. Shell. Elsevier: North-Holland.

Kan, R., and G. Zhou. 1999. A critique of the stochastic discount factor methodology. *Journal of Finance* 54: 1221–48.

Kirby, C. 1998. The restrictions on predictability implied by rational asset pricing models. *Review of Financial Studies* 11: 343–82.

Kosowski, R., A. Timmermann, R. Wermers, and H. White. 2006. Can mutual fund 'stars' really pick stocks? New evidence from a bootstrap analysis. *Journal of Finance* 61: 2551–95.

Krahnen, J.P., F. Schmid, and E. Theissen. 2006. Investment performance and market share: A study of the German mutual fund industry. In *Börsen, Banken und Kapitalmärkte*, ed. W. Bessler. Berlin: Duncker and Humblot.

Kwiatkowski, D., P. Phillips, P. Schmidt, and Y. Shin. 1992. Testing the null hypothesis of stationarity against the alternative of a unit root. *Journal of Econometrics* 54: 159–78.

Lakonishok, J., A. Shleifer, and R. Vishny. 1994. Contrarian investment, extrapolation, and risk. *Journal of Finance* 49: 1541–78.

Lewellen, J. 2004. Predicting returns with financial ratios. *Journal of Financial Economics* 74: 209–35.

Malkiel, B. 1995. Return from investing in equity mutual funds 1971 to 1991. *Journal of Finance* 40: 549–72.

Malkiel, B. 2003. Passive investment strategies and efficient markets. *European Financial management* 9: 1–10.

Maurer, R. 2004. Institutional investors in Germany. In *The German financial system,* eds J. Krahnen, and R. Schmidt, 106–38. Oxford: Oxford University Press.

Mehra, R., and E. Prescott. 1985. The equity premium: A puzzle. *Journal of Monetary Economics* 15: 145–62.

Ostdiek, B. 1998. The world ex ante risk premium: An empirical investigation. *Journal of International Money and Finance* 17: 967–99.

Paape, C. 2003. Currency overlay and performance evaluation. *Financial Analysts Journal* 59: 55–68.

Rey, D. 2004. Stock market predictability and tactical asset allocation. Ph.D Thesis, University of St. Gallen.

Roll, R. 1978. Ambiguity when performance is measured by the securities market line. *Journal of Finance* 33: 1051–69.

Roll, R., and S. Ross. 1994. Cross-sectional relation between expected returns and betas. *Journal of Finance* 49: 101–21.

Sargan, J. 1958. The estimation of economic relationships using instrumental variables, *Econometrica* 26: 393-415.

Schwert, G.W. 2002. Anomalies and market efficiency. In *Handbook of the economics of finance*, eds G. Constantinides, M. Harris, and R. Stulz. Elsevier: North Holland.

Shanken, J. 1990. Intertemporal asset pricing: An empirical investigation. *Journal of Financial Economics* 45: 99–120.

Sharpe, W. 1991. The arithmetic of active management, *Financial Analysts Journal* 47: 7–9.

Silva, F., M. Ceu Cortez, and M. Armada. 2003. Conditioning information and European bond fund performance, *European Financial Management* 9: 201–230.

Söderlind, P. 1999. An interpretation of SDF based performance measures. *European Finance Review* 3: 233–7.

Stambaugh, R. 1999. Predictive regressions. *Journal of Financial Economics* 54: 375–421.

Theissen, E. 2004. Organized equity markets. In *The German financial system*, eds J. Krahnen, and R. Schmidt, 139–62. Oxford: Oxford University Press.

Torous, W., R. Valkanov, and S. Yan. 2004. On predicting stock returns with nearly integrated explanatory variables. *Journal of Business* 77: 937–66.

White, H. 1980. A heteroscedasticity-consistent covariance matrix estimator and a direct test for heteroscedasticity. *Econometrica* 48: 817–38.

Zimmermann, H. 1998. *State Preference Theorie und Asset Pricing: Eine Einführung*. Heidelberg: Physica-Springer.

Conditioning information in mutual fund performance evaluation: Portuguese evidence

Paulo Armada Leite[a] and Maria Ceu Cortez[b]

[a] School of Management, Polytechnic Institute of Cávado and Ave, 4750-117 Barcelos, Portugal; [b] School of Economics and Management, University of Minho, Gualtar, 4710-057 Braga, Portugal

We estimate and compare the performance of Portuguese-based mutual funds that invest in the domestic market and in the European market using unconditional and conditional models of performance evaluation. Besides applying both partial and full conditional models, we use European information variables, instead of the most common local ones, and consider stochastically detrended conditional variables in order to avoid spurious regressions. The results suggest that mutual fund managers are not able to outperform the market, presenting negative or neutral performance. The incorporation of conditioning information in performance evaluation models is supported by our findings, as it improves the explanatory power of the models and there is evidence of both time-varying betas and alphas related to the public information variables. It is also shown that the number of lags to be used in the stochastic detrending procedure is a critical choice, as it will impact the significance of the conditioning information. In addition, we observe a distance effect, since managers who invest locally seem to outperform those who invest in the European market. However, after controlling for public information, this effect is slightly reduced. Furthermore, the results suggest that survivorship bias has a small impact on performance estimates.

1. Introduction

Portfolio performance evaluation is one of the most interesting topics in finance. Having not only attracted the attention of practitioners, this field has also motivated many studies in the academic literature. Besides being relevant, this issue is also controversial since it raises some complex questions related to capital market efficiency, a concept that is central to asset pricing theory.

Although performance evaluation has evolved considerably over the last decades, the standard (unconditional) measures applied in portfolio performance evaluation, proposed in the 1960s, are still extensively employed. The majority of the empirical studies carried out so far indicate that portfolio managers perform poorly in relation to the market. An implication is that if performance is indeed as weak as these studies suggest, then active fund management would tend to be replaced by passive investment strategies. This hypothesis, however, is contradicted by the size and expansion of this industry. As an attempt to address some of these concerns, a recent approach that has been advocated to re-examine fund performance is conditional performance evaluation. By taking into account the public information (represented by a set of predetermined lagged instruments) available to investors at the time the returns were generated, allowing both expected returns and risk to be time-varying, conditional measures, at least theoretically, are expected to produce more reliable inferences on performance (Chen and Knez 1996; Ferson and Schadt 1996).

Research on mutual fund performance has remained geographically narrow (Khorana, Servaes, and Tufano 2005). Conclusions from previous studies might therefore be sample specific. In fact, with the exception of the UK market, little is known about the conditional performance of other European markets. The Portuguese market, in particular, is still largely unexplored. On the other hand, the motivation for this study was further stimulated by the results of these few studies, which indicate that, outside the USA, the use of conditioning information in performance evaluation does not seem as pertinent as for the USA (e.g., Bauer, Otten, and Rad 2006; Blake, Lehmann, and Timmermann 2002; Otten and Bams 2002; Sawicki and Ong 2000).

This paper contributes to the international mutual fund performance literature by providing evidence on the impact of using conditioning information in evaluating the performance of Portuguese-based mutual funds investing in local as well as in European Union stocks. Additionally, our study explores both the distance effect and the survivorship bias topics in a conditional framework. Considering the tendency of European stock markets towards integration, we further innovate by considering European information variables instead of the most common used local ones.

The importance of using stochastically detrended conditional variables, in order to prevent spurious regression biases, deserves special emphasis. In fact, although the conditional evaluation framework implies the incorporation of a set of public information variables, the potential biases that may arise when these variables behave as persistent time series have been largely overlooked in previous research. In this context, the question of whether previous results on the impact of incorporating conditioning information might be attributed to spurious regressions motivates further analysis of this issue. We therefore contribute by showing that the number of lags used is a critical issue, as different selections may impact the significance of conditioning information.

The paper is organized as follows: Section 2 discusses the main motivations for using conditional models in performance evaluation. Section 3 describes the methodology. Section 4 describes the data. Section 5 presents and discusses the empirical results. In this section, we first analyse stock return predictability. Then, we discuss the performance of our sample of funds on the basis of unconditional and conditional measures of performance. Finally, Section 6 summarizes the main results and presents some concluding remarks.

2. Motivations for a conditional approach to performance evaluation

The efficiency of traditional mutual fund performance evaluation measures (Jensen 1968; Sharpe 1966; Treynor 1965) has been widely questioned in the literature, as criticisms at both the conceptual and the econometric level have been pointed out. One of those limitations is related to the fact that these measures assume the existence of a constant risk measure over the evaluation period. In fact, these measures represent an unconditional approach to performance evaluation in the sense that they do not consider the publicly available information about the state of the economy in the estimation of expected returns and risk, thus assuming that these are constant over time.

In reality, both expected returns and risk are time-varying. Under these circumstances, unconditional approaches tend to produce incorrect performance estimates, since they can confound the normal variation in risk and risk premiums with manager's performance. In fact, these measures have been recognized as biased when portfolio managers exhibit market timing skills or engage in dynamic investment strategies resulting in time-varying risk (Dybvig and Ross 1985; Grant 1977; Grinblatt and Titman 1989b; Jensen 1972).

Additionally, some public information variables, such as dividend yields or interest rates, have been shown relevant in predicting both stock and bond returns (e.g., Fama and French 1989; Ilmanen 1995; Pesaran and Timmermann 1995; Silva, Cortez, and Armada 2003). These findings have motivated important developments on asset pricing models and on performance evaluation measures. The underlying argument is straightforward: as these indicators are public and allow for an assessment of the state of the economy, investors can use them to update their predictions on expected returns. As a consequence, performance measures should incorporate this time variation (Ferson and Schadt 1996).

Conditional models evaluate portfolio managers taking into account the public information available to investors at the time the returns were generated (Farnsworth 1997). In a conditional model, both expected returns and risk are time-varying, as public information changes. By controlling for this source of potential bias inherent to unconditional measures, conditional models allow for a better assessment of performance. In fact, when empirically applied (e.g., Chen and Knez 1996; Christopherson, Ferson, and Glassman 1998; Christopherson, Ferson, and Turner 1999; Ferson and Qian 2004; Ferson and Schadt 1996; Ferson and Warther 1996), conditional models seem to generate more reliable estimates in terms of statistical significance. In addition to the argument that this approach may generate more accurate performance estimates, conditional models are also relevant from an economic point of view because of their ability to detect patterns in fund betas, somewhat allowing the investor to monitor the dynamic behaviour of mutual fund managers (Otten and Bams 2004).

The majority of conditional performance evaluation studies examine the US and the UK markets (e.g., Christopherson, Ferson, and Glassman 1998; Ferson and Schadt 1996; Otten and Bams 2004). Outside the USA, evidence suggests that the incorporation of public information variables in performance evaluation is not so pertinent (e.g., Bauer, Otten, and Rad (2006), in the New Zealand market; Sawicki and Ong (2000), in the Australian market; Blake, Lehmann, and Timmermann (2002) and Otten and Bams (2002), in several European markets).

In the particular case of the Portuguese market, the only study we are aware of, that focuses on the conditional performance evaluation of stock funds, is that of Cortez and Silva (2002), whose results are supportive of the conditional framework. Although limited to the partial version of the conditional model, a particular finding of this study in relation to the majority of other empirical studies is that conditional alphas are lower than their unconditional counterparts, which reflects a positive correlation between expected market returns and the conditional beta. Similar evidence was found by Bessler, Drobetz, and Zimmermann (2007) for German equity funds.

In fact, most studies show that the inclusion of conditioning information makes the average performance of funds look better (e.g., Ferson and Schadt 1996; Ferson and Warther 1996; Otten and Bams 2004; Sawicki and Ong 2000). This type of finding may seem puzzling because conditional performance measures require a superior set of information in order to achieve better results. However, as Ferson and Qian (2004) point out, this may occur because in a conditional framework a fund is not penalized for patterns in its risk exposures that are predictable based upon public information, even if that predictability causes a decrease in average returns.

The key to understand the differences between unconditional and conditional alphas is determined by the average value of the interaction terms, i.e., the nature of the covariance between conditional betas and market expected returns. If this covariance is positive (negative), the conditional alpha will be lower (higher) than the unconditional alpha (Ferson and Warther 1996). What most empirical studies have reported is the existence of a negative correlation between conditional betas and market expected returns. This indicates that fund managers tend to decrease (increase) their risk exposure when an increase (decrease) in the market return is expected. Ferson and Schadt (1996) and Ferson and Warther (1996) suggest two potential reasons for this type of relationship: the first is that betas of underlying assets may change in an opposite way to market performance; second, when expected market returns are high, considerable cash inflows can come into the funds, and these might not be immediately invested, causing beta to decline.

3. Methodology

3.1 *Unconditional model*

The unconditional model used in this study is based on Jensen's (1968) alpha. Based on the capital asset pricing model, this measure is the intercept (α_p) of the following regression:

$$r_{p,t} = \alpha_p + \beta_p r_{m,t} + \varepsilon_{p,t} \tag{1}$$

where $r_{p,t}$ represents the excess return of portfolio p over period t, $r_{m,t}$ represents the market's excess return during the same period, β_p is the systematic risk of the portfolio and $\varepsilon_{p,t}$ is an error term with the following properties: $E(\varepsilon_{p,t}) = 0$, $Var(\varepsilon_{p,t}) = \sigma^2_{\varepsilon_{p,t}}$, $Cov(\varepsilon_{p,t}, R_{m,t}) = Cov(\varepsilon_{p,t}, \varepsilon_{j,t}) = 0$. A statistically significant positive (negative) alpha indicates a superior (inferior) performance of the manager in relation to the market. In this model, both alphas and betas are constant.

3.2 *Partial conditional model*

The conditional approach of Ferson and Schadt (1996), also known as the partial conditional model, allows betas to be time-varying. The alphas, however, remain constant. The conditional beta is a linear function of a vector of predetermined information variables, Z_{t-1}, that represents the public information available at time $t - 1$ for predicting returns at time t:

$$\beta_p(Z_{t-1}) = \beta_{0p} + \beta'_p z_{t-1}, \tag{2}$$

where $z_{t-1} = Z_{t-1} - E(Z)$ represents a vector of the deviations of Z_{t-1} from the (unconditional) average values, β'_p is a vector that measures the response of the conditional beta to the information variables and β_{0p} is an average beta which represents the (unconditional) mean of the conditional betas: $E(\beta_p(Z_{t-1}))$.

Substituting Equation (2) into Equation (1) gives the following model:

$$r_{p,t} = \alpha_p + \beta_{0p} r_{m,t} + \beta'_p (z_{t-1} r_{m,t}) + \varepsilon_{p,t} \tag{3}$$

where $E(\varepsilon_{p,t}|Z_{t-1}) = E(\varepsilon_{p,t} r_{m,t}|Z_{t-1}) = 0$ and α_p represents a conditional performance measure. If a manager uses only publicly available information, contained in Z_{t-1}, the conditional alpha will be equal to zero, indicating neutral performance. This is consistent with the semi-strong form of market efficiency of Fama (1970).

Regression (3) may also be interpreted as a multi-factor model in which the market excess return is the first factor and the products of the market excess return with each of the lagged information variables are the additional factors. These additional factors can be interpreted as the returns from dynamic investment strategies that consist in holding z_{t-1} units of the market index and borrowing or selling z_{t-1} units of treasury bills. The dynamic strategies are constructed with the objective of replicating the dynamic behaviour of the fund's market beta through time.

A positive alpha means that the manager's average return is higher than the average return of the dynamic strategies.

In the partial conditional model, the covariance between the fund's betas and the market expected returns, given Z_{t-1}, is captured by the factor $z_{t-1}r_{m,t}$, which represents the products of those expected returns with each of the information variables. Therefore, this covariance is somewhat 'controlled' with the use of the conditioning information.

3.3 *Full conditional model*

As betas can be dynamic and change with market conditions, alphas might exhibit a similar behaviour. In fact, if a manager's performance varies throughout time, then a partial conditional model, which assumes constant alphas, will not provide much power in detecting superior performance.

In a partial conditional model, the conditional alpha should be zero if the managers' portfolio weights are no more informative about future returns than the public information variables in Z_{t-1}. If the manager uses more information than the one contained in this vector, the portfolio weights will be conditionally correlated with future returns, given Z_{t-1}, and the conditional alpha will be a function of this conditional covariance.

Christopherson, Ferson, and Glassman (1998) extend the model of Ferson and Schadt (1996) by also allowing alphas to be time-varying. In this full conditional model, alpha is a linear function of the vector Z_{t-1}:

$$\alpha_p(Z_{t-1}) = \alpha_{0p} + A_p' z_{t-1}, \tag{4}$$

where α_{0p} is an average alpha and the vector A_p' measures the response of the conditional alpha to the information variables. If we apply Equation (4) to the partial conditional model, we obtain the following regression, which allows us to estimate conditional alphas and track their variation in time as public information changes:

$$r_{p,t} = \alpha_{0p} + A_p' z_{t-1} + \beta_{0p} r_{m,t} + \beta_p'(z_{t-1}r_{m,t}) + \varepsilon_{p,t}. \tag{5}$$

4. Data description

4.1 *Samples*

Two different samples of Portuguese-owned open end equity funds were created, over the period of June 2000 to June 2004,[1] taking into consideration mergers, name changes and investment policy changes of funds. The first sample, described in Appendix 1, consists of 24 funds in existence at the end of June 2004, i.e., the surviving funds. This sample includes 10 National funds and 14 European Union funds.[2] The motivation to use and compare the performance of funds belonging to these two categories arises from the growing tendency towards European stock market integration, a fact that has increased Portuguese investors' participation in other markets. Moreover, the consideration of these two categories also allows for the investigation of the distance effect topic, both in a conditional and in an unconditional framework.

In order to assess the performance of each category of funds, two equally weighted portfolios of the surviving funds were formed. Thus, the performance of each category was estimated through the construction of a fund of funds and not just by calculating the average of the individual funds' results. This choice is justified by the fact that the Portuguese mutual fund industry is highly concentrated[3] and, in this situation, a size weighted portfolio would tend to be dominated by a very small number of large funds. It is worthwhile noting that the Portuguese mutual fund market has another small market characteristic: mutual fund companies have traditionally been dominated by the banking industry. This fact can condition the investors' behaviour towards a close involvement with the bank/fund company group and, consequently, may potentially explain why they tend to remain in poorly performing funds (Cortez, Paxson, and Armada 1999).

A major issue associated with the composition of the sample and that may have an impact on performance estimates is survivorship bias. This type of bias may arise from considering samples that contain only funds that survived throughout the entire evaluation period. Indeed, a sampling scheme that only selects the returns of surviving funds, whereas those of disappearing funds (inferior performers) are omitted, might overstate measured performance. However, among the authors that address this question, there is no consensus as to the magnitude and significance of this bias: some studies suggest that its impact is very small and/or not statistically significant (e.g., Brown and Goetzmann 1995; Brown et al. 1992; Grinblatt and Titman 1989a; Romacho and Cortez 2006), some suggest that it has a significant impact on performance estimates (e.g., Blake and Timmermann 1998; Malkiel 1995), whereas others still argue that it depends on investors' disposition to move away from poor performing funds (e.g., Shukla and Trzcinka 1994).

Since survivorship bias affects the vast majority of fund performance evaluation studies, including the pioneer studies on the conditional framework (e.g., Christopherson, Ferson, and Glassman 1998; Ferson and Schadt 1996; Ferson and Warther 1996), we empirically address this issue in Section 5.3. The estimation of survivorship bias using conditional models is still a largely unexplored research topic (the only study we are aware of is by Ayadi and Kryzanowski (2004)). In order to perform such an analysis, we consider a second sample, described in Appendix 3, which includes the non-surviving funds (20 funds).[4] This sample, composed of 12 National funds and eight European Union funds, was then used to construct two equally weighted portfolios containing all funds (surviving and non-surviving) that existed in the Portuguese market, in each category, during the sample period.

4.2 Fund returns and benchmark portfolios

Monthly data required to calculate the fund's returns, namely net asset values (NAVs) and distributed dividends, were obtained from the mutual fund companies. Fund returns are calculated as follows:

$$R_{p,t} = \ln\left[\frac{\text{NAV}_{p,t} + D_{p,t}}{\text{NAV}_{p,t-1}}\right],$$

where $R_{p,t}$ is the total return of portfolio p at time t, $\text{NAV}_{p,t}(\text{NAV}_{p,t-1})$ is the NAV of portfolio p at time t $(t-1)$ and $D_{p,t}$ is the dividend distributed at time t by portfolio p.

Since returns are calculated using NAVs, fund returns are net of operating expenses, but gross of any sales charge, with reinvestment of dividends. Table 1 presents some summary statistics for the equally weighted portfolios of funds. We can observe that monthly returns are, on average and for the sample period, negative and normally distributed.[5]

The benchmark portfolios used are the PSI-20 TR index for National funds, collected from Euronext Lisbon, and the Morgan Stanley Capital International (MSCI) Europe TR index for the European Union funds, obtained from MSCI. Both indices are adjusted for dividends. Just as fund returns, market returns are continuously compounded.

Table 1. Summary statistics on the returns of the equally weighted portfolios of funds.

	Portfolios of National funds		Portfolios of European Union funds	
	Surviving	All	Surviving	All
Mean	−0.5587	−0.5158	−1.1348	−1.1934
Median	−0.9112	−0.8389	−0.1070	−0.3474
Maximum	9.7203	9.6234	7.7410	7.8792
Minimum	−11.9435	−11.9627	−12.3647	−12.5993
Standard deviation	4.9619	4.9355	5.0648	5.1536
Skewness	−0.1651	−0.1670	−0.5067	−0.4939
Kurtosis	2.5329	2.5497	2.4731	2.4839
Jarque–Bera (JB)	0.6544	0.6285	2.6091	2.4840
p-val (JB)	0.7209	0.7303	0.2713	0.2888
Number of funds	10	22	14	22

Note: Some summary statistics for monthly raw returns (expressed in percentage) of the equally weighted portfolios of National and European Union funds computed for the period of June 2000 to June 2004. "All" includes both surviving and non-surviving funds. p-val (JB) is the probability that the Jarque–Bera statistic exceeds (in absolute value) the observed value under the null hypothesis of a normal distribution.

To calculate excess returns, the risk-free rate is proxied by the 1-month Euribor (Euro Interbank Offered Rate), obtained from the Portuguese Central Bank.[6]

4.3 Conditioning information

4.3.1 Predetermined information variables

As public information variables, we use three 1-month lagged instruments: the dividend yield of a market index, a measure of the slope of the term structure and a measure of the level of short-term interest rates. These variables, also used in most of the empirical studies conducted so far (e.g., Christopherson, Ferson, and Glassman 1998; Cortez and Silva 2002; Ferson and Schadt 1996; Sawicki and Ong 2000), follow from previous findings that have shown their relevance in predicting stock returns (e.g.: Fama and French 1989; Pesaran and Timmermann 1995).

In this particular study, we use European information variables instead of the most common local ones. This choice arises from the establishment of the European Monetary Union and the adoption of the Euro, which have caused a convergence in European interest rates, inflation rates, bond returns and an ever-increasing degree of integration in European stock markets (e.g., Fratzscher 2002; Hardouvelis, Malliaropulos, and Priestley 2006; Kim, Moshirian, and Wu 2005). In fact, in the second half of the 1990s, European stock markets converged towards full integration, i.e., their expected returns became more and more determined by EU-wide market risk and less by local risk (Hardouvelis, Malliaropulos, and Priestley 2006).

The dividend yield variable is the dividend payments in the prior 12 months divided by the current price of the MSCI Europe index, obtained from MSCI. The slope of the term structure is measured by the annualized yield spread between the German listed Federal securities with a residual maturity of 9–10 years, obtained from the European Central Bank, and the 3-month Euribor rate,[7] collected from the Portuguese Central Bank. The annualized 3-month Euribor rate was also used as an indicator of the short-term interest rate level. As in Ferson and Schadt (1996), these variables will be demeaned in the conditional tests in order to avoid biases in the regressions and allow an easier interpretation of the estimated coefficients.

4.3.2 Spurious regression biases

The importance of the lagged information variables in predicting stock excess returns can be questioned, as serious concerns may arise when persistent regressors are used (e.g., Ferson, Sarkissian, and Simin 2003b). In fact, variables such as interest rates or dividend yields tend to have high correlation coefficients. Thus, the accuracy of their econometric treatment is particularly critical in a conditional framework in order to avoid possible spurious regression biases. Many of the empirical studies conducted so far have not taken this issue into consideration, thus meaning that the significance of the conditional variables used can be attributed to this source of bias.

We conduct a detailed study of the time series related to the predetermined information variables. As we can verify in Appendix 5, which presents some summary statistics for the information variables, we have not only high correlations among the three variables, but also very high first-order autocorrelation coefficients for all series, which range from 92% to 96%. Besides this, we tested the stationarity of these variables using the augmented Dickey–Fuller (1979) test and concluded that, for a MacKinnon critical value of 5%, we cannot reject the null hypothesis of a unit root for most cases. Thus, following the suggestion of Ferson, Sarkissian, and Simin (2003a), the information variables were stochastically detrended by subtracting a trailing moving average of their own past values. This procedure, advocated by Campbell (1991), is used to alleviate any spurious regression biases and is quite appealing because it does not require any parameter estimation. The objective of this method is to diminish the persistence of the regressors, resulting in autocorrelations that fall under the level in which spurious regressions become a problem.

A practical dilemma that is implied by this procedure is the selection of the number of lags used to perform the detrending. Although this decision should not be arbitrary, it usually lacks proper justification. Campbell (1991) uses a 12-month lag for monthly data, a suggestion which is followed by Ferson, Sarkissian, and Simin (2003a) and Silva, Cortez, and Armada (2003), among others. This choice actually becomes critical because different lags can produce different performance estimates and also different conclusions regarding the significance of conditioning information. In fact, we tested several detrending periods (from 2 to 12 months) and, as shown in Table 2, found that the longer the detrending period, the higher the first-order autocorrelation coefficients of the three series. So, it seems that by increasing the number of lags we are "inducing" correlations in the series instead of reducing them. Besides this, the correlations among the variables were substantially smaller with the 2-month detrending than with the 12-month alternative. Therefore, the information variables were stochastically detrended by subtracting a trailing moving average over a period of 2-months.

The use of stochastically detrended conditional variables leads to considerably lower correlations between the variables (now varying between −16% and −51%) and diminishes the first-order autocorrelation coefficients of the three series to levels of persistence in which spurious regression is not a significant issue, as we can verify in Appendix 6. Moreover, the problems of non-stationarity seem to disappear, since we can reject the null hypothesis of a unit root in most cases.[8]

5. Performance evaluation

5.1 Stock return predictability

We start by analysing the statistical significance of conditioning information in order to determine if funds' returns are somewhat related to public information. We run both simple and multiple regressions of the excess returns of the equally weighted portfolios of funds on the information variables lagged 1-month, demeaned and stochastically detrended by subtracting a moving average over a period of 2 months. Table 3 presents the results of these regressions.

Table 2. First-order autocorrelation coefficients of the information variables.

Detrending period	DY	EUR	TS
2	0.4150	0.5727	0.4661
3	0.5771	0.7166	0.6571
4	0.6368	0.7771	0.7520
5	0.6975	0.8134	0.7921
6	0.7578	0.8439	0.8305
7	0.7837	0.8640	0.8618
8	0.8107	0.8805	0.8817
9	0.8218	0.8904	0.8949
10	0.8346	0.8960	0.9037
11	0.8443	0.9023	0.9116
12	0.8551	0.9122	0.9190

Note: First-order autocorrelation coefficients of the three information variables used (DY, dividend yield; EUR, short-term interest rate level; TS, slope of the term structure) for several monthly detrending periods.

In the case of simple regressions, we find that the most significant variables appear to be the dividend yield and the short-term interest rate level, but only for the National funds (at the 5% level). In the context of the European Union funds, their predictive power is weak, with no evidence of statistically significant information variables. The sign of the coefficients obtained for the slope of the term structure (positive) and the short-term interest rate level (negative) variables are as expected, since lower short-term interest rate levels predict higher stock returns. However, the sign of the coefficient (negative) obtained for the dividend yield variable is contrary to what is expected, since higher dividend yields predict higher stock returns.[9]

As to multiple regressions, once again the variables are significant only for National funds, with an adjusted R^2 of about 7%. In this case, the null hypothesis of the Wald test that the variables are jointly equal to zero is rejected at the 1% significance level, meaning that the expected portfolio excess returns vary over time as public information changes.

It should be stressed that if stochastically detrended variables had not been used, stock return predictability would have been overstated. Indeed, in the simple regressions, practically all the variables would have been significant and, in the case of multiple regressions, the null hypothesis of the Wald test would be rejected for both portfolios at the 5% level. However, that increased significance would be spurious and entirely related to the use of persistent regressors.

5.2 *Estimates of mutual fund performance*

The performance of our sample of surviving funds was analysed both in aggregate terms, using an equally weighted portfolio for each fund category, and for each individual fund.

Table 4 presents estimates of performance using the unconditional model. The results suggest that mutual fund managers are not able to outperform the market, presenting on average negative or neutral performance, an inference that is consistent with most empirical studies conducted so far. The adjusted coefficients of determination are relatively high for both portfolios.

The contrast between the two fund categories is very interesting: whereas the portfolio of National funds has a positive but not statistically significant alpha, the portfolio of European

Table 3. Regressions of the excess returns of the equally weighted portfolios of funds on the lagged information variables.

Variables	National funds	European Union funds
DY		
Coef.	−6.1117	−2.1821
t-stat	−2.4428**	−0.8026
R^2(adj.)	2.58%	−7.20%
EUR		
Coef.	−6.6585	−3.7709
t-stat	−2.2356**	−1.1013
R^2(adj.)	2.89%	−6.09%
TS		
Coef.	6.1499	2.6365
t-stat	1.3886	0.6940
R^2(adj.)	3.26%	−6.79%
DY		
Coef.	−6.7438	−2.7392
t-stat	−2.4093**	−0.9031
EUR		
Coef.	−6.7883	−4.0951
t-stat	−1.9703*	−1.0523
TS		
Coef.	1.7334	0.2296
t-stat	0.3344	0.0604
R^2(adj.)	6.75%	−9.67%
Wald	0.0011	0.7057

Note: The dependent variable in the regressions is the monthly excess return of an equally weighted portfolio of National or European Union surviving funds. This table presents the results for simple and multiple regressions including all variables: dividend yield (DY), short-term interest rate level (EUR) and the slope of the term structure (TS). All of these variables are demeaned, lagged 1-month and are stochastically detrended by subtracting a moving average over a period of 2 months. The coefficients and t-statistics for each of the variables are presented (standard errors are heteroskedasticity and autocorrelation adjusted errors following Newey and West, 1987). R^2 (adj.) is the adjusted coefficient of determination, expressed in percentage. Wald corresponds to the probability values of the χ^2 statistic of the Newey and West (1987) Wald test for the null hypothesis that all variables have a coefficient equal to zero. Asterisks are used to represent the statistically significant coefficients at 1% (***), 5% (**) and 10% (*) significance levels.

Union funds has a negative and statistically significant alpha at the 1% level. In terms of the individual funds, the results are similar: whereas all National funds' alphas are not statistically different from zero, eight European Union funds exhibit negative and statistically significant alphas at the 5% level. This evidence suggests the existence of a distance effect, since managers who invest locally seem to outperform those who invest in the European market.[10] Our results are therefore consistent with those of Coval and Moskowitz (2001), Engström (2003) and Romacho and Cortez (2006), which have shown that fund managers who invest in local markets have slightly higher stock selection abilities than those investing in more remote markets. The rationale for

Table 4. Performance and risk estimates using the unconditional model.

Portfolios	α_p	β_p	R^2 (adj.)
National funds	0.0680 $N+7$ [0] $N-3$ [0]	0.8530***	85.59%
European Union funds	−0.5157*** $N+1$ [0] $N-13$ [8]	0.8947***	91.48%

Note: Estimates of performance (alphas expressed in percentage) and risk for the two equally weighted portfolios of surviving funds using the unconditional model. R^2 (adj.) is the adjusted coefficient of determination, expressed in percentage. Asterisks are used to represent the statistically significant coefficients at 1% (***), 5% (**) and 10% (*) significance levels, based on heteroskedasticity and autocorrelation adjusted errors (following Newey and West (1987)). The number of individual funds presenting positive ($N+$) or negative ($N-$) alphas is also reported, as well as the number of those that are statistically significant at the 5% level, reported in brackets.

this phenomenon is that it is more costly to operate far away, i.e., larger investment universes imply higher costs associated with the search for information. Thus, the results are supportive of the existence of an information advantage that makes fund managers investing nearby better stock-pickers.

Another possible explanation for the underperformance of European Union funds in relation to National funds may be the fact that the former assume higher levels of risk, both specific (since they have a greater number of stocks in which they can invest) and systematic, as measured by the unconditional betas. In fact, as we can see in Table 4, European Union funds have, on average, higher betas than National funds.

The results of the partial conditional model are presented in Table 5. The incorporation of the lagged information variables in the model, allowing for time-varying betas, leads to an improvement in the explanatory power of the models. This is consistent with the findings of Christopherson, Ferson, and Glassman (1998), Ferson and Schadt (1996) and Otten and Bams (2004), among others. Although mutual fund performance estimates remain neutral (negative but not statistically different from zero) for the portfolio of National funds and negative and statistically significant at the 1% level for the portfolio of European Union funds, there is a slight decrease in the alphas in the first case and a very small increase in the latter case. Once again, we observe a distance effect, which seems to be slightly reduced with the use of the partial conditional model.

In terms of individual funds, there is one European Union fund whose performance, at the 5% significance level, changed from neutral to negative. For 22 of the 24 funds studied, the adjusted R^2's are higher, with increases that range from 0.05% to 3.18%.

The significance of the conditional variables, which add explanatory power to the models, was tested both individually (through t-tests) and jointly (using the Wald test). For both portfolios, we reject the hypothesis, at the 1% level, that the coefficients of the additional variables are jointly equal to zero, a finding that strongly suggests the existence of time-varying betas. In terms of individual funds, 19 funds reject the same hypothesis at the 5% level. In fact, we find that the term structure variable is the only statistically significant variable at the 5% level for both portfolios (as well as for 13 individual funds). The other two information variables present no evidence of being important predictors. However, these results are different to what we found in stock return predictability. It is important to emphasize that if we had used the 12-month detrending

Table 5. Performance and risk estimates using the partial conditional model.

Portfolios	α_p	β_{0p}	DY	EUR	TS	R^2 (adj.)	Wald
National	−0.0022	0.8954***	0.0426	−0.0105	0.5853**	86.97%	0.0082
funds	$N+$ 7 [0]		5 [0]	5 [0]	10 [8]		
	$N-$ 3 [0]		5 [0]	5 [0]	0 [0]		
European	−0.5147***	0.9430***	−0.1749	−0.0161	0.5272***	92.89%	0.0000
Union funds	$N+$ 0 [0]		4 [0]	8 [0]	13 [5]		
	$N-$ 14 [9]		10 [0]	6 [0]	1 [0]		

Note: Estimates of performance (alphas expressed in percentage), the average conditional beta(s) and the coefficient estimates for the conditional beta function (i.e., the cross-products between the excess market return and each of the three predetermined information variables: the dividend yield (DY), the short-term interest rate level (EUR) and the slope of the term structure (TS)), for the two equally weighted portfolios of surviving funds using the partial conditional model. All information variables are demeaned, lagged 1-month and stochastically detrended by subtracting a moving average over a period of 2 months. R^2 (adj.) is the adjusted coefficient of determination, expressed in percentage. Asterisks are used to represent the statistically significant coefficients at 1% (***), 5% (**) and 10% (*) significance levels, based on heteroskedasticity and autocorrelation adjusted errors (following Newey and West, 1987). The number of individual funds presenting positive ($N+$) or negative ($N-$) coefficients with respect to the alphas and the estimates for the conditional beta function are also reported, as well as the number of those which are statistically significant at the 5% level, reported in brackets. *Wald* corresponds to the probability values of the χ^2 statistic of the Newey and West (1987) Wald test for the null hypothesis that the coefficients on the additional variables, i.e., the conditional betas, are jointly equal to zero.

alternative, we would have obtained no evidence of statistically significant information variables in the models. This fact underlines the importance that the choice of the number of lags used in the detrending may have in the significance of conditioning information.

The results show a significant positive relation (at the 5% level) between the term structure variable and the conditional beta of both portfolios, which could explain why conditional alphas are lower than unconditional ones. However, this is only observed for the portfolio of National funds. The portfolio of European Union funds exhibits a very small increase in the alphas from the unconditional to the partial conditional model, probably due to the correlations between the information variables. So, we do not find a negative correlation between conditional beta and future expected returns, as in Ferson and Schadt (1996), but a positive correlation between the two, as reported by Cortez and Silva (2002) and Bessler, Drobetz, and Zimmermann (2007). According to the literature, a potential reason for the existence of such a negative correlation is the impact of new cash flows into the funds. However, this explanation seems to be unlikely in the case of the Portuguese market, because fund companies are dominated by the banking industry and this tends to induce investors to maintain a close involvement with the bank/fund company.

When a full conditional model is used, the explanatory power of the models is further improved, as we can see in Table 6. Besides this, for both portfolios we reject the hypothesis, at the 1% level, that the coefficients of the conditional betas and those of conditional alphas and betas are jointly equal to zero. Moreover, we also reject the hypothesis that the coefficients of the conditional alphas are jointly equal to zero for both the portfolio of National funds (for a 5% significance level) and the portfolio of European Union funds (for a 1% significance level), which suggests the existence of time-varying alphas.

When we analyse the estimates of the conditional alpha function in detail, we observe that the dividend yield variable is statistically significant (with a negative sign), at the 5% level, for both portfolios and for 14 individual funds. The other two information variables present little evidence of being important predictors. This evidence indicates that managers are obtaining lower risk-adjusted abnormal performance when dividend yields are high. Since high dividend

Table 6. Performance and risk estimates using the full conditional model.

Portfolios	α_{0p}	DY	EUR	TS	β_{0p}	R^2 (adj.)	W_1	W_2	W_3
National funds	−0.0698	−2.4797**	−1.5345	1.5800	0.8645***	88.12%	0.0316	0.0003	0.0000
	$N+$ 4 [0]	1 [0]	0 [0]	10 [1]					
	$N-$ 6 [0]	9 [7]	10 [1]	0 [0]					
European Union funds	−0.5183***	−2.0041***	−0.9559	0.9347	0.9411***	93.42%	0.0001	0.0000	0.0000
	$N+$ 0 [0]	2 [0]	5 [0]	14 [0]					
	$N-$ 14 [10]	12 [7]	9 [0]	0 [0]					

Note: The average conditional alpha(s), the coefficient estimates for the conditional alpha function and the average conditional beta(s) for the two equally-weighted portfolios of surviving funds using the full conditional model. The predetermined information variables are the dividend yield (DY), the short-term interest rate level (EUR) and the slope of the term structure (TS). All these variables are demeaned, lagged 1-month and stochastically detrended by subtracting a moving average over a period of 2 months. R^2(adj.) is the adjusted coefficient of determination, expressed in percentage. Asterisks are used to represent the statistically significant coefficients at 1% (***), 5% (**) and 10% (*) significance levels, based on heteroskedasticity and autocorrelation adjusted errors (following Newey and West, 1987). The number of individual funds presenting positive ($N+$) or negative ($N-$) coefficients with respect to the average conditional alphas and the estimates for the conditional alpha function are also reported, as well as the number of those which are statistically significant at the 5% level, reported in brackets. W_1, W_2 and W_3 correspond to the probability values of the χ^2 statistic of the Newey and West (1987) Wald test for the null hypothesis that the coefficients of conditional alphas, conditional betas and conditional alphas and betas, respectively, are jointly equal to zero.

yields predict high stock returns, this means that conditional alphas are negatively correlated with expected market returns, a fact that contradicts the argument that it is easier for a fund manager to look good in an up-market. In this way, our results contrast with the evidence obtained (without stochastically detrended conditional variables) by Christopherson, Ferson, and Glassman (1998), who find a positive correlation between conditional alphas and expected market returns.

Comparatively to the partial conditional model, the full conditional model presents similar results for the conditional beta function (even though we detect a decrease in the average conditional beta of the National funds' portfolio) and slightly lower performance estimates. In terms of individual funds, the only difference is that one of the European Union funds' performance (measured by the average of the conditional alpha) has gone from neutral to negative at the 5% level.

Once again, the use of a conditional model (in its full version now) seems to reduce the distance effect (in relation to both unconditional and partial conditional specifications). This finding suggests that this effect may be overstated in an unconditional framework.

Our results show significant evidence of time-varying alphas, dependent on the dividend yield variable, and an increase in the explanatory power of the models from the partial to the full conditional specification. In this way, they are consistent with those of Christopherson, Ferson, and Glassman (1998).

In summary, the use of conditional models leads to a slight decline of fund performance relatively to the unconditional framework, a fact which means that, even when conditional information effects are controlled, fund managers in our sample are not able to outperform the market.

5.3 Survivorship bias and performance

In this section, we study the impact of survivorship bias in performance estimates, using both raw returns and risk-adjusted returns and, in the latter case, considering both unconditional and conditional models.

As we can observe in Table 7, the results suggest that, in terms of raw returns, survivorship bias has a very small impact on performance estimates, reaching monthly values of -0.0429% for National funds and 0.0586% for European Union funds, which correspond to annual values of, approximately, -0.51% and 0.70%, respectively. These results are, in absolute value and given their magnitude, similar to those of Brown and Goetzmann (1995) and Elton, Gruber, and Blake (1996), but considerably smaller than the ones reported by Blake and Timmermann (1998) and Malkiel (1995). Besides this, for a 5% significance level, we cannot reject the hypothesis of equal means between the series of "surviving" and "all" funds (for both categories).[11]

In this table, two outcomes should be emphasized: first, European Union funds show higher survivorship bias than National funds. This finding is consistent with the evidence of Blake and Timmermann (1998) and may be related to the fact that the former assume higher levels of risk (both systematic and specific). Secondly, National funds exhibit negative survivorship bias, which means that the non-surviving funds' impact on the "all" funds' returns is positive and not negative, as expected.

As Elton, Gruber, and Blake (1996) point out, in most cases, funds disappear from databases not because they are liquidated but rather as a consequence of being merged/incorporated into other funds belonging to the same fund company. This type of strategy is an attempt to "erase" their poor performing records. In this particular case, the majority of the 20 non-surviving funds (more precisely 16) were also merged/incorporated into other funds. In the Portuguese market, these mergers/incorporations (especially in 2000 and 2002) seem to be more a result of concentration movements that occurred in the banking industry, which dominates the mutual fund market, than a consequence of poor performances.

In Table 8, we present the estimates of survivorship bias using risk-adjusted returns. As can be observed in the table, survivorship bias estimates are slightly smaller than those obtained with raw returns, corresponding to annual values that range, approximately, from -0.46% to -0.48% for National funds and from 0.54% to 0.57% for European Union funds. These values are, in absolute terms, slightly larger than those obtained by Grinblatt and Titman (1989a), but identical to the results of Elton, Gruber, and Blake (1996). However, despite being small in magnitude, there is evidence of a negative and statistically significant bias in the case of National funds. This finding reinforces the argument that non-surviving funds did not disappear as a consequence of being poor performers but due to the concentration movements that occurred in the Portuguese banking industry.

Table 7. Survivorship bias estimates using raw returns.

	Portfolios of National funds	Portfolios of European Union funds
Surviving (%)	-0.5587	-1.1348
All (%)	-0.5158	-1.1934
Survivorship bias (%)	-0.0429	0.0586
p-val.	0.9662	0.9553

Note: Raw returns (monthly and expressed in percentage) for the equally weighted portfolios of National and European Union funds for the period of June 2000 to June 2004. *All* includes both surviving and non-surviving funds. *Survivorship bias* is the difference between the values of "Surviving" and "All". *p*-val is the probability value of the *t*-test for the equality of means between these two series.

Table 8. Survivorship bias estimates using risk-adjusted returns.

	Portfolios of National funds	Portfolios of European Union funds
Unconditional model		
Surviving (%)	0.0680	−0.5157***
All (%)	0.1065	−0.5635***
Survivorship bias (%)	−0.0385**	0.0478*
Partial Conditional model		
Surviving (%)	−0.0022	−0.5147***
All (%)	0.0375	−0.5597***
Survivorship bias (%)	−0.0397**	0.0450
Full conditional model		
Surviving (%)	−0.0698	−0.5183***
All (%)	−0.0294	−0.5638***
Survivorship bias (%)	−0.0404**	0.0455

Note: Estimates of alphas/average of the conditional alphas (monthly and expressed in percentage) for the equally weighted portfolios of National and European Union funds for the period of June 2000 to June 2004. *All* includes both surviving and non-surviving funds. *Survivorship bias* is the difference between the values of "Surviving" and "All". Asterisks are used to represent the statistically significant coefficients at 1% (***), 5% (**) and 10% (*) significance levels, based on heteroskedasticity and autocorrelation adjusted errors (following Newey and West (1987)).

In both fund categories, the results are relatively stable across the different models used, which is consistent with the evidence of Ayadi and Kryzanowski (2004). However, in contrast with these authors, we find a slight increase in the magnitude of the National funds' survivorship bias with both partial and full conditioning; for the European Union funds, the estimates are not statistically different from zero at the 5% significance level.

6. Conclusions

One of the most recent developments in portfolio performance evaluation is related with the use of conditional models, which evaluate portfolio managers considering the public information available at the time the returns were generated. In this study, instead of just assuming a set of information variables, we previously analysed their ability in predicting stock excess returns, taking into account possible spurious regression biases. In order to do so, we used stochastically detrended variables and found that dividend yields and short-term interest rates, especially, seem to be useful predictors. However, we emphasize that the choice of the number of lags used in detrending is a critical decision since it can lead to different conclusions regarding the significance of conditioning information. In terms of broader implications, this discussion, as well as its extension to other markets, is important as it may question the significance of conditioning information found in previous empirical studies.

The results of the unconditional model indicate that, in general, National funds show neutral performance, whereas European Union funds present negative performance, a finding that suggests the existence of a distance effect. Consistent with previous studies (e.g., Ferson and Schadt 1996), incorporating the information variables in the models leads to an improvement of their explanatory power. However, unlike most empirical studies, our results show that the inclusion of conditioning information can lead to a slight decrease in mutual fund performance estimates. This reflects a positive correlation between expected market returns and the conditional beta. The negative performance obtained within the context of conditional models shows that, even when conditional information effects are controlled, fund managers are not able to beat the market.

The importance of using conditional models is reinforced by the evidence that both conditional betas and alphas appear to be time-varying, dependent on the slope of the term structure and dividend yield variables, respectively. Furthermore, our results suggest that the distance effect might be overstated in an unconditional framework, as we found that it is less evident when public information variables are incorporated in the model. In fact, it seems to lessen when we shift from the unconditional to the partial conditional model and from the latter to the full conditional specification.

In relation to survivorship bias, our evidence shows that it has a small impact on performance estimates and it is relatively stable across different performance models and metrics.

Further research regarding the use of multi-index conditional models or the decomposition of the managers' performance in a conditional framework is a natural extension of this paper. Another attractive subject for future investigation is conditional performance evaluation using portfolio weights (Ferson and Khang, 2002), which might allow for a better assessment of performance.

Notes

1. Although a longer evaluation period would be desirable, it would substantially reduce the number of funds. On the one hand, the Portuguese mutual fund industry is a very recent one when compared with the major markets (US and UK). On the other, the availability of data regarding the public information variables represented an additional constraint on the length of the sample period.
2. The average size of these funds is presented in Appendix 2.
3. In December 2004, the five largest equity fund management companies represented, in terms of net asset values, around 91% of the market.
4. The composition of this sample was checked with the Portuguese Unit Trust Association (APFIPP) and the Portuguese Securities Market Commission (CMVM).
5. Although not reported in the paper, the average monthly returns for individual funds are negative for all surviving funds and for 15 of the non-surviving funds. Using the Jarque–Bera statistic, only one fund (ESAE) rejects the null hypothesis of a normal distribution of returns (at a 5% significance level).
6. Appendix 4 presents some summary statistics for market returns (both negative, on average, and normally distributed) and for the risk-free rate, over the sample period.
7. Even though it would be preferable to use a German government bond rate as the short-term rate, we could not obtain that data due to the non-existence of a liquid Treasury bill market.
8. Using lags of up to six periods and a 5% MacKinnon critical value, the hypothesis of a unit root is rejected for all variables.
9. This result would have been different without the stochastic detrending of the information variables, since we found that without this procedure the sign of the coefficient would be positive, as expected.
10. This effect is not merely a consequence of the indexes used as benchmarks. In fact, additional tests showed that even if we had used the same benchmark for the two fund categories, National funds would still perform better than European Union funds.
11. Similar evidence is obtained by comparing the mean raw returns of surviving and non-surviving funds.

References

Ayadi, M. and L. Kryzanowski. 2004. Performance of Canadian fixed-income mutual funds. Paper presented at the Portuguese Finance Network (PFN) Meeting, July 15–16, in Lisbon, Portugal.

Bauer, R., R. Otten, and A.T. Rad. 2006. New Zealand mutual funds: Measuring performance and persistence in performance. *Accounting and Finance* 46: 1–17.

Bessler, W., W. Drobetz, and H. Zimmermann. 2007. Conditional performance evaluation for German mutual equity funds. Paper presented at the European Financial Management Association (EFMA) Meeting, June 27–30, in Vienna, Austria.

Blake, D. and A. Timmermann. 1998. Mutual fund performance: Evidence from the UK. *European Finance Review* 2: 57–77.

Blake, D., B. Lehmann, and A. Timmermann. 2002. Performance clustering and incentives in the UK pension fund industry. *Journal of Asset Management* 3: 173–94.

Brown, S. and W. Goetzmann. 1995. Performance persistence. *Journal of Finance* 50: 679–98.

Brown, S., W. Goetzmann, R. Ibbotson, and S. Ross. 1992. Survivorship bias in performance studies. *Review of Financial Studies* 5: 553–80.

Campbell, J. 1991. A variance decomposition for stock returns. *The Economic Journal* 101: 157–79.

Chen, Z. and P. Knez. 1996. Portfolio performance measurement: Theory and applications. *Review of Financial Studies* 9: 511–55.

Christopherson, J., W. Ferson, and D. Glassman. 1998. Conditioning manager alphas on economic information: Another look at the persistence of performance. *Review of Financial Studies* 11: 111–42.

Christopherson, J., W. Ferson, and A. Turner. 1999. Performance evaluation using conditional alphas and betas. *Journal of Portfolio Management* 26: 59–72.

Cortez, M.C. and F. Silva. 2002. Conditioning information on portfolio performance evaluation: A reexamination of performance persistence in the Portuguese mutual fund market. *Finance India* 16: 1393–408.

Cortez, M.C., D. Paxson, and M.R. Armada. 1999. Persistence in Portuguese mutual fund performance. *European Journal of Finance* 5: 342–65.

Coval, J. and T. Moskowitz. 2001. The geography of investment: Informed trading and asset prices. *Journal of Political Economy* 109: 811–41.

Dickey, D. and W. Fuller. 1979. Distribution of the estimators for autoregressive time series with a unit root. *Journal of the American Statistical Association* 74: 427–31.

Dybvig, P. and S. Ross. 1985. Differential information and performance measurement using a security market line. *Journal of Finance* 40: 383–99.

Elton, E., M. Gruber, and C. Blake. 1996. Survivorship bias and mutual fund performance. *Review of Financial Studies* 9: 1097–120.

Engström, S. 2003. Costly information, diversification and international mutual fund performance. *Pacific-Basin Finance Journal* 11: 463–82.

Fama, E. 1970. Efficient capital markets: A review of theory and empirical work. *Journal of Finance* 25: 383–417.

Fama, E. and K. French. 1989. Business conditions and expected returns on stocks and bonds. *Journal of Financial Economics* 25: 23–49.

Farnsworth, H. 1997. Conditional performance evaluation. In *Blackwell encyclopedic dictionary of finance*, ed. D. Paxson and D. Wood, 23–24. Blackwell Business.

Ferson, W. and K. Khang. 2002. Conditional performance measurement using portfolio weights: Evidence for pension funds. *Journal of Financial Economics* 65: 249–82.

Ferson, W. and M. Qian. 2004. *Conditional performance evaluation revisited.* Research Foundation Monograph of the CFA Institute, 84 pages. Research Foundation of CFA Institute, ISBN 0-943205-69-7. http://www-rcf.usc.edu/~ferson/

Ferson, W. and R. Schadt. 1996. Measuring fund strategy and performance in changing economic conditions. *Journal of Finance* 51: 425–61.

Ferson, W. and V. Warther. 1996. Evaluating fund performance in a dynamic market. *Financial Analysts Journal* 52: 20–28.

Ferson, W., S. Sarkissian, and T. Simin. 2003a. Is stock return predictability spurious? *Journal of Investment Management* 1: 1–10.

Ferson, W., S. Sarkissian, and T. Simin. 2003b. Spurious regressions in financial economics? *Journal of Finance* 58: 1393–413.

Fratzscher, M. 2002. Financial market integration in Europe: On the effects of EMU on stock markets. *International Journal of Finance and Economics* 7: 165–93.

Grant, D. 1977. Portfolio performance and the "cost" of timing decisions. *Journal of Finance* 32: 837–46.

Grinblatt, M. and S. Titman. 1989a. Mutual fund performance: An analysis of quarterly portfolio holdings. *Journal of Business* 62: 393–416.

Grinblatt, M. and S. Titman. 1989b. Portfolio performance evaluation: Old issues and new insights. *Review of Financial Studies* 2: 393–421.

Hardouvelis, G., D. Malliaropulos, and R. Priestley. 2006. EMU and European stock market integration. *Journal of Business* 79: 365–92.

Ilmanen, A. 1995. Time-varying expected returns in international bond markets. *Journal of Finance* 50: 481–506.

Jensen, M. 1968. The performance of mutual funds in the period 1945–1964. *Journal of Finance* 23: 389–416.

Jensen, M. 1972. Optimal utilization of market forecasts and the evaluation of investment performance. In *Mathematical methods in investment and finance*, ed. G. Szego and K. Shell, 310–35. North-Holland. http://papers.ssrn.com/so13/papers.cfm?abstract_id=350426

Khorana, A., H. Servaes, and P. Tufano. 2005. Explaining the size of the mutual fund industry around the world. *Journal of Financial Economics* 78: 145–85.

Kim, S., F. Moshirian, and E. Wu. 2005. Dynamic stock market integration driven by the European monetary union: An empirical analysis. *Journal of Banking and Finance* 29: 2475–502.

Malkiel, B. 1995. Returns from investing in equity mutual funds 1971 to 1991. *Journal of Finance* 50: 549–72.

Newey, W. and K. West. 1987. A simple positive semi-definite, heteroskedasticity and autocorrelation consistent covariance matrix. *Econometrica* 55: 703–8.

Otten, R. and D. Bams. 2002. European mutual fund performance. *European Financial Management* 8: 75–101.

Otten, R. and D. Bams. 2004. How to measure mutual fund performance: Economic versus statistical relevance. *Journal of Accounting and Finance* 44: 203–22.

Pesaran, M. and A. Timmermann. 1995. Predictability of stock returns: Robustness and economic significance. *Journal of Finance* 50: 1201–28.

Romacho, J. and M.C. Cortez. 2006. Timing and selectivity in Portuguese mutual fund performance. *Research in International Business and Finance* 20: 348–68.

Sawicki, J. and F. Ong. 2000. Evaluating managed fund performance using conditional measures: Australian evidence. *Pacific-Basin Finance Journal* 8: 505–28.

Sharpe, W. 1966. Mutual fund performance. *Journal of Business* 39: 119–38.

Shukla, R. and C. Trzcinka. 1994. Persistent performance in the mutual fund market: Tests with funds and investment advisers. *Review of Quantitative Finance and Accounting* 4: 115–35.

Silva, F., M.C. Cortez, and M.R. Armada. 2003. Conditioning information and European bond fund performance. *European Financial Management* 9: 201–30.

Treynor, J. 1965. How to rate management of investment funds. *Harvard Business Review* 43: 63–75.

Appendix 1. Sample 1: surviving funds

National funds

AF Acções Portugal (AFAP)
Banif Acções Portugal (BAP)
Barclays Premier Acções Portugal (BPAP)
BPI Portugal (BPIP)
Caixagest Acções Portugal (CAP)
Caixagest Gestão Lusoacções (CGLA)
Espírito Santo Portugal Acções (ESPA)
Finicapital[†] (FINI)
Postal Acções (POST)
Santander Acções Portugal (SAP)

European Union funds

AF Eurocarteira (AFEUR)
AF Investimentos Acções Europa (AFIAE)
Banif Euro Acções (BEA)
BBVA Bolsa Euro (BBVA)
BNC Acções (BNCA)
BPI Europa Crescimento (BPIEC)
BPI Europa Valor (BPIEV)
Caixagest Acções Europa (CAE)
Caixagest Gestão Euroacções (CGEA)
Espírito Santo Acções Europa (ESAE)
MG Acções (MGA)
MG Acções Europa (MGAE)
Raiz Europa (RZE)
Santander Acções Europa (SAE)

[†]This fund is presently classified as a European Union fund, but until May 2003 it was a National fund. Since it belonged to this last category for the majority of the period studied, we chose to maintain this classification.

Appendix 2. Average size of the surviving funds

This appendix shows the average size (measured by the total net assets) of the surviving funds over the sample period (June 2000 to June 2004).

National Funds	Average size (10^6€)	European Union funds	Average size (10^6€)
AFAP	105.60	AFEUR	153.59
BAP	6.54	AFIAE	53.47
BPAP	20.74	BEA	10.82
BPIP	12.49	BBVA	6.19
CAP	42.78	BNCA	2.67
CGLA	6.36	BPIEC	91.96
ESPA	16.64	BPIEV	124.18
FINI	4.79	CAE	89.66
POST	6.25	CGEA	39.32
SAP	58.26	ESAE	44.92
		MGA	25.81
		MGAE	3.50
		RZE	8.41
		SAE	42.82

Source: Portuguese Securities Market Commission.

Appendix 3. Sample 2: non-surviving funds

National funds
AF Investimentos Acções Portugal
Atlântico Acções
BNU Acções
Caixagest Valorização
DB Investimento
Europa Portugal Acções
Fipor Poupança Investimento
Mello Acções Portugal
Novo Fundo Capital
Raiz Valorização
Santander Capital Portugal
Uniacções Portugal

European Union funds
AF Acções Euro
BIG Eurocapital
BNU Acções Europa
BNU Gestão Activa Acções
Espírito Santo Acções Rendimento
Mello Acções Euro
Santander Iberfundo Acções
Uniacções Europa

Appendix 4. Summary statistics for the market indices and the risk-free rate

This appendix shows some summary statistics (expressed in percentage) for monthly market returns and the risk-free rate over the period of June 2000 to June 2004. p-val. (JB) is the probability that the Jarque–Bera statistic exceeds (in absolute value) the observed value under the null hypothesis of a normal distribution.

	PSI20-TR	MSCI Europe TR	Risk-free rate
Mean	−0.7825	−0.7246	0.2773
Median	−0.7226	−0.0673	0.2779
Maximum	10.6610	10.5455	0.4193
Minimum	−18.1019	−14.8687	0.1687
Standard deviation	5.3992	5.4235	0.0860
Skewness	−0.5208	−0.4166	0.2342
Kurtosis	3.8705	2.8784	1.6912
Jarque–Bera (JB)	3.6853	1.4181	3.8651
p-val (JB)	0.1584	0.4921	0.1448

Appendix 5. Summary statistics for the information variables (without stochastic detrending)

This appendix presents some summary statistics for the lagged information variables for the period of June 2000 to June 2004: dividend yield (DY), short-term interest rate level (EUR) and the slope of the term structure (TS). Table A1 presents various statistics for these variables (annual, demeaned and expressed in percentage) as well as their autocorrelation coefficients of order 1, 3, 6 and 12. Table A2 presents the correlation matrix among the instruments.

Table A1. Descriptive statistics and autocorrelations.

	DY	EUR	TS
Mean	0.0000	0.0000	0.0000
Median	0.0217	−0.0143	0.2243
Maximum	1.1767	1.7627	0.9808
Minimum	−0.8413	−1.4193	−1.2462
Standard Deviation	0.5222	1.0446	0.7057
Skewness	0.0997	0.2021	−0.4329
Kurtosis	2.2104	1.6825	1.9261
ρ_1	0.9217	0.9598	0.9460
ρ_3	0.7476	0.8477	0.8273
ρ_6	0.5658	0.6361	0.5464
ρ_{12}	0.1403	0.2220	0.0475

Table A2. Correlation matrix

	DY	EUR	TS
DY	1.0000		
EUR	−0.7933	1.0000	
TS	0.6656	−0.9375	1.0000

Appendix 6 – Summary statistics for the information variables (with stochastic detrending)

This appendix presents some summary statistics for the lagged information variables for the period of June 2000 to June 2004: dividend yield (DY), short-term interest rate level (EUR) and the slope of the term structure (TS). These variables are stochastically detrended by subtracting a trailing moving average over a period of 2 months. Table A3 presents various statistics for these variables (annual, demeaned, detrended and expressed in percentage) as well as their autocorrelation coefficients of order 1, 3, 6 and 12. Table A4 presents the correlation matrix among the instruments.

Table A3. Descriptive statistics and autocorrelations.

	DY	EUR	TS
Mean	0.0000	0.0000	0.0000
Median	−0.0180	0.0218	−0.0073
Maximum	0.4463	0.3643	0.5457
Minimum	−0.4102	−0.6221	−0.3753
Standard Deviation	0.1907	0.1799	0.2011
Skewness	0.1412	−0.6538	0.3777
Kurtosis	2.9195	4.7538	2.9822
ρ_1	0.4150	0.5727	0.4661
ρ_3	−0.1394	0.2123	0.2818
ρ_6	0.3136	−0.0989	−0.1153
ρ_{12}	0.0283	−0.3239	−0.3313

Table A4. Correlation matrix

	DY	EUR	TS
DY	1.0000		
EUR	−0.1570	1.0000	
TS	−0.2042	−0.5121	1.0000

Performance and characteristics of mutual fund starts

Aymen Karoui and Iwan Meier

HEC Montréal, 3000 Chemin de la Côte-Sainte-Catherine, Montréal, Québec, Canada H3T 2A7

We study the performance and portfolio characteristics of 828 newly launched US equity mutual funds over the period 1991–2005. These fund starts initially earn, on average, higher excess returns and higher abnormal returns. Their risk-adjusted performance is also superior to existing funds. Furthermore, we provide evidence for short-term persistence among top-performing fund starts, however, a substantial fraction of funds drop from the top to the bottom decile over two subsequent periods. Analyzing portfolio characteristics, we find that returns of fund starts exhibit higher ratios of unsystematic to total risk. Portfolios of new funds are typically also less diversified in terms of number of stocks and industry concentration and are invested in smaller and less liquid stocks.

1. Introduction

A large number of new equity mutual funds have emerged over the past two decades. Total net assets (TNA) managed by domestic US open-end equity funds increased from 239 billion at the end of 1990 to 6.9 trillion in 2007. Despite the slowdown of net inflows into equity funds after the downturn on stock markets in 2000, net inflows over this period total $2.3 trillion, which corresponds to 136 billion per year. The number of funds increased over the same time span from 1191 to 4767 and substantial dollar amounts flowed into recently launched funds.[1] An investor typically attempts to infer manager skill from past performance. However, this task is complicated in the case of fund starts as they provide, by definition, only a short track record of returns. For delegated portfolio management it is, therefore, important to learn whether there exist systematic patterns in risk-adjusted performance, risk taking, or portfolio characteristics after the inception of new funds. In this study we analyze the performance and characteristics, such as the ratio of unsystematic risk to total risk, diversification, and liquidity of the portfolio holdings of 828 equity fund starts over the period 1991–2005.

Starting with the seminal work of Jensen (1968), a large literature has discussed the performance of mutual funds. However, relatively little attention has been paid to the performance evaluation of emerging funds over the first months after inception. One notable exception is Blake and Timmermann (1998) who study a large sample of UK open-end mutual funds. They find weak evidence for superior performance of new funds and report an average, risk-adjusted excess return of 0.8% over the first year. For UK data on mutual funds Cuthbertson, Nitzsche, and O'Sullivan (2008) indirectly draw a similar conclusion. When excluding younger funds (less than 3 years old), the average alpha in their sample decreases slightly. A number of studies examine the relationship between fund age and performance in a multivariate regression framework. Ferreira, Miguel, and Ramos (2006) study a large sample of actively managed open-end equity funds in 19 countries and find evidence for a negative relation between fund age and abnormal performance, in particular, for foreign and global funds. For a survivorship-bias controlled sample of 506 funds from five important European fund countries (UK, Germany, France, Netherlands, and Italy), Otten and Bams (2002) draw the same conclusion.[2] Similarly, Liang (1999) finds a negative relationship for a sample of hedge funds. Two studies on socially responsible investments (or ethical funds) report an underperformance of fund starts: Gregory, Matako, and Luther (1997) for 18 UK funds, and Bauer, Koedijk, and Otten (2005) using a database of 103 German, UK, and US ethical mutual funds.[3] We find that the mean fund return over the first year after inception, net of fees and in excess of the 1-month Treasury bill rate, exceeds the mean return over the subsequent year by 0.12% per month. When we estimate the risk-adjusted performance as the intercept of the Carhart (1997) four-factor model, we report a decrease in the means over two non-overlapping 3-year windows after inception of 0.08% per month. Both results are significantly different from zero at the 5% level. Fund starts also outperform older funds on a risk-adjusted basis over the first 12 and 36 months after the launch date by 0.09% and 0.12% per month, respectively. When we look at unsystematic risk and estimates of factor loadings, we observe that fund starts are typically exposed to a higher fraction of unsystematic risk, are less sensitive to market risk, and load up on small stocks. We provide evidence that the observed decrease in excess returns and risk-adjusted performance is driven by changes in risk taking and not a mere effect of diseconomies of scale.

Hendricks, Patel, and Zeckhauser (1993) triggered a series of studies on the performance persistence in mutual fund returns. They document that skilled managers persistently provide superior performance relative to their peers ('hot hands' phenomenon). Other studies, such as Goetzmann and Ibbotson (1994), Brown and Goetzmann (1995), and Gruber (1996) also associate the existence of persistence over 1–3-year horizons with manager skill. Grinblatt, Titman, and Wermers (1995) and Carhart (1997) contest these results. Carhart (1997) concludes that the short-term persistence in fund returns disappears after controlling for the momentum anomaly discussed in Jegadeesh and Titman (1993). More recently, Bollen and Busse (2004) measure returns over intervals much shorter than monthly and find that the persistence is statistically significant – although they question the economic significance. We document that fund starts, using monthly returns and including a momentum factor, exhibit some degree of persistence. However, a relatively high fraction of funds drop from the decile of top-performing funds to the lowest decile over two subsequent 3-year windows, which indicates a high degree of risk taking by fund starts. Another result of Carhart's (1997) study is that there exists more likely an 'icy hands' phenomenon. We find only weak evidence of persistence among poorly performing fund starts.

Another contribution of our paper is the analysis of individual portfolio holdings of fund starts. For each fund in our sample we observe quarterly holdings and compute two measures of diversification: We count the number of different stock positions in the portfolio and compute the industry concentration index of Kacperczyk, Sialm, and Zheng (2005). To measure the liquidity of the reported portfolio, we calculate for all individual stock positions the Amihud (2002) illiquidity ratio and aggregate using market capitalization weights. This enables us to draw conclusions regarding changes in the selection of stocks over time not only from estimated factor loadings but also directly from portfolio holdings. We find that fund starts typically hold a smaller number of stocks, hold more industry concentrated portfolios, invest more in small-cap stocks, and the stock positions tend to be less liquid.[4]

Our results are consistent with several explanations:

(1) Berk and Green (2004) propose a model where managers have differential skills to generate positive excess returns. They assume that with increasing fund size future expected fund returns become competitive and no longer exceed a passive benchmark. In their model, rational investors infer manager skill from past performance and allocate money to funds with superior past performance. This behavior generates inflows to those funds and causes excess returns to deteriorate. These diseconomies of scale are consistent with small startup funds outperforming larger incumbent funds. A number of empirical studies such as Indro et al. (1999) and Chen et al. (2004) corroborate their conjecture that excess performance decreases with size. Chen et al. (2004) attribute this negative relationship between size and performance to increased indirect costs of price impact when larger volumes are traded. This view is contested by Otten and Bams (2002) and Ferreira, Miguel, and Ramos (2006) who report a positive coefficient for the impact of size on abnormal performance (economies of scale).

(2) Managers of emerging funds have a particularly high incentive to devote a lot of effort to the portfolio selection process as they build their career and reputation. In fact, the fund flow literature shows that top-performing funds are disproportionally rewarded with high inflows, which in turn will likely have a positive impact on the fund manager's salary. Chevalier and Ellison (1999a) find that younger fund managers tend to outperform their older peers. They attribute some of the superior performance to a survivorship bias due to the higher likelihood of being fired for poor performance when you are a young manager with short tenure. To explain the residual superior performance by younger managers, the authors put forward effort and career concerns. On the other hand, one might argue that new funds have less favorable terms to execute trades, limited research resources, and that new fund managers may lack experience and are more likely to commit costly mistakes.

(3) Prendergast and Stole (1996) suggest that young managers exaggerate their own opinion and take risk to signal high ability. With longer tenure managers become increasingly reluctant to take on risk. Our finding that fund starts are subject to a higher fraction of unsystematic risk is consistent with their argument. However, this decrease in the ratio of unsystematic to total risk differs from Chevalier and Ellison (1999b). Their results show that managers of young age are more likely to be replaced or demoted to a smaller fund if they do not deliver satisfying performance. They argue that this gives an incentive to young managers to avoid unsystematic risk and to herd. Our study, though, does not directly evaluate manager age (and education) but rather fund age. Moreover, our data set with 828 fund starts (1,374 funds in total) over a 15-year period 1991–2005 is hardly comparable with their total of 1,320 annual observations on the two investment objective categories growth and growth and income over the period 1993–1995. Most importantly, Chevalier and Ellison (1999b) define unsystematic risk as the fraction of the variance that cannot be explained by the market beta (Jensen's model), whereas in our analysis unsystematic risk is one minus the R^2 from the Carhart four-factor model.

(4) Reuter (2006) shows that funds paying substantial commissions to lead underwriters benefit from larger allocations of underpriced IPOs. If fund families favor newly launched funds in an attempt to build a successful return history, attract fund inflows, and increase fee income, this would result in superior performance of young funds. Gaspar, Massa, and Matos (2006) test whether fund complexes offer preferential treatment to young funds in IPO allocations but find no conclusive evidence.

(5) Malkiel (1995) discusses the issue of survivorship bias. He annotates that even after correcting for survivorship bias his data set may still suffer from an incubation bias. Fund families often

allocate seed money to a number of newly created portfolios ('incubator' funds). After these portfolios have established an initial track record, the fund complex decides which ones of these incubator portfolios will be opened and advertised to the public. The return series of the portfolios that are terminated are typically not added to mutual fund databases because these portfolios were never assigned a ticker. Evans (2008) estimates that 39.4% of his sample compiled from the Center for Research in Security Prices (CRSP) Survivor-Bias-Free US Mutual Fund Database are incubated. Artega, Ciccotello, and Grant (1998) provide another example of the existence of an incubation bias. Our findings that funds start out as less diversified portfolios, take sector bets, and carry more unsystematic risk are consistent with the existence of an incubation bias. If the strategy is successful and the fund is made publicly available, the fund further diversifies its portfolio and reduces unsystematic risk in an attempt to maintain a good track record and attain a favorable Sharpe ratio.

The remainder of the paper is organized as follows. Section 2 describes the sample. The performance of new funds is analyzed in Section 3. Section 4 examines the characteristics of fund starts and Section 5 concludes.

2. Data

Morningstar provided quarterly portfolio holdings of US domestic equity mutual funds going back to January 1991 and ending in December 2005. Monthly fund returns are retrieved from the Survivor-Bias-Free US Mutual Fund Database compiled by the CRSP. We match the two databases and for each fund portfolio we retain the return series of the oldest share class. Zhao (2005) and Nanda, Wang, and Zheng (2005) stress the importance to differentiate between the decision to start a new fund portfolio and the decision to introduce new share classes. We consider the first appearance of a new ICDI number, the primary and unique identifier in the CRSP mutual fund database, as a fund start. If a fund changes its name it will keep the ICDI number as long as it corresponds to essentially the same fund portfolio. The fund may also change its style orientation and/or fund manager and continue to be recorded under the same ICDI. The final sample comprises 1,374 US domestic equity mutual funds and 828 fund starts over the period 1991–2005. Sixty-four fund starts stop operation during our sample period, 24 funds within 3 years. While the CRSP database is free of survivorship bias (but does not include holdings prior to 2003), the Morningstar database suffers from this bias to some extent (Blake, Elton, and Gruber 2001). We include dead funds in our merged data set, however, coverage may not be comprehensive.

All returns are net of fees and we subtract the 1-month Treasury bill rate as a proxy for the risk-free rate to compute excess returns. To assess the risk-adjusted performance, we estimate the intercept (alpha) of the four-factor model introduced by Carhart (1997). The returns on these four factors are downloaded from Kenneth French's website.[5]

Fund characteristics are compiled from three sources: (i) monthly TNA under management, annual fees, and turnover are from the CRSP mutual fund database, (ii) the general industry classification (GIC) for each stock held in the portfolio is from the Morningstar database, and (iii) the size quantile rankings of stocks and the Amihud (2002) liquidity ratios are from Joel Hasbrouck's website.[6] For each fund portfolio we compute the industry concentration index of Kacperczyk, Sialm, and Zheng (2005), using the GICs of individual stock positions along with their portfolio weights, the average market capitalization rankings of reported stock positions, and the average illiquidity measure of Amihud (2002). Details on the computation of these measures follow in Section 4 where we discuss the characteristics of fund starts.

Table 1. Style classification and fund family affiliations.

Style	Number of funds (%)		TNA (in millions)	
			1991	2005
Panel A: Style classifications				
Small company growth	248	(18.05)	6,530	214,772
Other aggressive growth	195	(14.19)	11,974	153,412
Growth	424	(30.86)	63,545	676,040
Income	48	(3.49)	21,315	110,621
Growth and income	284	(20.67)	64,155	719,644
Sector funds	170	(12.37)	9,614	102,947
Not specified	5	(0.36)	1,269	134
Total	1,374	(100.00)	178,402	1,977,571

Number of portfolios	Number of fund families	TNA (in millions)	
		1991	2005
Panel B. Fund family characteristics			
1	171	4,313	111,676
2–5	153	21,489	258,009
6–10	38	43,350	459,469
11–50	25	80,819	732,085
>50	1	28,432	416,333
Total	388	178,402	1,977,571

Panel A reports the number of funds, the percentage of funds, and total net assets (TNA) under management sorted by self-declared investment style. Panel B reports the number of fund families for each category of family size (number of portfolios) and TNA at the beginning and end of the sample period. The sample covers 1,374 US equity mutual funds over the period 1991–2005.

Table 1 is split into two panels. Panel A shows the style classification of the sample funds. For each style classification, we tabulate number of funds, percentage of funds, and the market capitalization at the beginning and end of the sample period. When funds are sorted by these self-reported investment styles, it is evident that growth funds constitute almost one-third of the sample (30.9%). Panel B summarizes the size of the fund families in our sample. We count a total of 388 fund family affiliations. Most families are represented by 1–5 portfolios. Only 26 families are represented by more than 11 equity funds. However, the sum of the TNA of the 26 largest families exceeds the market capitalization of all other 362 families, which underlines the domination of the mutual fund industry by large fund families.

3. The performance of mutual fund starts

In this section, we analyze the returns of fund starts. First, we study the evolution of cumulative monthly excess returns and cumulative abnormal returns over the first 6 years after inception. Second, we compare the performance over two subsequent time windows. Third, instead of comparing the fund with any benchmark, we compare the risk-adjusted performance over time to test whether the performance of fund starts declines. Fourth, we compare the risk-adjusted performance of each fund start with the average risk-adjusted performance of all incumbent funds over the same time period. Finally, we study whether the decrease in (risk-adjusted) performance we find is driven by diseconomies of scale or changes in risk exposure.

3.1 *Estimating the performance of mutual fund starts*

For each fund, we regress the fund returns net of fees, R_i, and in excess of the 1-month Treasury bill rate, RF, on a constant and the returns of the standard four factors as in Carhart (1997). RMRF denotes the excess return of the CRSP value-weighted index over the 1-month Treasury bill rate, SMB and HML the returns on the factor-mimicking portfolios for small cap minus large cap and high book-to-market minus low book-to-market as defined by Fama and French (1993), and MOM captures the momentum anomaly documented by Jegadeesh and Titman (1993).

$$R_{i,t} - \text{RF}_t = \alpha_i + \beta_{1,i}\text{RMRF}_t + \beta_{2,i}\text{SMB}_t + \beta_{3,i}\text{HML}_t + \beta_{4,i}\text{MOM}_t + \varepsilon_{i,t} \tag{1}$$

We choose a 2-year estimation period. Using the estimated coefficients of the four factors, $\hat{\beta}_{j,i}$ for $j = 1$ to 4, we compute monthly expected returns. The abnormal return is the difference between the observed fund return and the expected return.

$$\text{AR}_{i,t} = R_{i,t} - (\hat{\beta}_{1,i}\text{RMRF}_t + \hat{\beta}_{2,i}\text{SMB}_t + \hat{\beta}_{3,i}\text{HML}_t + \hat{\beta}_{4,i}\text{MOM}_t) \tag{2}$$

We use the same factor loadings estimated over the first 2 years to compute abnormal returns for months $t = 1$ to $t = 24$. Thus, by construction the abnormal returns over the first 2 years are determined in-sample. The abnormal returns of months $t = 25$ to $t = 72$ are based on the factor loadings estimated from returns over months $t - 24$ to $t - 1$. Similar to Aggarwal and Jorion (2008), who study the performance of emerging hedge fund managers, we consider each fund start as an event. We take the first appearance of the fund in the CRSP Survivor-Bias-Free US Mutual Fund Database as the inception date. Cumulative excess and cumulative abnormal returns over the first k months after inception are computed as

$$\text{CAR}_{i,k} = \sum_{t=1}^{k} \frac{1}{N(t)} \sum_{i=1}^{N(t)} R_{i,t}^* \tag{3}$$

where $R_{i,t}^*$ is alternatively the excess return, $R_{i,t} - \text{RF}_t$, or the abnormal return, $\text{AR}_{i,t}$, of fund i over month t after inception, and $N(t)$ the number of fund starts. The number of fund starts is slightly decreasing with k due to the 64 fund exits in our sample. Figure 1 shows the cumulative excess returns and cumulative abnormal returns of the 828 fund starts in our sample.[7]

Cumulative excess returns begin to flatten out after 4 years. The cumulative abnormal return over the first 12 months of 0.72% is similar to the 0.8% that Blake and Timmermann (1998) find for UK open-end mutual funds. Cumulative abnormal returns become negative after 4 years. Table 2 displays the mean abnormal returns for each of the first 8 years after inception. Mean returns are significantly positive at the 10% level for the first 2 years and then become negative in the third year, which is consistent with the drop in cumulative abnormal returns in Figure 1.

To formally test whether the initial risk-adjusted performance is significantly larger, we estimate the intercept of the Carhart four-factor model (1) over two subsequent 36-month periods. This time window corresponds to the cutoff point that is also used, e.g., by Cuthbertson, Nitzsche, and O'Sullivan (2008). We trim the top and bottom 1% before reporting means and performing tests in means to mitigate the impact of potential outliers. The mean difference for alpha is 0.08% per month, which is significantly different from zero at the 1% level (t-statistics 2.73). To check the robustness of this result, we relax the assumption of a 36-month window and vary the length from $k = 12$ to 48 months. Figure 2 shows the mean difference (first minus second period) and the corresponding 95% confidence intervals. The mean difference, plotted as a solid line,

Panel A: Cumulative excess returns.

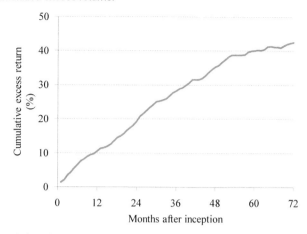

Panel B: Cumulative abnormal returns.

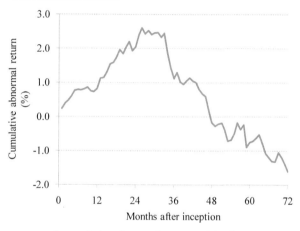

Figure 1. Cumulative excess returns and cumulative abnormal returns of fund starts. The graphs show the cumulative average excess return (Panel A) and cumulative average abnormal return (Panel B) of fund starts over the first 6 years. Excess returns equal fund returns net of management fees minus the 1-month Treasury bill rate. For each fund we estimate the coefficients of a Carhart four-factor regression over a 2-year window. Abnormal returns are computed as net fund return minus expected return, where the expected return is the sum of the returns on the four factors multiplied by the coefficient estimates. Monthly averages are equally-weighted portfolio returns of all fund starts aligned by inception date. The sample covers 828 fund starts over the period 1991–2005.

gradually decreases as we increase the length of the time window. With an increasing window size the precision of the mean estimate increases and the confidence bounds narrow. The line graph illustrates that for windows shorter than 27 months, the hypothesis that the performance over the first period is superior to the performance over the subsequent window of equal length can be rejected at the 5% level. This finding is in line with Figure 1. The positive abnormal returns of fund starts begin to deteriorate after 3 years. Therefore, if we compare two windows shorter than 27 months, the second window still includes many observations of the period of high abnormal returns and we find no significant difference in performance. Hence, testing the decline in fund performance crucially depends on the selected window size.

Table 2. Annualized abnormal returns after inception.

Number of years after inception	Mean	t-statistics
1	0.63*	1.81
2	0.72**	2.08
3	−0.40	−0.69
4	−0.25	−1.80
5	−0.72	−0.51
6	−0.32	−1.18
7	−0.44	−0.94
8	−0.95**	−3.41

Annualized average monthly abnormal returns are presented for the first 8 years after inception and expressed in percentage per year. For each fund we estimate the coefficients of a Carhart four-factor regression. Abnormal returns are computed as net fund return minus expected return, where the expected return is the sum of the returns on the four factors multiplied by the coefficient estimates.
*Significance at the 10% level.
**Significance at the 5% level.

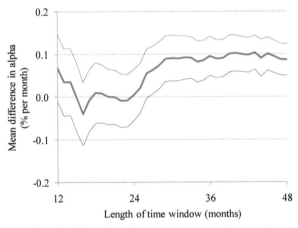

Figure 2. The difference in the risk-adjusted performance over two subsequent non-overlapping time windows of increasing length. The graph shows the difference in the mean risk-adjusted performance over two subsequent, non-overlapping time windows after inception (mean over the first interval minus mean over the second interval). We vary the window lengths from $k = 12$ to 48 months. Risk-adjusted performance is measured by the alpha from the Carhart four-factor model and reported in % per month. The thin lines indicate the upper and lower bounds of the 95% confidence interval. The sample covers 828 fund starts over the period 1991–2005.

3.2   Persistence in the returns of mutual fund starts

So far, we have documented a decrease in initial fund performance. Next, we address the question whether some fund starts persistently outperform their peers. Following Carhart (1997), we construct a contingency table of the decile rankings over two subsequent intervals. We rank the fund starts into deciles over an initial and subsequent time window based on their risk-adjusted performance. Then, we count the frequencies that a fund ends up in one of the deciles over the second period conditional on its ranking over the first period. This exercise is different from Carhart (1997) in that we sort funds into deciles based on event time. Instead of forming performance deciles over, e.g., years 1991 and 1992 (calendar time), we construct the deciles over each of the 2 years after inception (event time).

Panels A and B of Figure 3 illustrate the frequencies for 1-year and 3-year windows, respectively. The corner bar lined up with decile 10 for the initial period, and decile 10 for the subsequent period represents the number of funds whose performance persistently ranks among the top 10 percent over both intervals. Both graphs illustrate the existence of short-term persistence among top-performing funds ('hot hands'). There is only weak evidence for persistence among poorly performing fund starts ('icy hands'). The general pattern for different window sizes is fairly robust.

Panel A: Transition frequencies for decile rankings over years 1 and 2.

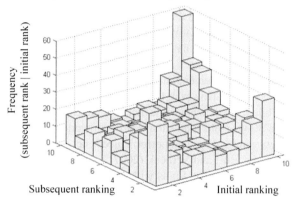

Panel B: Transition frequencies for decile rankings over years 1–3 and 4–6.

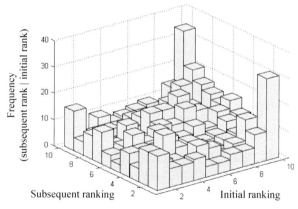

Figure 3. Performance persistence of fund starts. The 828 fund starts over the period 1991-2005 are ranked into deciles based on their average risk-adjusted performance. The risk-adjusted performance is measured by the alpha from the Carhart four-factor model. The bar chart plots the transition frequencies $f(l, m)$ that a fund with an initial decile rank l over the first period (initial rank) is sorted into decile m over the subsequent period (subsequent ranking). Panel A shows the conditional frequencies for a window length of 1 year, and Panel B the results for a 3-year window. Decile 1 comprises the funds with the lowest risk-adjusted performance and decile 10 the top-performing funds.

The most important observation is a decrease of the persistent top performers when we move from a 1-year to a 3-year window. Coupled with the substantial fraction of funds that drop from the top decile 10 to the bottom decile 1 these findings indicate that some funds earn a high alpha over the initial period due to luck or risk taking and not necessarily due to manager skill.

3.3 *The performance of new vs. old funds*

We proceed by testing whether fund starts outperform existing funds over the first 3 years after inception. As before, we focus on alpha estimates from Carhart (1997) four-factor regressions. The difference in means of 0.12% per month is statistically significant at the 1% level (*t*-statistics 2.77). Similar to Section 3.1 we check the robustness of this result and change the size of the time window after inception. Figure 4 plots the difference in means between alphas of new funds minus alphas of existing funds. The results are very robust to the selection of the window length and the differences start to decline beyond 48 months.

In the introduction, we discussed the literature on the performance of young funds. Blake and Timmermann (1998) plot the cumulative abnormal return of fund starts. In addition, two alternative methodologies were proposed to analyze the relationship between fund age and performance. Otten and Bams (2002) run a panel regression of risk-adjusted performance on fund age (in addition to assets under management and expense ratio) to study the performance of 506 funds from five European countries. However, this linear relationship between fund alphas and fund age is too restrictive. While it appears plausible that new funds exhibit superior performance initially, it is not clear why a 30-year-old fund should perform worse compared with a 20-year-old fund. This relationship between fund age and performance is not expected to be linear for all fund ages. The second approach by Huij and Verbeek (2007) separates funds into two groups. One group contains all fund starts (defined as funds with an inception date less than 5 years ago) and the remainder forms the second group. The authors then compare the risk-adjusted performance of the

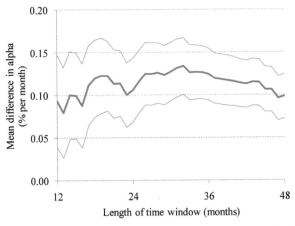

Figure 4. The difference in the risk-adjusted performance of fund starts vs. existing funds for an increasing time windows after inception. After each fund start we estimate the alpha of the Carhart four-factor model over the first *k* months and subtract the mean alpha of all existing funds over the same time span. The bold line plots the mean difference between the alphas and the thin lines indicate the upper and lower bounds of the 95% confidence interval for time windows from *k* = 12 to 48 months. The sample includes 1,374 funds and 828 fund starts over the period 1991–2005.

two groups. This approach provides a snapshot for the given sample period, and fund returns of new and existing funds are not evaluated over the same time span as new funds will be introduced throughout the sample period. We estimate the alpha of a given fund start over a specific period. To illustrate the evolution over time we select three periods: the first year, years 2 and 3, and years 4 and 5. Over the same calendar time window as the fund start, we then compute the alphas of all existing funds and sort them into deciles. Finally, we assign the fund start to one of the deciles formed by the existing funds. We repeat these steps for all 828 fund starts in our sample. This nonparametric ranking methodology is not influenced by outliers and avoids the criticisms raised above. The bar chart in Figure 5 shows the frequencies of the decile rankings of new funds among existing funds.

The proportion of new funds is higher among top-performing deciles (especially decile 10) over the first 12 months, and to some smaller degree during the period 12–36 months. Overall, the histogram shows a U-shaped pattern for the first year. Fund starts are not only more frequently ranked among the top-performing funds (decile 10) but also among the worst-performing funds (decile 1). A χ^2-test rejects the null hypothesis that all the proportions are equal for the first 12 months (χ^2-statistics 49.93) and the period 12–36 months (29.10) at the 1% level. However, the null hypothesis of equality cannot be rejected over the period 36–60 months (p-value of 0.24). Hence, while funds initially are more prominent among top winners and, to some lesser extent, bottom losers, the effect fades away after 3 years.

3.4 *What return characteristics can explain the pattern?*

We further examine whether this U-shape pattern in Figure 5 is explained by risk taking of young funds. We use the loadings on the four factors of the Carhart (1997) model and one minus the R^2 from the four-factor regression to capture the fraction of unsystematic risk relative to total risk.

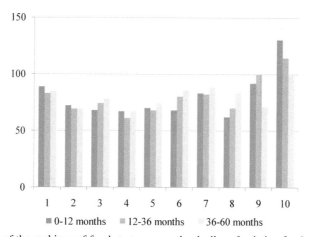

Figure 5. Histogram of the rankings of fund starts among the deciles of existing funds. For a fund start we estimate the alpha of the Carhart four-factor model for the first year, years 2 and 3, and years 4 and 5. Next, we sort existing funds into deciles within each of the same three time spans and assign the fund start to one of the deciles in each period. We repeat this procedure for all 828 fund starts in the sample of 1,374 funds from 1991 to 2005. The bar chart illustrates the frequencies of the rankings over the three time windows after inception. Decile 1 comprises the funds with the lowest risk-adjusted performance and decile 10 the top-performing funds.

Table 3. Tests of differences in the performance of fund starts over time and between fund starts and existing funds.

Number of years after inception	Excess return	Carhart (1997) four-factor model						Number of observations
		α	RMRF	SMB	HML	MOM	R^2	
Panel A: Monthly mean excess returns, coefficient estimates, and R^2 over time								
1	0.87	0.04	93.28	28.68	−3.42	5.95	84.92	828
2	0.75	−0.02	96.11	26.64	−3.78	5.32	86.71	824
3	0.91	0.12	94.59	25.44	−2.32	2.13	86.69	820
4	0.81	−0.02	95.39	25.45	4.10	4.86	87.30	816
5	0.64	−0.09	97.94	27.20	5.98	3.71	88.44	784
6	0.56	−0.02	97.21	24.59	8.65	4.37	88.83	735
7	0.45	−0.04	96.95	23.20	8.31	3.83	88.15	678
8	0.26	−0.05	97.14	23.55	8.11	6.80	89.11	569

Difference	Excess return	Carhart (1997) four-factor model					
		α	RMRF	SMB	HML	MOM	R^2
Panel B: Differences over 12-month and 36-month horizons							
First vs. second 12 months	0.12	0.06	−2.85	2.08	0.34	0.63	−1.78**
	(1.48)	(1.17)	(1.56)	(0.82)	(0.12)	(0.30)	(−2.54)
First vs. second 36 months	0.15***	0.08***	−2.22*	2.68	−8.81***	−0.93	−2.36***
	(2.77)	(2.73)	(−1.75)	(1.30)	(−3.85)	(−0.79)	(−3.11)
New vs. old funds, 12 months	0.03	0.09**	−1.92	14.43***	−6.51***	2.49*	−1.23***
	(0.41)	(2.29)	(−1.43)	(7.73)	(−3.20)	(1.77)	(−3.02)
New vs. old funds, 36 months	0.15**	0.12***	−1.66*	14.59***	−8.88***	0.39	−0.68*
	(2.23)	(5.63)	(−1.95)	(9.61)	(−5.34)	(0.43)	(−1.70)

Panel A tabulates average monthly excess returns and average coefficient estimates from the Carhart four-factor model for each of the first 8 years after inception. Excess returns are fund returns net of management fees minus the 1-month Treasury bill rate. α is the intercept of the Carhart four-factor regression, RMRF is the exposure to the CRSP value-weighted market index minus the 1-month treasury bill rate, SMB the small cap minus big cap factor, HML the high minus low book-to-market factor, and MOM the 1-year momentum factor. All means are in percentages per month and the top and bottom 1% of the differences are trimmed. The top part of Panel B tests for differences in means between first minus second period. The period length is alternatively 12 or 36 months. The bottom part of Panel B tests for differences between fund starts and existing funds over the first 12 and 36 months after inception. The values in brackets show the t-statistics for a two-sided t-test on the equality of the means. The sample period is from 1991 to 2005.
*Significance at the 10% level.
**Significance at the 5% level.
***Significance at the 1% level.

Panel A of Table 3 reports means return and risk characteristics for each of the first 8 years after inception. The top part of Panel B tabulates the differences in means for 12-month and 36-month windows and tests for significant differences. The lower part of Panel B tests for differences in means between fund starts and existing funds over the first 12 and 36 months after inception. To avoid distortions by outliers we trim again the top and bottom 1% of the observations when reporting means and testing whether the means are drawn from the same population.

The exposure to market risk, quantified by the average coefficient of RMRF, increases gradually over time (with the exception of year 2). The loadings on SMB decrease while those on HML increase over time and change signs. Overall, the explanatory power of the four-factor model increases. There is no consensus in the literature on the exposure of mutual funds to small/large and value/growth stocks. Gruber (1996) and Carhart (1997) argue that funds tend to invest more often in small growth stocks, whereas Falkenstein (1996) documents a preference for large value stocks.

The top part of Panel B in Table 3 tests whether these changes over time are statistically significant. We repeat the comparison of two subsequent windows after inception with window lengths of 12 and 36 months. Excess returns are significantly different (0.15% per month) between subsequent 36-month windows. As discussed in Section 3.1, for fund starts the decline in alpha becomes significant at the 5% level beyond a time window with a length of 27 months. The difference in the mean loadings over two subsequent 36-month windows significantly increases for RMRF (at the 10% level) and HML (at the 1% level). The difference for SMB is positive, indicating that fund starts invest more in small stocks, but not significant. The difference in HML indicates that in the longer run young funds increase their investments in high book-to-market stocks. There is no evident pattern in the exposure to the momentum factor (MOM). The increase in R^2 means that a higher percentage of the variation in mutual fund returns is explained by the four factors, corresponding to a decrease in unsystematic risk.

The bottom part of Panel B compares the means of fund starts with the means of existing funds. We check for robustness by comparing means over the first 12 and 36 months after inception. New funds have somewhat less market risk. In this comparison, the difference in SMB is significant (at the 1% level) at both horizons. Coupled with the positive but insignificant difference for SMB in the previous analysis, this reflects the slow but gradual decrease in the exposure to small-cap stocks. Again, the mean coefficient for HML is lower for fund starts and also the exposure to RMRF slightly increases over time. When comparing the R^2 with existing funds the difference is statistically different at the 1% level for the 12 month horizon and at the 10% level for 36 months, which corroborates our finding that the fraction of unsystematic to total risk decreases after inception.

Next, we apply again the methodology that we introduced in the previous section and sort new funds into the deciles formed by old funds based on these return and risk measures. Table 4 reports the frequencies of the decile rankings. χ^2-statistics along with the p-values for testing the null hypothesis of equality of the proportions are added at the bottom of the table.

A substantially higher fraction of fund starts rank in decile 10 for excess returns. Fund starts also rank more often in the lower deciles 1–4 for R^2, indicating a higher degree of unsystematic risk. Furthermore, fund starts are over-represented in the top decile for SMB and the bottom decile for HML. Carhart (1997) attributes the 'hot hands' phenomenon detected by Hendricks, Patel, and Zeckhauser (1993) to investments in momentum stocks. Compared with existing funds, young funds appear to more often follow either a contrarian (decile 1 for MOM) or a momentum strategy (decile 10). This may partially explain why we do not detect any systematic difference in means between two subsequent time periods or between new and old funds.

3.5   *Does alpha decrease due to fund inflows?*

In their model with rational investors Berk and Green (2004) illustrate how fund performance is competed away by new funds flowing to recently successful managers. The predictions of their model reproduce two empirical results we find; a decrease in alpha and the lack of performance persistence for most funds – even though it would not explain why the most successful funds in the top decile exhibit some degree of performance persistence. In the previous section we suggest that changes in risk taking are associated with the decrease in excess performance of fund starts. The following panel regression analysis attempts to differentiate whether the decrease in performance

Table 4. Frequency table for the rankings of fund starts among the deciles formed by existing funds based on return and risk characteristics.

Decile	Excess return	Carhart (1997) four-factor model					
		α	RMRF	SMB	HML	MOM	R^2
1	87	66	90	88	114	106	95
2	74	57	80	75	87	78	75
3	78	77	85	76	69	73	117
4	82	63	82	51	79	83	98
5	76	77	81	61	88	73	75
6	64	69	79	81	76	72	60
7	75	62	74	81	73	64	65
8	80	82	64	70	56	72	59
9	74	90	87	99	71	76	67
10	132	155	76	116	85	101	87
χ^2-statistics	37.49	90.30	6.11	38.42	26.79	20.40	40.75
p-value	0.00	0.00	0.73	0.00	0.00	0.02	0.00

After the inception of a new fund, all existing US equity mutual funds are sorted into decile portfolios based on fund characteristics over the first 3 years. The new fund is then attributed to one of the deciles. The table reports the frequencies of fund starts among the deciles of existing funds for the mean excess return over 3 years after inception and the loadings of the Carhart (1997) four-factor model. Decile 1 contains the funds with the lowest values for the returns, risk measures, or loadings, decile 10 the ones with the highest values. RMRF is the excess return of the CRSP value-weighted stock market portfolio over the 1-month Treasury bill rate. α represents the intercept of the four-factor model. SMB, HML, and MOM are the factor-mimicking size, book-to-market, and 1-year momentum portfolios as defined by Fama and French (1993) and in the case of MOM by Carhart (1997). The last two rows report the χ^2-statistics along with the p-values for testing the null hypothesis that the frequencies across all deciles are equal. The sample includes returns from 1,374 funds (828 fund starts) over the period 1991–2005.

is an effect of inflows and/or due to systematic changes in the risk exposure of new funds. We follow a recent methodology proposed by Amihud and Goyenko (2008) that essentially regresses alpha from the Carhart four-factor model on size, the R^2 from the four-factor model, and control variables such as turnover, expenses, and fund age. They find that R^2 is negatively related to alpha. This is consistent with our results that young funds have higher alphas and higher degrees of unsystematic risk relative to total risk (lower R^2).

We run panel regressions with fund fixed effects and year dummies to explore the impact of fund flows, fund age, and unsystematic risk on alpha. Fund flows are measured as a percentage of TNA (see Section 4.1 for more details). Our focus is on the behavior of fund starts and we therefore define an age dummy variable that takes zero for funds up to 3 years and one if the fund is older than 3 years. As in Amihud and Goyenko (2008) we use a logistic transform of the R^2 from the Carhart four-factor regressions to proxy for the ratio of unsystematic to total risk. This transformation is necessary as these R^2 are clustered around 0.90 and the transformation produces the preferred symmetric distribution.

$$\text{TR}^2 = \log \left[\frac{\sqrt{R^2}}{1 - \sqrt{R^2}} \right] \qquad (4)$$

When regressing alternatively alpha on 1-year lagged fund flows or the age dummy variable, both coefficients are negative but only significantly negative in the case of age. Table 5, models (1) and (2), presents the results. Assuming that the negative effect of fund size on alpha, or the negative

Table 5. Determinants of fund alpha.

Lagged variables	(1)	(2)	(3)	(4)	(5)	(6)
Log(TNA)			−0.154***			
			(−4.14)			
Log(TNA)^2			0.003			
			(0.74)			
Flows	−0.057		−0.323***	−0.133**	−0.227***	−0.554***
	(−1.27)		(−5.19)	(−2.69)	(−3.01)	(−3.26)
Age		−0.091***		−0.128***	−0.126*	−0.136***
		(−3.75)		(−4.50)	(−1.73)	(−3.29)
Age × flows				0.001	0.006	
				(0.05)	(0.33)	
TR^2					−0.113***	
					(−5.53)	
Age × TR^2					0.007	
					(0.34)	
Expenses						26.010***
						(4.36)
Turnover						−0.002
						(−0.35)
Number of stocks						0.000
						(−0.35)
ICI						−0.063
						(−0.78)
Size						−0.002**
						(−1.94)
Illiquidity ratio × 10^3						0.071
						(0.15)
Number of fund years	15,268	15,526	13,785	12,392	11,878	7,691
R^2	0.00	0.00	0.01	0.00	0.01	0.01

Panel regression with fund fixed effects and year dummies. The dependent variable is the intercept (alpha) from the Carhart four-factor model. Alpha is regressed on lagged flow, age, risk, and control variables. Flows are in percentage of total net assets (TNA). Age is a dummy variable that is zero for funds that are up to 3 years old, and 1 otherwise. TR^2 is the logistic transformation of the R^2 for the Carhart four-factor model: $TR^2 = \log\left[\sqrt{R^2}/1 - \sqrt{R^2}\right]$. The control variables include the number of different stock positions, the industry concentration index (ICI) of Kacperczyk, Sialm, and Zheng (2005), the average size quantile rankings of all stock positions (from 1 for micro-cap to 20 for giant-cap), and the illiquidity ratio is defined as in Amihud (2002). t-statistics are in brackets. The sample period is 1991–2005.
*Significance at the 10% level.
**Significance at the 5% level.
***Significance at the 1% level.

impact of large inflows, is not linear in size, we include in the fund flow regression (3) not only size, measured by the logarithm of TNA, but also the square of it. Indeed, as in Amihud and Goyenko (2008), the coefficient for log(TNA)^2 is positive, which mitigates the negative relation with alpha for the largest funds. TNA and flows simultaneously are both negative and significant at the 5% level.

Next, we compare the effect of flows and the age dummy in model (4). Both coefficients remain negative as in the individual regressions (1) and (2). The interaction term between age and flows does not add any explanatory power. We avoid including TNA in the estimation as TNA and age are highly correlated (Spearman rank order correlation of 0.35). Specification (5) shows that part of the age dummy proxies for the higher unsystematic risk of young funds. Amihud and Goyenko (2008) document that higher TR^2 has a negative predictive effect on alpha. Our previous results show that young funds are subject to higher unsystematic risk and thus lower TR^2. To check whether our finding that both, flows and the age dummy, are negatively related to alpha, we include control variables for expenses, turnover, diversification, and liquidity. We discuss these variables in more detail in the next section. The only control variables that show up significantly are expenses and average market capitalization of stock positions (size). Highly actively managed funds typically charge higher fees and have low R^2 in a Carhart four-factor regression (low TR^2). Thus, the positive coefficient for expenses is likely related to the effect of unsystematic risk on alpha.

In summary, we find that flows have a negative and young fund age a positive impact on fund performance. Part of the young age effect may be attributed to their lower R^2 in the Carhart four-factor regressions.

4. Characteristics of mutual fund starts

In this section, we examine the portfolio characteristics of new funds: TNA, fund flows, management fees, turnover, number of stocks in reported portfolios, industry concentration, and illiquidity ratio. So far, we have shown that new funds initially outperform existing funds and from exploring these characteristics we gain further insight on the main determinants of this superior performance. Table 6 shows descriptive statistics of the characteristics for the full sample. The increase in TNA reflects the growth in the mutual fund industry. For the other variables we observe no particular trend over the period 1991–2005.[8]

4.1 *Variable definitions and hypotheses*

Successful fund starts typically receive large inflows relative to their assets under management. This facilitates shifting portfolio allocations as these funds do not need to sell off positions to

Table 6. The change in mutual characteristics over time.

Fund characteristics	1991	1995	2000	2005
TNA	91.2	129.2	210.2	267.9
Fund flows (as % of TNA)	0.14	0.47	−0.11	−0.74
Fees (%)	1.15	1.15	1.15	1.19
Turnover (%)	58.0	64.0	69.0	54.0
Number of stocks	62.0	77.0	81.2	82.0
ICI	0.16	0.15	0.15	0.14
Size	10.6	10.8	16.8	16.4
Illiquidity ratio $\times 10^3$	0.272	0.086	0.001	0.004
Number of funds	568	992	1345	1211

This table shows the development of average characteristics of the 1,374 US equity mutual funds in our sample. Total net assets (TNA) in million dollars as of year-end. Fund flows are computed monthly as a percentage of TNA and the cells in the table contain the average value over the given year across all funds. ICI is the industry concentration index as defined by Kacperczyk, Sialm, and Zheng (2005), size, the average size quantile rankings of all stock positions (from 1 for micro-cap to 20 for giant-cap), and the illiquidity ratio is defined as in Amihud (2002).

substantially change the portfolio composition. Chen et al. (2004) argue that larger fund entities additionally suffer from indirect costs of price impact as they need to execute larger trades. Therefore, we expect to find economically relevant changes for fund starts over the first few years after inception.

We measure monthly fund flow as a percentage of fund size, where TNA is total net assets under management at time t and R_t the fund return from month $t-1$ to t.

$$\text{Flows}_t = \frac{\text{TNA}_t - (1 + R_t)\text{TNA}_{t-1}}{\text{TNA}_{t-1}} \tag{5}$$

As a new fund enters the market, its size is typically relatively small compared with existing funds. Given the favorable performance we documented previously, we expect that fund starts will succeed in attracting higher than average fund inflows.

Next, we define the following holdings-based fund characteristics: the industry concentration index (ICI) of Kacperczyk, Sialm, and Zheng (2005), the average size quantile rankings of stock positions, and the Amihud (2002) illiquidity ratio. Similar to the Herfindahl–Hirschman index, ICI quantifies the degree of diversification across $j = 10$ broadly defined industries, where $w_{j,t}$ is the weight of the reported mutual fund holdings in industry j at time t.

$$\text{ICI}_t = \sum_{j=1}^{10} w_{j,t}^2 \tag{6}$$

By construction, ICI varies between 0.1 (perfect diversification) and 1.0 (the portfolio is fully invested in one industry). Thus, higher values of ICI indicate a lower degree of diversification. Another proxy for portfolio diversification is the number of different stock positions. In an attempt to outperform their peers it appears plausible that new funds will invest in a less diversified portfolio and take bets on individual stocks or sectors. We, therefore, expect portfolios of new funds to have a smaller number of stocks and a higher concentration in a few industries. This view is also consistent with the higher ratio of unsystematic to total risk we documented in the previous section. Furthermore, failure of the timing of sector bets or stock picks could help to explain the lack of long-term persistence in the return pattern of new funds. In fact, the literature does not provide much evidence of market timing skills of fund managers. An exception is Bollen and Busse (2001) who find some timing ability in the very short run. Shawky and Smith (2005) discuss the trade-off to decide on the optimal number of stocks from the perspective of a mutual fund. On one hand, the diversification argument encourages managers to increase the number of stocks in their portfolio. On the other hand, improving analyst coverage favors a smaller number of stocks. Fund starts may have limited research resources and focus on covering fewer stocks or industries.

The estimated coefficients of the Carhart (1997) four-factor regressions may not fully capture the premium earned by small, illiquid stocks due to estimation errors. To corroborate our previous result that fund starts have a higher exposure to small stocks, we study the portfolio composition of new and incumbent funds using the average size quantile rankings of stock positions, and the Amihud (2002) illiquidity ratio. Hasbrouck (2006) sorts all stocks in CRSP into 20 quantiles (where the stocks in quantile 1 are micro-cap and in quantile 20 stocks issued by the largest firms). We assess the value-weighted average of all stock positions in the reported portfolio. On average, we succeed to match 94.1% of the holdings. The Amihud ratio measures the impact of dollar volume on returns.

$$IR_t = \frac{|R_{i,t}|}{T_{i,t}P_{i,t}} \tag{7}$$

where $R_{i,t}$ is the daily return on stock i from $t-1$ to t, $T_{i,t}$ the number of stocks traded over the same day, and $P_{i,t}$ the stock price at the end of the day. We use aggregated and annualized illiquidity ratios and compute a value-weighted average over all stock positions in the quarterly holdings.

4.2 Persistence in fund characteristics

First, we examine whether managers of fund starts systematically adjust the portfolio character-istics over time. Figure 6 shows the changes in average characteristics over the first 5 years after inception. Average TNA and fees exhibit a smooth upward trend. Fund flows as a percentage of TNA decay a few months after inception. Turnover decreases with fund age. Given the growth in assets under management the absolute turnover in dollars may still increase but the annual turnover as a percentage of TNA decreases. The number of stocks increases along with a decrease

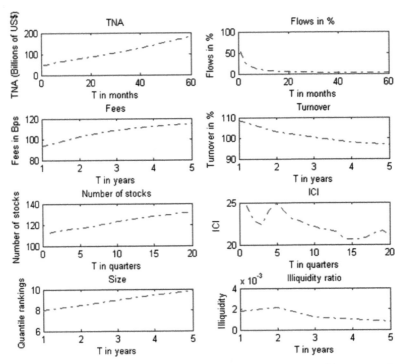

Figure 6. Persistence in characteristics of fund starts. We report the development of the average characteristics of fund starts over the first 5 years after inception. Total net assets (TNA) and fund flows (as a % of TNA) are available monthly. Fees and turnover are annual. Number of stocks in the fund portfolio, the Kacperczyk, Sialm, and Zheng (2005) industry concentration index (ICI), the average size quantile rankings of all stock positions (from 1 for micro-cap to 20 for giant-cap), and the average Amihud (2002) illiquidity ratio are computed from quarterly holdings.

in ICI over time. Thus, funds become more diversified which is consistent with the reduction in unsystematic risk we observed in Section 3.4. The last two plots at the bottom of Figure 6 support our earlier finding that young funds initially exhibit larger coefficient estimates for SMB. The average size quantile ranking of all stock positions in the reported portfolios is initially lower. In line with this finding, managers allocate a larger fraction of their assets to illiquid stocks, i.e. the average Amihud (2002) illiquidity ratio is higher.

4.3   Differences in characteristics of new vs. old funds

In order to test whether these changes in the fund characteristics are significant, we analyze the changes over two subsequent 3-year windows. Table 7 reports the results. The first two rows show the differences in mean characteristics over two subsequent 3-year periods (along with t-statistics in brackets) and the last two rows the differences between fund starts and existing funds over the first 3 years after inception. Not surprisingly, the size of new funds is smaller and they attract higher percentage inflows (significant at the 1% level). Fees are also significantly higher, however, economically hardly relevant and more an artifact of the low dispersion in fees. Fund portfolios of young funds are typically less diversified. However, the average number over 3 years does not exceed the number of stocks held by incumbent funds. The reason is that fund starts adjust their low number of stocks over a relatively short period and the difference over a 3-year period does not capture this effect. Similarly, the major decrease in ICI and the illiquidity ratio occurs over the first 3 years (as Figure 6 illustrates). When we compare the difference over the first year only (not reported here) the difference is significant. New funds are also more actively managed than existing funds (turnover is statistically significantly higher).

As a final step, we apply our ranking methodology outlined in Section 3.3. We take the average fund characteristic of each fund start over the first 3 years of existence and compare it with the cross-section of all existing funds over the same time period. We do this by sorting existing funds

Table 7. Persistence in fund characteristics over time and differences in fund characteristics between fund starts and existing funds.

Difference	TNA	Flows (%)	Fees (% of TNA)	Turnover (%)	Number of stocks	ICI	Size	Illiquidity ratio $\times 10^3$
First vs. second 36 months	−138.26***	0.04***	0.00**	−0.00	−10.05	−0.00	−2.69***	−0.001
t-statistics	(−5.75)	(15.03)	(2.61)	(−0.39)	(−0.99)	(−0.57)	(−3.84)	(−0.73)
New vs. old funds	−770.52***	0.05***	0.00**	0.18**	0.85	0.00	−1.02**	0.001
t-statistics	(−53.57)	(10.81)	(3.26)	(2.11)	(0.10)	(−0.29)	(−2.35)	(1.22)

The first two rows show the differences in means between the initial 36 month period minus the subsequent 36 month period after inception. The last two rows describe the differences in means between fund starts minus existing funds over the first 36 months after inception. TNA is total net assets and fund flows are measured as a percentage of TNA. For each fund portfolio we compute the number of different stock positions, the industry concentration index (ICI) of Kacperczyk, Sialm, and Zheng (2005), the average size quantile rankings of all stock positions (from 1 for micro-cap to 20 for giant-cap), and a value-weighted average Amihud (2002) illiquidity ratio. The values in brackets show the t-statistics for a two-sided t-test on the equality of the means.
*Significance at the 10% level.
**Significance at the 5% level.
***Significance at the 1% level.

Table 8. Frequency table for the rankings of fund starts among the deciles formed by existing funds based on fund characteristics.

Decile	TNA	Flows (% of TNA)	Fees (%)	Turnover (%)	Number of stocks	ICI	Size	Illiquidity ratio
1	170	13	86	76	107	90	111	73
2	146	9	72	66	103	81	84	67
3	123	13	52	74	109	77	72	74
4	99	23	74	84	88	76	55	74
5	104	32	72	90	78	76	87	70
6	78	45	74	89	58	86	87	72
7	53	97	77	85	72	69	77	72
8	37	143	104	71	65	90	78	80
9	15	210	108	95	52	95	75	98
10	3	243	109	95	91	77	60	106
χ^2-statistics	109.71	883.30	232.36	95.38	19.03	29.38	38.58	54.48
p-value	0.00	0.00	0.00	0.00	0.02	0.00	0.00	0.00

After the inception of a new fund all existing US equity mutual funds are sorted into decile portfolios based on fund characteristics over the first 36 months. The new fund is then attributed to one of the deciles. The table reports the frequency of fund starts among the deciles of existing funds for total net assets (TNA), fund flows as a percentage of TNA, management fees, annual turnover, number of stock positions in the portfolio, industry concentration index (ICI) of Kacperczyk, Sialm, and Zheng (2005), average size quantile rankings of all stock positions (from 1 for micro-cap to 20 for giant-cap), and the value-weighted average Amihud (2002) illiquidity ratio. Decile 1 contains the funds with the lowest values for the specific characteristic and decile 10 the funds with the highest values. The last two rows report the χ^2-statistics along with the p-values for testing the null hypothesis that the frequencies across all deciles are equal. The sample includes returns from 1,374 funds (828 fund starts) over the period 1991–2005.

over the same 3 years into deciles based on a given characteristic and determine the rank of the decile to which the fund start belongs to. Table 8 reports the frequencies of the decile rankings along with a χ^2-statistics for an equality test of these frequencies across all deciles. Most fund starts rank in the lower TNA deciles and only three are classified in the top decile within 3 years. However, most emerging funds grow quickly in relative terms. Management fees tend to be above the median of old funds, and young funds are also more prominent in the top two deciles for turnover. The majority of new funds hold a smaller number of stocks and the stock positions tend to be less liquid. The evidence for industry concentration is mixed.

5. Conclusions

We study the returns and matched portfolio holdings of US domestic equity mutual fund starts over the period 1991–2005. In particular, we investigate how performance and risk characteristics of fund starts change over the first years after inception. Our results show that, on average, new US equity mutual funds outperform their peers by 0.15% per month over the first 3 years. However, cumulative abnormal returns of fund starts decline after the initial 3 years. This decline in performance cannot be explained by diseconomies of scale alone as these funds mature and grow in size. We find distinct patterns in superior risk-adjusted performance estimated using Carhart's (1997) four-factor model. There is some performance persistence among top-performing fund starts. However, a relatively large number of top-performing funds over the first 3 years also drop directly to the bottom decile rankings over the next 3-year period. These results suggest that the initially favorable performance is to some extent due to risk taking and not necessarily superior manager skill. Scrutinizing the returns further confirms that fund starts exhibit higher unsystematic risk that cannot be explained by the risk exposure to the four factors of the Carhart model. Active management in the form of sector bets, rotation in factor loadings, and holding undiversified portfolios reduces the R^2 from these four-factor regressions. Based on factor loadings and characteristics of portfolio holdings we find that fund starts invest more actively in small-cap stocks and hold less diversified portfolios. They gradually increase their exposure to market risk and reduce unsystematic risk relative to total risk.

Acknowledgements

This paper has benefited from the comments of Bruno Rémillard, Chintal Desai, as well as participants at the 2007 Optimization Days at HEC Montréal, the 2008 Midwest Finance Association conference in San Antonio, the Desjardins Global Asset Management workshop, the 2008 Financial Management Association (Europe) meetings in Prague, and two anonymous referees. Aymen Karoui was supported by a grant from CREF and Iwan Meier acknowledges the research support from the Institut de Finance Mathématique de Montréal (IFM2).

Notes

1. ICI Mutual Fund Factbook 2008: www.ici.org, 'Data Tables'; 'Section 1: US Mutual Fund Totals'; Tables 3, 5, and 48.
2. Another strand of literature studies the impact of fund family affiliation. For example, Berzins (2006) analyzes institutional money managers and finds that the performance of a newly launched fund tends to fall into the same performance decile than the existing funds of the same family.
3. Peterson et al. (2001) and Prather, Bertin, and Henker (2004) report no significant difference in the performance of new and existing mutual funds.
4. The focus of Khorana and Servaes (1999), who study 1163 emerging funds over the period 1979–1992 (including other fund classes than equity funds), is on the determinants of mutual fund starts. They conclude that generating additional fees is the driving factor for fund openings. Fund families that outperformed their peers, larger fund families, and those who added new funds in the recent past are more likely to create a new fund. Fund families also more likely add a new fund when the largest fund families open new funds in a given investment style category.
5. http://mba.tuck.dartmouth.edu/pages/faculty/ken.french; Section 'Data Library,' 'US Research Returns Data.' The website also details the portfolio formation methodology to construct these factor returns.
6. http://pages.stern.nyu.edu/ ~jhasbrou; Section 'Research and Working Papers.'
7. To check whether sample selection has an impact on our results on cumulative performance, we also tested with an alternative sample where we select funds from the CRSP Survivors-Bias-Free US Mutual Fund Database following the sample selection methodology of Pastor and Stambaugh (2002). The authors provide a list of ICDI (named ICDI_Obj in MFDB), Wiesenberger (Obj) and Strategic Insight (SI_obj) classifications to identify US equity mutual funds in the CRSP mutual fund database and eliminate balanced funds, bond funds, flexible funds, international funds, mortgage-backed funds, money market funds, multi-manager funds, and specialized funds. Multiple share classes have been introduced starting in the 1990s and we use a name algorithm to exclude share classes as in Nanda, Wang, and Zheng (2005). Qualitatively, the results are similar: The performance declines rather quickly after the initial 3 years and the difference is significant over two subsequent 3-year windows.
8. When we consider the trend starting in 1962, then average fees have increased over time.

References

Aggarwal, Rajesh K., and Philippe Jorion. 2008. The performance of emerging hedge fund managers. Working Paper, University of Minnesota.

Amihud, Yakov. 2002. Illiquidity and stock returns: Cross-section and time-series effects. *Journal of Financial Markets* 5: 31–56.

Amihud, Yakov, and Ruslan Goyenko. 2008. Mutual fund R^2 as predictor of performance. Working Paper, New York University.

Artega, Kenneth R., Conrad S. Ciccotello, and C. Terry Grant. 1998. New equity funds: Marketing and performance. *Financial Analysts Journal* 54: 43–9.

Bauer, Rob, Kees C.G. Koedijk, and Rogér Otten. 2005. International evidence on ethical mutual fund performance and investment style. *Journal of Banking and Finance* 29: 1751–67.

Berk, Jonathan B., and Richard C. Green. 2004. Mutual fund flows and performance in rational markets. *Journal of Political Economy* 112, no. 6: 1269–95.

Berzins, Janis. 2006. Do families matter in institutional money management industry: The case of new portfolio openings. Working Paper, Indiana University.

Blake, Christopher R., Edwin J. Elton, and Martin J. Gruber. 2001. A first look at the accuracy of the CRSP mutual fund database and a comparison of the CRSP and Morningstar databases. *Journal of Finance* 56: 2415–30.

Blake, David, and Allan Timmermann. 1998. Mutual fund performance: Evidence from the UK. *European Finance Review* 2: 57–77.

Bollen, Nicolas P.B., and Jeffrey A. Busse. 2001. On the timing ability of mutual fund managers. *Journal of Finance* 56: 1075–94.

Bollen, Nicolas P.B., and Jeffrey A. Busse. 2004. Short-term persistence in mutual fund performance. *Review of Financial Studies* 18, no. 2: 569–97.

Brown, Stephen J., and William N. Goetzmann. 1995. Performance persistence. *Journal of Finance* 50: 679–98.

Carhart, Mark M. 1997. On persistence in mutual fund performance. *Journal of Finance* 52, no. 1: 57–82.

Chen, Joseph S., Harrison G. Hong, Ming Huang, and Jeffrey D. Kubik. 2004. Does fund size erode mutual fund performance? The role of liquidity and organization. *American Economic Review* 94, no. 5: 1276–302.

Chevalier, Judith, and Glenn Ellison. 1999a. Are some mutual fund managers better than others? Cross-sectional patterns in behavior and performance. *Journal of Finance* 54, no. 3: 875–99.

Chevalier, Judith, and Glenn Ellison. 1999b. Career concerns of mutual fund managers. *Quarterly Journal of Economics* 114, no. 2: 389–432.

Cuthbertson, Keith, Dirk Nitzsche, and Niall O'Sullivan. 2008. UK mutual fund performance: Skill or luck? *Journal of Empirical Finance* 15: 613–34.

Evans, Richard B. 2008. The incubation bias. Working Paper, University of Virginia.

Falkenstein, Eric G. 1996. Preferences for stock characteristics as revealed by mutual fund portfolio holdings. *Journal of Finance* 51, no. 1: 11–135.

Fama, Eugene F., and Kenneth R. French. 1993. Common risk factors in the return on bonds and stocks. *Journal of Financial Economics* 33: 3–53.

Ferreira, Miguel A., António F. Miguel, and Sofia Ramos. 2006. The determinants of mutual fund performance: A cross-country study. Swiss Finance Institute Research Paper Series No. 06-30. Available at SSRN: http://ssrn.com/abstract=947098

Gaspar, José-Miguel, Massimo Massa, and Pedro Matos. 2006. Favoritism in mutual fund families? Evidence on strategic cross-fund subsidization, *Journal of Finance* 61, no. 1: 73–104.

Goetzmann, William N., and Roger G. Ibbotson. 1994. Do winners repeat? Patterns in mutual fund performance. *Journal of Portfolio Management* 20: 9–18.

Gregory, A., J. Matako, and R. Luther. 1997. Ethical unit trust financial performance: Small company effects and fund size effects. *Journal of Business Finance and Accounting* 24: 705–25.

Grinblatt, Mark, Sheridan Titman, and Russ Wermers. 1995. Momentum investment strategies, portfolio performance, and herding: A study of mutual fund behavior. *American Economic Review* 85: 1088–105.

Gruber, Martin J. 1996. Another puzzle: The growth of actively managed mutual funds. *Journal of Finance* 51: 783–810.

Hasbrouck, Joel. 2006. Trading costs and returns for US equities: Estimating effective costs from daily data. Working Paper, New York University.

Hendricks, Darryll, Jayendu Patel, and Richard Zeckhauser. 1993. Hot hands in mutual funds: Short-run persistence of performance, 1974–88. *Journal of Finance* 48: 93–130.

Huij, Joop, and Marno Verbeek. 2007. Cross-sectional learning and short-run persistence in mutual fund performance. *Journal of Banking and Finance* 31, no. 3: 973–97.

Indro, D., C. Jiang, M. Hu, and W. Lee. 1999. Mutual fund performance: Does fund size matter? *Financial Analysts Journal* 55, no. 3: 74–87.

Jegadeesh, Narasimhan, and Sheridan Titman. 1993. Returns to buying winners and selling losers: Implications for stock market efficiency. *Journal of Finance* 48: 65–91.

Jensen, Michael C. 1968. The performance of mutual funds in the period 1945-1964. *Journal of Finance* 23: 389–416.

Kacperczyk, Marcin, Clemens Sialm, and Lu Zheng. 2005. On the industry concentration of actively managed equity mutual funds. *Journal of Finance* 60, no. 4: 1983–2011.

Khorana, Ajay, and Henri Servaes. 1999. The determinants of mutual funds starts. *Review of Financial Studies* 12, no. 5: 1043–74.

Liang, Bing. 1999. On the performance of hedge funds. *Financial Analysts Journal* 55, no. 4: 72–85.

Malkiel, Burton G. 1995. Returns from investing in equity mutual funds 1971 to 1991. *Journal of Finance* 50, no. 2: 549–72.

Nanda, Vikram K., Z. Jay Wang, and Lu Zheng. 2005. The ABCs of mutual funds: On the introduction of multiple share classes. Working Paper, University of Michigan.

Otten, Roger, and Dennis Bams. 2002. European mutual fund performance. *European Financial Management* 8, no. 1: 75–101.

Pastor, Lubos, and Robert F. Stambaugh. 2002. Mutual fund performance and seemingly unrelated assets. *Journal of Financial Economics* 63, no. 3: 315–49.

Peterson, James D., Paul A. Pietranico, Mark W. Riepe, and Fran Xu 2001. Explaining the performance of domestic equity mutual funds. *Journal of Investing* 10: 81–92.

Prather, Laurie, William J. Bertin, and Thomas Henker 2004. Mutual fund characteristics, managerial attributes and fund performance. *Review of Financial Economics* 13: 305–26.

Prendergast, Canice, and Lars Stole. 1996. Impetuous youngsters and jaded old-timers: Acquiring a reputation for learning. *Journal of Political Economy* 104, no. 6: 1105–34.

Reuter, Jonathan. 2006. Are IPO allocations for sale? Evidence from mutual funds. *Journal of Finance* 61, no. 5: 2289–323.

Shawky, Hany A., and David M. Smith. 2005. Optimal number of stock holdings in mutual fund portfolios based on market performance. *Financial Review* 40: 481–95.

Zhao, Xinge. 2005. Entry decisions by mutual fund families. In *Stock exchanges, IPOs, and mutual funds*, ed. E. Kline, 151–79. New York: Nova Science Publishers, Inc.

Individual home bias, portfolio churning and performance

Stockholm University School of Business, Finance Department, S-106 91 Stockholm, Sweden

This study investigates economic consequences of individual investors' home bias and portfolio churning in their personal pension accounts. The empirical analysis is carried out within a Heckman style two-stage framework to account for selection bias with respect to individuals' investment activity, and to allow for an endogenously determined home bias, portfolio churning and performance. Results indicate that home bias induces a worse risk-adjusted performance. Home-biased individuals' relatively bad performance originates in insufficient risk-reduction, due to a lack of international diversification. A higher degree of portfolio churning also deteriorates performance, despite the fact that churning is not associated with any direct transaction costs. However, home-biased individuals do not churn portfolios as often as individuals with a larger share of international asset holdings, which diminishes the negative effects of home bias on performance. Overconfidence is driven by a return-chasing behavior, where overconfident individuals favor international assets with high historical returns. Individuals with actual skill are more often men than women, are not tempted by high historical returns, and use international assets for the right reason – diversification.

1. Introduction

One of the most intriguing puzzles of international portfolio investment is investor home bias. The fact that investors have a tendency for concentrating equity investments to their domestic market has been known for a long time. French and Poterba (1991) estimate the domestic ownership share of the world's five largest stock markets to 92.2% for the USA, 95.7% for Japan, 92% for the UK, 79% for Germany and 89.4% for France (values for 1990). Many authors try to explain this home bias that runs counter to well-known benefits from international diversification.[1] A number of explanations for investor home bias are offered, including inflation hedging (Adler and Dumas 1983; Cooper and Kaplanis 1994), information asymmetries (Kang and Stulz 1997), investor sophistication (Grinblatt and Keloharju 2001; Karlsson and Nordén 2007; Bailey, Kumar, and Ng 2008), familiarity with domestic or local assets (Huberman 2001; Coval and Moscowitz 1999), investor overconfidence (Karlsson and Nordén 2007) and various demographic characteristics of individual investors (Karlsson and Nordén 2007; Kyrychenko and Shum 2006).

Although many studies analyze the potential reasons for individuals' home bias, only a few focus on the actual consequences for being home-biased. As an exception, Bailey, Kumar and Ng (2008) empirically estimate the potential benefits from international investing for US individual investors, with accounts at a large discount broker firm, by comparing investment performance of individuals who invest in foreign assets with corresponding individuals who hold only domestic assets. They find that investing abroad reduces portfolio risk more efficiently than domestic investments alone, but only for individuals holding under-diversified portfolios, with less than 12 assets. For individuals with well-diversified portfolios, Bailey, Kumar and Ng (2008) find no incremental benefits from international diversification. Moreover, they find no differences in actual performance between investors' portfolios with domestic holdings only and portfolios flavored with foreign assets.

Another stylized fact of individual investment behavior, documented by Odean (1999) and Barber and Odean (2000, 2001), is the tendency for investors to trade too frequently and thereby deteriorates portfolio performance. Recently, Graham, Harvey and Huang (2009) put forward a link between individual home bias and trading frequency, and argue that both behaviors are driven by the same underlying psychological bias, namely, the competence effect. Without considering the effects on performance, Graham, Harvey and Huang (2009) find that more competent investors trade more frequently, and are more likely to invest in international assets, than less competent investors.[2] In an early study, Tesar and Werner (1995) find that investors' turnover rate of foreign equity investments is higher than the corresponding home market turnover rate. In addition, Bohn and Tesar (1996) report evidence of a return-chasing behavior among US investors, whereby they excessively turn foreign assets over in search for higher returns. Bailey, Kumar and Ng (2008) suggest that the high turnover rate is due to overconfidence, where an overconfident investor is defined as someone who trades often and exhibits poor performance (Odean 1999). Barber and Odean (2001) propose that gender is a good indicator of overconfidence, where men are supposed to be more overconfident than women, as men are found to trade more often than women, and with relatively worse performance results.

The purpose of this study is to investigate economic consequences of home bias for individuals by studying portfolios formed within the newly defined contribution pension plan in Sweden. In addition, recognizing the link between individuals' home bias and trading frequency, this study performs a comprehensive analysis of the interrelations of home bias, portfolio churning and performance. Specifically, the analysis concentrates on four main hypotheses. First, individuals' home bias is hypothesized to negatively affect portfolio performance. Supposedly, since home-biased individuals do not fully utilize the benefits from international diversification, they will face higher portfolio risk and lower risk-adjusted returns. By analyzing portfolio returns, not adjusted for risk, it is also investigated that whether individuals with home bias achieve lower actual returns than people with a larger share of international assets in their portfolios.

The second investigated hypothesis is that portfolio churning deteriorates performance. According to Odean (1999) and Barber and Odean (2000, 2001), investor overconfidence is manifested in an excess portfolio rebalancing, which ultimately leads to lower returns. Hence, a negative effect from churning is expected on individuals' actual portfolio returns as well as the corresponding risk-adjusted performance measure. Third, the analysis aims at finding out whether home-biased individuals rebalance their portfolios less often than people with a larger share of international investments, as predicted by the competence effect according to Graham, Harvey and Huang (2009). The competence effect stipulates that individuals, who believe they are competent with respect to investment choices, trade more often and invest to a larger degree in international assets. Hence, individual portfolio churning is expected to be negatively related to home bias.

Fourth, and finally, this study directly analyzes the decisions of overconfident individuals with respect to portfolio choice and international investment. Following Odean (1999), an overconfident individual is someone who belongs to the group of individuals who trade most often and exhibit the worst performance. Specifically, the analysis is focussed on whether the overconfident individuals show less degree of home bias, as suggested by, e.g. Bailey, Kumar and Ng (2008), and whether they are relatively more prone to a return-chasing behavior, in lieu of Bohn and Tesar (1996), than people not 'suffering from' the behavioral bias of overconfidence. Moreover, the behavior of the overconfident individuals is contrasted to that of 'skilled' individuals, i.e. people who churn their portfolios equally often as the overconfident individuals, but who are also among the top performers in terms of high risk-adjusted returns.

The empirical analysis uses a Heckman (1979) style two-stage framework to account for a potential selection bias due to individuals' active investment participation, while allowing for an endogenous determined degree of home bias, portfolio churning and performance. The results indicate that the portfolios for individuals with a high degree of home bias show a significantly worse risk-adjusted performance than the corresponding portfolios for individuals who are relatively more heavily invested in international assets. On the other hand, individual home bias is not a significant determinant of portfolio returns, not adjusted for risk. The results are consistent with the idea that home-biased individuals hold less-diversified portfolios than people with a larger investment share of international assets. Thus, home-biased individuals on average incur a bad risk-adjusted performance due to an insufficient risk-reduction in their portfolio formation.

The results of this study also confirm that portfolio churning significantly deteriorates individuals' performance in their pension accounts. The result that portfolio churning deteriorates performance is not related to trading costs. The main conclusion of Barber and Odean (2000) is that it is the cost of trading and frequency of trading, not the portfolio allocation per se, that explain the poor individual performance in their sample. Interestingly, in a setting where individual investors do not meet transaction costs for rebalancing their portfolios, trading is still hazardous to individual wealth. Hence, individuals' portfolio churning in their pension accounts must in general be associated with bad reallocation choices and poor portfolio selections.

In addition, the results show that home-biased individuals churn their portfolios significantly less often than individuals with a larger share of international asset holdings. Consistent with the competence story from Graham, Harvey and Huang (2009), this latter effect indirectly diminishes the direct negative effect of home bias on performance. Thus, the analysis in this paper shows two sides of being home-biased. On the one hand, home-biased individuals give up benefits from international diversification, with a resulting deteriorating effect on risk-adjusted portfolio performance. On the other hand, home-biased individuals do not rebalance their portfolios too often, avoiding excessive trading to a larger extent than individuals with more exposure to international assets.

Finally, overconfident individuals are found to hold a larger share of international assets and to be more prone to return-chasing behavior than other people. Thus, overconfident investors show less tendency for home bias, but are instead inclined to invest in international assets with high historical returns, which results in a bad performance. In contrast, skilled high-performing individuals appear to use international investments for the right reasons, as they are found to hold a larger share of international assets, and to have a lower tendency for return-chasing behavior than less skilled individuals. Gender is an important determinant of skill, where men are more likely than women to rebalance their portfolios often with good performance, but not of overconfidence, since men and women are equally likely to trade often with mediocre results.

The analysis contributes to previous research in several aspects. First, this study is one of few that analyze the actual consequences of home bias for individual investors. Most previous works study the reasons for home bias, and often also on an aggregate basis. Second, as of this date, this study provides the most thorough simultaneous analysis of individuals' home bias, portfolio churning and performance. Hence, this study treats home bias and churning as endogenous determinants of performance, and puts forward the idea that the degree of home bias is a potential explanation for excessive trading, which in turn is well known to reduce portfolio performance. In addition, by using the two-stage approach according to Heckman (1979), the results of this study are robust against a possible bias arising from only observing the behavior of individuals choosing to be active investors. The endogeneity and selection bias issues are typically overlooked in the individual investor literature.[3]

Third, by analyzing the behavior of both overconfident and skilled individuals, this study is able to contribute to the issue of whether home bias is related to overconfidence. According to the competence hypothesis in Graham, Harvey and Huang (2009), people who regard themselves as competent with regard to investment decisions are less likely to be home-biased. Given the results of this study, the same observation is true for individuals who show actual competence in terms of a high portfolio performance. Moreover, the results in this study indicate that the most important difference between skilled and overconfident individuals is the latter individuals' tendency for return-chasing behavior. Thus, the lack of home bias is not the main determinant of investor overconfidence. Instead, the overconfident individuals appear to use international investments for the wrong reasons, chasing returns rather than diversifying their portfolios.

Finally, by using individual portfolios formed and maintained within the Swedish-defined benefit pension system, it is possible to analyze the choices of a representative sample of a nation's entire work force with a well-defined investment set.[4] All portfolios are formed at the same time, and investors are initially provided with the same information brochure regarding available mutual funds. Hence, the set up is rather close to a laboratory experiment in terms of choice under uncertainty, in a well-defined, relatively low-cost, setting. Moreover, the inclusion of assets in the pension portfolios is made entirely in the interest of future return performance. The investment process contains no corporate control dimension that can be of significant importance when the home-bias issue, and indeed individuals decisions to trade, is investigated in a stock market.[5] Unlike most previous studies, including Barber and Odean (2000), trading for liquidity reasons does not contaminate portfolio churning within the pension system. In addition, portfolio churning in the pension accounts is not associated with any transaction costs. The data enable a detailed categorization of individuals based on different demographic and socioeconomic features such as gender, age, education level, wealth, income and country of birth. Thus, while investigating the endogenous interrelationships between home bias, portfolio churning and performance, the analysis controls for exogenous factors as investor demographics.

The rest of the study is organized into four sections. Section 2 briefly presents the Swedish pension system, with an emphasis on individual choice in the defined contribution part, and on the data used in the analysis. Section 3 outlines the framework for analyzing the relationships between individuals' home bias, portfolio churning and performance. Additional explanatory variables, with motivation from previous research, are also presented. Section 4 contains an analysis of the empirical results. Finally, the study ends in Section 5 with some concluding remarks.

2. Portfolio choice within the defined contribution pension system

2.1 *The Swedish pension system*

In 2000, the Swedish pay-as-you-go pension system was redesigned into a partially self-financing system. Since then, the system consists of three parts. The first and largest part is the income pension, which is based on 16% of the annual income and is used to finance those who are retired today. The second part, the premium pension (PPM), is based on 2.5% of the annual income. In the introductory phase, in 2000, each participating individual invested 2.5% of the previous 4 years of income in mutual funds at his/her discretion and own account. The third part of the system is a guaranteed pension designed to ensure that no retiree will be completely without pension payments at the time of retirement, regardless of his/her previous income. In total, 18.5% of each individual's income is invested on an annual basis to finance the system.[6] However, an individual earning more than 7.5 income base amounts per year will only be accredited an upper limit of 7.5 income base amounts, although he/she will still pay 18.5% of his/her income to the system.[7]

2.2 *Individual choice of domestic and foreign assets*

In 2000, each individual was presented with an investment opportunity set of 464 mutual funds and invited to choose between one and five funds. If no choice was made, the allotted money was invested in the default alternative, the Seventh Swedish Pension Fund, which is a mutual fund run by the government. Each individual received a brochure containing the 464 mutual funds with accompanying information on risk, historical returns, fees and a few words briefly describing each fund.[8,9] Given the brief fund description, the proportion of domestic assets is assessed for each available mutual fund, and each individual's ratio of domestic holdings is calculated as the proportion of money allocated to domestic assets in the individual's portfolio of funds. In the brochure, the mutual funds are categorized into three different levels. Table 1 presents the different fund categories together with the associated average proportions of domestic and foreign assets. Unless the information in the brochure states otherwise, the following classification criteria are used: Swedish funds are classified as 100% domestic; Regional and Nordic funds are classified as 50% domestic and 50% foreign. European and Industry funds are classified as 100% foreign. Mixed funds and Generation funds are classified as 10%, two-thirds or 50% domestic. In the brochure, fixed income funds are sorted as 100% domestic or foreign or a mixture thereof. In the latter case, funds are classified as 50% domestic and 50% foreign.[10] The investment opportunity set using these criteria consists of 16.5% purely domestic funds, 70.8% purely foreign, whereas 12.7% of the funds contain a mixture of domestic and foreign assets. When funds containing both domestic and foreign assets proportionally are categorized as domestic or foreign, the opportunity set consists of 24% domestic and 76% foreign assets. Although the mutual funds with foreign assets clearly dominate the domestic-oriented funds, the Swedish market is still overrepresented relative to the corresponding country weight in the world market portfolio. Thus, the investment opportunity set is skewed toward a relatively high proportion of domestic investments.

2.3 *Data*

The data come from the first round of the new Swedish pension system, involving the investment choices of 4.4 million individuals in 2000.[11] For a sample of 15,651 individuals, the investment choices are linked to very detailed demographic and socioeconomic data collected by Statistics Sweden for the year 2000.[12] For each individual, the data set contains information on how much money, which funds and how many funds the individual have invested in. Also, the age, gender, country of birth, education, occupation, disposable income and net wealth for the same individual are included.[13] From the 15,651 individuals in the data set, 10,375 individuals (66.3%) made an active investment decision. For these individuals, the exact allocations of domestic and foreign assets in their portfolios are calculated. The remaining 5276 individuals (33.7%) did not make an active investment decision, and are assigned to the default alternative.

Apart from individuals' initial choices in 2000, the data set also contains information on the dynamics of the individual portfolios over the 4-year period, from the initiation of the new pension plan in 2000, through 2004. Hence, details of if and when each individual rebalances his/her

Table 1. Summary sample statistics for the mutual funds.

Category 1	Category 2	Category 3	Number of funds	Number of chosen funds	Allocated money	Mean domestic share	Mean fee (%)
Equity	Sweden	Sweden (normal)	28	4569	4,800,123,432	1	0.92
		Sweden small cap	6	561	506,386,580	1	1.16
		Sweden index	7	1063	1,105,700,786	1	0.41
	Regional	Swedish equity and foreign equity	11	3165	4,100,383,409	0.5455	0.74
		Nordic countries	12	564	507,253,768	0.5	1.27
		Europe	36	1735	1,606,165,272	0	1.11
		Euroland	8	312	319,545,930	0	0.99
		Europe small cap	9	418	301,211,933	0	1.23
		Europe index	7	383	392,557,592	0	0.48
		North America and USA	26	1225	1,121,788,615	0	1.05
		Asia and Far East	18	374	309,412,169	0	1.19
		Global	32	3731	4,031,305,960	0	1.01
		New markets	21	478	377,384,821	0	1.56
	Countries	Japan	20	442	346,927,964	0	1.06
		UK	6	23	23,448,653	0	1.21
		Other countries	19	399	324,268,144	0	1.25
	Industry	IT and Communication	19	2260	1,975,405,143	0	1.15
		Pharmaceutical	7	3372	3,036,806,146	0	1.36
		Other industries	16	2764	2,486,159,364	0.125	1.17
Mixture	Mixture	Swedish equity and fixed income	3	15	24,225,414	1	1.08
		Swedish equity, Swedish and foreign fixed income	28	1932	2,269,518,659	0.6577	0.74
		Foreign equity and fixed income	22	569	661,769,730	0	0.93
Generation	Generation	Pension in less than 10 years	5	638	907,300,443	0.2	0.46
		Pension in less than 20 years	6	971	1,644,690,232	0	0.46
		Pension in more than 20 years	21	2423	4,720,791,537	0.0714	0.46
Fixed income	Fixed income	Sweden, short maturity	15	242	229,219,643	1	0.46
		Sweden, long maturity	15	457	459,515,496	1	0.45
		Europe and Euroland	18	26	16,844,014	0	0.70
		Others	15	93	71,885,873	0.0333	0.79
Default			1	5276	17,160,328,449	Unknown	Unknown
All funds			457	40,480	55,838,325,171	0.2399	0.85

portfolio are also included. Moreover, the monthly returns, after transaction costs (annual fees), are reported for each investor's portfolio. In the analysis of individual portfolio performance, monthly returns on various market indices are obtained from Morningstar and Ecowin.

3. Modeling of individuals' activity, portfolio churning and performance

In order to investigate whether individuals' home bias affect their portfolio performance, and the likelihood of them rebalancing their portfolios, the measures of performance and rebalancing frequency are related to the share of domestic holdings together with a set of exogenous explanatory variables, including individuals' demographic and socioeconomic characteristics. However, it is important to take into account the sample selection issue arising from having 'passive' individuals in the sample, the ones not making an active choice or with preference for the default alternative. To simply ignore the 'passive' individuals would induce a selection bias if their characteristics prove to be different from those of the 'active' individuals. Hence, it is necessary to jointly model individuals' performance, rebalancing frequency and the likelihood of making an active choice. This is accomplished by using the two-step procedure according to Heckman (1979), where first a probit model is used to estimate the likelihood of making an active choice, and second, a regression analysis is performed to model individuals' performance and rebalancing frequency, taking the likelihood of activity into account.

3.1 *Individuals' activity choice*

First, consider individuals' activity choice. Let z be a nominal variable with two outcomes: $z = 1$ if the individual chooses to make an active investment decision and $z = 0$ if he/she chooses to be passive. Define $\Pr(z = 1)$ and $\Pr(z = 0)$ as the individuals' probability of making an active or passive choice, respectively. For each individual k, the choice of activity is modeled as

$$z_k = \boldsymbol{\gamma}' \mathbf{w}_k + \xi_k \tag{1}$$

where $\mathbf{w}_k$ is a vector of explanatory variables for the activity choice of individual k, $\boldsymbol{\gamma}$ is a vector of coefficients measuring the effect of each explanatory variable on the activity choice and ξ_k is a residual term. The coefficients in Equation (1) are estimated using the maximum likelihood probit estimation technique. Accordingly, $\Pr(z_k = 1) = \Phi(\boldsymbol{\gamma}' \mathbf{w}_k)$ and $\Pr(z_k = 0) = 1 - \Phi(\boldsymbol{\gamma}' \mathbf{w}_k)$, where $\Phi(\cdot)$ denotes the standard normal cumulative distribution function.

In the estimation of individual activity in Equation (1), explanatory variables are included in the vector $\mathbf{w}_k$ based on previous results.[14] The activity choice is related to the level of investor sophistication (Grinblatt and Keloharju 2001; Karlsson and Nordén 2007), represented by four sets of variables: (i) level of education, less than high school, high school or more than high school education, including dummy explanatory variables for less and more than high school education, (EDU_1 and EDU_3, respectively); (ii) the amount of money invested in the pension system (MONEY); (iii) the disposable income (INCOME) and (iv) net wealth (WEALTH). Related to the investor sophistication issue are individuals' total portfolios of financial holdings, apart from the investment in the defined contribution pension fund system. An individual is regarded as more sophisticated if he/she has prior experience with risky assets like stocks and mutual funds. Thus, the dummy variable EXP which equals one if an individual owns stocks or mutual funds prior to the pension investment, and zero otherwise, is included in the analysis.

Other explanatory variables in the probit model for activity are controls for individual employment, dummy variables for private employment (OCC_2), self-employment (OCC_3) and unemployment (OCC_4), to separate from the base case individuals who are government employees; gender and marital status, a dummy variable equal to one if the individual is a man (MALE), a dummy variable equal to one if the individual is married (MARRIED), and a dummy variable equal to one if the individual has children (KIDS); individual age (AGE) and whether the individual is an immigrant (IMM = 1).

3.2 *Individuals' portfolio churning*

The individual rebalancing frequency variable $CHANGE_k$ is related to a set of explanatory variables using ordinary least squares regression analysis of the individuals with an active choice only. To take the activity choice into account, a conditional regression analysis is performed with the dependent variable CHANGE$_k|z_k = 1$. Conditioning on the explanatory variables for individuals' rebalancing occurrence, and using the second step in Heckman's (1979) estimation procedure, the regression is formulated as

$$\text{CHANGE}_k = \boldsymbol{\beta}'\mathbf{x}_k + \beta_\lambda \lambda_k(\hat{\boldsymbol{\gamma}}'\mathbf{w}) + \eta_k \tag{2}$$

where $\mathbf{x}_k$ is a vector of explanatory variables, $\boldsymbol{\beta}$ is a vector of regression coefficients and η_k is a residual term. The function $\lambda_k(\hat{\boldsymbol{\gamma}}'\mathbf{w}) = \phi(\hat{\boldsymbol{\gamma}}'\mathbf{w})/\Phi(\hat{\boldsymbol{\gamma}}'\mathbf{w})$ is known as the inverse Mills ratio for the normal distribution from the probit estimation of Equation (1). Heckman (1979) motivates the inclusion of $\lambda_k(\hat{\boldsymbol{\gamma}}'\mathbf{w})$ as an explanatory variable in Equation (2). Given that only individuals who have made an active choice ($z_k = 1$) are used in the regression Equation (2), the regression coefficients in $\boldsymbol{\beta}$ can be consistently estimated without incurring a selection bias.

The vector $\mathbf{x}_k$ includes individuals' demographic and socioeconomic characteristics from the first-stage probit model in Equation (1).[15] Most importantly, the share of domestic holdings (SHARE) is included in order to test whether individual home bias affects portfolio churning. Since the degree of home bias is hypothesized to depend on the individual characteristics in $\mathbf{x}_k$, the variable SHARE clearly is of endogenous nature. Hence, the regression in Equation (2) is estimated using the two-stage least squares technique, treating SHARE as an endogenous variable. Included is also a dummy variable which equals one if the historical average return for the individual's chosen portfolio, obtained from the information folder, belongs to the top decile (RETCHASE). This variable is intended to capture the effect from individuals' return-chasing behavior on portfolio churning, which is expected to be positive. For control purposes, the number of funds chosen by each individual investor is used. Accordingly, the set of explanatory variables in Equation (2) contains dummy variables reflecting the number of funds chosen (FUND_1 to FUND_4), with the base case equal to five mutual funds in the individual's portfolio.

3.3 *Individuals' performance*

Individual performance PERF$_k$ is measured using both Jensen's alpha (risk-adjusted return) and excess return over the risk-free rate of interest (return not adjusted for risk). Each performance measure is related to a set of explanatory variables, and the inverse Mills ratio, according to

$$\text{PERF}_k = \boldsymbol{\delta}'\mathbf{v}_k + \delta_\lambda \lambda_k(\hat{\boldsymbol{\gamma}}'\mathbf{w}) + \varepsilon_k \tag{3}$$

where $\mathbf{v}_k$ is a vector of explanatory variables, $\boldsymbol{\delta}$ is a vector of regression coefficients and ε_k is a residual term. Following Heckman (1979), the inclusion of the inverse Mills ratio as an explanatory variable in Equation (3) enables a consistent estimation of the coefficients in $\boldsymbol{\delta}$. The vector $\mathbf{v}_k$ contains the same explanatory variables as $\mathbf{x}_k$ in Equation (2), plus the rebalancing frequency variable CHANGE. The regression in Equation (3) is estimated using the two-stage least squares technique, where the variables SHARE and CHANGE are treated as endogenous variables in the investigation of whether home bias and portfolio churning affect performance.

As the first performance measure, Jensen's alpha is computed for each individual portfolio using monthly returns over the 4-year period from the initiation of the new pension plan in 2000, through 2004. Each individual's alpha is estimated in the following regression model:

$$\text{RETURN}_{k,t} = \text{ALPHA}_k + \sum_{s=1}^{S} \text{BETA}_{k,s}(I_{s,t} - r_{f,t}) + e_{k,t} \tag{4}$$

where $\text{RETURN}_{k,t} = r_{k,t} - r_{f,t}$, $r_{k,t}$ is the portfolio return (less the mutual fund fees) for individual k in month t, $r_{f,t}$ is the risk-free rate of return in month t, ALPHA_k is Jensen's alpha for individual k, $I_{s,t}$ is the return on index s in month t, $\text{BETA}_{k,s}$ is the sensitivity of individual k portfolio return to index s and $e_{k,t}$ is the corresponding residual return for individual k in month t.

Jensen's alpha measures the return an individual earns in excess of what he/she would have earned if he/she held a portfolio with broad market indices with the same risk.[16] The results from Karlsson and Nordén (2006) are used to specify the appropriate indices in Equation (4), representing market factors generating the mutual fund portfolio returns that are contained in the individual accounts. Accordingly, for all individuals alike, a six-index model is used to calculate individual alphas, with the MSCI World index, the MSCI Japan index, the MSCI Far East (excluding Japan), the Serfiex DEMI Euro Zone T-bill index, Handelsbanken Swedish 5–10 Years Government Bond index and the Merrill Lynch Euro High Yield index. Monthly returns on the Swedish 1-month Treasury bill rate are used as a proxy for the risk-free interest rate.

The second measure of individual performance is the monthly excess portfolio return $\text{RETURN}_{k,t}$, i.e. the left-hand-side variable in Equation (4). The analysis of portfolio returns, not adjusted for risk, allows for a comparison of the effects of individual home bias on both alpha and excess return. Individuals' home bias is hypothesized to negatively affect portfolio performance. This hypothesis is expected to hold since home-biased individuals do not fully utilize the benefits from international diversification, leading to higher portfolio risk, and lower risk-adjusted returns. By analyzing portfolio returns, not adjusted for risk, it is also investigated whether individuals with home bias achieve lower returns per se than people with a larger share of international assets in their portfolios. In addition, portfolio churning is expected to reduce performance. Barber and Odean (2000, 2001) conclude that investor overconfidence is manifested in an excess portfolio rebalancing, which ultimately leads to lower returns.

3.4 Portfolio churning: overconfidence or skill?

Individual overconfidence OVERCON_k is measured using a dummy variable, which is equal to 1 if the individual is in both the highest portfolio rebalancing quintile and the lowest performance (alpha) quintile. The overconfidence measure is related to the same set of explanatory variables, including the inverse Mills ratio, as the measure of portfolio churning in Equation (2):

$$\text{OVERCON}_k = \varphi' x_k + \phi_\lambda \lambda_k(\hat{\gamma}' w) + \zeta_k \tag{5}$$

where x_k is a vector of explanatory variables, φ is a vector of regression coefficients and ζ_k is a residual term. The model can be used to investigate whether overconfident individuals are more home-biased and/or more prone to return-chasing behavior than other people, by analyzing the coefficients associated with the explanatory variables SHARE and RETCHASE in Equation (5). In addition, by including the gender dummy variable MALE in the regression, an explicit test of whether men are more overconfident than women can be carried out.

Similarly, an individual's skill $SKILL_k$ is represented by a dummy variable, which is equal to 1 if the individual is in the highest portfolio rebalancing quintile and at the same time in the highest performance (alpha) quintile. This particular definition of individual skill is made in order to provide a benchmark against overconfidence. The overconfidence measure, adopted from Odean (1999), includes individuals who rebalance their portfolio often with a bad performance. Hence, as defined in this study, the skilled individuals are also rebalancing frequently, but with good performance results. As for the overconfidence variable, individual skill is regressed on the vector of explanatory variables $\mathbf{x}_k$, and the inverse Mills ratio

$$SKILL_k = \boldsymbol{\theta}'\mathbf{x}_k + \theta_\lambda \lambda_k(\hat{\boldsymbol{\gamma}}'\mathbf{w}) + \varsigma_k \qquad (6)$$

where $\boldsymbol{\theta}$ is a vector of regression coefficients and ς_k is a residual term.

By comparing the coefficients associated with the variable SHARE from the regressions in Equations (5) and (6), it is analyzed whether home bias, or international investment, is a driver of overconfidence or skill. Moreover, the inclusion of the variable RETCHASE in both equations enables a test of whether return-chasing behavior relates to overconfidence or skill. Finally, the gender issue, i.e. if men are more skilled and/or overconfident than women, is directly investigated by estimating the corresponding coefficients for the gender dummy variable MALE.

4. Empirical results

4.1 *Descriptive statistics*

Table 2 displays average values for the quantitative variables in the analysis, organized according to level of domestic share, portfolio churning, performance and the default alternative. In the first five rows of Table 2, the variable averages are displayed with respect to five different levels of the share of domestic holdings (SHARE). Noteworthy is that individual performance, as measured by Jensen's alpha (ALPHA) and excess return not adjusted for risk (RETURN), is on average increasing in the share of domestic holdings, whereas portfolio risk, measured as standard deviation of excess returns (STDEV), is virtually identical for the different categories of SHARE, indicating that home bias appear not to hurt individuals' performance. Also, relatively home-biased individuals appear to have a tendency for not rebalancing their portfolios, as the variable CHANGE is decreasing in share of domestic holdings. Moreover, the variables INCOME and MONEY are decreasing in SHARE, consistent with the story from Karlsson and Nordén (2007) that home bias is driven by investor sophistication. The variable FEE is also decreasing in SHARE, indicating that portfolios with a larger proportion of international assets are more costly.

In rows six through eight of Table 2, the variable averages are displayed with respect to three different categories of portfolio rebalancing (NOCHANGE, no churning; 1CHANGE, the portfolio is churned once only; MCHANGE, churning on multiple occasions). On average, risk-adjusted performance (ALPHA), and share of domestic holdings (SHARE), is lower when individuals' portfolios are more frequently rebalanced. In addition, people who rebalance relatively often do, on average, choose more costly mutual funds, as the variable FEE is increasing in the rebalancing frequency. Note, however, that the transaction costs are annual mutual fund fees, and not associated with portfolio churning.

Rows 9–11 display the variable averages according to three different levels of risk-adjusted performance (ALPHA). Accordingly, the share of domestic holdings (SHARE) is increasing in performance, which indicates that home bias on average indeed is not hurting individuals' risk-adjusted returns. However, one need to keep in mind that the average values in Table 2 are

Table 2. Summary statistics, average values.

	N	ALPHA	RETURN	STDEV	CHANGE	SHARE	AGE	INCOME	WEALTH	MONEY	FEE
SHARE < 0.2	3073	−0.0069	−0.0125	0.1959	0.5975	0.0614	43.32	382,061	526,928	13,789	0.8025
0.2 ≤ SHARE < 0.4	3119	−0.0061	−0.0127	0.2058	0.5614	0.2945	41.19	369,665	392,106	14,298	0.8226
0.4 ≤ SHARE < 0.6	2725	−0.0038	−0.0110	0.2040	0.4510	0.4904	42.64	349,030	403,965	13,283	0.6947
0.6 ≤ SHARE < 0.8	984	−0.0015	−0.0088	0.1923	0.3760	0.6711	45.05	346,909	368,031	13,199	0.6383
SHARE ≥ 0.8	474	0.0016	−0.0065	0.2051	0.2553	0.9383	47.51	351,056	510,066	10,736	0.6252
NOCHANGE	7390	−0.0046	−0.0115	0.2021	0.0000	0.3517	43.10	360,381	431,165	13,362	0.7245
1CHANGE	1975	−0.0055	−0.0119	0.1960	1.0000	0.3421	42.18	371,998	471,843	14,040	0.7945
MCHANGE	1010	−0.0061	−0.0116	0.2036	3.2990	0.2714	42.39	384,168	424,505	14,622	0.9170
ALPHA < −0.002	6987	−0.0071	−0.0138	0.2095	0.5205	0.2721	41.94	366,449	452,728	13,882	0.8209
−0.002 ≤ ALPHA < 0.002	2828	−0.0014	−0.0077	0.1756	0.3536	0.4642	44.90	359,434	364,265	13,190	0.5827
ALPHA ≥ 0.002	560	0.0041	−0.0030	0.2240	1.1964	0.5980	45.76	373,326	631,423	12,401	0.8310
Default	5276	−0.0021	−0.0079	0.1625	–	–	43.37	326,432	444,108	11,373	0.4800
All	15,651	−0.0040	−0.0103	0.1881	0.3930	0.3421	43.03	364,131	455,608	12,858	0.7579

Note: This table presents average sample values for the variables: ALPHA, Jensen's alpha as measure of individual portfolio performance over the sample period; RETURN, the average monthly excess return (portfolio return less the Swedish 1-month Treasury bill rate) over the sample period; STDEV, annualized standard deviation of the monthly excess returns over the sample period; CHANGE, individual rebalancing frequency (churning); SHARE, the individual domestic share of invested pension funds; AGE, in years of the individual; INCOME, individual's disposable income in SEK; WEALTH, market value in SEK of financial assets and real estate holdings, net of debt for each individual; MONEY, amount in SEK of the total initial investments in pension funds for each individual; FEE, percentage transaction cost (fee) for the individual investments. Average sample values are presented with respect to five groups based on the level of SHARE, three groups based on whether individuals have churned their portfolios or not; NOCHANGE, no churning; 1CHANGE, portfolio is churned once; MCHANGE, portfolio is churned more than once. The row labeled 'All' contains overall averages for all individuals, whereas 'Default' represents individuals who ended up in the default alternative. N, the number of individuals in each row-wise group.

calculated without considering the endogenous nature of home bias, churning and performance, with respect to a common set of exogenous explanatory variables.

Table 3 displays the categorical variables with respect to the domestic share levels, categories of portfolio rebalancing, performance levels and the default alternative. From the proportion values alone, it is difficult to discern distinct patterns for the main variables of interest, portfolio churning (CHANGE) and performance measured as ALPHA. Nevertheless, a larger share of the highly educated (EDU_3) and experienced (EXP) individuals tends to rebalance their portfolio relative the corresponding share among less educated (EDU_1 and EDU_2) and inexperienced people. Moreover, risk-adjusted performance appears to be related to gender, as the proportion of men is larger in the group of high-performing individuals relative to the other groups with average- and low-performers.

4.2 *Activity choice results*

Table 4 presents the results from the estimation of the first-stage probit model for activity choice according to Equation (1). Specification (1) contains all explanatory variables motivated by previous research, whereas specification (2) excludes the explanatory variables with insignificant coefficients at the 10% level. Variables are excluded sequentially, one at the time, starting with the highest associated p-value (INCOME) in specification (1). Since the purpose of the probit regression model is to provide the first stage in the two-stage procedure according to Heckman (1979), in order to avoid a selection bias in the second-stage estimations, the results from specification (2), the most parsimonious specification, are retained. As can be seen in Table 4, the two specifications produce virtually identical estimated values, and significance levels, for the retained coefficients.[17]

The activity choice is significantly related to a number of individual characteristics. In line with the results from Engström and Westerberg (2003) and Karlsson and Nordén (2007), individuals are significantly more likely to make an active choice the younger they are, if their gender is female, the more money they put into the pension system, if they have previous experience with risky assets, if they are not self- or unemployed, if they have not less than high-school education, if they are married, if they have no children and if they are not immigrants.[18] On the whole, the activity results are consistent with the idea that more-sophisticated individuals are more likely to make an active investment decision in their pension accounts.

4.3 *Portfolio churning results*

Table 5 contains the results from the estimation of the second-stage estimation of the regression model for individuals' portfolio churning (CHANGE) according to Equation (2). In the estimation, a set of exogenous variables is used as instruments for the share of domestic holdings (SHARE). The instruments are chosen in accordance with Karlsson and Nordén (2007), including the inverse Mills ratio (LAMBDA) from the first-stage probit model estimation for CHOICE. Specification (1) contains the full set of explanatory variables $\mathbf{x}_k$, whereas specification (2) is a parsimonious version excluding the insignificant explanatory variables. The estimation results show a significantly negative relationship between the portfolio rebalancing frequency and (the instrument for) SHARE. Hence, after controlling for the exogenous variables, and taking a potential selection bias from the activity choice into account, home-biased individuals, with a high domestic share, are less likely to rebalance their portfolios than individuals with a larger share of international assets. This result is consistent with the competence effect, stipulated by Graham, Harvey and

Table 3. Summary statistics, proportion of individuals.

	N%	MALE	OCC_1	OCC_2	OCC_3	OCC_4	EDU_1	EDU_2	EDU_3	EXP	IMM
SHARE < 0.2	0.1963	0.5181	0.2769	0.5988	0.0446	0.0797	0.1523	0.5142	0.3336	0.6736	0.0888
0.2 ≤ SHARE < 0.4	0.1993	0.4941	0.3046	0.5909	0.0349	0.0696	0.1282	0.5220	0.3498	0.7002	0.0786
0.4 ≤ SHARE < 0.6	0.1741	0.4815	0.3160	0.5589	0.0433	0.0818	0.1747	0.5361	0.2892	0.6437	0.1017
0.6 ≤ SHARE < 0.8	0.0629	0.5122	0.3028	0.5884	0.0254	0.0833	0.2195	0.5213	0.2591	0.5691	0.1189
SHARE ≥ 0.8	0.0303	0.5401	0.2722	0.5274	0.0464	0.1540	0.2068	0.4958	0.2975	0.6160	0.1013
NOCHANGE	0.4722	0.5047	0.2930	0.5817	0.0402	0.0851	0.1774	0.5303	0.2923	0.6529	0.0950
1CHANGE	0.1262	0.4744	0.3078	0.5732	0.0425	0.0765	0.1296	0.5099	0.3605	0.6537	0.0835
MCHANGE	0.0645	0.5327	0.3129	0.5980	0.0297	0.0594	0.0901	0.4861	0.4238	0.7366	0.0921
ALPHA < −0.002	0.4464	0.4938	0.3011	0.5798	0.0421	0.0770	0.1401	0.5287	0.3312	0.6884	0.0837
−0.002 ≤ ALPHA < 0.002	0.1807	0.4961	0.3016	0.5873	0.0276	0.0835	0.1994	0.5145	0.2861	0.5951	0.1057
ALPHA ≥ 0.002	0.0358	0.6286	0.2357	0.5768	0.0696	0.1179	0.2054	0.4786	0.3161	0.6554	0.1357
Default	0.3371	0.5237	0.2640	0.5119	0.0633	0.1600	0.2233	0.4956	0.2811	0.5017	0.1785
All	1.0000	0.5091	0.2866	0.5582	0.0476	0.1076	0.1812	0.5132	0.3056	0.6074	0.1215

Note: This table displays the proportion of individuals according to each column-wise characteristic, with respect to the row-wise groups: five groups based on the degree of home bias (SHARE), three groups based on whether individuals have churned their portfolios or not; NOCHANGE, no churning; 1CHANGE, portfolio is churned once; MCHANGE, portfolio is churned more than once. The row labeled 'All' contains overall averages for all individuals, whereas 'Default' represents individuals who ended up in the default alternative. $N\%$, the proportion of individuals in each row-wise group; MALE, dummy variable equal to 1 if the individual is male; OCC_1, dummy variable equal to 1 if the individual is employed by the government; OCC_2, dummy variable equal to 1 if the individual is employed in the private sector; OCC_3, dummy variable equal to 1 if the individual is self-employed; OCC_4, dummy variable equal to 1 if the individual is unemployed or not registered; EDU_1, dummy variable equal to 1 if the education level of the individual is below high school; EDU_2, dummy variable equal to 1 if the education level is high school; EDU_3, dummy variable equal to 1 if the education level is above high school; EXP, dummy variable equal to 1 if the individual has other risky holdings; IMM, dummy variable equal to 1 if the individual is an immigrant.

Table 4. Estimation results from the probit regression model of active choice.

	(1)		(2)	
	Coefficient	p-Value	Coefficient	p-Value
CONSTANT	0.0594	0.3028	0.0865	0.1037
AGE	$-3.81e-3$	0.0005	$-4.30e-3$	0.0001
INCOME	$1.92e-8$	0.4384		
WEALTH	$-1.02e-8$	0.1715		
MALE	-0.1152	0.0000	-0.1064	0.0000
MONEY	$2.25e-5$	0.0000	$2.24e-5$	0.0000
EXP	0.3200	0.0000	0.3126	0.0000
OCC_2	0.0296	0.2754		
OCC_3	-0.1787	0.0007	-0.2030	0.0000
OCC_4	-0.2135	0.0000	-0.2318	0.0000
EDU_1	-0.1373	0.0000	-0.1180	0.0000
EDU_3	-0.0388	0.1272		
MARRIED	0.3009	0.0000	0.3053	0.0000
IMM	-0.3432	0.0000	-0.3444	0.0000
KIDS	-0.0503	0.0478	-0.0528	0.0374
N	15,651		15,651	
R^2	0.0695		0.0690	

Note: This table contains results from the first-stage probit regression model for individual active investment (CHOICE) according to Equation (1). The explanatory variables are AGE (in years), INCOME
(individual's disposable income in SEK), WEALTH (market value in SEK of financial assets and real
estate holdings, net of debt for each individual), MALE (dummy variable equal to 1 if the individual is
male), MONEY (total initial investments in pension funds for each individual in SEK), EXP (a dummy
variable equal to 1 if the individual has other risky holdings), OCC_2–OCC_4 (dummy variables for
individuals occupation, where OCC_2 represents private sector employment, OCC_3 self-employment,
OCC_4 unemployment, and the base case represents government employment), EDU_1 (a dummy variable equal to 1 if the education level of the individual is below high school), EDU_3 (a dummy variable
equal to 1 if the education level is above high school, and where the base case represents education level
below high school), MARRIED (a dummy variable equal to 1 if the individual is married) and IMM (a
dummy variable equal to 1 if the individual is an immigrant). Model (2) is a parsimonious version of Model
(1), excluding the insignificant explanatory variables in a step-wise fashion. Each model is estimated using
the maximum likelihood technique outlined in Berndt et al. (1974), and the heteroskedasticity-consistent
covariance matrix according to White (1980).

Huang (2009), according to which people who believe they are competent investors, trade more
often and invest more in international assets.

The rebalancing decision is significantly positively related to age, previous experience with risky
assets and the dummy variable indicating more than high-school education, as well as significantly
negatively (positively) related to the dummy variable indicating less (more) than high-school
education. These results are consistent with the idea that more-sophisticated individuals churn
their portfolios more often than less-sophisticated individuals. Some evidence is also found (at
least at the 5% significance level) that men are rebalancing their portfolios more often than women.
This gender result goes well in hand with previous evidence in, e.g. Barber and Odean (2000,
2001). In addition, the dummy variables for the initial number of chosen funds – one, two or
three – are significantly different from zero, indicating that people who choose four or five mutual
funds tend to rebalance their portfolios more often than those with fewer funds. The LAMBDA
coefficient is significantly positive at the 5% level in specification (1), and at the 1% level in

Table 5. Estimation results from the regression model of portfolio churning.

	(1)		(2)	
	Coefficient	p-Value	Coefficient	p-Value
CONSTANT	1.0161	0.0000	1.0512	0.0000
AGE	5.99e − 3	0.0000	6.00e − 3	0.0116
INCOME	1.30e − 8	0.5183		
WEALTH	−2.20e − 8	0.0342	−2.01e − 8	0.0398
MALE	0.0460	0.0944	0.0519	0.0388
MONEY	1.70e − 6	0.5456		
EXP	0.0738	0.0335	0.0629	0.0384
EDU_1	−0.0877	0.0151	−0.0834	0.0183
EDU_3	0.0878	0.0031	0.0906	0.0021
FUND_1	−0.6046	0.0000	−0.5907	0.0000
FUND_2	−0.1655	0.0002	−0.1578	0.0000
FUND_3	−0.1382	0.0002	−0.1283	0.0000
FUND_4	−0.0282	0.4690		
SHARE	−2.5628	0.0000	−2.5224	0.0000
RETCHASE	−0.0464	0.3617		
LAMBDA	0.3173	0.0133	0.2432	0.0099
N	10,375		10,375	
R^2	0.0351		0.0329	

Note: This table contains results from the second stage in the Heckman style estimation procedure, of the regression model for portfolio churning (CHANGE) according to Equation (2). The explanatory variables are AGE (in years), INCOME (individual's disposable income in SEK), WEALTH (market value in SEK of financial assets and real estate holdings, net of debt for each individual), MALE (dummy variable equal to 1 if the individual is male), MONEY (total initial investments in pension funds for each individual in SEK), EXP (a dummy variable equal to 1 if the individual has other risky holdings), EDU_1 (a dummy variable equal to 1 if the education level of the individual is below high school), EDU_3 (a dummy variable equal to 1 if the education level is above high school, and where the base case represents education level below high school), FUND_1–FUND_4 (dummy variables reflecting the number of mutual funds the individual has invested in, one–four, where the base case is an investment in five funds), SHARE (the instrument for the share of domestic holdings in the individual's portfolio) and RETCHASE (a dummy variable equal to one if the individual is in the highest historical portfolio return decile). LAMBDA is the inverse Mills ratio from the estimation of the first-stage probit model for CHOICE. Model (2) is a parsimonious version of Model (1), excluding the insignificant explanatory variables in a step-wise fashion. Each model is estimated using the maximum likelihood technique outlined in Berndt et al. (1974), and the heteroskedasticity-consistent covariance matrix according to White (1980). The variable SHARE is treated as endogenous in the estimations.

specification (2), which illustrates the importance of using the Heckman approach to account for a potential selection bias.

4.4 *Portfolio performance results*

Table 6 contains the results from the second-stage regression model according to Equation (3), where portfolio performance (ALPHA) is related to instruments for SHARE and CHOICE, the exogenous variables and the inverse Mills ratio LAMBDA. Specification (1) is estimated using all explanatory variables in the vector $\mathbf{v}_k$, whereas specification (2) excludes the insignificant variables INCOME, WEALTH, MALE and EXP. The coefficient for SHARE is significantly negative, which indicates that performance is significantly lower for home-biased individuals.

Table 6. Estimation results from the regression model of performance (Alpha).

	(1)		(2)	
	Coefficient	p-Value	Coefficient	p-Value
CONSTANT	$2.26e-3$	0.1371	$1.11e-3$	0.4039
AGE	$4.22e-5$	0.0002	$3.79e-5$	0.0000
INCOME	$-6.22e-12$	0.9683		
WEALTH	$-5.98e-11$	0.5668		
MALE	$7.77e-5$	0.6961		
MONEY	$3.12e-8$	0.1324	$4.37e-8$	0.0085
EXP	$-3.39e-4$	0.2009		
EDU_1	$-6.35e-4$	0.0226	$-6.54e-4$	0.0145
EDU_3	$1.01e-3$	0.0000	$9.40e-4$	0.0000
FUND_1	$-3.18e-3$	0.0000	$-2.99e-3$	0.0000
FUND_2	$-1.48e-3$	0.0007	$-1.43e-3$	0.0007
FUND_3	$-1.55e-3$	0.0000	$-1.50e-3$	0.0000
FUND_4	$-8.49e-4$	0.0034	$-8.30e-4$	0.0030
SHARE	$-5.65e-3$	0.0095	$-4.70e-3$	0.0250
CHANGE	-0.0184	0.0000	-0.0177	0.0000
RETCHASE	$-3.97e-3$	0.0000	$-3.93e-3$	0.0000
LAMBDA	$1.42e-3$	0.1364	$2.21e-3$	0.0010
N	10,375		10,375	
R^2	0.2736		0.2729	

Note: This table contains results from the second stage in the Heckman style estimation procedure, of the regression model for portfolio performance according to Equation (3), with Jensen's alpha (ALPHA) as a measure of performance. The explanatory variables are AGE (in years), INCOME (individual's disposable income in SEK), WEALTH (market value in SEK of financial assets and real estate holdings, net of debt for each individual), MALE (dummy variable equal to 1 if the individual is male), MONEY (total initial investments in pension funds for each individual in SEK), EXP (a dummy variable equal to 1 if the individual has other risky holdings), EDU_1 (a dummy variable equal to 1 if the education level of the individual is below high school), EDU_3 (a dummy variable equal to 1 if the education level is above high school and where the base case represents education level below high school), FUND_1–FUND_4 (dummy variables reflecting the number of mutual funds the individual has invested in, one–four, where the base case is an investment in five funds), SHARE (the instrument for the share of domestic holdings in the individual's portfolio), CHANGE (the instrument for portfolio churning) and RETCHASE (a dummy variable equal to one if the individual is in the highest historical portfolio return decile). LAMBDA is the inverse Mills ratio from the estimation of the first-stage probit model for CHOICE. Model (2) is a parsimonious version of Model (1), excluding the insignificant explanatory variables in a step-wise fashion. Each model is estimated using the maximum likelihood technique outlined in Berndt et al. (1974), and the heteroskedasticity-consistent covariance matrix according to White (1980). The variables SHARE and CHANGE are treated as endogenous in the estimations.

The significantly negative relationship between risk-adjusted performance and home bias highlights the potential costs for individuals not pursuing international diversification. This negative relationship is not observed in Table 2, where average ALPHA appears to be an increasing function of SHARE, but only after the interrelations between SHARE, CHANGE and the exogenous individual characteristics are taken into consideration.

The coefficient for CHANGE is significantly negative. Consistent with previous studies, e.g. Odean (1999) and Barber and Odean (2000, 2001), and in accordance with expectations, portfolio churning deteriorates performance. In addition, the coefficient for RETCHASE is significantly negative, which implies that return-chasing individuals perform significantly worse than other individuals. Performance is also significantly positively related to individual age and to the amount of money the individual puts into the portfolio (at least in the more parsimonious specification), whereas individuals with less (more) than high-school education have significantly lower (higher) performance, at the 5% (1%) significance level, than the high-school-educated individuals. These results are consistent with the idea that more-sophisticated individuals show better risk-adjusted performance than less-sophisticated people. Moreover, performance is significantly lower in individuals' portfolios with less than five funds, rather than the maximum amount of five funds, which is consistent with that diversification matters for performance.

To further examine the effects of individuals' home bias and churning on portfolio performance, the results from the regression of excess return (RETURN), not adjusted for risk, are presented in Table 7. Specification (1) includes all explanatory variables in the vector $\mathbf{v}_k$, whereas specification (2) excludes the variables INCOME, WEALTH and MALE, which are not significantly different from zero at the 10% level. One major contrast between the results from Tables 6 and 7 has been

Table 7. Estimation results from the regression model of performance (excess return).

	(1)		(2)	
	Coefficient	p-Value	Coefficient	p-Value
CONSTANT	-0.0114	0.0000	-0.0116	0.0000
AGE	$6.63e-5$	0.0000	$6.32e-5$	0.0000
INCOME	$3.17e-11$	0.7849		
WEALTH	$-1.07e-11$	0.1940		
MALE	$7.65e-6$	0.9640		
MONEY	$3.97e-8$	0.0244	$3.91e-8$	0.0116
EXP	$-5.51e-4$	0.0141	$-5.94e-4$	0.0047
EDU_1	$-6.17e-4$	0.0103	$-5.87e-4$	0.0129
EDU_3	$8.86e-4$	0.0000	$8.47e-4$	0.0000
FUND_1	$-1.25e-3$	0.0521	$-1.12e-3$	0.0800
FUND_2	$-1.55e-3$	0.0001	$-1.52e-3$	0.0001
FUND_3	$-1.38e-3$	0.0000	$-1.35e-3$	0.0000
FUND_4	$-9.93e-4$	0.0001	$-9.85e-4$	0.0001
SHARE	$5.41e-3$	0.0200	$6.08e-3$	0.0090
CHANGE	-0.0144	0.0000	-0.0139	0.0000
RETCHASE	$-5.70e-3$	0.0000	$-5.67e-3$	0.0000
LAMBDA	$8.38e-4$	0.3103	$7.57e-4$	0.3230
N	10,375		10,375	
R^2	0.2883		0.2873	

Note: This table contains results from the second stage in the Heckman style estimation procedure, of the regression model for portfolio performance according to Equation (3), with excess return (RETURN) as a measure of performance. The explanatory variables are AGE (in years), INCOME (individual's disposable income in SEK), WEALTH (market value in SEK of financial assets and real estate holdings, net of debt for each individual), MALE (dummy variable equal to 1 if the individual is male), MONEY (total initial investments in pension funds for each individual in SEK), EXP (a dummy variable equal to 1 if the individual has other risky holdings), EDU_1 (a dummy variable equal to 1 if the education level of the individual is below high school), EDU_3 (a dummy variable equal to 1 if the education level is above high school, and where the base case represents education level below high school), FUND_1–FUND_4 (dummy variables reflecting the number of mutual funds the individual has invested in, one–four, where the base case is an investment in five funds), SHARE (the share of domestic holdings in the individual's portfolio) and CHANGE (portfolio churning). LAMBDA is the inverse Mills ratio from the estimation of the first-stage probit model for CHOICE, and is included in model specification (1) and excluded in model specification (2). Each model is estimated using the maximum likelihood technique outlined in Berndt et al. (1974), and the heteroskedasticity-consistent covariance matrix according to White (1980). The variables SHARE and CHANGE are treated as endogenous in the estimations.

Table 8. Estimation results from the regression model of investor overconfidence.

	(1)		(2)	
	Coefficient	p-Value	Coefficient	p-Value
CONSTANT	0.1186	0.0000	0.1332	0.0000
AGE	$2.12e-4$	0.2488		
INCOME	$1.45e-9$	0.5923		
WEALTH	$-5.35e-10$	0.6662		
MALE	$1.55e-3$	0.6887		
MONEY	$-7.13e-7$	0.0952	$-7.40e-7$	0.0348
EXP	$1.64e-3$	0.7311		
EDU_1	$-4.94e-3$	0.2872		
EDU_3	$2.96e-3$	0.4809		
FUND_1	-0.0433	0.0000	-0.0446	0.0000
FUND_2	$2.69e-3$	0.6507		
FUND_3	0.0160	0.0053	0.0126	0.0074
FUND_4	$8.09e-3$	0.1403		
SHARE	-0.2880	0.0000	-0.2750	0.0000
RETCHASE	0.0415	0.0000	0.0425	0.0000
LAMBDA	0.0105	0.5716	$1.82e-3$	0.8902
N	10,375		10,375	
R^2	0.0334		0.0332	

Note: This table contains results from the second stage in the Heckman style estimation procedure, of the regression model for individual overconfidence (OVERCON) according to Equation (5). An individual is regarded as overconfident if he or she belongs to the lowest risk-adjusted performance (Alpha) quintile, and the highest portfolio churning quintile. The explanatory variables are AGE (in years), INCOME (individual's disposable income in SEK), WEALTH (market value in SEK of financial assets and real estate holdings, net of debt for each individual), MALE (dummy variable equal to 1 if the individual is male), MONEY (total initial investments in pension funds for each individual in SEK), EXP (a dummy variable equal to 1 if the individual has other risky holdings), EDU_1 (a dummy variable equal to 1 if the education level of the individual is below high school), EDU_3 (a dummy variable equal to 1 if the education level is above high school, and where the base case represents education level below high school), FUND_1–FUND_4 (dummy variables reflecting the number of mutual funds the individual has invested in, one through four, where the base case is an investment in five funds), SHARE (the instrument for the share of domestic holdings in the individual's portfolio) and RETCHASE (a dummy variable equal to one if the individual is in the highest historical portfolio return decile). LAMBDA is the inverse Mills ratio from the estimation of the first-stage probit model for CHOICE. Model (2) is a parsimonious version of Model (1), excluding the insignificant explanatory variables in a step-wise fashion. Each model is estimated using the maximum likelihood technique outlined in Berndt et al. (1974), and the heteroskedasticity-consistent covariance matrix according to White (1980). The variable SHARE is treated as endogenous in the estimations.

found. In Table 7, the excess return is significantly positively related to the share of domestic assets (SHARE), whereas in Table 6, the corresponding relationship between ALPHA and SHARE is significantly negative. Hence, when performance is measured as risk-adjusted return (ALPHA), home bias is bad for performance, whereas home bias actually appears to be good for performance measured as return – not adjusted for risk. The results are consistent with the fact that home-biased individuals do not fully utilize the risk-reducing benefits from international diversification, and thereby achieve significantly lower risk-adjusted performance.

Another notable difference between the results in Tables 6 and 7 is the negative significance of the coefficient for the variable EXP in the regression of excess return. Accordingly, when individual performance is measured by excess return (alpha), previous experience with risky asset holdings has a significantly (insignificantly) negative influence on performance. This result is

Table 9. Estimation results from the regression model of investor skill.

	(1)		(2)	
	Coefficient	p-Value	Coefficient	p-Value
CONSTANT	0.0388	0.0208	0.0476	0.0000
AGE	$7.46e-4$	0.0000	$7.70e-4$	0.0000
INCOME	$6.34e-10$	0.5999		
WEALTH	$-2.08e-9$	0.0522	$-1.86e-9$	0.0608
MALE	0.0129	0.0001	0.0134	0.0000
MONEY	$1.34e-7$	0.6869		
EXP	$2.50e-3$	0.5502		
EDU_1	$-6.96e-3$	0.0797	$-7.65e-3$	0.0464
EDU_3	$3.14e-3$	0.3748		
FUND_1	-0.0326	0.0000	-0.0330	0.0000
FUND_2	$4.81e-4$	0.9322		
FUND_3	-0.0107	0.0104	-0.0109	0.0007
FUND_4	$-2.71e-4$	0.9542		
SHARE	-0.1785	0.0000	-0.1822	0.0000
RETCHASE	-0.0137	0.0161	-0.0137	0.0134
LAMBDA	0.0193	0.1683	0.0117	0.2083
N	10,375		10,375	
R^2	0.0069		0.0062	

Note: This table contains results from the second stage in the Heckman style estimation procedure, of the regression model for individual skill (SKILL) according to Equation (6). An individual is regarded as skilled if he or she belongs to the highest risk-adjusted performance (Alpha) quintile, and the highest portfolio churning quintile. The explanatory variables are AGE (in years), INCOME (individual's disposable income in SEK), WEALTH (market value in SEK of financial assets and real estate holdings, net of debt for each individual), MALE (dummy variable equal to 1 if the individual is male), MONEY (total initial investments in pension funds for each individual in SEK), EXP (a dummy variable equal to 1 if the individual has other risky holdings), EDU_1 (a dummy variable equal to 1 if the education level of the individual is below high school), EDU_3 (a dummy variable equal to 1 if the education level is above high school, and where the base case represents education level below high school), FUND_1–FUND_4 (dummy variables reflecting the number of mutual funds the individual has invested in, one through four, where the base case is an investment in five funds), SHARE (the instrument for the share of domestic holdings in the individual's portfolio) and RETCHASE (a dummy variable equal to one if the individual is in the highest historical portfolio return decile). LAMBDA is the inverse Mills ratio from the estimation of the first-stage probit model for CHOICE. Model (2) is a parsimonious version of Model (1), excluding the insignificant explanatory variables in a step-wise fashion. Each model is estimated using the maximum likelihood technique outlined in Berndt et al. (1974), and the heteroskedasticity-consistent covariance matrix according to White (1980). The variable SHARE is treated as endogenous in the estimations.

rather surprising, and goes against the hypothesis that more experienced, and thereby sophisticated, individuals make relatively sound investment choices. The remaining results in Table 7 conform to those from Table 6. Thus, whether individual performance is measured by risk-adjusted or unadjusted returns, younger, lowly educated individuals – who rebalance their portfolio often, and have a tendency for chasing returns – perform significantly worse than older, highly educated individuals, who do not rebalance their portfolio or chase returns.

4.5 *Overconfidence or skill?*

In the final part of the empirical analysis, focus is on the individuals who rebalance their portfolios most often. The purpose with the analysis is to disentangle the characteristics of the skilled individuals, who rebalance their portfolios with good results, and of those who can be regarded as overconfident, i.e. they rebalance frequently with poor portfolio performance. Table 8 contains the results obtained from estimating the regression in Equation (5), where the overconfidence measure (OVERCON) is related to the same set of explanatory variables as the measure of portfolio churning (CHANGE) in Equation (2). OVERCON is a dummy variable, which is equal to one for individuals in both the highest portfolio churning quintile and the lowest risk-adjusted performance quintile. As before, specification (1) uses the full set of explanatory variables, whereas the parsimonious specification (2) excludes variables with insignificant coefficients at the 10% level in a step-wise fashion. The results show that investor overconfidence is significantly negatively related to the variable SHARE, which imply that individuals with a relatively large share of international assets are more likely to be overconfident than home-biased individuals. This result is consistent with the prediction in Bailey, Kumar and Ng (2008). Overconfidence is significantly positively related to the variable RETCHASE. Hence, confirming the notion from Bohn and Tesar (1996), return-chasing individuals are more likely to be overconfident than individuals who are not regarded as return-chasers. Interestingly, gender is not a significant determinant of overconfidence, which rebukes the evidence presented in, e.g. Barber and Odean (2001).

Table 9 presents the results from the regression of the measure of investor skill (SKILL) on the same set of explanatory variables. An individual is regarded as skilled if he or she is in both the highest portfolio churning quintile and the highest risk-adjusted performance quintile. The definition of the variable SKILL enables a direct comparison of the overconfident individuals, who churn their portfolios often with bad performance, with the skilled people, who also exhibit a frequent portfolio rebalancing, but with good results in terms of high alphas. Focussing on the results from the more parsimonious specification (2) in Table 9, the variable SHARE is a significantly negative determinant of skill. In other words, consistent with the results from the performance regression analysis in Table 6, international diversification is beneficial for generating alphas. In addition, relative to the overconfident individuals, the skilled people appear to exhibit a significantly lower propensity to chase returns, as the coefficient for the variable RETCHASE is significantly negative (at the 5% level). The characteristic skill is also highly significantly positively correlated with the MALE dummy variable.

In summary, both overconfident and skilled individuals are more inclined to invest in international assets than 'average' individual investors. However, their return-chasing behavior is quite different. Overconfident individuals appear to invest to a relatively high degree in funds with high historical returns, whereas skilled people are less inclined to do so. Moreover, gender appears to be an important determinant of skill, while men and women appear to be equally likely to be overconfident.

5. Concluding remarks

This study investigates the economic consequences of individual investors' home bias by studying the portfolios formed within the newly defined contribution pension plan in Sweden. The main purpose of the study is to analyze whether home bias affects portfolio performance. A relationship between home bias and portfolio churning is suggested, where the degree of home bias affects the likelihood of an individual to rebalance his/her portfolio, which in turn deteriorates performance. Thus, this study provides a thorough simultaneous analysis of individuals' home bias, portfolio churning and performance, while also taking their decisions to make an active investment into account. In addition, the behavior of overconfident individuals is contrasted to that of skilled individuals. Particularly, the analysis focuses on whether overconfident individuals are relatively more home-biased, and whether they are relatively more inclined to show a return-chasing behavior, than skilled people.

The examination of the interrelations between individuals' home bias, portfolio churning and performance is performed using the individual initial choices within their own pension accounts, and the same individuals' portfolio maintenance during the following 4-year period. Hence, the data contain detailed information of the share of domestic to foreign assets in the individual portfolios, when the individuals have rebalanced their portfolios, and also the monthly returns, after transaction costs, for all individual portfolios. The portfolio formation within the Swedish pension system constitutes a setting where barriers to international investments and information asymmetries are virtually non-existing, and where the investments contain no corporate control dimension. In addition, in this setting, trading for liquidity needs does not contaminate individuals' decisions to churn their portfolios. The empirical framework also allows for an endogenously determined degree of home bias, portfolio churning and performance.

The findings of this study indicate that the portfolios for individuals with a high degree of home bias show a significantly worse risk-adjusted performance than the corresponding portfolios for individuals who are relatively more heavily invested in international assets. On the other hand, home bias is not a significant determinant of actual portfolio returns, not adjusted for risk. Hence, home bias incurs a bad risk-adjusted performance due to an insufficient international diversification. The results also show that portfolio churning significantly deteriorates performance, although churning is not associated with any transaction costs, apart from fixed annual fees, which are incurred irrespective of whether a portfolio is rebalanced or not. Moreover, home-biased individuals tend not to churn their portfolios as often as individuals with a larger share of international asset holdings, which diminishes the negative effect of home bias on performance.

Overconfident individuals are found to hold a larger share of international assets and to be more inclined to a return-chasing behavior than other people. Hence, home-biased individuals are less likely to be overconfident. Instead, the results are consistent with overconfidence being driven by a desire to invest in international assets with high historical returns, which on average results in a bad performance. In contrast, skilled individuals, who exhibit high performance, appear to use international investments for the right reasons, as they are found to hold a larger share of international assets, and to have a lower tendency for return-chasing behavior. Interestingly, gender is an important determinant of skill, where men are more likely than women to rebalance their portfolios often with good performance, but not of overconfidence, since men and women are equally likely to trade often with mediocre performance.

Acknowledgements

This study has benefited from comments and suggestions from two anonymous referees, Sebastian Lobe and Anders Anderson. We have also received valuable input from seminar participants at Stockholm University, the 2008 Campus for Finance – Research Conference, and the 2007 Arne Ryde Workshop in Financial Economics.

Notes

1. See Lewis (1999) and Karolyi and Stulz (2002) for excellent overviews and summaries of the home bias literature.
2. Note that Graham, Harvey and Huang (2009) relate competence to individuals who perceive themselves as competent with respect to financial investments, which not necessarily coincides with actual competence or knowledge in the matter.
3. For example, Bailey, Kumar and Ng (2008) neglect to treat measures of home bias as endogenous variables in their analysis of whether home bias affects portfolio performance of individual investors. For this reason, their results might be driven by a bias of an unknown magnitude.

4. Previous studies of home bias at the individual level often use less general data, limited to a certain type of individual investors. For example, Bailey, Kumar and Ng (2008) use the data from Barber and Odean (2000), based on individual investors' accounts with only a single US discount broker.

5. Dahlquist et al. (2003) argue that in a country like Sweden, where controlling shareholders are economically important, a large home bias is expected on an aggregate level.

6. Sundén (2006) provides a more detailed description of the Swedish pension system.

7. For the year 2000, one income base amount equals SEK 38,800.

8. The brochure contains fund-specific information on percentage return for the last 5 years, which equals the compounded annual growth rate of return for the years 1995–1999. The information on risk corresponds to an annualized percentage standard deviation of 3-year monthly historical fund returns. The brochure also presents a categorized risk measure, where the risk is categorized into five different classes, and colors, with respect to standard deviation; Class 1: very low risk, dark green, percentage standard deviation in the range 0–2; Class 2: low risk, light green, 3–7; Class 3: average risk, yellow, 8–17; Class 4: high risk, orange, 18–24; Class 5: very high risk, red, 25–.

9. All mutual funds charge uniform management fees. Load and switch fees are prohibited, and management fees are generally much lower than for the same funds offered outside PPM.

10. Note that the assessment of funds' domestic and foreign investment proportions is based entirely on information from the brochure, and is thus available to each individual investor at the time of the portfolio formation.

11. This study uses the same data set as that of Karlsson and Nordén (2007).

12. Data sources from Statistics Sweden are, HEK 2000; a report on household economy, IoF 2000; income report and SUN 2000; educational status. These three reports are for the total population in Sweden. They are linked to a survey on 15,000 households, conducted in the year 2000 by Statistics Sweden, reporting in-depth wealth statistics. In addition, information on individuals' country of birth is obtained from Statistics Sweden.

13. Disposable income represents income after tax plus government subsidies. Net wealth is financial wealth plus market value of real estate minus debt. Financial wealth is reported in detail, how much is held in stocks, mutual funds and risk-free assets. Note that disposable income and net wealth are reported on a household level.

14. Engström and Westerberg (2003) model the activity choice using a probit regression model, with a set of similar data from the introduction of the Swedish-defined contribution pension system. Karlsson and Nordén (2007) model the activity choice jointly with the choice of share of domestic holdings in a multinomial logit setup. They use data on the same individuals as in this study, excluding immigrants, and focus on the determinants of home bias.

15. For identification reasons, the following explanatory variables are used in the first-step probit model, but not in the second-step regression analysis: OCC_2, OCC_3, OCC_4, MARRIED, KIDS and IMM.

16. The overwhelming evidence is that alpha on average is negative for mutual funds, see e.g. Elton, Gruber and Blake (1996), Grinblatt and Titman (1989), Jensen (1968), Sharpe (1966) and Chen, Jegadeesh and Wermers (2000). Hence, a negative individual alpha on average is not inconsistent with individuals picking better performing funds, see Elton, Gruber and Blake (2007). Note also that the focus of the analysis is on the relative performance for different types of individuals, not individual performance per se.

17. For robustness, all second-stage regressions are estimated using the inverse Mills ratio from both first-stage model specifications, with almost identical results. Only the second-stage results from using specification (2) in the first stage are reported. The unreported specification (1) based results are available from the authors upon request.

18. Note that Engström and Westerberg (2003) use a larger sample of individuals from the same population as in this study, but with a less detailed set of individual characteristics data. Karlsson and Nordén (2007) use the same set of data as in this study, excluding immigrants. Moreover, Karlsson and Nordén (2007) analyze the determinants of home bias and the activity choice jointly in a multinomial logit model setup.

References

Adler, M., and B. Dumas. 1983. International portfolio choice and corporate finance: A synthesis. *Journal of Finance* 38: 925–984.

Bailey, W., A. Kumar, and D. Ng. 2008. Foreign investments of US individual investors: Causes and consequences. *Management Science* 54: 443–459.

Barber, B., and T. Odean. 2000. Trading is hazardous to your wealth: The common stock performance of individual investors. *Journal of Finance* 55: 773–806.

Barber, B., and T. Odean. 2001. Boys will be boys: Gender, overconfidence, and common stock investment. *Quarterly Journal of Economics* 141: 261–292.

Berndt, E., B. Hall, R. Hall, and J. Hausmann. 1974. Estimation and inference in non-linear structural models. *Annals of Economic and Social Measurement* 3: 653–665.

Bohn, H., and L. Tesar. 1996. US equity investment in foreign markets: Portfolio rebalancing or return chasing? *American Economic Review* 86: 77–81.

Chen, H., N. Jegadeesh, and R. Wermers. 2000. The value of active mutual fund management: An examination of the stockholdings and trades of fund managers. *Journal of Financial and Quantitative Analysis* 35: 343–368.

Cooper, I., and E. Kaplanis. 1994. Home bias in equity portfolios, inflation hedging, and international capital market equilibrium. *Review of Financial Studies* 7: 45–60.

Coval, J., and T. Moscowitz. 1999. Home bias at home: Local equity preference in domestic portfolios. *Journal of Finance* 54: 2045–2107.

Dahlquist, M., L. Pinkowitz, R. Stulz, and R. Williamson. 2003. Corporate governance and the home bias. *Journal of Financial and Quantitative Analysis* 38: 87–110.

Elton, E., M. Gruber, and C. Blake. 1996. The persistence of risk-adjusted mutual fund performance. *Journal of Business* 69: 133–157.

Elton, E., M. Gruber, and C. Blake. 2007. Participant reaction and the performance of funds offered by 401(k) plans. *Journal of Financial Intermediation* 16: 249–271.

Engström, S., and A. Westerberg. 2003. Which individuals make active investment decisions in the new Swedish pension system? *Journal of Pension Economics and Finance* 2: 1–21.

French, K., and J. Poterba. 1991. International diversification and international equity markets. *American Economic Review* 81: 222–226.

Graham, J., C. Harvey, and H. Huang. 2009. Investor competence, trading frequency, and home bias. *Management Science* (forthcoming).

Grinblatt, M., and M. Keloharju. 2001. Distance, language, and cultural bias: The role of investor sophistication. *Journal of Finance* 46: 1053–1073.

Grinblatt, M., and S. Titman. 1989. Mutual fund performance: An analysis of quarterly portfolio holdings. *Journal of Business* 62: 393–416.

Heckman, J. 1979. Sample selection bias as a specification error. *Econometrica* 47: 153–161.

Huberman, G. 2001. Familiarity breeds investment. *Review of Financial Studies* 14: 659–680.

Jensen, M. 1968. The performance of mutual funds in the period 1945–1964. *Journal of Finance* 23: 389–416.

Kang, J., and R. Stulz. 1997. Why is there a home bias? An analysis of foreign portfolio equity ownership in Japan. *Journal of Financial Economics* 46: 3–28.

Karlsson, A., and L. Nordén. 2006. Benefits of contribution: Individual asset allocation and performance in a defined contribution pension system. Working Paper, Stockholm University, School of Business.

Karlsson, A., and L. Nordén. 2007. Home sweet home: Home bias and international diversification among individual investors. *Journal of Banking and Finance* 31: 317–333.

Karolyi, A., and R. Stulz. 2002. Are financial assets priced locally or globally? In *Handbook of the Economics of Finance*, ed. G. Constantinides, M. Harris, and R. Stulz. Amsterdam: Elsevier.

Kyrychenko, V., and C. Shum. 2006. Foreign contents in US household portfolios. Working Paper, York University.

Lewis, K. 1999. Trying to explain home bias in equities and consumption. *Journal of Economic Literature* 37: 571–608.

Odean, T. 1999. Do investors trade too much? *American Economic Review* 89: 1279–1298.

Sharpe, W. 1966. Mutual fund performance. *Journal of Business* 39: 119–138.

Sundén, A. 2006. The Swedish experience with pension reform. *Oxford Review of Economic Policy* 22: 133–148.

Tesar, L., and I. Werner. 1995. Home bias and high turnover. *Journal of International Money and Finance* 14: 467–492.

White, H. 1980. A heteroskedasticity-consistent covariance matrix estimator and a direct test for heteroskedasticity. *Econometrica* 48: 817–838.

Diversification benefits for bond portfolios

Wassim Dbouk[a] and Lawrence Kryzanowski[b]

[a] Department of Accounting, Finance and Managerial Economics, Suliman S. Olayan School of Business, American University of Beirut, Bliss Street, P.O. Box 11-0236, Beirut, Lebanon; [b] Department of Finance, John Molson School of Business, Concordia University, 1455 de Maisonneuve Blvd West, Montreal, P.Q., Canada H3G 1M8

Finance research has focused primarily on the diversification of stock portfolios. Various metrics are used herein to assess the diversification benefits, and the optimal bond portfolio sizes (PSs) for investment opportunity (IO) sets differentiated by issuer type, credit ratings and term-to-maturity. While PSs of 25–40 bonds appear optimal for the marginal reduction of dispersion with increasing PS, larger (smaller) PSs are optimal if the investor is concerned about left tail weight (positive skewness or reward-to-downside risk). Although the marginal reduction of dispersion is less than 1% beyond these optimal PSs, much potential diversification benefits still remain unrealized for many of the IO sets studied herein.

1. Introduction

A cornerstone of the modern portfolio theory is the study by Markowitz (1952), which illustrates the benefits of forming portfolios with less than perfectly positively correlated assets. The subsequent literature, which has focused on the benefits and drawbacks of using this approach primarily for equity portfolios, reaches different conclusions concerning the minimum portfolio size (henceforth, PS) needed to achieve a 'well-diversified' equity portfolio. Early studies find a required PS for US equities that varies from eight to ten (Evans and Archer 1968; Latane and Young 1969; Elton and Gruber 1977) to 15 (Jennings 1971; Kryzanowski et al. 1985) to 30 (Statman 1987) to at least 100 (Fama 1965). More recent studies find that the required number of stocks has increased to 50 (Malkiel and Xu 2006) or as high as 300 (Statman 2004; Statman and Scheid 2005) due to increases in idiosyncratic volatility, increases in the correlations between stocks, and a change in the size and structure of industries (Bennett and Sias 2006). Other empirical studies find that stock diversification benefits diminish with large negative movements in stock returns (Silvapulle and Granger 2001) due to higher firm-level return dispersions when market returns are largely negative (Demirer and Lien 2004), and that the increasing importance of correlations during market downturns is related to the market's tail distribution (Sancetta and Satchell 2007). Van Nieuwerburgh and Veldkamp (2005) argue that informational advantages explain the observation that investors tend to hold fewer assets than suggested by the literature on diversification benefits.

Numerous authors document improved return-risk combinations from international diversification in stocks or in stocks and bonds (Solnik et al. 1996; Chollerton et al. 1986; Jorion 1987, 1989; Kaplanis and Schaefer 1991; Thomas 1989; De Santis and Sarno 2008). Cappiello et al. (2006) and Hunter and Simon (2004, 2005) find that the average correlation in the international bond market has increased over time but not to the same extent as observed in the equity market by Goetzman et al. (2005), among others. Hunter and Simon (2004) find that US investors who hold a well-diversified portfolio of domestic fixed-income and equity investments can obtain incremental diversification benefits from investing in international government bonds if currency risk is hedged. Varotto (2007) finds that interest rate factors followed by maturity diversification are important and credit rating and seniority diversification effects are unimportant causes of diversification of total portfolio returns in international corporate bond portfolios. He also finds that industry diversification, unlike interest rate and maturity diversifications, have little impact on the volatility of corporate bond portfolios.

The study by McEnally and Boardman (1979) appears to the only study that investigates how many bonds are necessary to obtain a target level of diversification benefits in terms of volatility risk reduction for IO sets differentiated by bond ratings. These authors conclude that eight to sixteen bonds significantly reduce volatility risk in bond portfolios. They also find that diversified portfolios of high-yield bonds have lower systematic risk than portfolios of investment grade bonds, which could be attributed to an industry effect since the lowest risk bonds are in the utility sector, whereas the high risk bonds are industrial bonds.

However, the implications of the results of McEnally and Boardman may not be applicable to more recent periods for a number of reasons. First, they examine a randomly chosen sample of 515 corporate *straight* bonds for the period 1972–1976. Second, their findings are likely to be outdated and limited because the bond opportunity set has not only expanded substantially in terms of credit quality, industry, country and bond maturity, but the operational efficiency of the market has improved. Third, as McEnally and Boardman (1979) note, this time period is characterized by extreme instability in the corporate bond market in terms of interest rate volatility and default premia. As a result, Moody's re-rated approximately one-fourth of the bonds in their sample during the studied period. Fourth, the only metrics used to assess diversification benefits in their study is unconditional variance. More recent tests of the benefits of equity diversification use a much broader set of metrics that reflect higher-order moments, alternate definitions of risk, and reward-to-risk measures.

Thus, the primary purpose of this article is to re-examine the diversification benefits associated with different-sized portfolios of bonds using various metrics. These metrics investigate the diversification benefits in terms of dispersion of returns, reward to risk, downside risk and the probability of underperforming a target rate of return. In addition, the IO sets are categorized by industry sector and credit ratings. Also, the impact on the minimum PSs of an investor's preference for long- versus short-term investments is assessed by dividing the IO sets by maturities of more than and less than 10 years.

This article makes five contributions to the literature. The first contribution deals with the benefits of diversification of bond portfolios for IO sets that are differentiated not only by credit ratings but also by industry sectors, domesticity and/or maturities. The second contribution is the investigation of not only the straight bonds previously investigated in the literature but also bonds with additional characteristics such as callability, puttability and convertibility. The third contribution is an examination of the diversification benefits using various metrics, including some that were only recently introduced into the literature on stock diversification benefits. Fourth, we show that there is no minimum PS. The choice of the minimum PS depends on the objectives of investors in terms of risk, return and bond maturity, and on issuer and bond characteristics, such as industry and rating. Finally, we show that while the marginal reduction of dispersion with increasing PS is achieved with PSs of 25–40 bonds, much potential diversification benefits still remain unrealized for many of the IO sets studied herein. Together with the investment cost of obtaining such portfolios on own account, this may explain while individuals purchase bond mutual funds although studies find that bond mutual funds exhibit neutral and under performance when evaluated using gross and net-of-fees returns, respectively (Kahn and Rudd 1995).

The remainder of the article is organized as follows. The sample, data and IO sets are discussed in the next section. In Section 3, we report our results for the various performance metrics and discuss the minimum PS beyond which most of the marginal diversification benefits are exhausted. In Section 4, we conduct a sensitivity analysis to determine if our results change materially for a straight bond sample or different sample years. Section 5 concludes the article.

2. Samples and data

Our bond sample is extracted from the Lehman Brothers Fixed Income Database distributed by Warga (1998), which ceased to be updated in March 1998, and has been widely used in various bond studies (Elton et al. 2001; Liu et al. 2007). The database consists of 39,132 bonds and 1,289,010 monthly bond prices from January 1985 until December 1997. The database contains monthly quoted and matrix prices, and descriptive bond information, such as industry, rating, duration, convexity, monthly total dollar returns, coupons, maturities, and embedded option features. Since monthly dollar returns are reported in the database, the monthly rate of return at time $t + 1$ is calculated using the formula:

$$r_{t+1} = \frac{C_{t+1} + P_{t+1} + A_{t+1} - P_t - A_t}{P_t + A_t}, \qquad (1)$$

where P_t and P_{t+1} are the clean (bid) prices at time t and $t + 1$, respectively; A_t and A_{t+1} are the accrued interest at time t and $t + 1$, respectively; and C_{t+1} is the coupon payment at time $t + 1$. The monthly rate of return is obtained by dividing the total dollar return (numerator) by the beginning of the period dirty price.

Our initial sample includes all bonds with quoted bid prices. This initial sample is divided into many IO sets depending on the deemed preferences of our hypothetical investor (Table 1).[1] There are 27,497 unique bonds and 939,267 bond prices when differentiating by issuer type, and 30,758 unique bonds with 927,295 bond prices when differentiating by credit ratings.

3. Diversification benefits measured using various metrics

In this section of the article, various metrics are used to measure the benefits of portfolio diversification and to identify the minimum PS needed to diversify a specific percentage of nonsystematic risk or to capture a specific percentage of the reward from bearing risk. This is implemented by selecting bonds randomly using a Monte Carlo approach in order to create 5000 portfolios for each IO set j and each portfolio size s. We test for a PS ranging from 2 to 100 and 'All', where the latter includes $N - 1$ bonds and N is the number of bonds in the IO set j.

Since the form of the distribution changes as the IO set, metric and PS change, the values of the dispersion metrics used in the determination of the minimum PS also will change. Therefore, we examine various metrics for different PS and different IO sets to determine how the optimal PS changes when the return distribution is time varying.

Table 1. Sample sizes for the IO sets differentiated by issuer type and credit rating.

Characteristic	IOs differentiated by issuer type						IOs differentiated by credit rating					
	All	Tr./Ag.	Industrial	Utility	Financial	Foreign	All	Aaa	Aa	A	Baa	Spec.
Panel A: Sample sizes for IO sets differentiated by issuer type and credit rating												
Unique bonds(#)	27,497	9113	7511	4453	4991	1429	30,758	10,206	3714	7442	4722	4674
Bond prices (#)	939,267	291,229	260,869	159,892	163,108	64,169	927,295	340,761	112,965	238,113	120,663	114,793
Average coupon (%)	7.69	5.43	7.57	8.54	8.42	8.49	8.30	5.55	8.39	8.35	8.80	10.42
Average maturity (years)	12.04	11.59	11.61	16.56	7.92	12.50	11.89	11.47	14.22	12.13	12.66	8.99
Panel B: Statistics for IO set differentiated by issuer type and credit rating and with maturities < 10 years												
Unique bonds (#)	19,194	5841	5741	2477	4145	990	21,355	7195	2233	5016	3083	3828
Bond prices (#)	546,547	162,281	165,061	57,911	126,021	35,273	549,376	201,504	54,677	139,772	69,209	84,214
Average coupon (%)	7.75	5.99	7.90	7.90	8.48	8.51	8.27	6.28	8.08	8.15	8.59	10.24
Average maturity (years)	5.44	4.12	5.31	5.98	5.00	5.87	5.43	4.20	5.20	5.43	5.77	6.57
Panel C: Statistics for IO set differentiated by issuer type and credit rating and with maturities > 10 years												
Unique bonds (#)	11,497	3,899	2960	2554	1421	663	12395	3741	1812	3176	2067	1599
Bond prices (#)	392,702	128,939	95,806	101,979	37,085	28,893	377,902	139,247	58,285	98,340	51,451	30,579
Average coupon (%)	7.48	4.73	7.09	8.90	8.23	8.47	8.36	4.51	8.68	8.64	9.09	10.90
Average maturity (years)	20.53	20.99	20.68	22.57	17.83	20.59	20.78	22.00	22.69	21.64	21.93	15.64

Note: This table summarizes the sample sizes in terms of the total number (#) of unique bonds, the total number (#) of bond prices, the average coupon (%), and average maturity in years (yrs.) in the IO sets investigated in this article. These IO sets are differentiated by issuer type and credit rating (panel A) and maturities (short maturities in panel B and long maturities in panel C). 'Tr./Ag.' refers to Treasury/Agency and 'Spec.' refers to Speculative. Note that the sum of sample sizes for short maturities and long maturities does not add up to the size of the IO sets not differentiated by maturity because a unique bond could be listed both in short and long maturities if its time to maturity moves from more than 10 years to less than 10 years.

The most common method used to estimate the overall benefits of diversification as PS increases is to estimate the ratio in percentage terms of the potential benefits that are achieved, on average, for the specific PS versus the potential benefits achievable from holding all the assets in the IO set. The most common method for estimating the marginal benefits of diversification as the PS increases is to estimate the speed at which the value of the diversification metric changes (Campbell et al. 2001). Since the average correlation among security returns limits the power of diversification to reduce risk, a PS level should be reached at which an increase in PS produces only a small change in the metric measuring the marginal benefits of diversification. Due to the costs associated with further diversification, rational investors will be adverse to increasing the PS when the diversification benefits from incrementing the PS to the next larger PS are 'small', which is taken herein to be a marginal change in the value of the diversification metric of 1% or less. However, this criterion for the determination of a 'minimum' PS, which is based on a small marginal benefit (SMB), may leave a substantial proportion of the overall potential benefits from further diversification unrealized, as is shown below.

3.1 Correlations of bond returns

The first metric used in this section is the correlation of bond returns. This metric enables us to identify which IO sets have low or negative correlations, on average, and consequently may produce the highest diversification benefits. For each month, for each IO set j (un)differentiated by issuer type, rating category and maturity, the cross-sectional mean of the correlations between every unique pair of bonds contained therein is calculated using only the bonds with at least 27 returns over the 36-month moving window ending during that month.[2]

Summary statistics for various time-series distributions of the cross-sectional mean correlations for the (un)differentiated IO sets are reported in Table 2. The industrial and financial sectors have the lowest means and medians for the time-series of cross-sectional mean correlations over the studied period. For a fixed PS, portfolios composed of bonds issued by industrial or financial firms can be expected to eliminate idiosyncratic risk faster than portfolios consisting of bonds issued by firms of the other issuer types. As is the case for short- versus long-term maturity bonds (i.e., less than versus greater than 10 years), speculative grade bonds have a lower mean for the time-series of cross-sectional mean correlations over the studied period. All else held equal, this implies that investors may achieve diversification benefits faster, on average, for any PS by holding bonds with shorter maturities or lower quality ratings.

Summary statistics for this metric for various pairs of the differentiated IO sets are reported in Table 3. The potentially superior diversification properties of speculative grade bonds persist. The maximum and minimum time-series correlations for speculative grade bonds are 0.19 and 0.03 for A- and Aaa-rated bonds, respectively. Furthermore, the time-series correlations between speculative grade bonds with maturities less than 10 years and the other IO sets even become negative. Similarly, the categories of utilities and foreign bonds show relatively low levels of time-series average correlations with the other differentiated IO sets. For instance, utilities and foreign bonds are negatively correlated with the treasury/agency category for bonds with maturities longer than 10 years.[3]

3.2 Dispersion of bond return metrics

The first metric examined in this sub-section of the article is the excess standard or mean derived deviation (MDD) for a randomly selected portfolio, which is defined as the difference between

Table 2. Summary statistics for the time-series of the cross-sectional mean correlations of all individual bond-return pairing within each IO set differentiated by issuer type and credit rating.

Statistic	IOs differentiated by issuer type						IOs differentiated by credit rating					
	All	Tr./Ag.	Industrial	Utility	Financial	Foreign	All	Aaa	Aa	A	Baa	Spec.
Panel A: Statistics for IO sets differentiated by issuer type or credit rating												
Mean	0.347	0.526	0.224	0.419	0.27	0.426	0.324	0.458	0.414	0.365	0.329	0.108
Median	0.311	0.533	0.218	0.444	0.243	0.448	0.316	0.48	0.407	0.339	0.314	0.108
Standard deviation	0.080	0.101	0.073	0.067	0.097	0.063	0.044	0.063	0.061	0.083	0.092	0.039
Minimum	0.244	0.353	0.106	0.276	0.151	0.324	0.264	0.357	0.301	0.256	0.202	0.046
Maximum	0.482	0.687	0.342	0.524	0.455	0.514	0.435	0.557	0.528	0.521	0.493	0.176
Panel B: Statistics for IO set differentiated by issuer type or credit rating and with maturities < 10 years												
Mean	0.268	0.409	0.173	0.291	0.249	0.351	0.245	0.344	0.321	0.303	0.278	0.098
Median	0.239	0.387	0.169	0.28	0.229	0.356	0.223	0.335	0.293	0.281	0.247	0.099
Standard deviation	0.078	0.096	0.056	0.096	0.091	0.069	0.046	0.055	0.083	0.085	0.096	0.035
Minimum	0.175	0.282	0.103	0.149	0.131	0.241	0.197	0.268	0.213	0.179	0.141	0.044
Maximum	0.399	0.574	0.273	0.459	0.421	0.467	0.362	0.482	0.478	0.462	0.449	0.162
Panel C: Statistics for IO set differentiated by issuer type or credit rating and with maturities > 10 years												
Mean	0.513	0.817	0.363	0.484	0.385	0.53	0.531	0.728	0.506	0.476	0.416	0.163
Median	0.479	0.841	0.323	0.515	0.345	0.543	0.500	0.752	0.528	0.453	0.409	0.149
Standard deviation	0.109	0.10	0.130	0.075	0.130	0.075	0.106	0.098	0.075	0.092	0.094	0.079
Minimum	0.348	0.415	0.139	0.321	0.229	0.384	0.383	0.518	0.353	0.333	0.266	0.055
Maximum	0.688	0.928	0.546	0.587	0.635	0.648	0.714	0.884	0.642	0.63	0.573	0.310

Note: Summary statistics for the time-series of cross-sectional mean correlations of all individual bond return pairings within IO sets differentiated by issuer type and credit rating but undifferentiated by maturity are reported in panel A of this table. Summary statistics for these IO sets, when further differentiated by maturities of less than and more than 10 years, are reported in panels B and C, respectively. For each month, the mean cross-sectional correlation for each differentiated IO set j is calculated from the correlations between every unique pair of bonds that have at least 27 monthly returns over a 36-month moving window. 'Tr./Ag.' refers to Treasury/Agency.

Table 3. Correlations between the time-series of cross-sectional mean correlations of monthly returns for various IO sets differentiated by issuer type and credit rating.

IO	All [All]	Tr./Ag. [Aaa]	Industrial [Aa]	Utility [A]	Financial [Baa]	Foreign [Spec.]
Panel A: Correlations for IO sets differentiated by issuer type and by credit rating						
All [All]	1.00 [1.00]					
Tr./Ag. [Aaa]	0.89 [0.89]	1.00 [1.00]				
Industrial [Aa]	0.93 [0.22]	0.78 [0.32]	1.00 [1.00]			
Utility [A]	0.45 [0.58]	0.12 [0.38]	0.28 [0.94]	1.00 [1.00]		
Financial [Baa]	0.94 [0.62]	0.74 [0.52]	0.82 [0.92]	0.65 [0.98]	1.00 [1.00]	
Foreign [Spec.]	0.63 [0.08]	0.47 [0.03]	0.42 [0.06]	0.75 [0.19]	0.67 [0.12]	1.00 [1.00]
Panel B: Correlations for IO sets differentiated by issuer type, credit rating and maturity						
All [All]	1.00 [1.00]	0.84 [0.91]	0.97 [0.33]	0.23 [0.84]	0.90 [0.74]	0.34 [0.76]
Tr./Ag. [Aaa]	0.92 [0.83]	1.00 [1.00]	0.87 [0.07]	−0.13 [0.57]	0.62 [0.44]	−0.07 [0.82]
Industrial [Aa]	0.94 [0.86]	0.81 [0.49]	1.00 [1.00]	0.08 [0.71]	0.83 [0.81]	0.17 [0.15]
Utility[A]	0.92 [0.74]	0.73 [0.42]	0.84 [0.98]	1.00 [1.00]	0.55 [0.97]	0.92 [0.48]
Financial [Baa]	0.94 [0.90]	0.79 [0.67]	0.84 [0.97]	0.98 [0.97]	1.00 [1.00]	0.64 [0.39]
Foreign [Spec.]	0.83 [−0.21]	0.85 [−0.21]	0.72 [0.21]	0.74 [0.10]	0.76 [0.11]	1.00 [1.00]

Note: This table reports the correlations between the time-series of cross-sectional mean correlations of monthly returns for the IO sets differentiated by issuer type and credit rating in panel A, where the latter are reported in the brackets. For each month, the mean cross-sectional correlation for each differentiated IO set j is calculated from the correlations between every unique pair of bonds in the IO set for bonds that have at least 27 monthly returns over a 36-month moving window. The correlations, which are further differentiated by bond maturity, are reported in panel B, where the values not in and in the brackets are based on maturities less than and greater than 10 years, respectively. 'Tr./Ag.' refers to Treasury/Agency and 'Spec.' refers to Speculative.

the time-series standard deviations of the random portfolio and the whole IO set to which that portfolio belongs. This metric, which is calculated for 5000 randomly selected portfolios for each (un)differentiated IO set, is given by[4]

$$\text{MDD}_{j,s} = \bar{\sigma}_{j,s} - \sigma_J, \tag{2}$$

where $\bar{\sigma}_{j,s}$ is the mean of the standard deviations for the 5000 randomly selected portfolios with a PS or PS of s for (un)differentiated IO set j, and σ_J is the average standard deviation of all the bonds in (un)differentiated IO set j.[5]

As expected, the MDD decreases with increasing PS (see Figures 1 and 2). The minimum PS that satisfies the SMB criterion ranges from 35 to 45 bonds for IO sets differentiated by issuer type. The overall diversification benefit at this minimum PS is substantial (MDD reductions range from 75% to 96%). For issuer-type-differentiated IO sets for bond maturities less than 10 years, we observe not only lower SMB-determined PSs in the range of 30 to 35 bonds but also similar

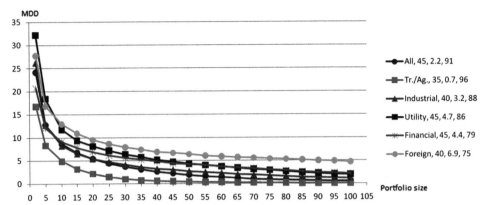

Figure 1. Excess Standard Deviations (MDDs) for IO Sets Differentiated by issuer type and maturity.
This figure depicts the excess standard deviations (MDDs) multiplied by 100 of quoted returns (i.e., differences between the standard deviations of the 5000 random portfolios and an equally weighted index of all bonds in that IO set j for the whole period) differentiated by PS and issuer type for all maturities for various PSs. The optimal PS is reached when the reduction in the MDD is not more than 1% from incrementing the PS to the next larger PS provided that the difference in the mean MDDs for PS s of two and All are significantly different at the 0.05 level. 'Tr./Ag.' refers to Treasury/Agency. The series name, optimal PS, the MDD value, and the percentage reduction in the MDD from a benchmark PS of two when the optimal PS is reached are reported in that order for each series in the legend to the figure.

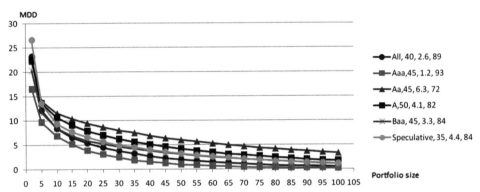

Figure 2. Excess Standard Deviations (MDDs) for IO Sets Differentiated by credit rating.
This figure depicts the excess standard deviations (MDDs) multiplied by 100 of quoted returns (i.e., differences between the standard deviations of the 5000 random portfolios and an equally weighted index of all bonds in the IO set j) differentiated by PS and rating category for all maturities for various PSs. The optimal PS is reached when the reduction in the MDD is not more than 1% from incrementing the PS to the next larger PS provided that the difference in the mean MDDs for PS s of two and All are significantly different at the 0.05 level. 'Tr./Ag.' refers to Treasury/Agency. The series name, optimal PS, the MDD value, and the percentage reduction in the MDD from a benchmark PS of two when the optimal PS is reached are reported in that order for each series in the legend to the figure.

reductions in the MDD of 75 to 95% (except for the 62% reduction in the MDD for the foreign IO set). A comparison of the MDD for a specific PS for shorter versus longer maturities clearly shows that the former is never smaller with a wide range of PS of 35–55 bonds but with a similar range of overall reductions in MDDs of 72–97%. This is due, most probably, to the higher sensitivity of long-term bonds to changes in economic factors.

The IO sets differentiated by rating category have a wider range for SMB-determined PS than the issuer-type-differentiated IO sets. For the rating category IO sets, the SMB-determined PS range from 35 to 50 bonds with an overall reduction in MDD ranging between 72 and 93%. When differentiated by maturities, the short maturities IO sets also show in general lower SMB-determined PS (40–55 bonds) than the longer maturities (35–60 bonds), except for the Baa and Speculative IO sets where the shorter maturities have a higher SMB-determined PS. The overall reductions in MDD are considerable for both long and short maturities (80–96%), except for the Aa short maturity IO set that exhibits a slightly lower reduction in MDD of 65%.

The second metric examined in this sub-section is the average cross-sectional standard deviation (de Silva et al. 2001; Ankrim and Ding 2002), which sometimes is referred to as the mean realized dispersion (MRD). When cross-sectional variations in returns are high, a fund manager is operating in a high-risk environment where the probabilities of market over- and under-performance are high. Consequently, risk-averse managers seek to reduce their exposure to higher MRDs, which for a fixed PS s and IO set j is given by

$$\text{MRD}_{j,s} = \frac{1}{N} \sum_{\tau=1}^{N} \sigma_{j,s,\tau}, \qquad (3)$$

where $\sigma_{j,s,\tau}$ is the cross-sectional standard deviation for the 5000 randomly selected portfolios for IO set j with a PS of s for month τ; and N is the number of months in the sample (i.e., 156 months from January 1985 until December 1997). The diversification benefits, which are shown in Figures 3 and 4, exhibit similar patterns across all (un)differentiated IO sets. The overall MRD is reduced, on average, by 76–80% for a SMB-determined PS of 35–40 bonds.

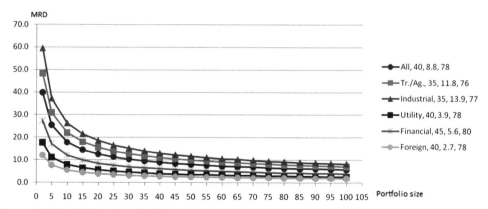

Figure 3. MRDs Differentiated by issuer type.
This figure depicts the MRDs multiplied by 100 of quoted returns (i.e., the mean of the cross-sectional standard deviations of IO set j for the whole period) differentiated by (PSs) and issuer type for all maturities. The optimal PS is reached when the reduction in the MRD is not more than 1% from incrementing the PS to the next larger PS provided that the difference in the mean MRDs for PS s of two and All are significantly different at the 0.05 level. 'Tr./Ag.' refers to Treasury/Agency. The series name, optimal PS, the MRD value, and the percentage reduction in the MRD from a benchmark PS of two when the optimal PS is reached are reported in that order for each series in the legend to the figure.

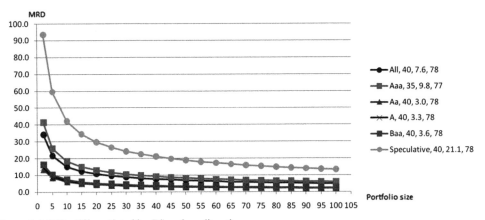

Figure 4. MRDs differentiated by PS and credit rating.
This figure depicts the MRDs multiplied by 100 of quoted returns (i.e., the mean of the cross-sectional standard deviations of IO set j for the whole period) differentiated by PS and rating category for all maturities. The optimal PS is reached when the reduction in the MRD is not more than 1% from incrementing the PS to the next larger PS provided that the difference in the mean MRDs for PS s of two and All are significantly different at the 0.05 level. 'Tr./Ag.' refers to Treasury/Agency. The series name, optimal PS, the MRD value, and the percentage reduction in the MRD from a benchmark PS of two when the optimal PS is reached are reported in that order for each series in the legend to the figure.

3.3 *Composite return and risk metrics*

Investors are interested in holding portfolios that provide the best return-risk tradeoffs. Consequently, a diversification strategy, such as increasing PS, which diminishes risk also, needs to result in a higher return-to-risk tradeoff. Accordingly, we now examine how different return-to-risk metrics react to a changing PS for the various IO sets.

Metrics commonly used for this purpose normalize the excess return over the risk-free rate of the portfolio by the risk of that portfolio. One such metric is the Sortino ratio, which is defined as

$$Sor_{j,s} = (\bar{r}_{j,s} - \bar{r}_f)/\bar{\sigma}_{j,s}, \qquad (4)$$

where $\bar{r}_{j,s}$ is the mean return on the portfolios of size s for IO set j; $\bar{\sigma}_{j,s}$, the average semi standard deviation of returns for portfolios of size s for IO set j; and $\bar{r}_f$, the mean risk-free rate.

The results for the Sortino metrics are shown in Figures 5 and 6.[6] Based on the results for IO sets differentiated by issuer type, the SMB-determined minimum PSs range between 20 and 45 bonds for all IO sets, and the associated overall increases in their Sor are in the range of 72–94%. Based on a further differentiation by maturity, the SMB-determined minimum PSs are in the range of 20–65 bonds for short-term maturity IO sets (with associated increases in their overall Sor of 74–98%). They are in the range of 10 (foreign) to 30 (Tr./Ag.) bonds for the long-term maturity IO sets (with associated increases in their overall Sor of 74–95%).

3.4 *Metrics based on higher-order moments*

Although the metrics used so far have the advantage of being simple, robust and independent of any reference index, they do not capture higher dimensions of risk that may differ across PSs for the same IO sets. For example, the Sortino ratio ignores the existence of third and fourth moments (i.e., skewness and kurtosis), which may be unfavorable to the investor. Similarly, lower second

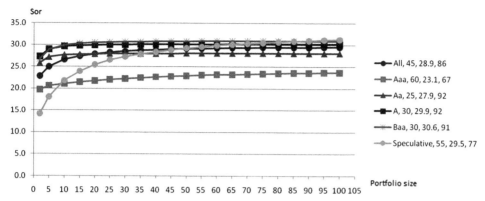

Figure 5. Sortino ratios differentiated by PS and issuer type.
This figure depicts the Sortino ratios (Sor) multiplied by 100 of quoted returns differentiated by PS and issuer type for all maturities. The optimal PS is reached when the reduction in the Sor is not more than 1% from incrementing the PS to the next larger PS provided that the difference in the mean Sor for PS s of two and All are significantly different at the 0.05 level. 'Tr./Ag.' refers to Treasury/Agency. The series name, optimal PS, the Sor value, and the percentage reduction in the Sor from a benchmark PS of two when the optimal PS is reached are reported in that order for each series in the legend to the figure.

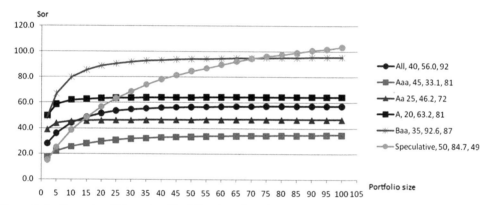

Figure 6. Sortino ratios differentiated by PS and credit rating.
This figure depicts the Sortino ratios (Sor) multiplied by 100 of quoted returns differentiated by PS and rating category for all maturities. The optimal PS is reached when the reduction in the Sor is not more than 1% from incrementing the PS to the next larger PS provided that the difference in the mean Sor for PS s of two and All are significantly different at the 0.05 level. 'Tr./Ag.' refers to Treasury/Agency. The series name, optimal PS, the Sor value, and the percentage reduction in the Sor from a benchmark PS of two when the optimal PS is reached are reported in that order for each series in the legend to the figure.

return moments may occur for PSs along with fatter tails. In addition, the Sortino ratio can be manipulated by transferring part of the risk from the first and second-order moments to the third and fourth-order moments (Lo 2001).[7]

   The time-series mean of the cross-sectional Skew and Kurt for a fixed PS s and IO set j are given by

$$\mu_{\text{Skew}_{j,s}} = \frac{1}{N} \sum_{\tau=1}^{N} \text{Skew}_{j,s,\tau} \quad \text{and} \quad \mu_{\text{Kurt}_{j,s}} = \frac{1}{N} \sum_{\tau=1}^{N} \text{Kurt}_{j,s,\tau}, \tag{5}$$

where Skew$_{j,s,\tau}$ and Kurt$_{j,s,\tau}$ are the cross-sectional skewness and kurtosis, respectively, for the 5000 randomly selected portfolios for IO set j with a PS of s for month τ; and N is the number of cross-sections.

The literature documents that investors prefer to construct portfolios with positive skewness given that the mean of returns generally falls above the median (Harvey and Siddique 2000; Premaratne and Tay 2002). Consequently, an increase in PS that makes skewness more positive or less negative is considered valuable. Based on Figures 7 and 8, the mean of the time-series of cross-sectional mean skewnesses is highly positive at a PS of two, and decreases monotonically as the PS increases from 2 to all bonds for all IO sets. Thus, the SMB-determined minimum PS of two bonds is preferred for skewness for all IO sets. These results are consistent with those documented by Kryzanowski and Singh (2009) for Canadian equity IO sets where further diversification diminishes the positive skewness associated with not well-diversified portfolios. Interestingly, the returns of the 'All' portfolio are negatively skewed, which is consistent with the results of many studies that find negative skewness for an index (French et al. 1987; Brown et al. 1993; and Campbell and Hentschel 1992, where the latter authors claim that the price reaction tends to be greater for unfavorable compared with favorable events).

In contrast, the kurtosis metric, as shown in Figures 9 and 10, decreases monotically with an increase in PS from 2–100 for all IO sets. If risk-averse investors weigh potential downside returns more than potential upside returns, then these investors will prefer a distribution with low kurtosis, since the tails are more likely to fall closer to the mean. Thus, the risk of an extreme loss decreases as PS increases from 2–100 bonds.[8] PSs of 20–30 bonds capture most of the decrease in kurtosis as PS increases (84–88% except for the 46% for the foreign IO set). When differentiated by short maturities, the minimum PS range remains at 20–30 bonds with the corresponding average decreases in kurtosis in the range of 41–89%. The minimum PS range drops to 15–25 bonds for longer maturities, and the corresponding average reductions range from 25 (foreign IO set) to 86% ('All' IO set). When further differentiated by credit rating, the range of minimum PS is 20–30 bonds, and the corresponding average reductions in kurtosis range from 55 to 87%.

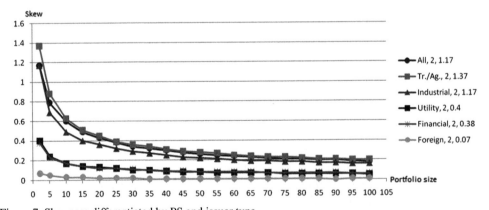

Figure 7. Skewness differentiated by PS and issuer type.
This figure depicts the skewnesses (Skews) of quoted returns differentiated by PS and issuer type for all maturities. The optimal PS is reached when the reduction in the Skew is not more than 1% from incrementing the PS to the next larger PS provided that the difference in the mean Skews for PS s of two and All are significantly different at the 0.05 level. 'Tr./Ag.' refers to Treasury/Agency. The series name, optimal PS, and the Skew value are reported in that order for each series in the legend to the figure.

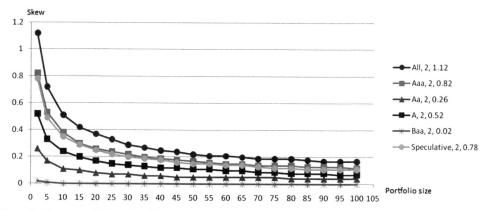

Figure 8. Skewness differentiated by PS and credit rating.
This figure depicts the skewnesses (Skews) of quoted returns differentiated by PS and rating category for all maturities. The optimal PS is reached when the reduction in the Skew is not more than 1% from incrementing the PS to the next larger PS provided that the difference in the mean Skews for PS s of two and All are significantly different at the 0.05 level. 'Tr./Ag.' refers to Treasury/Agency. The series name, optimal PS, and the Skew value are reported in that order for each series in the legend to the figure.

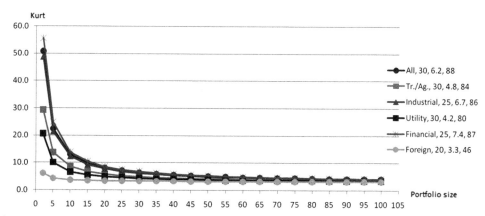

Figure 9. Kurtosises differentiated by PS and issuer type.
This figure depicts the kurtosises (Kurts) of quoted returns differentiated by PS and issuer type for all maturities. The optimal PS is reached when the reduction in the Kurt is not more than 1% from incrementing the PS to the next larger PS provided that the difference in the mean Kurts for PS s of two and All are significantly different at the 0.05 level. 'Tr./Ag.' refers to Treasury/Agency. The series name, optimal PS, the Kurt value, and the percentage reduction in the Kurt from a benchmark PS of two when the optimal PS is reached are reported in that order for each series in the legend to the figure.

Most interestingly, the relation between kurtosis and PS or s is convex; first decreasing as PS increases, and then increasing as PS increases further so that the kurtosis at a PS of All is considerably higher than its corresponding value at a PS of two for all (un)differentiated IO sets. This illustrates a potential difficulty when interpreting changes in kurtosis in isolation. Kurtosis not only measures the tail heaviness of a distribution relative to that of the normal distribution, but it also measures the peakedness of that distribution, and their relative impacts on the kurtosis measure can vary with changing PS.[9] Specifically, the convex relation between skewness and PS

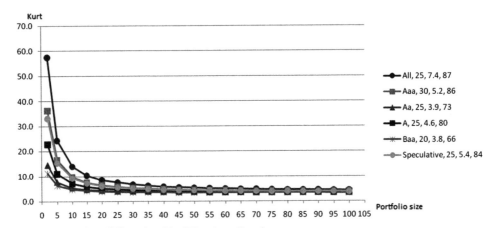

Figure 10. Kurtosises differentiated by PS and credit rating.
This figure depicts the kurtosises (Kurts) of quoted returns differentiated by PS and rating category for all maturities. The optimal PS is reached when the reduction in the Kurt is not more than 1% from incrementing the PS to the next larger PS provided that the difference in the mean Kurts for PSs of two and All are significantly different at the 0.05 level. 'Tr./Ag.' refers to Treasury/Agency. The series name, optimal PS, the Kurt value, and the percentage reduction in the Kurt from a benchmark PS of two when the optimal PS is reached are reported in that order for each series in the legend to the figure.

for a fixed IO set j for month τ occurs because the ratio, $(\sum_{i=1}^{5000}(r_{i,j,s,\tau} - \bar{r}_{j,s,\tau})^4)/\sigma_{j,s,\tau}^4$, first declines in value and then increases in value as s increases, where $(r_{i,j,s,\tau} - \bar{r}_{j,s,\tau})$ is the return deviation for the ith portfolio of size s for IO set j for month τ from its cross-sectional mean return for that month, and $\sigma_{j,s,\tau}$ is the cross-sectional standard deviation of returns for the portfolios of size s for IO set j for month τ. In turn, this means that $\sum_{i=1}^{5000}(r_{i,j,s,\tau} - \bar{r}_{j,s,\tau})^4$ initially declines at a faster rate than $\sigma_{j,s,\tau}^4$ as PS increases, and later declines at a slower rate than $\sigma_{j,s,\tau}^4$ as PS increases further. In contrast, the skewness, which is based on raising mean return deviations and the standard deviation of returns to the third and not fourth power declines monotonically with increasing PS.

To measure the left and right tails, we use the left (LQW) and right (RQW) quantile robust measures of tail weight as introduced by Brys et al. (2006).[10] These measures are not sensitive to the presence of outliers and provide robust measures of tail heaviness. Similar to Brys et al. (2006), we choose to measure the tail weight of the left and right 1/8 quantiles. The LQW(0.125) results are shown in Figures 11 and 12.[11] In all IO sets (without exception), the tail weight for the PS of 'All' is significantly higher than those of the PS of 100. This clearly contributes to the high Kurtosis measures of a PS of 'All'. More interestingly, however, is that the tail weight of a PS of 'All' is not always the highest reported for the IO sets. In fact, some PSs have a higher tail weight (e.g., the tail weight of the IO set 'All' for a PS of 10 is 0.380, whereas it is 0.360 for a PS of 'All'). Given the fact that the kurtosis measures for 'All' are the highest in the IO set even if some PS have a higher-tail weight leads us to conclude that the main factor contributing to the high kurtosis is the peakedness of the distribution.[12]

Unlike the other metrics examined above, the difference between the left tail weight (LTW) metric values at PSs of two and All are not helpful in measuring diversification benefits. This is due to the nonlinear relationship between the tail weights and the PSs, which results in some of the maximum and/or minimum LTW values being associated with a PS different than two or All. Consequently, the total potential diversification benefit for this metric is redefined as the

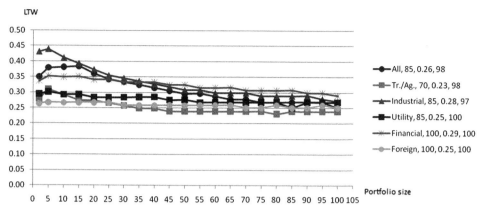

Figure 11. Left tail weights differentiated by PS and issuer type.
This figure depicts the left tail weights (LTWs) of quoted returns differentiated by PS and issuer type for all maturities. The optimal PS is reached when the reduction in the LTW based on the difference between the maximum and minimum LTW values for the IO set is not more than 1% from incrementing the PS to the next larger PS. 'Tr./Ag.' refers to Treasury/Agency. The series name, optimal PS, the LTW value, and the percentage reduction in the LTW from a benchmark PS of 2 when the optimal PS is reached are reported in that order for each series in the legend to the figure.

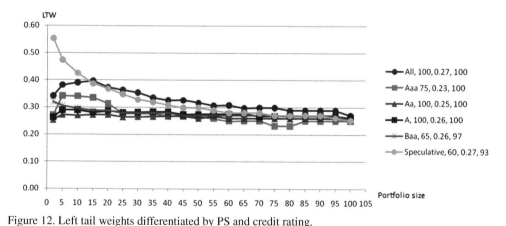

Figure 12. Left tail weights differentiated by PS and credit rating.
This figure depicts the left tail weights (LTWs) of quoted returns differentiated by PS and rating category for all maturities. The optimal PS is reached when the reduction in the LTW based on the difference between the maximum and minimum LTW values for the IO set is not more than 1% from incrementing the PS to the next larger PS. 'Tr./Ag.' refers to Treasury/Agency. The series name, optimal PS, the LTW value, and the percentage reduction in the LTW from a benchmark PS of two when the optimal PS is reached are reported in that order for each series in the legend to the figure.

difference between the maximum and minimum LTW values, and the optimal PS is redefined as the PS beyond which no other PS provides a marginal reduction of more than 1% in this measure of total potential diversification benefits. The optimal PSs are between 80 and 100 bonds for the IO sets differentiated by issuer type. Exceptions occur mainly in the long-term maturity IO sets where the optimal PSs for TR/Ag., Foreign and Industrial are 25, 45 and 65 bonds, respectively.

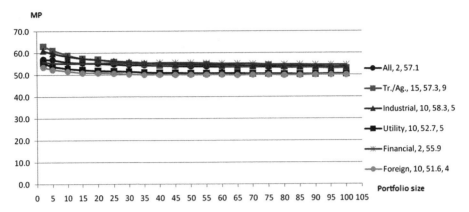

Figure 13. Probabilities of observing market underperformance differentiated by PS and issuer type.
This figure depicts the mean probabilities (MPs) multiplied by 100 that a portfolio of size s that is randomly drawn from IO set j differentiated by issuer type will, on average, underperform the market return over holding periods of 3 years. The optimal PS is reached when the reduction in the MP is not more than 1% from incrementing the PS to the next larger PS provided that the difference in the MPs for PS s of two and All are significantly different at the 0.05 level. 'Tr./Ag.' refers to Treasury/Agency. The series name, optimal PS, the MP value, and the percentage reduction in the MP from a benchmark PS of two when the optimal PS is reached are reported in that order for each series in the legend to the figure.

The optimal PSs are 60–100 bonds for the credit-rating IO sets when undifferentiated by maturity, and are wider at 45–100 and 35–100 bonds for short- and long-term maturities, respectively.

3.5 *Probability of underperforming a target rate of return*

The literature documents that investors are concerned about the probability of portfolio returns falling below a target rate of return (Mao 1970; Xu 2003; Byrne and Lee 2004). We now investigate the probability that the cumulative holding-period return of a portfolio of size s is lower than the cumulative return over the same holding period for an equal-weighted portfolio of all the bonds in the IO set.[13]

Based on the results summarized in Figures 13 and 14, the probability that a portfolio of size s underperforms the market varies somewhat across IO set and PS. Not unexpectedly, the probability of underperforming the market is almost zero, on average, when the PS is one less than all the available bonds in the IO set. The SMB minimum PS does not exceed 15 bonds for any IO set with corresponding potential benefits that do not exceed 9%. We find a higher probability of market underperformance for speculative compared with investment grade bonds for the various PSs. We caution that drawing an inference of relative underperformance of speculative bonds based solely on this metric would be incorrect. As we found earlier, the return-to-risk rewards as captured by the Sortino ratios (Figure 6) for portfolios of speculative bonds, on average, exceed the Sortino ratios for all other bond portfolios with the exception of Baa bonds at PSs above 25 bonds and exceed all other bond portfolios at PSs greater than 75 bonds.

4. Sensitivity analysis

In this section, we conduct various sensitivity analyses to investigate if our choice of bond sample affects the optimal PS. We begin with three samples of time periods of equal length (i.e.,

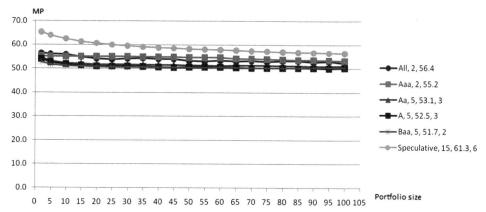

Figure 14. Probability of observing market underperformance differentiated by PS and credit rating.
This figure depicts the mean probabilities multiplied by 100 that a portfolio of size s that is randomly drawn from IO set j differentiated by rating category will, on average, underperform the market return over holding periods of three years. The optimal PS is reached when the reduction in the MP is not more than 1% from incrementing the PS to the next larger PS provided that the difference in the MPs for PS s of two and All are significantly different at the 0.05 level. 'Tr./Ag.' refers to Treasury/Agency. The series name, optimal PS, the MP value, and the percentage reduction in the MP from a benchmark PS of two when the optimal PS is reached are reported in that order for each series in the legend to the figure. Note that the Aa series is eclipsed by the A series.

1986–1989, 1990–1993 and 1994–1997), and investigate the SMB-determined minimum PSs using the MRD metric differentiated by issuer type for the different sample periods. Based on untabulated results, we find that there are no significant changes in the SMB-determined PSs across the samples even though the metric values, potential diversification benefits and the form of distribution differ across these three time periods. In general, the optimal PS is about 40 bonds with associated diversification benefits of about 80%.[14] Second, we restrict our bond choice to straight bonds by excluding bonds with embedded options. Based on untabulated results, we find that in general there is not much difference between the optimal PS for the straight bond IO sets and that for the IO sets that also include bonds with embedded options. The optimal PS for the IO sets of straight bonds exhibit an optimal PS of 30–40 bonds for the MRD metric compared with 35–40 bonds for the samples that include the bonds with embedded options. Similarly, the optimal PS using the skewness metric of two bonds and the kurtosis metric of 20–30 bonds are the same for the IO sets (with)out the bonds with embedded options.

5. Conclusion

In this article, the minimum PSs required to capture most of the diversification benefits from increasing PS for various measures of diversification benefits are examined for IO sets differentiated by issuer type or bond rating, and further differentiated by term to maturity. Most of the diversification benefits are defined herein as the PS for which the marginal benefits from further diversification are less than 1%.

Based on the results summarized in Table 4, we find that the minimum PSs vary not only by issuer type, term-to-maturity and bond rating but also by the metric used to measure the marginal benefits of further diversification. Further, while the marginal benefits of further diversification are generally achieved with PSs of 25–40 bonds, the untapped benefits of full diversification (i.e., holding all bonds in the IO set) at these PSs are still sizeable compared with IO sets of

Table 4. Summary of the minimum portfolio sizes beyond which the marginal benefits of increasing PS are less than 1%.

IO sets differentiated by issuer type							IO sets differentiated by credit rating						
IO set	MDD	MRD	Skew	LTW	Sor	Prob3yr.	IO set	MDD	MRD	Skew	LTW	Sor	Prob3yr.
Panel A: Minimum PS for IO sets differentiated by issuer type for all maturites													
All	45	40	2	85	35	2	All	40	40	2	100	35	2
Tr./Ag.	35	35	2	70	50	15	Aaa	45	35	2	75	45	2
Industrial	40	35	2	85	45	10	Aa	45	40	2	100	25	5
Utility	45	40	2	85	25	10	A	50	40	2	100	30	5
Financial	45	45	2	100	30	2	Baa	45	40	2	65	30	5
Foreign	40	40	2	100	30	10	Spec.	35	40	2	60	30	15
Panel B: Minimum PS for IO sets differentiated by issuer type for maturities < 10 years													
All	35	35	2	95	30	2	All	40	40	2	100	35	2
Tr./Ag.	35	40	2	85	25	2	Aaa	45	40	2	90	25	2
Industrial	30	40	2	85	35	5	Aa	45	40	2	90	30	5
Utility	35	35	2	85	30	15	A	55	40	2	95	25	2
Financial	35	35	2	100	35	2	Baa	55	35	2	45	25	2
Foreign	35	35	2	80	20	2	Spec.	45	35	2	70	35	10
Panel C: Minimum PS for IO sets differentiated by issuer type for maturities > 10 years													
All	50	40	2	95	35	2	All	50	40	2	95	35	2
Tr./Ag.	35	40	2	25	5	2	Aaa	60	40	2	100	45	2
Industrial	45	40	2	65	35	10	Aa	60	40	2	95	30	10
Utility	55	40	2	85	30	5	A	60	40	2	95	35	10
Financial	50	45	2	85	40	10	Baa	45	40	2	45	30	5
Foreign	35	45	2	45	25	10	Spec.	35	40	2	35	35	10

Note: This table reports the minimum PSs beyond which the marginal benefits of increasing the PS to the next PS are less than 1% for various diversification metrics. These include: MDD (mean excess standard deviation), MRD (mean cross-sectional dispersion), skewness (skew), left tail weight (LTW), Sor (Sortino ratio), and probabilities of earning less than the market return over a 3-year holding period (Prob3yr.). 'Tr./Ag.' refers to Treasury/Agency; and 'Spec.' refers to Speculative.

equities. This may explain the empirical findings that unlike equity funds, bond funds generally are value-neutral for unit holders based on gross returns and value-destroying based on net returns (Kahn and Rudd 1995). This is caused by the difficulty and cost for retail investors of forming their own bond portfolios that capture a high percentage of the potential benefits of full diversification and to earn value-neutral benchmark- and risk-adjusted returns through self management.

Acknowledgements

Financial support from the Concordia University Research Chair in Finance, IFM2, SSHRC and SSQRC-CIRPÉE are gratefully acknowledged. The usual disclaimer applies.

Notes

1. Since the foreign bonds are issued in US dollars by non-US companies from all sectors, all of our returns are based on US dollars. Clearly, the number of foreign bonds is much smaller than the number of US bonds, which means that our study has an investor home bias. Nevertheless, it accurately reflects the home-bias selection followed by investors that are referred to as 'the home bias puzzle' in the literature, since international diversification not subject to his bias could achieve higher diversification benefits.

2. The decision to require a minimum of 27 monthly returns to compute the correlations is based on a number of considerations. Requiring fewer monthly returns leads to a bias in the correlations due to the increase in missing observations, whereas requiring no missing values would result in the elimination of too many bonds from our sample. Having 75% of the observations as nonmissing, in our opinion, is an appropriate balance between the negative consequences of requiring too many or too few returns in order to include more bonds (i.e., a more representative sample of bonds) in our correlation computations.

3. When the number of bonds for a specific month is less than 101, the PS of 'All' represented by a portfolio of $N - 1$ bonds is lower in size than a PS of 100. Consequently, we eliminate months from our metric calculations where the number of bonds available for selection is less than 101. This results in the elimination of four months for the foreign (short maturities) IO set, one month for financial (long maturities) IO set, one month for foreign (long maturities) IO set, and 32 months for speculative grade (long maturities) IO set.

4. We also examine the normalized portfolio variance metric of Goetzmann and Kumar (2008) that is equal to the ratio of the two variances in the MDD metric, and not to the difference of their standard deviations. Based on untabulated results, a SMB-determined minimum PS of around 20–30 bonds captures a high percentage of potential diversification benefits of 91–98% (except for a capture of only 83% for the foreign IO set for both short and long maturities). Similar results are found for most IO sets differentiated by credit rating. Their SMB-determined minimum PSs are 20–40 bonds that correspond to the capture of 87–98% of the potential overall benefits of diversification.

5. Equal weights are used in forming the portfolios given the findings reported in the literature for equities that no sample-based mean–variance portfolio formation strategy is consistently better in terms of out-of-sample performance than using equal weights. To illustrate, DeMiguel et al. (2007) find that none of the 14 models that they evaluate across seven empirical data sets is consistently better than the $1/N$ rule in terms of Sharpe ratio, certainty-equivalent return, or turnover. They conclude that this indicates that the out-of-sample gain from optimal diversification is more than offset by estimation error.

6. The SMB-determined minimum PSs for the Sharpe ratio range from 30 (Utility) to 50 (industrial) bonds, and the relative increase in the Sharpe ratios range from 80 (Tr./Ag.) to 95% (foreign) for IO sets differentiated by issuer type. The SMB-determined minimum PSs range from 25 (Aa) to 60 (Aaa) bonds with associated relative overall increases of 67% (Aaa) to 92% (Aa-A) for IO sets differentiated by credit rating.

7. By selling out-of-the-money put options on the S&P 500, Lo (2001) obtains a Sharpe ratio of 1.94 for the period from January 1992 to December 1999. This is higher than the corresponding Sharpe ratio of 0.98 for the S&P 500. In Lo's example, the maximum loss for his fund is -18.3% compared with -8.9% for the S&P 500.

8. Unlike the other metrics, diversification benefits are captured by the decrease in kurtosis between a PS of two, and the PS under investigation since measuring the potential diversification benefits as the difference in the kurtosises between a PS of two and PS of 'All' bonds is not applicable due to the very high kurtosis for a PS of 'All' bonds.

9. According to Ruppert (1987), kurtosis measures both peakedness and tail weight, because if probability mass is moved from the flanks to the center of a distribution, then mass has to be moved from the flanks to the tail to keep the scale fixed. As a result, Brys et al. (2006) conclude that, since no agreement exists on what kurtosis really estimates, its use is often restricted to symmetric distributions. They also note that the kurtosis coefficient is very sensitive to outliers in the data.

10. For a continuous univariate distribution F, $\mathrm{LQW}_F(p) = [Q((1 - p)/2) + Q(P/2) - 2Q(0.25)]/[Q((1 - p)/2) - Q(P/2)]$ and $\mathrm{RQW}_F(q) = [Q((1 + q)/2) + Q(1 - (q/2)) - 2Q(0.75)]/[Q((1 + q)/2) - Q(1 - (q/2))]$ in which $0 < p < 1/2$ and $1/2 < q < 1$ and where $Q(p) = Q_F(p) = F^{-1}(P)$ is the quantile function. The results of the right tail weight are not reported to conserve valuable journal space.

11. We also test the left medcouple and right medcouple robust measures of tail weight, and the results emit similar implications as those discussed herein (for further details about these tests refer to Brys et al. 2006). We also test the tail behavior for up to 20,000 randomly selected portfolios and again the results have the same patterns. The right tail weight tables are not reported to conserve valuable journal space.

12. We also examine semi-variance with the risk-free rate as the target return given the evidence that bond return distributions are not symmetric and investors dislike negative returns. Based on untabulated results, the SMB minimum PS range is 20–25 bonds, and the overall reductions in the semi-variances range between 93 and 96% for IO sets differentiated by issuer type. Similar results are observed for further differentiation by maturities and for the various IO sets differentiated by credit ratings (un)differentiated by maturities.

13. For each month, the cumulative holding-period return is first calculated. Then, the probability is calculated based on the number of times that the holding-period returns for the specific PS underperforms the holding-period return on the market (the target return).

14. The results reported in this section tend to have the same pattern for the IO sets differentiated by rating category.

References

Ankrim, E., and Z. Ding. 2002. Cross-sectional volatility and return dispersion. *Financial Analyst Journal* 58, no. 5: 67–73.

Bennett, J., and R. Sias. 2006. Why company-specific risk changes over time. *Financial Analysts Journal* 62, no. 5: 89–100.

Brown, K., W. Harlow, and S. Tinic. 1993. The risk and required return of common stock following major price innovations. *Journal of Financial and Quantitative Analysis* 28, no. 1: 101–16.

Brys, G., H. Mia, and A. Struyf. 2006. Robust measures of tail weight. *Computational Statistics and Data Analysis* 50, no. 3: 733–59.

Byrne, P., and S. Lee. 2004. Different risk measures: Different portfolio compositions? *Journal of Property Investment and Finance* 22, no. 6: 501–11.

Campbell, J., and L. Hentschel. 1992. An asymmetric model of changing volatility in stock returns. *Journal of Financial Economics* 31: 281–318.

Campbell, J., M. Lettau, B. Malkiel, and Y. Xu. 2001. Have individual stocks become more volatile? An empirical exploration of idiosyncratic risk. *Journal of Finance* 56, no. 1: 1–43.

Cappiello, L., R. Engle, and K. Sheppard. 2006. Asymmetric dynamics in the correlations of global equity and bond returns. *Journal of Financial Econometrics* 4, no. 4: 537–72.

Chollerton, K., P. Pieraerts, and B. Solnik. 1986. Why invest in foreign currency bonds. *Journal of Portfolio Management* 12, no. 4: 4–8.

DeMiguel, V., L. Garlappi, and R. Uppal. 2007. Optimal versus naive diversification: How inefficient is the 1/N portfolio strategy? *The Review of Financial Studies* (forthcoming).

Demirer, R., and D. Lien. 2004. Firm-level return dispersion and correlation asymmetry: Challenges for portfolio diversification, *Applied Financial Economics* 14, no. 6: 447–56.

De Santis, R., and L. Sarno. 2008. Assessing the benefits of international portfolio diversification in bonds and stocks. Working Paper number 883, European Central Bank. Available at SSRN: http://ssrn.com/abstract=1105383

De Silva, H., S. Sapra, and S. Thorley. 2001. Return dispersion and active management. *Financial Analyst Journal* 57, no. 5: 29–42.

Elton, E., and M. Gruber. 1977. Risk reduction and portfolio size: An analytical solution. *Journal of Business* 50, no. 4: 415–37.

Elton, E., M. Gruber, D. Agrawal, and C. Mann. 2001. Explaining the rate spread on corporate bonds. *Journal of Finance* 56: 247–77.

Evans, J., and S. Archer. 1968. Diversification and the reduction of dispersion: An empirical analysis, *Journal of Finance* 23: 761–67.

Fama, E. 1965. Portfolio analysis in a stable paretian market. *Management Science* 11, no. 3: 404–19.

French, K., W. Schwert, and R. Stambaugh. 1987. Expected stock returns and volatility. *Journal of Financial Economics* 19: 3–29.

Goetzmann, W., and A. Kumar. 2008. Equity portfolio diversification. *Review of Finance* 12, no. 3: 433–63.

Goetzmann, W., L. Li, and K. Rouwenhorst. 2005. Long-term global market correlations. *Journal of Business* 78, no. 1: 1–38

Harvey, C., and A. Siddique. 2000. Conditional skewness in asset pricing tests, *Journal of Finance* 55: 1263–95.

Hunter, D., and D. Simon. 2004. Benefits of international bond diversification. *Journal of Fixed Income* 13: 57–72.

Hunter, D., and D. Simon. 2005. A conditional assessment of the relationships between the major world bond markets. *European Financial Management* 11, no. 4: 463–82.

Jennings, E. 1971. An empirical analysis of some aspects of common stock diversification. *Journal of Financial and Quantitative Analysis* 6, no. 2: 797–813.

Jorion, P. 1987. Why buy international bonds? *Investment Management Review* (September/October): 19–28.

Jorion, P. 1989. Asset allocation with hedged and unhedged foreign stocks and bonds. *The Journal of Portfolio Management* 15, no. 4: 49–54.

Kahn, R.N., and A. Rudd. 1995. Does historical performance predict future performance? *Financial Analysts Journal* 51, no. 6: 43–52.

Kaplanis, E., and S. Schaefer. 1991. Exchange risk and international diversification in bond and equity portfolios. *Journal of Economics and Business* 43, no. 4: 287–307.

Kryzanowski, L., A. Rahman, and A. Sim. 1985. Diversification, the reduction of dispersion, and the effect of Canadian regulations and self-imposed limits on foreign investment, Working Paper, Concordia University.

Kryzanowski, L., and S. Singh. 2009. Should minimum portfolio sizes be prescribed for achieving sufficiently well-diversified equity portfolios? *Frontiers in Finance and Economics* (forthcoming).

Latane, H., and W. Young. 1969. Test for portfolio building rules. *Journal of Finance* 24: 595–612.

Liu, S., J. Shi, J. Wang, and C. Wu. 2007. How much of the corporate bond spread is due to personal taxes?, *Journal of Financial Economics* 85, no. 3: 599–636.

Lo, A. 2001. Risk management for hedge funds: Introduction and overview. *Financial Analysts Journal* 57: 16–33.

Malkiel, B., and Y. Xu. 2006. Idiosyncratic risk and security returns, Working Paper, University of Texas.

Mao, J. 1970. Survey of capital budgeting: Theory and practice. *Journal of Finance* 25, no. 2: 349–60.

Markowitz, H. 1952. Portfolio selection. *Journal of Finance* 7, no. 1: 77–91.

McEnally, R., and C. Boardman. 1979. Aspects of corporate bonds portfolio diversification. *Journal of Financial Research* 2: 27–36.

Premaratne, G., and A. Tay. 2002. How should we interpret evidence of time varying conditional skewness? Working Paper, University of Singapore.

Ruppert, D. 1987. What is kurtosis? An influence function approach. *The American Statistician* 41: 1–5.

Sancetta, A., and S.E. Satchell. 2007. Changing correlation and equity portfolio diversification failure for linear factor models during market declines. *Applied Mathematical Finance* 14, no. 3: 227–42.

Silvapulle, P., and C. Granger. 2001. Large returns, conditional correlation and portfolio diversification: A value-at-risk approach. *Quantitative Finance* 1, no. 2: 542–51.

Solnik, B., C. Boucelle, and Y. Le Fur. 1996. International market correlation and volatility. *Financial Analysts Journal* 52, no. 5: 17–33.

Statman, M. 1987. How many stocks make a diversified portfolio. *Journal of Financial and Quantitative Analysis* 22, no. 3: 353–63.

Statman, M. 2004. The diversification puzzle. *Financial Analysts Journal* 60, no. 4: 44–53.

Statman, M., and J. Scheid. 2005. Global diversification. *Journal of Investment Management* 3, no. 2: 53–63.

Thomas, L. 1989. The performance of currency-hedged foreign bonds, *Financial Analysts Journal* 45, no. 3: 25–31.

Van Nieuwerburg, S., and L. Veldkamp. 2005. Information acquisition and portfolio under-diversification. Working Paper, New York University.

Varotto, S. 2007. Total return and credit spread diversification in international bond portfolios. Working Paper, ICMA Centre. Available at SSRN: http://ssrn.com/abstract=963762.

Warga, A. 1998. Fixed income database, University of Houston, Houston, TX.

Xu, Y. 2003. Diversification in the Chinese stock market. Working Paper, University of Texas at Dallas.

International bond diversification strategies: the impact of currency, country, and credit risk

Mats Hansson, Eva Liljeblom and Anders Löflund

Department of Finance and Statistics, Hanken School of Economics, P.O. BOX 479, 00101 Helsinki, Finland

We investigate the incremental role of emerging market debt and corporate bonds in internationally diversified government bond portfolios. Contrary to earlier results, we find that international diversification among government bonds does not yield significant diversification benefits. This result is obtained using mean–variance spanning and intersection tests, with restrictions for short sales, both for currency unhedged and hedged internationally developed market government bonds. Currency hedged international corporate bonds in turn do offer some diversification benefits, and emerging market debt, in particular, significantly shifts the mean–variance frontier for a developed market investor. Since especially unconstrained mean–variance spanning and intersection tests can indicate significant diversification benefits, but lead to frontier portfolios with extreme weights, we also consider some ex-ante global government bond portfolio strategies. We find that passive global benchmarks such as GDP-weighed government bond portfolios perform quite well within developed countries.

1. Introduction

Many institutional investors are restricted by policy to holdings in the bond market. Also investors with multi-asset class allocation objectives frequently decentralize bond portfolio construction and consider total portfolio allocation from pre-aggregated sub-asset classes. While there is ample international evidence on diversification issues concerning international equity portfolios, and also several papers at least mainly dealing with the benefits of international diversification in a mixed stock and bond portfolio framework,[1] there are surprisingly few studies focusing on efficient international diversification strategies within the asset class of bonds. Moreover, typically other studies have analyzed diversification benefits from the perspective of a US- or UK-based investor alone, or focused only on some bond category such as government bonds.[2] While lack of good data to a great extent explains this prior focus, current better availability of bond indices now enables a study of the full spectrum of international bond diversification possibilities including both international government bonds, emerging market debt as well as international corporate bonds.

The main purpose of this paper is to investigate the incremental diversification benefits of emerging market debt and corporate bonds for international government bond investors. Our approach separately and jointly considers three different risks in international bond portfolios:

currency, country, and credit risk. Currency risk is assessed by studying currency hedged versus unhedged portfolios, while country and credit risks are analyzed by including emerging market and corporate bond indices. We study diversification benefits from the perspective of investors from different country origins. Contrary to earlier results, we find that when mean–variance spanning tests with restrictions for short sales are conducted, neither unhedged or hedged international government bonds provide significant diversification benefits for investors from different country origins. However, hedged corporate bonds do offer some diversification benefits and emerging market debt significantly shifts the mean–variance frontier for a developed market investor.

We contribute to the existing literature in several ways. First, we study simultaneously international diversification benefits over several classes of bonds with varying risk. The analysis allows us to answer several interesting questions concerning both the relative importance of currency risk, the optimality of hedging, as well as the benefits of including emerging market debt and corporate bonds into an international bond portfolio. Second, given previous evidence of increasing correlations, substantial diversification benefits in bond investments can be questioned, and updated evidence is called for. Our data, ranging from January 1997 to May 2006, indeed show evidence of reduced benefits in pure government bond investments. Third, we study bond portfolio diversification from the perspectives of several different investor categories including the USA as well as European and Japanese perspectives. Since bond return correlations vary a lot depending on the pair of countries analyzed (higher between geographically or culturally connected countries, see, e.g. Levy and Lerman (1988), for more recent data, e.g. Hunter and Simon (2004)), diversification benefits may look different depending on investor origin.[3] Finally, we use mean–variance spanning tests with non-negativity portfolio weight constraints derived by De Roon, Nijman, and Werker (2001) in addition to more informal assessments of mean–variance frontiers and Sharpe ratios for different ex-ante portfolio strategies. Such tests have not been used for bond portfolios earlier.

The structure of the paper is the following. In Section 2, we review some related literature and formulate our research questions. In Sections 3 and 4, the method and the data used in the study are presented, together with descriptive statistics. Results are presented in Section 5, robustness is discussed in Section 6, and Section 7 summarizes our findings.

2. Prior research on bond diversification

Early studies of international market bond correlations tell a mixed story of the relative benefits of international bond diversification for investors from different countries. In Levy and Lerman (1988), correlations between government bond returns for geographically closely related countries were found to be rather high compared with corresponding stock market correlations. However, also very low correlations, such as for Japan, were detected. From the perspective of a US-based investor, the correlations between foreign and domestic bond returns were typically lower than corresponding equity market correlations, leading to the result in Levy and Lerman (1988) that an internationally diversified bond portfolio (the frontier of bonds) for the US investor dominated an internationally diversified stock portfolio (the frontier of stocks). Despite these apparent benefits, at least for the US investor, the home bias in US bond portfolios was higher than that in stock portfolios as late as in 1990 (Tesar and Werner 1995). Differences in transaction cost for stocks versus bonds may explain the contradiction between these early findings.

Evidence by, e.g. Solnik, Boucrelle, and Le Fur (1996) and Cappiello, Engle, and Sheppard (2006) document some increased correlations between bond returns over time but not systematically higher for all pairs of countries.[4] In line with previous research, Cappiello, Engle, and

Sheppard (2006) found higher within-region correlations, the distinct regions for government bonds being Europe,[5] North America, and Japan. The time-series evidence indicates increasingly correlated business conditions between the USA and Europe, but not between the USA and Japan. However, these increased correlations do not seem to have eliminated diversification benefits of currency hedged foreign bonds to a US multi-asset portfolio (Hunter and Simon 2004).[6]

These prior studies on government bonds, mainly from the US perspective, give rise to the question of whether foreign bonds bring in diversification benefits in a domestic bond portfolio for other than US-based investors. Given changed correlations, it is also of interest what the current state of such benefits is. Using recent data, we will study diversification benefits from three continental perspectives (North America, Europe, and Japan). For Europe, we will use Germany (within/entering Eurozone) and UK (outside Eurozone) as investor origin.

Another interesting aspect is the question of currency risk, which is more critical for bond portfolios as compared with equities, because exchange risk typically accounts for a larger part of the total asset risk for bonds than equities (e.g. Odier and Solnik 1993). On the other hand, currency hedging is easier than for stocks, since the future value of the asset in local currency is less uncertain (i.e. the concept of a 'perfect hedge' is not equally unattainable as for stocks). Consequently, hedging is much more common among bond investors as compared with stock investors, and also shown to typically improve performance (see, e.g. Jorion 1989; Eun and Resnick 1994).

However, it is possible that increased bond correlations and relatively high currency risk eliminate diversification benefits. Thus, the question of whether unhedged bonds still offer diversification benefits is an interesting one. In an early study (years 1977–1990), Levich and Thomas (1993) found that US-based investors would have earned higher returns on unhedged foreign bonds than on US bonds. On the other hand, later Burger and Warnock (2003) conclude that for US investors, optimal government bond portfolios rarely include unhedged positions in foreign currency denominated bonds. This result is also confirmed by Hunter and Simon (2004) for a US multi-asset portfolio. Our study updates the results on currency risk for the US investor perspective and expands the analysis by including European and Asian perspectives.

Most international bond diversification studies have been conducted using ex-post frontiers. Formal mean–variance spanning tests have only been used by Hunter and Simon (2004) who do not impose a non-negativity weight constraint. Since it may, in some cases, be harder to short government bonds, and especially emerging market debt and corporate bonds, as it is to short stocks, not allowing for negative weights is even more motivated here as in the case of stock diversification studies. It is also well known that unconstrained mean–variance frontiers frequently yield extreme portfolio weights not easily replicable in practice and making the analysis vulnerable to possible estimation errors in sample return moments. In this study, we contribute by providing more robust assessment of diversification benefits using a mean–variance spanning test with short sales constraints, developed by De Roon, Nijman, and Werker (2001).

Most international bond diversification studies have focused on government bonds from developed countries. With increasing correlations between developed market bonds, emerging market debt might offer additional diversification benefits. However, the evidence from equity markets is ambiguous concerning the benefits of emerging market assets. While, De Santis (1994) and Harvey (1995) show that the mean–variance frontier for stocks significantly shifts away only when emerging stock markets are included, De Roon, Nijman, and Werker (2001) find that when short sales constraints are enforced, and small transaction costs included, the significant diversification benefits from emerging market stocks disappear. Chances are that the results may be similar for emerging market government bonds, since several recent studies on emerging market credit spreads have documented significant co-movement in spreads for sovereign debt issues by emerging market countries. For example, Cifarelli and Paladino (2002) find convincing evidence of co-movement, more so within geographical areas than between them. Mauro, Sussman, and Yafeh (2002) find larger co-movement in the 1990s than in 1870–1913 and argue that investors pay less attention to country-specific events than earlier.

Besides geographical diversification into emerging market debt, bond investors typically consider international corporate bonds, a market that has recently been subject to extensive growth. Corporate bonds also offer a different type of exposure by including firm risk. Varotto (2003) studied the role of country, industry, as well as. credit ratings category diversification of corporate debt in a large sample of individual corporate bonds. The results indicate that geographical diversification is more effective in reducing portfolio risk than any of the other investment strategies tested. However, there is a lack of studies of the role of corporate bonds in multi-asset portfolios. We contribute by assessing the marginal diversification benefits of international corporate bonds in a broadly diversified government bond portfolio. We will use country/region-based corporate bond indices as proxies for national well-diversified corporate bond portfolios.

Summarizing, we will test the following six hypotheses:

Question 1: What are the diversification benefits from including international government bonds into a local bond portfolio, especially for other than US investors?

Question 2: How have these benefits changed (e.g. in the euro regime) for different countries within and outside Europe? i.e. what is the current level of these benefits?

Question 3: Does the mean–variance frontier significantly shift outward only when currency hedged (as compared with unhedged) international bonds are included?

Question 4: Does restricting for short sales produce results different from those of studies so far, where constraints for short sales have not been used?

Question 5: Does emerging market debt (currency hedged) provide additional diversification benefits into an internationally diversified developed market bond portfolio?

Question 6: Are there additional diversification benefits from including unhedged or hedged corporate bonds into an internationally diversified bond portfolio?

3. Method

We apply mean–variance intersection and spanning tests with and without short sales constraints to assess benefits of extended diversification. These test procedures are well known and standard, with excellent summaries given, e.g. by De Roon and Nijman (2001) covering the case with short sales allowed (see their Section 3.3.) and by De Roon, Nijman, and Werker (2001) who derive the inequality restrictions imposed by short sales constraints. The test statistics in the short sales constrained case (De Roon, Nijman, and Werker (2001, Equation (16)) for the case of intersection) is asymptotically distributed as a mixture of χ^2 distributions, for which case Kodde and Palm (1986) provide statistical tables to assess statistical significance. Before De Roon, Nijman, and Werker (2001), regression-based mean–variance spanning tests have been conducted by Huberman and Kandel (1987) and Bekaert and Urias (1996), whereas De Santis (1994), Hansen, Heaton, and Luttmer (1995), Chen and Knez (1996), and Dahlquist and Soderlind (1999) employed generalized method of moments-based (GMM) tests.[7] Other earlier methods include those by Jobson and Korkie (1989) and Glen and Jorion (1993), who both investigated Sharpe ratios. The relative benefit of the Wald test by De Roon, Nijman, and Werker (2001) as compared with these earlier alternatives is that the short sales constraints can now be analyzed separately, and that the power of the test is sufficiently high.

Spanning and intersection tests involve testing statistically whether addition of 'test assets' to a set of 'benchmark' assets significantly shifts the mean–variance frontier outward. The test assets in our tests include the following sub-sets: (1) Morgan Stanley Capital International (MSCI) developed country government bond indices for 11 countries, (2) 10 emerging country government bond indices, and (3) five developed country corporate bond indices. We also consider diversification into multiple sub-sets jointly. We choose four different scenarios for the benchmark asset: (1) Merrill Lynch Developed Country Global Government Bond index, (2) a developed country GDP-weighted government bond index,[8] (3) a pure 100% USD home market government bond investor investing in MSCI US Government bond index,[9] and (4) a mean–variance frontier of 11 developed country government bonds. When there is a single benchmark index, we test for mean–variance intersection using local 1-month TBill return as the zero beta rate. Rejection of null hypothesis indicates that the chosen benchmark index is not mean–variance efficient with respect to the test assets, i.e. non-zero weights in the test assets offer significant diversification benefits compared with investing in the benchmark only (see restrictions corresponding to Equation (15) in De Roon, Nijman, and Werker (2001)). In case the benchmark assets by themselves form a frontier we test for mean–variance spanning, i.e. a comparison of the two frontiers is made for all feasible zero beta rates (restrictions corresponding to Equation (20) in De Roon, Nijman, and Werker (2001)).

We also investigate the impact of currency hedging on mean–variance spanning. We assume a perfect money market hedge through covered interest rate parity. In this case, the monthly currency hedged excess return of an international long-term bond investment is simply the local long bond return minus the local 1-month TBill return, i.e unaffected by the exchange rate movement between home and overseas currency (see the Appendix for currency hedging assumptions).

Throughout the paper, we focus exclusively on unconditional mean–variance intersection and spanning tests and leave extensions to conditional investment strategies for future research. The unconditional analysis covers an interesting benchmark case and while conditional strategies may further enhance portfolio performance, monthly global bond portfolio revisions do entail much higher transaction costs than the passive buy and hold type of allocations considered in this paper.

4. The data

The return data used in this study are monthly total returns for the three categories of bond indices from January 1997 to May 2006. We categorize these as follows: Group 1 includes the government bond indices from 11 developed countries, denoted in local currencies; Group 2 the bond indices from 10 emerging markets, all denominated in USD; and Group 3 the corporate bond indices from five developed markets, in local currencies. We also use monthly money market returns in the reference currencies to calculate monthly excess returns in intersection tests. When needed, end-of-month currency exchange rates are used to convert bond index returns into currency unhedged returns or hedged excess returns in the desired currency. The calculation of the four indices used as benchmarks for the intersection and spanning tests is explained in Section 3.

The bond index returns are obtained from Datastream and are originally provided to Datastream by Morgan Stanley (Group 1), Lehman Brothers (Group 2), or Merrill Lynch (Group 3). These three data providers were selected for respective groups of data based on best possible geographical coverage and earliest possible start date for the return series to maximize sample size. These indices are widely used as benchmarks on the markets and their coverage is generally considered as representative. The correlations between the few major available indices furthermore indicate that the choice between these major indices does not seem to be crucial.[10]

If available, the corporate bond indices selected are classified as industrial or non-financial and investment grade. If several indices meet the investment grade rating criteria an index with issuers rated in the lower end of investment grade was selected to allow for a larger amount of credit risk premia to clearly separate these indices from the indices in Group 1. If an industrial or non-financial index was not available a broad corporate index was selected.[11]

All indices used are total return indices, i.e. coupons and principal payments are reinvested in the index. The description of the three index categories (Groups 1–3) are summarized in Table 1.

Descriptive statistics on continuously compounded monthly returns in the currency of denomination for the indices in all three groups are provided in Table 2. The highest average returns as well as the highest standard deviations are found among the emerging market indices (Group 2), with some markets having average monthly returns in excess of 1%. These indices also exhibit some very large positive and negative returns. All returns in excess of $\pm 10\%$ were checked for errors in the original total return index data, but only one index value was judged to be erroneous and replaced with the average of the preceding and following index value.[12]

Beginning-of-month point estimates of currency spot rates quoted against the USD are used to calculate currency unhedged returns for indices denominated in local currency (all the non-USD

Table 1. Description of the bond indices used in the study.

	Group 1	Group 2	Group 3
Bond index type included in group	Developed countries government	Emerging market	Corporate bond
Index family from which indices in group are selected from	Morgan Stanley Capital International (MSCI) sovereign debt indices	Lehman Brothers global emerging markets indices	Merrill Lynch corporate indices
Number of indices in group	11	10	5
Issuers of the bonds	Governments	Governments, agencies, local issues, corporates	Corporate
Rating (S&P)	BBB or higher	BBB+ or lower[a]	BBB– or higher
Maturity of bonds included	7–10 years	At least 1 year	At least 1 year
Currency of denomination	Local currency	USD	Local currency
Coupon	Fixed	Fixed or floating	Fixed
Individual country indices in group	USA, UK, Germany, Japan, Switzerland, Canada, Australia, New Zealand, Sweden, Denmark, Norway	Argentina, Brazil, Colombia, Indonesia, Lebanon, Mexico, Philippines, Russia, Turkey, Venezuela	USA, UK, EMU, Japan, Canada

The table describes the sources and characteristics of the different bond indices used in the study. For all indices, monthly total returns have been used. The time period for the data is from January 1997 to May 2006.

[a]Lehman Brothers defines any country that has a long-term foreign currency sovereign debt rating of Baa1/BBB+/BBB+, or below using the middle rating of Moody's, S&P, and Fitch as an emerging market. Individual bonds in the indices may have higher ratings, but in the quality breakdown as of 31 December 2006, only 1.6% of the bonds in the Lehman Brothers global emerging markets index had a rating of A or Aa using Moody's ratings scale.

Table 2. Descriptive statistics for bond returns.

Panel A. Group 1: developed countries

G1	USA	UK	GER	JPN	SWI	CAN	AUS	NZ	SWE	DEN	NOR	Average
Mean	0.0050	0.0056	0.0048	0.0024	0.0035	0.0056	0.0057	0.0062	0.0058	0.0056	0.0056	0.0051
Median	0.0060	0.0070	0.0071	0.0033	0.0045	0.0053	0.0054	0.0073	0.0093	0.0092	0.0057	0.0064
Standard deviation	0.0174	0.0145	0.0137	0.0137	0.0122	0.0137	0.0169	0.0152	0.0149	0.0134	0.0154	0.0146
Skewness	−0.4273	−0.1765	−0.4443	−1.3370	−0.0883	0.1216	0.2229	0.0279	−0.5919	−0.6115	−0.1742	−0.3162
Min	−0.0560	−0.0349	−0.0260	−0.0645	−0.0217	−0.0262	−0.0323	−0.0321	−0.0354	−0.0274	−0.0340	−0.0355
Max	0.0530	0.0472	0.0358	0.0392	0.0306	0.0470	0.0536	0.0537	0.0350	0.0339	0.0451	0.0431

Panel B. Group 2: emerging markets

G2	ARG	BRA	COL	IND	LEB	MEX	PHI	RUS	TUR	VEN	Average
Mean	−0.0018	0.0105	0.0077	−0.0027	0.0081	0.0072	0.0081	0.0117	0.0103	0.0104	0.0070
Median	0.0109	0.0171	0.0083	0.0067	0.0070	0.0078	0.0089	0.0164	0.0114	0.0145	0.0109
Standard deviation	0.0708	0.0582	0.0329	0.0692	0.0151	0.0254	0.0284	0.1350	0.0443	0.0486	0.0528
Skewness	−1.2476	−1.2185	−1.2297	−2.5413	0.4203	−2.5605	−0.6144	−5.7658	−1.1172	−2.4952	−1.8370
Min	−0.2583	−0.2619	−0.1425	−0.4211	−0.0525	−0.1563	−0.1358	−1.1472	−0.2088	−0.3149	−0.3099
Max	0.1617	0.1714	0.0943	0.1848	0.0830	0.0703	0.1184	0.3330	0.1429	0.1378	0.1498

Panel C. Group 3: corporate bonds

G3	USA	UK	EMU	JPN	CAN	Average
Mean	0.0051	0.0066	0.0052	0.0012	0.0059	0.0048
Median	0.0061	0.0073	0.0067	0.0012	0.0057	0.0054
Standard deviation	0.0144	0.0132	0.0122	0.0050	0.0119	0.0113
Skewness	−0.2114	0.0642	−0.2141	−0.5379	−0.0202	−0.1839
Min	−0.0386	−0.0287	−0.0217	−0.0182	−0.0181	−0.0251
Max	0.0390	0.0428	0.0378	0.0132	0.0317	0.0329

The table reports descriptive statistics (arithmetic means, medians, standard deviations, skewness, and minimum and maximum values) for continuously compounded monthly total returns, in the currency of denomination, for three groups of bond indices. Group 1 includes government bond indices for 11 developed countries: the USA, the UK, Germany, Japan, Switzerland, Canada, Australia, New Zealand, Sweden, Denmark, and Norway. Group 2 includes bond indices for 10 emerging markets: Argentina, Brazil, Colombia, Indonesia, Lebanon, Mexico, Philippines, Russia, Turkey, and Venezuela. Group 3 includes corporate bond indices for five countries/markets: the USA, the UK, the EMU area, Japan, and Canada. The data period is from January 1997 to May 2006.

Table 3. Descriptive statistics for currency returns.

	GBP	EUR	YEN	CHF	CAD	AUS	NZL	SEK	DKK	NOK	Average
Mean	−0.0008	−0.0001	−0.0003	−0.0008	−0.0019	0.0006	0.0010	0.0004	−0.0002	−0.0005	−0.0002
Median	0.0004	0.0002	0.0016	−0.0022	−0.0017	0.0024	−0.0032	−0.0012	−0.0004	0.0003	−0.0004
Standard deviation	0.0226	0.0286	0.0349	0.0300	0.0195	0.0324	0.0342	0.0307	0.0287	0.0295	0.0291
Skewness	−0.1242	−0.0939	−0.9243	−0.1913	0.1757	0.1421	0.3612	−0.0019	−0.0984	−0.0771	−0.0832
Min	−0.0606	−0.0728	−0.1663	−0.0681	−0.0494	−0.0777	−0.0785	−0.0856	−0.0694	−0.0657	−0.0794
Max	0.0556	0.0653	0.0763	0.0570	0.0486	0.0982	0.0880	0.0758	0.0646	0.0746	0.0704

The table reports descriptive statistics (arithmetic means, medians, standard deviations, skewness, and minimum and maximum values) for continuously compounded monthly changes in the foreign exchange rates for 10 currencies (GBP, EUR, YEN, CHF, CAD, AUS, NZL, SEK, DKK, and NOK) against the USD. A positive value means an appreciating currency. The data period is from January 1997 to May 2006.

ASSET MANAGEMENT AND INTERNATIONAL CAPITAL MARKETS

Table 4. Intra-group correlations and average between-group correlations.

G1	USA	UK	GER	JPN	SWI	CAN	AUS	NZ	SWE	DEN	NOR	G2	G3
Panel A. Group 1: developed countries													
USA	1.00											−0.01	0.56
UK	0.73	1.00										0.01	0.60
GER	0.78	0.87	1.00									0.01	0.61
JPN	0.22	0.13	0.19	1.00								−0.06	0.29
SWI	0.57	0.62	0.75	0.22	1.00							0.00	0.46
CAN	0.82	0.74	0.72	0.19	0.52	1.00						0.11	0.62
AUS	0.75	0.67	0.62	0.23	0.47	0.79	1.00					0.10	0.52
NZ	0.76	0.70	0.68	0.18	0.48	0.75	0.86	1.00				0.09	0.53
SWE	0.69	0.79	0.89	0.12	0.67	0.69	0.66	0.71	1.00			0.12	0.58
DEN	0.76	0.82	0.94	0.15	0.75	0.73	0.64	0.69	0.92	1.00		0.10	0.62
NOR	0.62	0.70	0.79	0.14	0.58	0.61	0.58	0.61	0.74	0.79	1.00	0.20	0.54
Average	0.61											0.06	0.54

G2	ARG	BRA	COL	IND	LEB	MEX	PHI	RUS	TUR	VEN		G1	G3
Panel B. Group 2: emerging markets													
ARG	1.00											0.11	0.13
BRA	0.45	1.00										−0.01	0.13
COL	0.31	0.70	1.00									0.11	0.24
IND	0.21	0.49	0.36	1.00								−0.01	0.05
LEB	0.02	0.13	0.18	0.02	1.00							0.15	0.23
MEX	0.42	0.73	0.68	0.57	0.14	1.00						0.25	0.31
PHI	0.29	0.55	0.53	0.49	0.03	0.65	1.00					0.07	0.18
RUS	0.26	0.56	0.49	0.64	−0.04	0.69	0.64	1.00				−0.08	0.01
TUR	0.35	0.63	0.54	0.57	0.06	0.61	0.55	0.62	1.00			−0.07	0.08
VEN	0.46	0.60	0.51	0.48	0.03	0.67	0.39	0.56	0.47	1.00		0.10	0.16
Average	0.43											0.06	0.15

G3	USA	UK	EMU	JPN	CAN							G1	G2
Panel C. Group 3: corporate bonds													
USA	1.00											0.59	0.27
UK	0.63	1.00										0.62	0.13
EMU	0.71	0.76	1.00									0.66	0.13
JPN	−0.07	−0.03	−0.08	1.00								0.19	−0.02
CAN	0.78	0.69	0.67	0.02	1.00							0.63	0.25
Average	0.41											0.54	0.15

The table reports, in all but the last two columns, intra-group correlations for the indices used in our study. In the last two columns, between-group correlations (correlations between a country index and an equally weighted index for countries in the other two groups) are reported, together with an overall average of these at the very end of each panel. Panel A reports correlations for Group 1, which includes government bond indices for 11 developed countries: the USA, the UK, Germany, Japan, Switzerland, Canada, Australia, New Zealand, Sweden, Denmark, and Norway. Group 2 (in Panel B) includes bond indices for 10 emerging markets: Argentina, Brazil, Colombia, Indonesia, Lebanon, Mexico, Philippines, Russia, Turkey, and Venezuela. Group 3 (in Panel C) includes corporate bond indices for five countries/markets: the USA, the UK, the EMU area, Japan, and Canada. The data period is from January 1997 to May 2006.

indices) in Groups 1 and 3 (Group 2 is entirely USD-denominated).[13] The source for the spot rates is also Datastream, expressed as foreign currency to USD. Descriptive statistics for currency returns are found in Table 3.

As can be seen in Table 3, the standard deviation of all currency returns exceeds the standard deviation of the corresponding government or corporate bond return. Leaving returns unhedged will thus notably increase risks unless counterbalanced by good reductions in correlations.

To give an overview of the correlations within each group and between a particular index and indices in other groups, we report intra-group correlations and the average correlation between an index and all indices in the two other groups. These correlations are reported in Table 4, the last two columns representing the average correlation of the index with all indices in the group indicated by the column heading.

As can be seen, the largest average intra-group correlation (0.61) can be found in the group for developed markets. It can also clearly be seen that the indices in the emerging markets group (Group 2) on average have low correlations against indices in Groups 1 and 3 (0.06, and 0.15, respectively), while the correlation between indices in Group 1 and 3 (0.54) is not much lower than the average intra-group correlation in the set of developed markets. There is, however, substantial within-group variation both within Group 1 (with a minimum correlation of only 0.12) as well as within the group of corporate bonds, where even negative correlations (between Japan and the other markets) are observed.[14]

The correlations of Group 2 with the other two groups are also the most unstable. For example, constructing equally weighted portfolios of all indices in each group and computing 12-month rolling correlations with the equally weighted portfolios of the other two groups gives an average

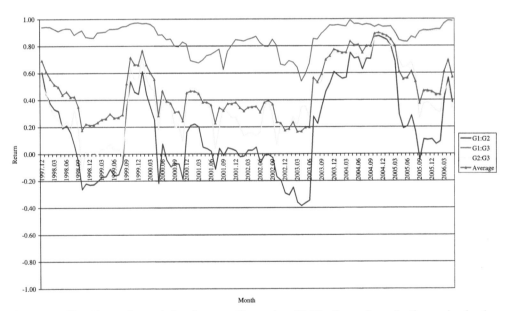

Figure 1. Rolling 12-month correlations between Groups 1 and 3. The figure shows the time series development of the between-group correlations for our three groups (G1: developed market bonds, G2: emerging market debt, and G3: corporate bonds) of bond index returns. For each group, based on the different individual bond index returns included in that group, equally weighted monthly portfolio returns have first been calculated. Then, 12-month rolling correlations have been calculated between each pair of group portfolios. A line showing the average correlation is also included. The time period is from December 1997 to May 2006.

Table 5. Individual correlations with ML global benchmark.

Group 1	USA	UK	GER	JPN	SWI	CAN	AUS	NZ	SWE	DEN	NOR	Average
ML global	0.60	0.45	0.47	0.26	0.36	0.54	0.54	0.56	0.44	0.42	0.36	0.45
Group 2	ARG	BRA	COL	IND	LEB	MEX	PHI	RUS	TUR	VEN		
ML global	0.10	−0.04	0.13	0.03	0.08	0.11	−0.08	−0.18	−0.06	0.10		0.02
Group 3	USA	UK	EMU	JPN	CAN							
ML Global	0.45	0.33	0.41	0.16	0.48							0.37

The table reports the correlation between each individual index on one hand, and the Merrill Lynch (ML) benchmark index on the other hand. The first two rows report this correlation for the countries in Group 1, which includes government bond indices for 11 developed countries: the USA, the UK, Germany, Japan, Switzerland, Canada, Australia, New Zealand, Sweden, Denmark, and Norway. The next two lines reports this correlation for countries in Group 2, which includes bond indices for 10 emerging markets: Argentina, Brazil, Colombia, Indonesia, Lebanon, Mexico, Philippines, Russia, Turkey, and Venezuela. The last row reports this for the indices in Group 3, which includes corporate bond indices for five countries/markets: the USA, the UK, the EMU area, Japan, and Canada. The data period is from January 1997 to May 2006.

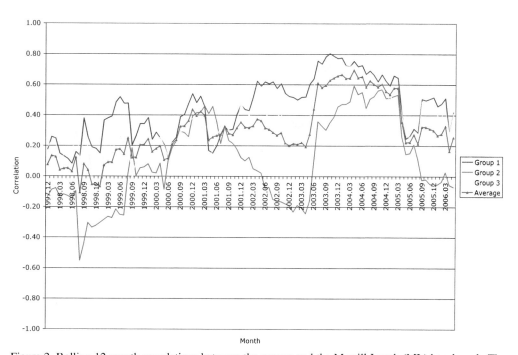

Figure 2. Rolling 12-month correlations between the groups and the Merrill Lynch (ML) benchmark. The figure shows the time series development of the correlations between the returns for the bond Groups 1–3 (G1: developed market bonds, G2: emerging market debt, and G3: corporate bonds) on one hand, and the ML benchmark index on the other hand. For each group, based on the different individual bond index returns included in that group, equally weighted monthly portfolio returns have first been calculated. Then, for each group portfolio, 12-month rolling correlations have been calculated between the returns for that group, and the ML benchmark. The time period is from December 1997 to May 2006.

rolling correlation of 0.17 between Groups 1 and 2, with a standard deviation of 0.33, a minimum value of −0.39, and a maximum of 0.87. The corresponding standard deviation between Groups 2 and 3 is 0.25, but between Groups 1 and 3 it is only 0.10, with a minimum value of 0.53. This is demonstrated graphically in Figure 1.

Also relevant for this study is the correlation with the benchmarks. To preserve space, we report the correlations of each index only with respect to one benchmark, the Merrill Lynch Global Government Index. These are reported in Table 5.

As can be seen, the correlations with the benchmark are lower than the average intra-group correlations reported in Table 4. The variability of these correlations is demonstrated in Figure 2, where average 12-month rolling correlations with the ML benchmark for equally-weighted indices for each group are shown. There seems to be an increasing time trend for both the correlations for Group 1 (developed markets) as well as Group 3 (corporate bonds), whereas the picture for Group 2 (emerging market debt) is more variable.[15]

5. Results

We start by reporting on the global diversification benefits for unhedged and hedged returns when allowing for short sales. We perform analyses from four investor perspectives: US, UK, German, and Japanese, but only report results for the first three.[16] For each investor perspective, we test four 'home market' benchmark cases against expanded asset ('test assets') sets. Three of the 'home market' benchmark cases are single index cases with either (1) the Merrill Lynch Developed Country Global Government Bond index, (2) a developed country GDP-weighted government bond index, or (3) a pure 100% home market government bond investor investing in the MSCI Government bond index for the investor's home country. The fourth 'home market' benchmark case (4) allows a developed country government bond investor to freely mean–variance-optimize their portfolios among 11 developed MSCI country government bond indices.

Note that we in cases (1)–(3), where the home market benchmark asset is a single index, only test for mean–variance intersection, choosing the risk-free rate as the intercept. Economically, as shown by Gibbons, Ross, and Shanken (1989), the mean–variance-intersection chi-square Wald-statistics is closely related to the increase in the maximum obtainable Sharpe ratio given the expanded asset set being tested. In the fourth case, we also test for mean–variance spanning as now the benchmark assets themselves yield a mean–variance frontier. Results are reported in Panels A–C (for the different country perspectives) of Tables 6 and 7 using unhedged and hedged returns, respectively.[17] Base case benchmark (maximum) Sharpe ratios are reported on the left of the tables.

Table 6, Panel A, first column, shows that bond diversification to developed country government bonds (Dev) on an unhedged basis does not offer significant diversification benefits for a USD-dominated investor, as none of the intersection tests for the three 'home-country' benchmarks rejects the null hypothesis. Panels B and C report similar results for UK and German investors.

Sharpe ratios are improved when the developed market government bonds are currency hedged, but the improvement is still insignificant for the USD-dominated investor (Table 7, Panel A, first column) as well as for the others (corresponding columns in Panels B and C). In summary, our results so far differ from those from a somewhat (but not fully) comparable, more recent study of Hunter and Simon (2004), who found significant diversification benefits when including hedged foreign bonds to a US multi-asset portfolio.[18]

Table 6. Diversification benefits from global bond diversification for US, UK, and German investors in Panels A–C (unhedged returns in local currency, portfolio optimization, and tests allowing for short sales).

Benchmark (Sharpe ratio)		Test assets						
		Dev	Em	CB	Dev+Em	Dev+CB	Em+CB	All
Panel A. Results for US investors								
Part I. Intersection tests of expanding a single asset benchmark with test assets								
USAMSCI (0.103)	ΔSharpe	0.176	0.412	0.160	0.534	0.273	0.560	0.683
	χ^2 (Intersection)	8.12	28.52	7.07	44.22	17.54	47.93	67.93
	(*p*-Value)	(0.617)	(0.001)	(0.216)	(0.001)	(0.287)	(0.000)	(0.000)
MLBENCH (0.053)	ΔSharpe	0.226	0.462	0.211	0.588	0.323	0.644	0.751
	χ^2 (Intersection)	9.08	29.55	8.14	45.96	18.81	54.42	72.55
	(*p*-Value)	(0.614)	(0.001)	(0.149)	(0.001)	(0.279)	(0.000)	(0.000)
GDPBENCH (0.086)	ΔSharpe	0.209	0.430	0.177	0.555	0.298	0.589	0.700
	χ^2 (Intersection)	10.39	29.09	7.46	45.30	19.22	50.29	68.54
	(*p*-Value)	(0.496)	(0.001)	(0.189)	(0.002)	(0.257)	(0.000)	(0.000)
Part II. Intersection and spanning tests of expanding a mean–variance frontier (Dev) with additional test assets								
ALL MSCI (0.289)[a]	ΔSharpe		0.349	0.087			0.498	
	χ^2 (Intersection)		33.66	8.79			55.77	
	(*p*-Value)		(0.000)	(0.118)			(0.000)	
	χ^2 (Spanning)		243.42	102.12			275.77	
	(*p*-Value)		(0.000)	(0.000)			(0.000)	
Panel B. Results for UK investors								
Part I. Intersection tests of expanding a single asset benchmark with test assets								
UKMSCI (0.094)	ΔSharpe	0.128	0.309	0.183	0.453	0.274	0.488	0.642
	χ^2 (Intersection)	7.34	17.26	8.61	**32.53**	18.58	**37.020**	**59.70**
	(*p*-Value)	(0.693)	(0.069)	(0.126)	**(0.038)**	(0.234)	**(0.001)**	**(0.000)**
MLBENCH (−0.025)	ΔSharpe	0.248	0.357	0.296	0.579	0.393	0.684	0.784
	χ^2 (Intersection)	8.35	15.11	8.95	**34.60**	19.93	**49.19**	**65.29**
	(*p*-Value)	(0.682)	(0.128)	(0.111)	**(0.031)**	(0.223)	**(0.000)**	**(0.000)**
GDPBENCH (−0.009)	ΔSharpe	0.241	0.334	0.279	0.567	0.384	0.633	0.746
	χ^2 (Intersection)	10.53	15.50	8.82	**35.14**	21.04	**44.02**	**61.38**
	(*p*-Value)	(0.484)	(0.115)	(0.117)	**(0.027)**	(0.177)	**(0.000)**	**(0.000)**
Part II. Intersection and spanning tests of expanding a mean–variance frontier (Dev) with additional test assets								
ALL MSCI (0.273)[a]	ΔSharpe		0.274	0.095			0.463	
	χ^2 (Intersection)		**23.64**	10.54			**49.14**	
	(*p*-Value)		**(0.009)**	(0.061)			**(0.000)**	
	χ^2 (Spanning)		**76.34**	**53.25**			**115.49**	
	(*p*-Value)		**(0.000)**	**(0.000)**			**(0.000)**	
Panel C. Results for German investors								
Part I. Intersection tests of expanding a single asset benchmark with test assets								
GERMSCI (0.156)	ΔSharpe	0.177	0.297	0.161	0.456	0.293	0.473	0.609
	χ^2 (Intersection)	9.57	**19.94**	8.39	38.64	19.88	**40.93**	**61.95**
	(*p*-Value)	(0.479)	**(0.030)**	(0.136)	(0.007)	(0.177)	**(0.000)**	**(0.000)**
MLBENCH (0.102)	ΔSharpe	0.231	0.302	0.212	0.515	0.348	0.584	0.685
	χ^2 (Intersection)	11.26	17.07	9.87	**41.40**	21.88	**51.48**	**68.13**
	(*p*-Value)	(0.422)	(0.073)	(0.079)	**(0.005)**	(0.147)	**(0.000)**	**(0.000)**

(*Continued*)

Table 6. Continued.

Benchmark (Sharpe ratio)		Test assets						
		Dev	Em	CB	Dev+Em	Dev+CB	Em+CB	All
GDPBENCH (0.099)	ΔSharpe	0.260	0.291	0.214	0.521	0.359	0.552	0.667
	χ^2 (Intersection)	13.32	15.91	9.83	**41.83**	22.86	**46.36**	**64.52**
	(p-Value)	(0.273)	(0.102)	(0.080)	**(0.004)**	(0.117)	**(0.000)**	**(0.000)**

Part II. Intersection and spanning tests of expanding a mean–variance frontier (Dev) with additional test assets

ALL MSCI (0.333)[a]								
	ΔSharpe		0.279	0.116				0.432
	χ^2 (Intersection)		**26.78**	9.49				**48.25**
	(p-Value)		**(0.003)**	(0.091)				**(0.000)**
	χ^2 (Spanning)		**80.93**	**49.84**				**116.51**
	(p-Value)		**(0.000)**	**(0.000)**				**(0.000)**

The table reports diversification benefits from global bond diversification for US, UK, and German investors in Panels A–C. Each panel has two parts. In Part I, we report Sharpe ratios and their improvements (ΔSharpe) as well as χ^2 values from intersection tests, together with their p-Values, for expanding the investment universe from one of the three alternative initial assets/benchmark portfolios: (1) the Morgan Stanley Capital International Government Bond index for the country in question (USAMSCI, UKMSCI, or GERMSCI), (2) MLBENCH, the Merrill Lynch World Government Bond index, and (3) GDPBENCH, a constructed annually GDP-weighted global government bond index. In Part II, we report results of intersection and spanning test for expanding the investment universe from a benchmark case ALL MSCI, i.e. a mean–variance frontier of 11 developed (=Dev) country government bond indices. The test assets are, when applicable: (1) Dev, all non-local developed (Group 1) country government bond indices, (2) Em, 10 emerging market (Group 2) indices, and (3) CB, the corporate bond indices for the USA, the UK, Japan, the Euro area, and Canada. Consult, e.g. Table 1 for countries included in the three groups. Combinations such as Dev+Em denote that test assets from two groups (here Dev and Em) are included. All in the last column denote Dev+Em+CB. Short sales are allowed for. Monthly local currency denominated unhedged raw returns (spanning tests) or returns in excess of the 1-month local (US, UK, or German) Tbill rate (intersection tests) in the period January 1997–May 2006 are used (113 observations). All statistics significant at the 5% level are in boldface.
[a]Maximum Sharpe ratio.

Diversifying only to corporate bonds (CB) also does not lead to significant improvements on an unhedged basis for US or foreign investors (column CB in Table 6, Panel A) as none of the intersection tests reject the null hypothesis. However, mean–variance spanning is clearly rejected in the fourth benchmark case, if diversification is into global corporate bonds. Given that mean–variance intersection is not rejected in this case, this result simply suggests that diversification benefits arise from outmost sections of the expanded frontier (very low or high risk) and not from expansion of the tangency region.

With currency risk removed, corporate bonds do offer significant diversification benefits at the 5% level for the US benchmark as well as for foreign investors (Table 7, column CB in Panels A–C), except in the case where free optimization across 11 developed country bond indices is allowed (ALL MSCI). In that case, there are no substantial performance improvements for other than Japanese investors (which is the country perspective not reported here), from including corporate bonds, except perhaps for the most risk tolerant investors (spanning is rejected).

Diversification into emerging countries clearly expands the frontier as indicated by significant Wald statistics for the mean–variance intersection or spanning test for the US investor (Table 6, Panel A) in all cases where emerging market government bond asset class ('Em') is included in the test. For the other investors, the improvement is mostly not significant for emerging market debt as such, but the combined effect of emerging market debt and corporate bonds is significant

Table 7. Diversification benefits from global bond diversification for US, UK, and German investors in Panels A–C (currency hedged returns, portfolio optimization, and tests that allow for short sales).

Benchmark (Sharpe ratio)		Test assets						
		Dev	Em	CB	Dev+Em	Dev+CB	Em+CB	All
Panel A. Results for US investors								
Part I. Intersection tests of expanding a single asset benchmark with test assets								
USAMSCI (0.103)	ΔSharpe	0.269	0.412	0.257	0.523	0.360	0.618	0.705
	χ^2 (Intersection)	14.63	**28.52**	**13.28**	**42.63**	22.83	**57.01**	**71.77**
	(*p*-Value)	(0.146)	**(0.001)**	**(0.021)**	**(0.002)**	(0.088)	**(0.000)**	**(0.000)**
MLBENCH (0.053)	ΔSharpe	0.324	0.462	0.309	0.575	0.411	0.638	0.760
	χ^2 (Intersection)	15.68	**29.55**	**14.45**	**44.10**	23.94	**53.54**	**74.08**
	(*p*-Value)	(0.153)	**(0.001)**	**(0.013)**	**(0.002)**	(0.091)	**(0.000)**	**(0.000)**
GDPBENCH (0.086)	ΔSharpe	0.290	0.430	0.278	0.542	0.378	0.609	0.724
	χ^2 (Intersection)	15.07	**29.09**	**14.08**	**43.37**	23.37	**53.40**	**72.83**
	(*p*-Value)	(0.179)	**(0.001)**	**(0.015)**	**(0.003)**	(0.104)	**(0.000)**	**(0.000)**
Part II. Intersection and spanning tests of expanding a mean–variance frontier (Dev) with additional test assets								
ALL MSCI (0.376)[a]	ΔSharpe		0.250	0.087			0.432	
	χ^2 (Intersection)		**24.77**	7.25			**50.54**	
	(*p*-Value)		**(0.006)**	(0.203)			**(0.000)**	
	χ^2 (Spanning)		**62.41**	**784.99**			**971.37**	
	(*p*-Value)		**(0.000)**	**(0.000)**			**(0.000)**	
Panel B. Results for UK investors								
Part I. Intersection tests of expanding a single asset benchmark with test assets								
UKMSCI (0.094)	ΔSharpe	0.278	0.418	0.315	0.532	0.369	0.595	0.714
	χ^2 (Intersection)	14.85	**28.44**	**17.79**	**42.91**	23.07	**52.32**	**72.10**
	(*p*-Value)	(0.137)	**(0.002)**	**(0.003)**	**(0.002)**	(0.083)	**(0.000)**	**(0.000)**
MLBENCH (0.053)	ΔSharpe	0.324	0.462	0.309	0.575	0.411	0.638	0.760
	χ^2 (Intersection)	15.68	**29.55**	**14.45**	**44.10**	23.94	**53.54**	**74.08**
	(*p*-Value)	(0.153)	**(0.001)**	**(0.013)**	**(0.002)**	(0.091)	**(0.000)**	**(0.000)**
GDPBENCH (0.086)	ΔSharpe	0.290	0.430	0.278	0.542	0.378	0.609	0.724
	χ^2 (Intersection)	15.07	**29.09**	**14.08**	**43.37**	23.37	**53.40**	**72.83**
	(*p*-Value)	(0.179)	**(0.001)**	**(0.015)**	**(0.003)**	(0.104)	**(0.000)**	**(0.000)**
Part II. Intersection and spanning tests of expanding a mean–variance frontier (Dev) with additional test assets								
ALL MSCI (0.376)[a]	ΔSharpe		0.250	0.087			0.432	
	χ^2 (Intersection)		**24.77**	7.25			**50.54**	
	(*p*-Value)		**(0.006)**	(0.203)			**(0.000)**	
	χ^2 (Spanning)		**61.14**	**902.27**			**1118.08**	
	(*p*-Value)		**(0.000)**	**(0.000)**			**(0.000)**	
Panel C. Results for German investors								
Part I. Intersection tests of expanding a single asset benchmark with test assets								
GERMSCI (0.166)	ΔSharpe	0.206	0.354	0.195	0.460	0.297	0.551	0.642
	χ^2 (Intersection)	12.52	**26.76**	**11.31**	**40.06**	20.59	**53.52**	**68.72**
	(*p*-Value)	(0.251)	**(0.003)**	**(0.046)**	**(0.005)**	(0.151)	**(0.000)**	**(0.000)**
MLBENCH (0.053)	ΔSharpe	0.324	0.462	0.309	0.575	0.411	0.638	0.760
	χ^2 (Intersection)	15.68	**29.55**	**14.45**	**44.10**	23.94	**53.54**	**74.08**
	(*p*-Value)	(0.153)	**(0.001)**	**(0.013)**	**(0.002)**	(0.091)	**(0.000)**	**(0.000)**

(Continued)

Table 7. Continued.

Benchmark (Sharpe ratio)		Dev	Em	CB	Dev+Em	Dev+CB	Em+CB	All
					Test assets			
GDPBENCH (0.086)	ΔSharpe	0.290	0.430	0.278	0.542	0.378	0.609	0.724
	χ^2 (Intersection)	15.07	**29.09**	**14.08**	**43.37**	23.37	**53.40**	**72.83**
	(p-Value)	(0.179)	**(0.001)**	**(0.015)**	**(0.003)**	(0.104)	**(0.000)**	**(0.000)**

Part II. Intersection and spanning tests of expanding a mean–variance frontier (Dev) with additional test assets

ALL MSCI (0.376)[a]	χ^2 (Spanning)		0.250	0.087				0.432
	(p-Value)		**24.77**	7.25				**50.54**
	ΔSharpe		**(0.006)**	(0.203)				**(0.000)**
	χ^2 (Intersection)		**56.96**	**967.01**				**1192.92**
	(p-Value)		**(0.000)**	**(0.000)**				**(0.000)**

The table reports diversification benefits from global bond diversification for US, UK, and German investors in Panels A–C. Each panel has two parts. In Part I, we report Sharpe ratios and their improvements (ΔSharpe) as well as χ^2 values from intersection tests, together with their p-Values, for expanding the investment universe from one of the three alternative initial assets/benchmark portfolios: (1); the Morgan Stanley Capital International Government Bond index for the country in question (USAMSCI, UKMSCI, or GERMSCI), (2) MLBENCH, the Merrill Lynch World Government Bond index, and (3) GDPBENCH, a constructed annually GDP-weighted global government bond index. In Part II, we report results of intersection and spanning test for expanding the investment universe from a benchmark case ALL MSCI, i.e. a mean–variance frontier of 11 developed (=Dev) country government bond indices. The test assets are, when applicable: (1) Dev, all non-local developed (Group 1) country government bond indices, (2) Em, 10 emerging market (Group 2) indices, and (3) CB, the corporate bond indices for the USA, the UK, Japan, the Euro area and Canada. Consult, e.g. Table 1 for countries included in the three groups. Combinations such as Dev+Em denote that test assets from two groups (here Dev and Em) are included, all in the last column denotes Dev+Em+CB. Short sales are allowed for. Monthly local currency denominated hedged raw returns (spanning tests) or hedged returns in excess of the 1-month local (US, UK, or German) Tbill rate (intersection tests) in period January 1997–May 2006 are used (113 observations). All statistics significant at the 5% level are in boldface.
[a] Maximum Sharpe ratio.

in all cases. Gauging by the Sharpe ratio improvements, these benefits are also quite substantial as compared with the low Sharpe ratios of benchmark investing only.

Next, diversification benefits are assessed under the more realistic assumption of no short sales. We use Kodde and Palm (1986) statistical table 1 to assess the statistical significance of the De Roon, Nijman, and Werker (2001) chi-square statistics, when taking into account the inequality restrictions implied by short sales constraint. Table 8, Panel A, reports the results for the USD-dominated investor, using unhedged returns.

As expected, constraining the frontiers by not allowing negative positions dramatically cuts the diversification benefits. The case against diversification through international government bonds is now even more apparent. However, emerging country bonds still offer significant diversification benefits, especially in the outer areas of the frontiers, as the mean–variance intersection tests generally do not reject but corresponding spanning tests do.[19] This result is driven by a few high-performing but high-risk emerging countries in our sample.[20] The results for two other countries are reported in Table 8, Panels B and C. The results for the German investor (and to some extent for the Japanese, not reported here) are in line with those for the USA. However, for the UK investor, none of the expanded diversification opportunities are statistically significant.

Can currency hedging offset some of the drawbacks with excluding possibilities to short government bonds observed in Table 8? Table 9, Panel A, shows that this is indeed the case: diversification

Table 8. Diversification benefits from global bond diversification for US, UK, and German investors in Panels A–C (unhedged returns in GBP, portfolio optimization, and tests that do not allow short sales).

Benchmark		Test assets						
(Sharpe ratio)		Dev	Em	CB	Dev+Em	Dev+CB	Em+CB	All
Panel A. Results for US investors								
Part I. Intersection tests of expanding a single asset benchmark with test assets								
USAMSCI (0.103)	ΔSharpe	0.076	0.269	0.105	0.276	0.105	0.281	0.281
	χ^2 (Intersection)	2.40	14.28	3.68	14.84	3.678	15.28	15.28
MLBENCH (0.053)	ΔSharpe	0.126	0.313	0.156	0.326	0.156	0.331	0.331
	χ^2 (Intersection)	5.19	14.77	6.83	18.15	7.44	17.26	18.84
GDPBENCH (0.086)	ΔSharpe	0.093	0.282	0.122	0.293	0.122	0.298	0.298
	χ^2 (Intersection)	6.11	14.35	5.46	21.23	10.29	16.08	22.22
Part II. Intersection and spanning tests of expanding a mean–variance frontier (Dev) with additional test assets								
ALL MSCI (0.179)[a]	ΔSharpe		0.200	0.029			0.205	
	χ^2 (Intersection)		12.18	3.91			13.33	
	χ^2 (Spanning)		**82.05**	23.03			**158.30**	
Panel B. Results for UK investors								
Part I. Intersection tests of expanding a single asset benchmark with test assets								
UKMSCI (0.094)	ΔSharpe	0.015	0.066	0.089	0.066	0.089	0.116	0.116
	χ^2 (Intersection)	0.34	1.88	4.67	1.88	4.67	5.40	5.40
MLBENCH (−0.025)	ΔSharpe	0.134	0.157	0.208	0.185	0.208	0.235	0.235
	χ^2 (Intersection)	4.41	2.67	6.26	7.84	7.14	8.06	9.83
GDPBENCH (−0.009)	ΔSharpe	0.118	0.141	0.192	0.169	0.192	0.219	0.219
	χ^2 (Intersection)	5.83	3.22	7.03	10.65	9.51	10.24	12.55

(Continued)

Table 8. Continued.

Benchmark (Sharpe ratio)		Test assets						
		Dev	Em	CB	Dev+Em	Dev+CB	Em+CB	All
Part II. Intersection and spanning tests of expanding a mean–variance frontier (Dev) with additional test assets								
ALL MSCI (0.109)[a]	ΔSharpe			0.074			0.101	0.135
	χ^2 (Intersection)			4.31			5.60	8.43
	χ^2 (Spanning)			18.57			25.63	

Panel C. Results for German investors

		Dev	Em	CB	Dev+Em	Dev+CB	Em+CB	All
Part I. Intersection tests of expanding a single asset benchmark with test assets								
GERMSCI (0.156)	ΔSharpe	0.088	0.096	0.098	0.133	0.107	0.122	0.135
	χ^2 (Intersection)	5.68	4.33	4.79	7.46	7.68	5.92	8.43
MLBENCH (0.102)	ΔSharpe	0.142	0.087	0.151	0.186	0.160	0.176	0.189
	χ^2 (Intersection)	7.71	2.86	7.20	13.45	9.91	9.12	14.42
GDPBENCH (0.099)	ΔSharpe	0.145	0.091	0.155	0.190	0.164	0.179	0.193
	χ^2 (Intersection)	9.33	3.15	8.48	18.22	13.50	11.83	19.43
Part II. Intersection and spanning tests of expanding a mean–variance frontier (Dev) with additional test assets								
ALL MSCI (0.244)[a]	ΔSharpe	0.045		0.019			0.047	
	χ^2 (Intersection)	3.68		4.31			6.36	
	χ^2 (Spanning)	**71.52****		38.82			**334.71****	

The table reports diversification benefits from global bond diversification for US, UK, and German investors in Panels A–C. Each panel has two parts. In Part I, we report Sharpe ratios and their improvements (ΔSharpe) as well as χ^2 values from intersection tests, together with their *p*-values, for expanding the investment universe from one of the three alternative initial assets/benchmark portfolios: (1) the Morgan Stanley Capital International Government Bond index for the country in question (USAMSCI, UKMSCI, or GERMSCI), (2) MLBENCH, the Merrill Lynch World Government Bond index, and (3) GDPBENCH, a constructed annually GDP-weighted global government bond index. In Panel B, we report results of intersection and spanning test for expanding the investment universe from a benchmark case ALL MSCI, i.e. a mean–variance frontier of 11 developed (=Dev) country government bond indices. The test assets are, when applicable: (1) Dev, all non-local developed (Group 1) country government bond indices, (2) Em, 10 emerging market (Group 2) indices, and (3) CB, the corporate bond indices for the USA, the UK, Japan, the Euro area, and Canada. Consult, e.g. Table 1 for countries included in the three groups. Combinations such as Dev+Em denote that test assets from two groups (here Dev and Em) are included. All in the last column denotes Dev+Em+CB. Short sales are allowed for. Monthly local currency denominated unhedged raw returns (spanning tests) or returns in excess of the 1-month local (US, UK, or German) Tbill rate (intersection tests) in period January 1997–May 2006 are used (113 observations). Short sales are not allowed for. All statistics significant at the 5% level are in boldface.

[a]Maximum Sharpe ratio.

*Significant χ^2-values according to the Kodde–Palm test (according to its higher and lower critical value) at the 5% level.

**Significant χ^2-values according to the Kodde–Palm test (according to its higher and lower critical value) at the 1% level. ¤Statistics significant at the 5% level using at least one Kodde–Palm 5% critical value.

Table 9. Diversification benefits from global bond diversification for US, UK, and German investors in Panels A–C (currency hedged returns, portfolio optimization, and tests that do not allow short sales).

Benchmark		Test assets						
(Sharpe ratio)		Dev	Em	CB	Dev+Em	Dev+CB	Em+CB	All
Panel A. Results for US investors								
Part I. Intersection tests of expanding a single asset benchmark with test assets								
USAMSCI (0.103)	ΔSharpe	0.157	0.269	0.214	0.329	0.220	0.351	0.358
	χ^2 (Intersection)	9.57	14.28	12.00*	21.05	13.42	22.00	23.82
MLBENCH (0.053)	ΔSharpe	0.207	0.313	0.264	0.380	0.270	0.401	0.409
	χ^2 (Intersection)	8.45	14.77	12.25*	21.86	12.95	23.46¤	24.67
GDPBENCH (0.086)	ΔSharpe	0.174	0.282	0.231	0.347	0.237	0.368	0.375
	χ^2 (Intersection)	8.55	14.35	12.25*	21.66	13.22	37.64**	24.45
Part II. Intersection and spanning tests of expanding a mean–variance frontier (Dev) with additional test assets								
ALL MSCI (0.260)[a]	ΔSharpe		0.173	0.063			0.201	
	χ^2 (Intersection)		12.63	6.21			16.59	
	χ^2 (Spanning)		259.30**	2862.30**			2793.03**	
Panel B. Results for UK investors								
Part I. Intersection tests of expanding a single asset benchmark with test assets								
UKMSCI (0.094)	ΔSharpe	0.166	0.274	0.223	0.338	0.229	0.360	0.367
	χ^2 (Intersection)	9.63	14.14	14.62¤	21.68	16.61	23.12¤	25.82
MLBENCH (0.053)	ΔSharpe	0.207	0.313	0.264	0.380	0.270	0.401	0.409
	χ^2 (Intersection)	8.45	14.77	12.25**	21.86	12.95	45.85**	24.67
GDPBENCH (0.086)	ΔSharpe	0.174	0.282	0.231	0.347	0.237	0.368	0.375
	χ^2 (Intersection)	8.55	14.35	12.25**	21.66	13.22	22.83	24.45

(*Continued*)

Table 9. Continued.

Benchmark (Sharpe ratio)	Test assets						
	Dev	Em	CB	Dev+Em	Dev+CB	Em+CB	All
Part II. Intersection and spanning tests of expanding a mean–variance frontier (Dev) with additional test assets							
ALL MSCI (0.260)[a]							
ΔSharpe		0.173	0.063				0.201
χ^2 (Intersection)		12.63	6.21				16.59
χ^2 (Spanning)		**253.23****	**756.66****				**2247.68****
Panel C. Results for German investors							
Part I. Intersection tests of expanding a single asset benchmark with test assets							
GERMSCI (0.166)							
ΔSharpe	0.094	0.214	0.151	0.267	0.157	0.288	0.295
χ^2 (Intersection)	6.23	12.78	8.62	27.24	11.06	19.53	21.38
MLBENCH (0.053)							
ΔSharpe	0.207	0.313	0.264	0.380	0.270	0.401	0.409
χ^2 (Intersection)	8.45	14.77	**12.25****	21.86	12.95	23.46[¤]	38.13
GDPBENCH (0.086)							
ΔSharpe	0.174	0.282	0.231	0.347	0.237	0.368	0.375
χ^2 (Intersection)	8.55	14.35	**12.25****	21.66	13.22	22.83	37.07
Part II. Intersection and spanning tests of expanding a mean–variance frontier (Dev) with additional test assets							
ALL MSCI (0.260)[a]							
ΔSharpe		0.173	0.063				0.201
χ^2 (Intersection)		12.63	6.21				16.59
χ^2 (Spanning)		**221.43****	**319.56****				**1515.18****

The table reports diversification benefits from global bond diversification for US, UK, and German investors in Panels A–C. Each panel has two parts. In Part I, we report Sharpe ratios and their improvements (ΔSharpe) as well as χ^2 values from intersection tests, together with their p-values, for expanding the investment universe from one of the three alternative initial assets/benchmark portfolios: (1) the Morgan Stanley Capital International Government Bond index for the country in question (USAMSCI, UKMSCI, or GERMSCI), (2) MLBENCH, the Merrill Lynch World Government Bond index, and (3) GDPBENCH, a constructed annually GDP-weighted global government bond index. In Panel B, we report results of intersection and spanning test for expanding the investment universe from a benchmark case ALL MSCI , i.e. a mean–variance frontier of 11 developed (=Dev) country government bond indices. The test assets are, when applicable: (1) Dev, all non-local developed (Group 1) country government bond indices, (2) Em, 10 emerging market (Group 2) indices, and (3) CB, the corporate bond indices for the USA, the UK, Japan, the Euro area, and Canada. Consult, e.g. Table 1 for countries included in the three groups. Combinations such as Dev+Em denote that test assets from two groups (here Dev and Em) are included. All in the last column denotes Dev+Em+CB. Short sales are allowed for. Monthly local currency denominated hedged raw returns (spanning tests) or hedged returns in excess of the 1-month local (US, UK, or German) Tbill rate (intersection tests) in period January 1997–May 2006 are used (113 observations). Short sales are not allowed for. All statistics significant at the 5% level are in boldface.

[a] Maximum Sharpe ratio.

*Significant χ^2-values according to the Kodde–Palm test (according to its higher and lower critical value) at the 5% level.

**Significant χ^2-values according to the Kodde–Palm test (according to its higher and lower critical value) at the 1% level.

¤Statistics significant at the 5% level using at least one Kodde–Palm 5% critical value.

into global corporate bonds significantly improves the performance of global benchmark or US only government bond investors.

As Table 9, Panel A, shows, the best improvements occur with diversification into both corporate bonds and emerging country bonds. As before, however, the benefits mostly result from positions in high-risk emerging country bonds given rejections only in our spanning tests. For investors from the other countries, the results are mainly likewise.

Monthly Sharpe ratio improvements also appear economically meaningful in the more realistic short sales constrained cases of Tables 8 and 9 ranging from about 0.13 (unhedged CB only) to about 0.30 (Em only) to about 0.37 (CB+EM) for the US investor. With benchmark asset monthly standard deviations around 1.8%, for example, a monthly Sharpe ratio improvement of 0.3 translates to an additional monthly excess return of approximately 0.54% with unchanged risk level for the investor. For a passive buy and hold investor (not engaging into currency hedging) this amounts to roughly 6.5% p.a. additional gross return. Diversifying into corporate bonds would improve Sharpe ratios, currency hedged, about 0.23 which would imply annual return improvements around $1.8\% \times 0.23 \times 12 = 5.0\%$ p.a. These gross numbers are economically large and probably remain meaningful even after considering the relatively high transaction and implementation costs arising from bid-ask spreads, hedging costs, tracking error costs due to imperfect index mimicking with a set of individual bonds, etc.[21] Launch of exchange traded funds (ETFs) replicating many of these benchmark indices should over time furthermore alleviate investability problems.[22]

Figures 3–5 summarizes our findings for the US investor, showing the shift of the frontier from the home-country benchmark (positioned near the frontier for developed market government bonds) to a frontier including also corporate bonds (in Figure 3), emerging country bonds (in Figure 4), and both (Figure 5).

6. Robustness tests

In this section, we report results from various robustness tests performed. We above all address two issues: concerns with the use of a mean–variance framework when the returns may not be normally distributed, as well as concerns with time stability and the use of an unconditional framework.

6.1 *Deviations from normality*

Our study is based on monthly bond returns, which, in general, are more normal than daily or weekly ones. The skewness statistics in Table 2 (and kurtosis statistics, not reported here) indicate that the developed market government and corporate bond series generally conform reasonably well to normality. However, the emerging market government bonds display negative skewness from being heavily influenced by a small number of large negative returns. They also exhibit large positive outliers. The mean–variance framework is clearly a simplification, and we want to address the concern that negative skewness, or perhaps outliers, may have distorted the inference. We thus perform two robustness controls regarding the normality assumption.

First, we check for the sensitivity of the results using downside risk-based Sortino ratios instead of Sharpe ratios when gauging the level of performance improvement. The Sortino ratios are computed as mean excess returns of optimal strategies divided by the root of downside semi-variance (i.e. standard deviation using lower tail negative excess return months only). We find that emerging market bonds are not favored by the mean-variance (MV) framework by ignoring their

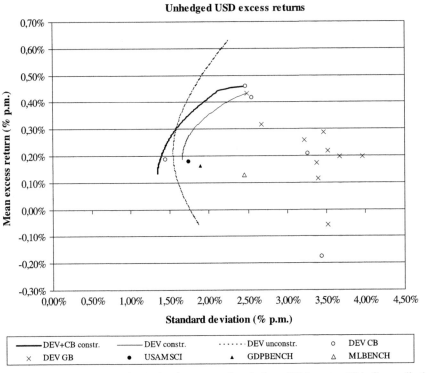

Figure 3. Diversification benefits of unhedged corporate bonds for a US investor. This figure displays the individual assets (developed country government bonds and corporate bonds), three benchmarks (USAMSCI, GDPBENCH, and MLBENCH), as well as three optimized frontiers: (1) the frontier optimized on the basis of all the developed country government bonds, allowing for short sales (the dotted line), (2) the same as before, but with a short sales constraint (the continuous thin line), and (3) the frontier when both developed market government bonds as well as corporate bonds are included as assets (the bold line). All returns are unhedged.

negative skewness, as the Sortino ratios are very similar, or in many cases in fact even higher, than Sharpe ratios.

Second, in order to gauge the leverage of possible positive outliers, especially in the emerging market bond series, we have re-estimated the essential results by truncating observations beyond two standard deviations in all bond series. We find that emerging market bonds strengthen rather than reduce their relative performance with this check, suggesting positive outliers are not a main cause of their success.[23]

6.2 Stability over time

While full scale conditional analysis is beyond the scope of this paper, we investigate stability over time by breaking up the sample period into the January 1997–December 2001 and the January 2002–May 2006 sub-periods. We find that rejections more often occur (i.e. significant diversification benefits are found) during the latter time period of 2002–May 2006. In fact, even unhedged for currency risk, emerging market bonds and corporate bonds offer significant diversification

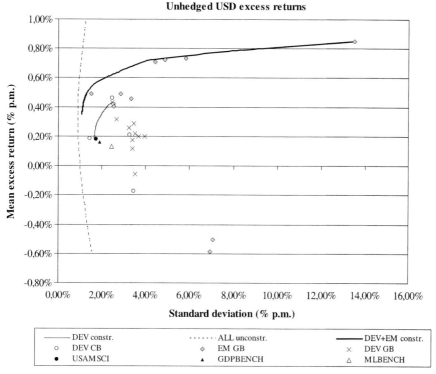

Figure 4. Diversification benefits of emerging market government bonds. This figure displays the individual assets (developed country government bonds and emerging market debt), three benchmarks (USAMSCI, GDPBENCH, and MLBENCH), as well as three optimized frontiers: (1) the frontier optimized on the basis of all the developed country government bonds, constraining for short sales (the thin continuous line), (2) the frontier when both developed market government bonds as well as emerging market debt are included as assets (the bold line), and (3) the unconstrained (i.e. short sales are allowed for) frontier of all these (the dotted line). The government bond returns are unhedged, whereas the emerging market debt is USD dominated.

benefits during this period. Thus, in general, the results do not seem to be driven by steadily increased correlations.

Hedged for currency risk, the rejection for corporate bonds stems from results for the sub-period of 1997–2001, with their Sharpe ratios improving over global Merrill Lynch Government bond and Global GDP weighted benchmarks. Since it is the full period intersection and spanning tests (Sharpe ratio improvements) that take the net effect of changing means, variances, and correlations into account simultaneously, our overall conclusion is still that currency hedging is beneficial for both corporate and emerging market bonds. Developed market government bonds never provide diversification benefits, not even in our sub-period analyses.

It is well known that unconditional mean–variance efficiency implies conditional mean–variance efficiency, while the converse is not true (Hansen and Richard 1987, 599). We restrict our analysis to the unconditional case, but note that for cases where we find no diversification benefits in the unconditional framework, we also would not find any in the conditional setting, because the unconditional case is a nested case of the corresponding conditional model (net of possible statistical power issues due to the larger problem of the conditional framework). Furthermore, our

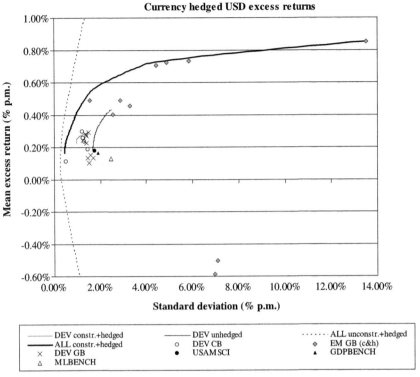

Figure 5. Effect of currency hedging on international bond diversification. This figure displays the individual assets (developed country government bonds, emerging market debt, and corporate bonds), the benchmarks (USAMSCI, GDPBENCH, and MLBENCH), as well as four optimized frontiers: (1) the frontier optimized on the basis of all the unhedged developed country government bonds (the thin continuous line), (2) the same as before, but hedged (the vague line), (3) the frontier when both unhedged developed market government bonds, unhedged corporate bonds, and USD dominated emerging market debt are included as assets (the bold line), and (4) the same as in (3) but hedged (the dotted line). Short sales are constrained for in each case.

results provide a meaningful benchmark case for more passively oriented bond investors, focusing on economizing on transaction costs. Attaining optimal portfolios resulting from a conditional framework would require costly frequent dynamic trading.

7. Summary and conclusion

Many investors, such as fixed income fund managers, dedicate their attention solely to the asset class of bonds. However, as compared with studies of international diversification benefits for stock portfolios, there are surprisingly few studies of fixed income diversification benefits only. This paper investigates bond diversification benefits and contributes to the earlier studies in several ways: we include several different categories of bonds such as government bonds, emerging market debt, and corporate bonds to assess broadly based international bond market diversification. Second, we assess diversification benefits using methods taking into account short sales constraints and currency hedging. Finally, a contribution of this study is consideration of investor's domicile of either USA, European (UK or Germany), or Japan.

We find increasing correlations within both government bonds as well as corporate bonds over time during our sample period of 1997–2006. The overall level of correlations between these asset classes is relatively high. Only emerging market debt differs by still offering lower correlations both within the asset class as well as with respect to other types of bonds.

First, we analyze international diversification benefits when short sales are allowed. Contrary to earlier studies, we do not find significant diversification benefits within the asset class of government bonds. This holds both for US investors as well as investors from UK, Germany, and Japan. Diversification benefits remain insignificant even if we assume perfect hedging of currency risk and are even smaller when constraining for short sales.

Diversification from government bonds into international corporate bonds also fails to offer significant improvements on a currency unhedged basis for both US and global investors. However, with currency risk removed, corporate bonds do offer significant diversification benefits for both US and non-US government bond investors, even in the case of constraining for short sales.

In contrast, diversification into emerging country debt clearly expands the frontier for investors for all developed country investors. Gauging by the Sharpe ratio improvements, these benefits are also economically quite substantial. Constraining the frontiers by disallowing negative positions dramatically reduces diversification benefits. However, USD denominated emerging country bonds do still offer some statistically significant diversification benefits. The best improvements occur with diversification into both currency hedged corporate bonds and emerging country bonds. However, the benefits have to be obtained by positions in high-risk emerging country bonds, given rejections only in our spanning tests.

The practical implications of our study are that there seems to be less arguments than earlier for extensive government bond diversification, even on a hedged basis. However, corporate bonds and especially emerging market debt seems to offer substantial Sharpe ratio improvements, even after comparison with estimates of transaction costs. These results maintain when downside risk only is considered.

Acknowledgements

Highly valuable comments by two anonymous referees are gratefully acknowledged. We are grateful for comments received at the Joint Finance Research Seminar in Helsinki, the conference on Asset Management and International Capital Markets in Frankfurt, the European Financial Management Association's Annual Meeting in Athens, and the Southern Finance Association's meeting in Florida.

Notes

1. Among the pioneers in this line are, e.g. Grauer and Hakansson (1987), Jorion (1989), and Odier and Solnik (1993). Although some analysis of bond portfolios is also included in such papers, the number of fixed income assets is typically low.
2. See, e.g. Dewachter and Maes (2001) studying US government bonds in UK portfolios, or Varotto (2003) studying various forms of diversification solely within the asset class of corporate bonds.
3. For equities, Chiou (2008) has shown that, as expected, developing countries benefit more from both regional and global diversification.
4. Interestingly, Hunter and Simon (2005) find that the mean and volatility spillovers are much weaker among major international bond markets than those between equity markets, and that the bond diversification benefits do not decrease during periods of high volatility or after extremely negative bond returns. These results are also supported by those of Polwitoon and Tawatnuntachai (2006) for international bond funds.
5. Later evidence for the euro-area by Baele et al (2004) indicates fully integrated money markets, a reasonably high integration in the government and corporate bond markets, whereas the credit market is the least integrated.
6. Fresh indirect international evidence on the existence of significant diversification benefits from foreign debt is offered by studies on home bias. Sørensen et al (2007) show that the home bias is actually smaller in the debt portfolios of

many countries than in the corresponding equity portfolios. If the markets behave rationally, this empirical evidence would indicate higher actual diversification benefits of foreign debt, and/or lower transaction costs or informational asymmetries for foreign debt securities. Evidence from fund managers' views by Lütje and Menkhoff (2007) also indicate lower informational advantages and less relative optimism for international bond managers, again supporting less home bias for bond investments. Polwitoon and Tawatnuntachai (2006) report international diversification benefits from global bond funds for a US investor.

7. Bekaert and Urias (1996) investigate small sample properties of mean-variance spanning test methods and find that regression-based methods appear to have better power than GMM-based alternatives.

8. The weights in the GDP index are annually rebalanced such that a particular year's weight is based on previous year's GDP converted to USD as reported by the International Monetary Fund (IMF) for each country in Group 1.

9. When analyzing diversification benefits from another investor perspective (UK, German, or Japanese investors), we correspondingly use the MSCI index for that country.

10. For example, the correlation between our choice for the US government bonds (the MSCI US 7–10 Year Sovereign Debt Index) and a potential alternative, the Merrill Lynch US Treasury 7–10 Year Index, is as high as 0.9958 during our study period.

11. Even if Merrill Lynch had the best geographical coverage and longest time-series of corporate indices, it was not possible to find exactly the same type of index for all countries. The indices for the USA and EMU are industrial/non-financial, while the indices for UK, Japan, and Canada are broad corporate indices. The ratings (Standard & Poor's) of the issuers included are BBB for the USA, A for Japan, and investment grade for the EMU, the UK, and Canada.

12. The return for the Lebanese index in November and December 1997 would else have been +151% and −148%, respectively. As we found no financial news to explain this, and as the price index data series in contrast to the total return index data used in our study did not exhibit the same extreme fluctuations, the November index value was smoothed. All other large returns were accompanied with either a simultaneous equity market return in the same direction, and/or a substantial weakening of the local currency.

13. Germany is the only country in our sample entering the Eurozone from the beginning of year 1999. For the German Government bond index in Group 1, we, therefore, use the DEM to USD currency rate up to the end of 1998, and the EUR to USD rate from 1999 onwards.

14. If Japan would be excluded, the average intra-group correlation for developed markets (Group 1) would rise to 0.71. For the group containing corporate bonds (Group 3), the exclusion of Japan would also increase the correlation to 0.71.

15. Regressing a time trend on the correlation for each group results in positive regression coefficients between 0.0040 and 0.0045. The coefficient estimates are statistically significant on at least a 5% level using heteroskedasticity and autocorrelation consistent standard errors (Andrews 1991).

16. The Japanese results can be available from the authors. Of these analyzed four perspectives, only one represents the Euro area. However, the integration of the money and bond markets in the Euro area has been fast, as reported in, e.g. Baele et al (2004). When we calculated the correlations between total return bond indices that could be found for our study period for both France, Italy, and Germany (Citigroup Government Bond Index, maturity 7–10 years), the correlation was 0.99 between the returns on German and French bonds during our study period, and 0.94 between each of these two against Italian bonds. Since also the currency risk for these countries is the same from 1999 onwards, and the money market benchmark (EURIBOR) is the same, we believe that our results for German investors can be rather representative also for the other Euro area investors.

17. In line with related literature we assume a perfect hedge. These calculations are detailed in the Appendix.

18. The main reason for reduced diversification benefits seems to lie in the more recent data used in our study. During our time period (from 1997 to May 2006), the average correlation between US and foreign government bonds was 0.67 (ranging from 0.62 to 0.82 for the different country pairs, see column 1 in Table 4, Panel A), while the correlations between the USA and three foreign bonds analyzed in the Hunter and Simon (2004) study (for the years from 1992 to September 2002) vary between 0.15 (USA–Japan) and 0.56 (USA–Germany) on a comparable basis. Given higher correlations in our study, there are less diversification benefits in the first place. Although the removal of exchange rate does lead to improvements in Sharpe ratios, these are not large enough to give significant diversification benefits.

19. While insignificant in the total sample period our sub-sample analysis shows that emerging market bonds do offer significant diversification benefits (intersection rejected) against all four benchmarks in the 2002–2006 sub-period. This is in line with the spanning test rejections and is due to the relatively higher Sharpe ratios in 2002–2006 compared with 1997–2001.

20. For example, considering the ML benchmark investor: He should abandon his benchmark offering a Sharpe ratio of 0.053 totally for a maximum Sharpe ratio ($0.053 + 0.313 = 0.366$, column 4 of Table 9) portfolio consisting of 74.6% India, 13.4% Mexico, 3.5% Russia, 5.6% Turkey, and 2.8% Venezuela. Note that currency risk and variability

in local short risk free rates used in computing excess returns can significantly alter return and risk levels compared with local raw returns in Table 3.

21. We also compared these benefits with measures for transaction costs in the bond and currencies markets. For example, Chordia, Sarkar, and Subrahmanyam (2005) report an average quoted spread of $0.022 per $100 par value for US government bonds around the start of our study period, indicating pretty low transaction costs. For corporate bonds, the bid-ask spreads are wider, e.g. Chen, Lesmond, and Wei (2007) report spreads of about 31 and 44 basis points (bp) for BBB bonds in maturity classes of 1–7 and 7–15 years. Developing market bonds exhibit a larger variation in spreads, ranging from low spreads of 5 bp for certain countries (e.g. Mexico, Chile, and Brazil) to 50–100 bp for Venezuela (Jeanneau and Tovar 2006). The hedging costs, in turn, can be approached by looking at bid-ask spreads on the currency markets. Hau, Killeen, and Moore (2002) report median post-euro spreads between 5 and 8 bp on the spot market for currencies such as USD, JPY, GBP, and EUR. The forward spreads are typically wider than the spot spreads. However, our analysis of these transaction costs as compared with the diversification benefits from our study indicate that there still would be sizable bond diversification benefits net of transaction costs.

22. During our study period, however, relatively few international bond market ETFs existed. According to Gebler and Tucker (2003), the first bond ETFs (both Canadian) were launched in 2000. In 2003, there were only four bond ETFs in the USA.

23. These normality-related robustness results are available from the authors upon request.

References

Andrews, D.W.K. 1991. Heteroskedasticity and autocorrelation consistent covariance matrix estimation. *Econometrica* 59: 817–58.

Baele, L., A. Ferrando, P. Hördahl, E. Krylova, and C. Monnet. 2004. Measuring European financial integration. *Oxford Review of Economic Policy* 20: 509–30.

Bekaert, G., and M.S. Urias. 1996. Diversification, integration, and emerging market closed-end funds. *Journal of Finance* 51: 835–70.

Burger, J.D., and F.E. Warnock. 2003. Diversification, original sin, and international bond portfolios. International Finance Discussion Papers 755, Board of Governors of the Federal Reserve System.

Cappiello, L., R.F. Engle, and K. Sheppard. 2006. Asymmetric dynamics in the correlations of global equity and bond returns. *Journal of Financial Econometrics* 4: 537–72.

Chen, Z., and P.J. Knez. 1996. Portfolio performance measurement: Theory and applications. *Review of Financial Studies* 9: 511–56.

Chen, L., D.A. Lesmond, and J. Wei. 2007. Corporate yield spreads and bond liquidity. *Journal of Finance* 62: 119–49.

Chiou, W.-J.P. 2008. Who benefits more from international diversification? *Journal of International Financial Markets, Institutions and Money* 18: 466–82.

Chordia, T., A. Sarkar, and A. Subrahmanyam. 2005. An empirical analysis of stock and bond market liquidity. *Review of Financial Studies* 18: 85–129.

Cifarelli, G., and G. Paladino. 2002. An empirical analysis of the co-movement among spreads on emerging-market debt. University of Florence Economics Working Paper 127.

Dahlquist, M., and P. Soderlind. 1999. Evaluating portfolio performance with stochastic discount factors. *Journal of Business* 72: 347–83.

De Roon, F.A., and T.E. Nijman. 2001. Testing for mean–variance spanning: A survey. *Journal of Empirical Finance* 8: 111–55.

De Roon, F.A., T.E. Nijman, and B.J.M. Werker. 2001. Testing for mean–variance spanning with short sales constraints and transaction costs: The case of emerging markets. *Journal of Finance* 56: 721–42.

De Santis, G. 1994. Asset pricing and portfolio diversification: Evidence from emerging financial markets. In *Investing in emerging markets*, ed. M. Howell. London, UK: Euromoney Books.

Dewachter, H., and K. Maes. 2001. An affine model for international bond markets. Working Paper, Catholic University of Leuven.

Eun, C.S., and B.G. Resnick. 1994. International diversification of investment portfolios: US and Japanese perspectives. *Management Science* 40: 140–61.

Gebler, A., and M. Tucker. 2003. Taking stock of bonds: ETFs reach the fixed income markets. Institutional Investor Investment Guide Series: Guide to Exchange-Traded Funds II, Fall 2003, 52–56.

Gibbons, M., S. Ross, and J. Shanken. 1989. A test of the efficiency of a given portfolio. *Econometrica* 57: 1121–52.

Glen, J., and P. Jorion. 1993. Currency hedging for international portfolios. *Journal of Finance* 48: 1865–86.

Grauer, R.R., and N.H. Hakansson. 1987. Gains from international diversification: 1968–85 returns on portfolios of stocks and bonds. *Journal of Finance* 42: 721–41.

Hansen, L.P., J. Heaton, and E.H.J. Luttmer. 1995. Econometric evaluation of asset pricing models. *Review of Financial Studies* 8: 237–74.

Hansen, L.P., and S.F. Richard. 1987. The role of conditioning information in deducting testable restrictions implied by dynamic asset pricing models. *Econometrica* 55, 587–613.

Harvey, C. 1995. Predictable risk and returns in emerging markets. *Review of Financial Studies* 8: 773–816.

Hau, H., W. Killeen, and M. Moore. 2002. The euro as an international currency: Explaining puzzling first evidence from the foreign exchange markets. *Journal of International Money and Finance* 21, 351–83.

Huberman, G., and S. Kandel. 1987. Mean–variance spanning. *Journal of Finance* 42: 873–88.

Hunter, D.M., and D.P. Simon. 2004. Benefits on international bond diversification. *Journal of Fixed Income* 13: 57–72.

Hunter, D.M., and D.P. Simon. 2005. A conditional assessment of the relationships between the major world bond markets. *European Financial Management* 11: 463–82.

Jeanneau, S., and C.E. Tovar. 2006. Domestic bond markets in Latin America: Achievements and challenges. *BIS Quarterly Review* 5: 51–64.

Jobson, J.D., and B.M. Korkie. 1989. A performance interpretation of multivariate tests of intersection, spanning and asset pricing. *Journal of Financial and Quantitative Analysis* 24: 185–204.

Jorion, P. 1989. Asset allocation with hedged and unhedged foreign stocks and bonds. *Journal of Portfolio Management* 15: 49–54.

Kodde, D. and F.C. Palm. 1986. Wald criteria for jointly testing equality and inequality restrictions. *Econometrica* 54: 1243–48.

Levich, R.M., and L.R. Thomas. 1993. Internationally diversified bond portfolios: The merits of active currency risk management. NBER Working Paper W4340.

Levy, H., and Z. Lerman. 1988. The benefits of international diversification in bonds. *Journal of Portfolio Management* 15: 49–54.

Lütje, T., and L. Menkhoff. 2007. What drives home bias? Evidence from fund managers' views. *International Journal of Finance and Economics* 12: 21–35.

Mauro, P., N. Sussman, and Y. Yafeh. 2002. Emerging market spreads: Then versus now. *Quarterly Journal of Economics* 117: 95–733.

Odier, P., and B. Solnik. 1993. Lessons from international asset allocation. *Financial Analysts Journal* 49: 63–77.

Polwitoon, S., and O. Tawatnuntachai. 2006. Diversification benefits and persistence of US-based global bond funds. *Journal of Banking and Finance* 30: 2767–86.

Solnik, B., C. Boucrelle, and Y. Le Fur. 1996. International market correlation and volatility. *Financial Analysts Journal* 52: 17–34.

Sørensen, B.E., Y.-T. Wu, O. Yosha, and Y. Zhu. 2007. Home bias and international risk sharing: Twin puzzles separated at birth. *Journal of International Money and Finance* 26: 587–605.

Tesar, L.L., and I.M. Werner. 1995. Home bias and high turnover. *Journal of International Money and Finance* 14: 467–92.

Varotto, S. 2003. Credit risk diversification: Evidence from the Eurobond market. Bank of England Working Paper 199, Bank of England.

Appendix. Currency hedging assumptions

Currency hedged monthly return of foreign country i investment measured from the point of view of a domestic investor (dom) is

$$R_{i,\text{dom}} = (1 + E[R_i])(1 + f_i) + (R_i - E[R_i])(1 + e_i) - 1$$

where R_i is the foreign market return in local currency, f_i the forward premium or discount of foreign currency against domestic currency, and e_i the exchange rate return.

We assume a 'perfect hedge' with $e_i = f_i$ (forward rates are unbiased forecasts of future spot rates) and $\text{cov}(R_i, f_i) = 0$ which allows simplification of hedged return to (approximately)

$$R_{i,\text{dom}} \approx R_i + f_i$$

Since covered interest rate parity states the forward premium or discount equals the (monthly) interest rate differential, $f_i = r_{\text{dom}} - r_i$, the currency hedged 'raw' return in domestic currency is

$$R_{i,\text{dom}} \approx R_i + r_{\text{dom}} - r_i$$

and are used in spanning tests with currency hedged returns.

Intersection tests utilize excess returns over domestic short-term interest rate whereby the currency hedged excess return is $R_{i,\text{dom}} \approx R_i + r_{\text{dom}} - r_i - r_{\text{dom}} \approx R_i - r_i$, or simply the foreign country excess return.

The performance of investment grade corporate bond funds: evidence from the European market

Leif Holger Dietze, Oliver Entrop and Marco Wilkens

Catholic University of Eichstätt-Ingolstadt, Ingolstadt, Germany

This paper examines the risk-adjusted performance of mutual funds offered in Germany which exclusively invest in the 'rather new' capital market segment of euro-denominated investment grade corporate bonds. The funds are evaluated employing a single-index model and several multi-index and asset-class-factor models. In contrast to earlier studies dealing with (government) bond funds, we account for the specific risk and return characteristics of investment grade corporate bonds and use both rating-based indices and maturity-based indices, respectively, in our multi-factor models. In line with earlier studies, we find evidence that corporate bond funds, on average, under-perform the benchmark portfolios. Moreover, there is not a single fund exhibiting a significantly positive performance. These results are robust to the different models. Finally, we examine the driving factors behind fund performance. As well as examining the influence of several fund characteristics, particularly fund age, asset value under management and management fee, we investigate the impact of investment style on the funds' risk-adjusted performance. We find indications that funds showing lower exposure to BBB-rated bonds, older funds, and funds charging lower fees attain higher risk-adjusted performance.

1. Introduction

The European corporate bond[1] market is a rapidly growing capital market sector which boasted a nominal value of approximately €1370 billion at the beginning of 2005 and growth rates of 16.8% in 2003 and 9.5% in 2004. The European Monetary Union in 1999 merged the formerly separate and comparatively small local markets for corporate bonds. Many European companies have started issuing bonds in order to benefit from the 'new opportunities' of this capital market segment. As a consequence, the European corporate bond market now attracts more diverse investor groups than it did 10 years ago. Another reason for this market's success among investors may be the fact that it achieved higher returns on average than both the euro-denominated government bond market and the European stock market over the recent period of 2000–05.

For private investors, given the highly asymmetrical distribution of corporate bond returns and the de facto existence of minimum investment amounts in this market, the most feasible way to take advantage of the risk and return characteristics of this sector is to invest in broadly diversified corporate bond mutual funds. However, a large number of mutual bond funds traditionally invest in government bonds or in a large variety of different bond types such as government, mortgage, corporate, foreign currency bonds, etc. In addition to these government or mixed bond funds, there is now a rapidly rising number of specialized mutual funds concentrating on the European corporate bond market which reflects their attractiveness for private investors. Surprisingly, to our knowledge, there is no published academic research dealing with the performance of these 'new' funds.

There are only a few studies on the performance of bond funds. Cornell and Green (1991) examine the performance of low-grade bond funds in the USA but their sample of funds serves as a proxy for the low-grade bond market, rather than for analyzing the performance of active fund management. Blake, Elton, and Gruber (1993) is the first major study to investigate the performance of bond funds in the USA. They apply single-index models (SIMs) and multi-index models (MIMs) and a multi-factor model similar to Sharpe (1988, 1992). In addition to their first study, Elton, Gruber, and Blake (1995) analyze the performance of US bond funds using APT-based MIMs. Kahn and Rudd (1995) measure performance employing an asset-class-factor model but their work focusses on performance persistence. Gallo, Lockwood, and Swanson (1997) and Detzler (1999) evaluate globally investing US-based bond funds using SIMs and MIMs. Ferson, Henry, and Kisgen (2006) are the first to apply conditional performance measures to the US government bond fund market using a stochastic discount factor approach. The Australian government bond fund market is examined by Gallagher and Jarnecic (2002) who apply conditional and unconditional factor models. None of these studies focuses on corporate bond funds.

The same holds for the very few studies of the European bond fund market. Maag and Zimmermann (2000) investigate the performance of German government bond funds using SIM and MIM and an asset-class-factor model. Silva, Cortez, and Armada (2003) analyze the bond fund market in Europe using conditional and unconditional factor models. They refer to a sample of bond funds for six European countries, but only the UK sample based in the non-euro zone explicitly contains a sub-sample that consists of funds that concentrate on corporate bonds.

Our study is the first to investigate a sample of mutual funds primarily investing in euro-denominated investment grade corporate bonds. We limit our analysis to investment grade corporate bond funds since, compared with the US, the European high-yield market is still poorly developed. Given their different focus, none of the studies mentioned above takes into account the specific risk profile of corporate bond funds that can be largely attributed to different rating classes. Hence, our paper also represents the first study to apply letter-rating-based indices, in addition to maturity-based indices, as factors that capture the risk and return characteristics of investment grade corporate bond funds in detail. In addition to investigating the fund performance itself, we analyze the relation between fund characteristics and performance. We examine the influence of the fund characteristics, chiefly management fee, fund size and age. Finally, we assess whether investment style is related to performance.

The paper is organized as follows. Section 2 outlines the research objectives and our hypotheses. The methodology is described in Section 3. Section 4 contains the data and specification of the models. The empirical results are discussed in Section 5.[2] Conclusions and implications are presented in Section 6.

2. Research objectives and hypotheses

The following investigation has been carried out to analyze the risk-adjusted performance of European corporate bond funds. For the US bond fund market, Blake, Elton, and Gruber (1993), Elton, Gruber, and Blake (1995), Kahn and Rudd (1995), Gallo, Lockwood, and Swanson (1997), Detzler (1999), and Ferson, Henry, and Kisgen (2006) report that fund managers under-perform or do not outperform passive benchmark portfolios. Gallagher and Jarnecic (2002) find significant under-performance in the Australian government bond mutual fund market. Analog results are found by Maag and Zimmermann (2000) and Silva, Cortez, and Armada (2003) for (government) bond mutual funds in Europe.

So far, most studies investigating the performance of actively managed bond mutual funds report under-performance or report non-superior performance. This result is robust to both the specific models and benchmark indices as well as the specific market under consideration. This indicates that the considered markets are at least so efficient that a possible out-performance (before costs) is outweighed by the cost of the funds.[3] Since we expect the same in the European corporate bond market, we hypothesize:

Hypothesis 1 (H1)   Funds under-perform passive benchmark portfolios, net of expenses.

In addition to the measurement of performance, a well-studied issue in the (government) bond fund market is the relation between expense ratios and performance. For the US market, Blake, Elton, and Gruber (1993) find that, for most of their fund subgroups and models, the expense ratios account for the major part of the under-performance. An analogous negative relation between the expense ratio and the performance is reported by Kahn and Rudd (1995). The findings of Blake, Elton, and Gruber (1993) imply that, on average, a percentage-point increase in expenses reduces performance by about one percentage-point. Detzler's (1999) results indicate an even more inverse relationship for the major part of her models, whereas Maag and Zimmermann (2000) find a less negative and not significant relation in the German government bond fund market. Since we expect the relationship between fees and performance to be similar in similar markets, we hypothesize for our bond fund sample:[4]

Hypothesis 2 (H2)   There is a negative relationship between the fund management fees and performance.

Another issue of interest is the relation between fund size and performance. Larger funds should achieve economies of scale that can be realized by spreading the fixed costs, e.g. reporting and marketing, over a larger amount of assets under management and by reducing variable costs, e.g. by efficiencies in security transactions and back-office functions (Collins and Mack 1997). Hence, they should operate at lower costs, as found by Malhotra and McLeod (1997) for US equity mutual funds. On the other hand, larger funds tend to have disadvantages in trading resulting from the price impact of purchasing or selling large amounts of securities when acting in comparatively non-liquid markets.

So far, the relation between fund size and performance has primarily been addressed by studies dealing with equity mutual funds, such as Grinblatt and Titman (1989). Based on US equity mutual fund data, they find an inverse relationship between fund size and performance when analyzing gross returns. In contrast, the performance based on net returns is unrelated to size. In a more recent study, Chen et al. (2004) find evidence that fund size erodes the performance of US equity mutual funds. This effect is more pronounced for small cap funds where it affects the performance significantly. This finding suggests that liquidity may be the driving factor reducing the performance of large-size funds in small markets, outweighing the possible advantage of a better cost structure.[5] As the corporate bond market in Europe is a small market, one might expect that the same holds for corporate bond funds. To test whether this is true, our third hypothesis is:

Hypothesis 3 (H3)   There is a negative relationship between the fund assets under management and performance.

In addition to a possible size effect, the performance may be related to fund age.[6] Malhotra and McLeod (1997) find that older US equity mutual funds tend to operate at lower cost.[7] If that were true for our sample and if H2 were valid, and assuming that lower costs result in lower fees, we would expect older funds to have higher risk-adjusted performance. Thus, we hypothesize for the European corporate bond fund market:

Hypothesis 4 (H4) There is a positive relationship between the fund age and performance.

Finally, performance could be related to investment style. The less developed (and efficient) a market is, the more rewarded research activities should be. As the BBB market is known to be less homogeneous and (in Europe) less developed than the higher rating classes, one could expect funds primarily investing in this segment to show higher risk-adjusted performance. Therefore, our last hypothesis for the European corporate bond fund market is as follows:

Hypothesis 5 (H5) There is a positive relationship between the engagement of a fund in BBB bonds and performance.

3. Models

As there is still no evidence on how to apply particular equilibrium models to fixed-income markets such as the corporate bond market, we follow the majority of the papers cited in Section 1 and employ SIMs and MIMs and asset-class-factor models to measure the risk-adjusted performance of the fund management.

In MIMs, the performance measure is the intercept in a regression of fund excess returns on benchmark excess returns, while the benchmark consists of different indices. The general form of the models is given by Blake, Elton, and Gruber 1993:

$$R'_{it} = \alpha_i + \sum_{j=1}^{K} \beta_{ij} I'_{jt} + \varepsilon'_{it}, \tag{1}$$

where R'_{it} is the 1-month excess return on fund i in month t, I'_{jt} the 1-month excess return on index j in month t, β_{ij} the sensitivity of fund i to index j, and ε'_{it} the residual for fund i in month t. α_i measures the risk-adjusted performance of fund i. K represents the number of indices which is simply one in the case of a SIM. Using discrete excess returns, the estimated sensitivities can be interpreted as weights in a passive portfolio, assuming the difference between 1 and the sum of βs is being invested in the risk-free asset. Therefore, excess returns of this benchmark portfolio represent the result of a passive strategy. The ordinary least squares (OLS) method selects βs and α in such a way that the risk of the resulting passive portfolio best mimics the risk of the examined fund.

The shortcoming of the model presented above is its failure to incorporate the restrictions facing the fund management. Negative βs would imply short positions in the corresponding indices, which is normally not allowed in fund management. A sum of the βs exceeding unity would imply a leverage of the fund which is generally not the case either. Both investment strategies, shorting and leverage, can be assumed to be even less feasible for an individual investor. To overcome these shortcomings, we additionally employ the constrained asset-class-factor model of Sharpe (1988, 1992):

$$R_{it} = \sum_{j=1}^{K+1} \beta_{ij} I_{jt} + \varepsilon_{it}, \tag{2}$$

where R_{it} is the 1-month return on fund i in month t, I_{jt} the 1-month return on index j in month t, and β_{ij} the sensitivity of fund i to index j. $I_{K+1,t}$ denotes the 1-month return of the risk-free asset class. ε_{it} is the residual for fund i in month t which accounts for a possible α of the fund, too. The aim is to find the best set of index exposures (βs) that conforms with fund restrictions (no leverage and no short sales). Following Sharpe (1987, 1988, 1992), we employ a quadratic optimization procedure that minimizes the variance of the residual. More specifically:

$$\min \ Var\left(R_i - \sum_{j=1}^{K+1} \beta_{ij} I_j\right) \quad \text{s.t.} \sum_{j=1}^{K+1} \beta_{ij} = 1 \text{ and } \beta_{ij} \geq 0, \quad \forall j = 1, \ldots, K+1. \tag{3}$$

Note that in order to keep the constraints simple, returns instead of excess returns are used. For that reason, the risk-free asset has to be included as a separate asset class. If the benchmark portfolio estimated by the unconstrained regression approach in a MIM does not imply a violation of fund constraints, i.e. if $\beta_{ij} \geq 0$ and sum of βs ≤ 1 holds in the MIM, the estimated weights of the benchmark indices of the corresponding asset-class-factor model are exactly the same.

In Sharpe's asset-class-factor model, the mean of the residuals is generally not equal to zero as the residuals still contain the α. Normally, having estimated the βs and, hence, determined the passive portfolio, performance in the sense of Sharpe (1992) is measured out-of-sample as the difference between fund return and return of the benchmark portfolio in the next month (selection return). In order to compare the performance based on the constrained model with that of the unconstrained model, we slightly modify the Sharpe procedure for the measurement of performance. We use our β estimates resulting from the return data of the whole observation period, not for determining the appropriate benchmark for the next month, but for the whole observation period. The risk-adjusted performance, α, is then measured in-sample as the difference between the average fund return and the average benchmark return, i.e. the average of the residuals.[8]

4. Data and model specification

We investigate the period from July 2000 to June 2005. The euro zone capital market in this period is characterized by, on average, declining government bond yields and a first declining and then rising equity market. However, the average return of the equity market over the whole sample period is negative.

In our analysis, we concentrate on those mutual funds primarily investing in euro-denominated investment grade corporate bonds that are offered in Germany, which is one of the largest markets for mutual funds in Europe. All fund data were provided by the German fund rating company Feri Trust according to their internal fund style classification as euro-denominated investment grade corporate bond funds. For each fund, we compared the style classification by Feri Trust with the portfolio classification provided in the latest available fund report.

To be included in our data sample, funds have to have a complete time-series history throughout the five-year period from July 2000 to June 2005 and more than €20 million assets under management, according to the latest available fund report. As reported by Feri Trust, only one fund with an inception date before July 2000 was liquidated during this time period. Hence, our later results should not be substantially affected by survivor-only conditioning, which can cause biased estimates of performance, i.e. survivorship bias in performance, and biased results concerning the relationship between performance and fund characteristics (Carhart et al. 2002). The resulting sample consists of 19 investment grade corporate bond funds. We examine monthly discrete total returns, net of management fees and other expenses, while load charges are not taken into account.

Table 1 shows major characteristics of the funds and descriptive statistics of their excess returns, where the excess return is calculated as the difference between fund return and the 1-month Euribor. The funds have an average age of 7.8 years, but most of them were founded in 1999 or 2000. The average asset value equals €356 million, five funds have an asset value of less than €100 million and one fund an asset value of more than €1000 million. The average mean monthly excess return of the funds is 0.263%. For most funds, the return distribution is slightly skewed to the left. Further, we find a kurtosis of less than 3 in most cases. Nevertheless, applying the Jarque–Bera test, we cannot reject the hypothesis of normal distribution except for two funds (Deka, HSBC Trinkaus).

As benchmark indices in our later regressions, we choose total return indices from the iBoxx € bond index family offered by International Index Company Ltd. Today, these indices are suitable to represent the euro-denominated investment grade corporate bond market. This is also reflected by the fact that banks start offering index-tracking exchange-traded funds based on iBoxx indices. The process of index construction and index calculation is transparent to a large extent, resulting in ex-ante information on all bonds constituting the indices and public availability of used bond prices and corresponding bond characteristics on a daily basis.[9]

Specifically, we use the total return iBoxx € Corporates index and its rating-specific and maturity-specific sub-indices. Thus, unlike the studies mentioned above, which typically apply just one overall investment grade index and (sometimes) one overall non-investment grade index to capture credit risk, we can have a closer look at the impact of credit quality within the investment grade corporate bond market. In the iBoxx € index family, there are four rating-specific indices (AAA, AA, A, BBB) that include (like the funds) financial and non-financial bonds with identical letter ratings, as well as five maturity-specific indices (1–3, 3–5, 5–7, 7–10, 10+ years) that include those bonds with similar (nominal) time to maturity.

In addition, we apply the total return iBoxx € Sovereigns index as a broad euro zone government bond index and the DJ Stoxx 600 performance index as a broad equity index. Apart from euro zone-based companies, the DJ Stoxx 600 also includes stocks of non-euro zone-based companies. However, we have also applied other (smaller) euro zone indices as well. As subsequent results do not change, we use the broad DJ Stoxx 600.

Table 2 presents the average Macaulay duration[10] of the bonds included in each index, the empirical duration of the indices and descriptive statistics for the monthly excess returns. The empirical duration is given by the negative of the slope that is obtained by regressing the index returns on the change of the 10-year German governmental spot rate. The mean excess returns of the BBB and the Sovereigns indices are striking. While one might expect the mean of the returns to increase with lower rating, i.e. with higher credit risk, this is not true of the mean of the BBB index (0.298%) which is lower than the AA (0.393%) and A (0.403%) means. This may be caused by the different durations of the indices, since a higher duration yields higher returns in general. Further, the returns of lower-rated bonds are generally more equity-linked than those of higher-rated bonds. Since we find a negative average excess return of the DJ Stoxx 600 (−0.460%) in our sample period, the comparatively low BBB mean return gains further plausibility. Furthermore, the mean and volatility of the Sovereigns index, consisting of government bonds, are higher than

Table 1. Fund characteristics and descriptive statistics for fund excess returns.

Fund	ISIN	Age	Asset value	Management fee per month (%)	Mean (%)	Volatility (%)	Skewness	Kurtosis	Jarque–Bera
ADIG	LU0011193892	16.74	127.00	0.067	0.277	0.736	0.054	2.379	0.992
Balzac	FR0000018483	5.64	99.89	0.042	0.272	0.769	−0.217	2.743	0.635
Bayern LB	LU0110699088	5.07	154.23	0.071	0.267	0.656	−0.121	3.259	0.313
CA	LU0119099819	6.02	717.03	0.067	0.311	0.783	−0.007	2.402	0.894
Capital Invest	AT0000859046	18.04	642.21	0.050	0.304	0.707	0.252	2.593	1.049
Deka	LU0112241566	5.16	693.60	0.071	0.181	0.917	−1.055	5.332	24.724***
dit	LU0079919162	7.83	220.40	0.083	0.276	0.759	0.169	2.187	1.936
Rothschild	LU0112663983	5.04	30.55	0.067	0.183	0.499	−0.079	2.511	0.660
Fortis	LU0083949205	7.39	800.01	0.063	0.288	0.744	−0.277	2.446	1.533
HSBC Trinkaus	DE0005152003	5.28	80.20	0.058	0.173	1.032	−1.246	8.048	79.231***
ING	LU0092545796	6.75	396.51	0.017	0.325	0.824	−0.430	2.846	1.907
KBC	LU0094437620	6.33	571.16	0.063	0.298	0.802	−0.331	2.683	1.343
LB	LU0783114985	11.12	40.90	0.042	0.180	0.635	−0.012	2.828	0.075
LODH	LU0095723387	6.40	304.37	0.063	0.306	0.734	−0.183	2.393	1.255
Pictet	LU0128470845	5.59	224.27	0.058	0.214	0.725	−0.205	2.573	0.874
Schroder	LU0113257694	5.00	281.50	0.083	0.246	0.755	−0.102	2.545	0.620
Spängler	AT0000768296	5.83	39.44	0.079	0.293	0.828	−0.028	2.528	0.566
UBAM	LU0095453105	6.31	253.67	0.079	0.298	0.826	−0.306	2.502	1.554
Uni	LU0045581039	12.25	1095.80	0.050	0.312	0.743	−0.016	2.734	0.179
Average		7.78	356.46	0.062	0.263	0.762	−0.218	3.028	6.334
Median		6.31	253.67	0.063	0.277	0.755	−0.121	2.573	0.992
Maximum		18.04	1095.80	0.083	0.325	1.032	0.252	8.048	79.231
Minimum		5.00	30.55	0.017	0.173	0.499	−1.246	2.187	0.075

This table reports main fund characteristics and descriptive statistics for monthly excess returns of funds over the period July 2000–June 2005. Age is given in years as of June 2005. The asset value under management is given in € million. Asset values and management fees were obtained from the funds' latest reports prior to June 2005. The excess return is calculated as the difference between the fund's discrete monthly total return and the 1-month Euribor. The last column shows the Jarque–Bera test for normality. *10% level. **5% level. ***1% level.

Table 2. Average duration and descriptive statistics for excess returns of the benchmark indices.

Index	ISIN	Average duration	Empirical duration	Mean (%)	Volatility (%)	Skewness	Kurtosis	Jarque–Bera
					Descriptive statistics of excess returns			
Corporates	DE0006301161	4.73	4.17	0.374	0.807	−0.224	2.476	1.188
Corporates AAA	DE0006304454	3.98	4.12	0.284	0.716	−0.290	2.728	1.027
Corporates AA	DE0006600083	5.33	5.39	0.393	0.916	−0.384	2.774	1.600
Corporates A	DE0006601024	4.95	4.54	0.403	0.845	−0.312	2.404	1.862
Corporates BBB	DE0006601362	4.15	3.13	0.298	1.000	−1.271	7.390	64.345***
Corporates 1–3	DE0006301187	1.94	1.76	0.177	0.402	−0.057	2.523	0.601
Corporates 3–5	DE0006301518	3.60	3.40	0.302	0.714	−0.226	2.560	0.996
Corporates 5–7	DE0006301534	5.16	4.94	0.411	0.943	−0.146	2.459	0.945
Corporates 7–10	DE0006301559	6.81	5.88	0.538	1.121	−0.209	2.576	0.886
Corporates 10+	DE0006301575	10.64	8.55	0.729	1.609	−0.194	2.879	0.412
Sovereigns	DE0009682831	5.54	5.40	0.340	0.911	−0.394	2.707	1.767
DJ Stoxx 600	EU0009658210	–	–	−0.460	4.971	−0.394	3.045	1.556
Average				0.316	1.246	−0.342	3.043	7.444
Median				0.357	0.914	−0.258	2.642	1.108
Maximum				0.729	4.971	−0.057	7.390	64.345
Minimum				−0.460	0.402	−1.271	2.404	0.412

This table reports the average Macaulay duration and the empirical duration of the benchmark indices and descriptive statistics for their monthly excess returns over the period July 2000–June 2005. The average Macaulay duration is the mean of the average Macaulay durations of the bonds included in each index as reported by International Index Company every month. We calculated the empirical duration by regressing the discrete monthly total returns of each index on the monthly change of the German governmental 10-year spot rate. It is given by the negative of the respective slope coefficient. The excess return is calculated as the difference between the fund's discrete monthly total return and the 1-month Euribor. The last column shows the Jarque–Bera test for normality.
*10% level. **5% level. ***1% level.

ROR

the respective values of the AAA index which could also be explained by the higher duration of the Sovereigns index.

To specify the SIM, we apply the iBoxx € Corporates as a broad index representing the whole market. Two types of multi-index- and asset-class-factor models are specified, the first one related to rating segments and the second one to maturity segments. The first type has four rating-based factors, the iBoxx € Corporates AAA, AA, A, and BBB, which represent all factors in the first MIM, called MIM-1. In the second and third MIM, MIM-2 and MIM-3, the iBoxx € Sovereigns index and the DJ Stoxx 600 are added. The latter also allows us to control for fund investments in non-investment grade bonds as well, since the stock market is well known to be more strongly correlated to the non-investment grade bond market than to the investment grade bond market (see Merton (1974) for theoretical and Cornell and Green (1991) for empirical evidence). The maturity-based model MIM-4 contains the five iBoxx € Corporates maturity indices. The DJ Stoxx 600 is added in the last model, called MIM-5. The five asset-class-factor models, ACFM-1 to ACFM-5, are specified in the same way as the MIMs, but the 1-month Euribor is added to represent the risk-free asset in each model. Table 3 provides a summary of our models.

Before presenting our empirical results, the (possible) problem of multicollinearity has to be addressed. Table 4 provides the correlations of the excess returns of the indices in our data sample. As expected, the AAA, AA, and A rating-specific indices and the Sovereigns index are highly correlated (above 0.9). From this strong dependence, it follows that the coefficients of these factors that are estimated later can be very sensitive to slight modifications of the data set. Therefore, in terms of style analysis, these coefficients need to be treated with caution. On the

Table 3. Specification of the MIMs and the asset-class-factor models.

MIM-1 (Rating)	MIM-2 (Rating + Sovereigns)	MIM-3 (Rating + Sovereigns + Stock)	MIM-4 (Maturity)	MIM-5 (Maturity + Stock)
Corporates AAA	Corporates AAA	Corporates AAA	Corporates 1–3	Corporates 1–3
Corporates AA	Corporates AA	Corporates AA	Corporates 3–5	Corporates 3–5
Corporates A	Corporates A	Corporates A	Corporates 5–7	Corporates 5–7
Corporates BBB	Corporates BBB	Corporates BBB	Corporates 7–10	Corporates 7–10
	Sovereigns	Sovereigns	Corporates 10+	Corporates 10+
		DJ Stoxx 600		DJ Stoxx 600
ACFM-1 (Rating)	ACFM-2 (Rating + Sovereigns)	ACFM-3 (Rating + Sovereigns + Stock)	ACFM-4 (Maturity)	ACFM-5 (Maturity + Stock)
Euribor	Euribor	Euribor	Euribor	Euribor
Corporates AAA	Corporates AAA	Corporates AAA	Corporates 1–3	Corporates 1–3
Corporates AA	Corporates AA	Corporates AA	Corporates 3–5	Corporates 3–5
Corporates A	Corporates A	Corporates A	Corporates 5–7	Corporates 5–7
Corporates BBB	Corporates BBB	Corporates BBB	Corporates 7–10	Corporates 7–10
	Sovereigns	Sovereigns	Corporates 10+	Corporates 10+
		DJ Stoxx 600		DJ Stoxx 600

This table reports the specification of the MIMs and the asset-class-factor models. For each model, the included factors are provided. Except for DJ Stoxx 600 and 1-month Euribor, the indices belong to the iBoxx € index family. The MIMs are based on the respective excess returns. The asset-class-factor models are based on the returns of the respective indices and the 1-month Euribor.

Table 4. Correlation between indices.

	AAA	AA	A	BBB	1–3	3–5	5–7	7–10	10+	Sovereigns	DJ Stoxx 600	Corporates
AAA	1.00											
AA	0.98	1.00										
A	0.91	0.95	1.00									
BBB	0.55	0.62	0.77	1.00								
1–3	0.80	0.81	0.88	0.78	1.00							
3–5	0.84	0.87	0.95	0.88	0.91	1.00						
5–7	0.88	0.92	0.97	0.80	0.89	0.95	1.00					
7–10	0.87	0.93	0.97	0.83	0.84	0.94	0.96	1.00				
10+	0.85	0.91	0.92	0.71	0.77	0.84	0.90	0.96	1.00			
Sovereigns	0.97	0.98	0.91	0.53	0.75	0.82	0.87	0.88	0.88	1.00		
DJ Stoxx 600	-0.49	-0.43	-0.29	0.11	-0.25	-0.18	-0.24	-0.20	-0.22	-0.47	1.00	
Corporates	0.88	0.92	0.98	0.85	0.90	0.98	0.98	0.99	0.93	0.87	-0.21	1.00

This table reports the correlations of the monthly excess returns of the respective indices over the period July 2000–June 2005. The excess return is calculated as the difference between the index's discrete monthly total return and the 1-month Euribor. Except for DJ Stoxx 600, the abbreviations refer to the respective indices of the iBoxx € index family.

other hand, the main focus of this paper is on the performance of the funds in comparison to a passive benchmark portfolio consisting of the indices. This performance is measured by the α, which is not in general affected by multicollinearity. The same observations hold for the maturity models. The only hypothesis in which we apply (a bit of) style analysis is hypothesis H5. Since we aim to regress the αs against the coefficients of the BBB index (as a measure of the BBB exposure of the funds) in Section 5.3, these coefficients must be reliable. The correlations of the BBB index to the other rating indices and the Sovereigns index are in a range from 0.77 (A) to 0.53 (Sovereigns). Moreover, we calculated the variance inflation factor (VIF) of the BBB index for each rating-based model. The VIF is smaller than 5 for all our models which means that multicollinearity should not be a statistical problem in our analysis (Kennedy 2003, 213).

5. Empirical results

5.1 *Performance*

In order to examine the risk-adjusted performance of the funds, we first apply the SIMs and the MIMs. We estimate the α and the βs of the funds by applying the OLS procedure. Significance tests are based on heteroscedasticity- and autocorrelation-adjusted covariance matrices according to Newey and West (1987). The αs and the average (adjusted) R^2 are summarized in Table 5 (Panel A). These adjusted R^2 are comparable to those reported, for instance, by Blake, Elton, and Gruber (1993) and Maag and Zimmermann (2000) for the US bond and the German government bond fund market, respectively. On the whole, the rating-based models provide a better fit than the maturity-based models.

Furthermore, a comparison of MIM-1 and MIM-2 shows that adding the iBoxx € Sovereigns index does not really improve the explanatory power of the models. The DJ Stoxx 600 does not add much explanatory power to the models either, which tells us that the funds do not exhibit a material equity exposure.[11] In addition, interpreting the stock index as a proxy for non-investment grade bonds, we can conclude that the funds in our sample do not participate significantly in the low-quality segment either. These results are in line with the fund policies, as we require the fund in our sample to invest primarily in high-quality corporate bonds.

The overall findings concerning the performance of our fund sample displayed in Table 5 support hypothesis H1. There are just two funds (Bayern LB, Capital Invest) that have a positive α. In contrast to this, 17 funds show a negative α. Depending on the model, we have statistical significance at the 10% level for 9 to 12 funds with negative αs.[12] The sign and significance of the αs are quite robust to different models. The average α of the fund sample (-0.051% per month) is slightly less negative than its average management fee (0.062% per month; Table 1).

Table 5 (Panel A) also provides the corresponding results for the asset-class-factor models. Again, there are only the same two funds (Bayern LB, Capital Invest) showing an average positive α. In contrast, again 17 funds have a negative α on average. For significance tests in the asset-class-factor models, we apply the method of Kim, White, and Stone (2005) and use Monte Carlo simulation for deriving the distributions of αs and β coefficients. Following Kim, White, and Stone (2005), we set the pretest level at 50% and the number of Monte Carlo draws at 5000. Depending on the model, we have statistical significance at the 10% level for 9 to 10 funds with negative αs. Again, sign and significance of the αs are quite robust to different models. The average α of the fund sample is -0.047% per month. The differences between the αs of the MIMs and the αs of the respective asset-class-factor models are small in comparison to the α size. However, the average fund αs

Table 5. Alphas.

	SIM and MIM							Asset-class-factor models					
	SIM	MIM-1	MIM-2	MIM-3	MIM-4	MIM-5	Average	ACFM-1	ACFM-2	ACFM-3	ACFM-4	ACFM-5	Average
Panel A: Single funds													
ADIG	-0.038	-0.011	-0.011	-0.011	-0.027	-0.026	-0.021	-0.011	-0.011	-0.011	-0.028	-0.028	-0.018
Balzac	-0.072**	-0.027	-0.020	-0.018	-0.065***	-0.064***	-0.044	-0.027*	-0.023	-0.023	-0.064**	-0.064***	-0.040
Bayern LB	-0.012	0.002	0.013	0.012	0.004	0.003	0.004	0.002	0.009	0.008	0.000	0.000	0.004
CA	-0.027	-0.001	-0.016	-0.016	-0.016	-0.016	-0.015	-0.001	-0.001	-0.001	-0.016	-0.016	-0.007
Capital Invest	0.020	0.040	0.044	0.044	0.006	0.006	0.027	0.040	0.044	0.044	0.012	0.012	0.031
Deka	-0.188**	-0.165**	-0.189***	-0.191***	-0.178**	-0.180**	-0.182	-0.156***	-0.156***	-0.162***	-0.169**	-0.166**	-0.162
dit	-0.041	-0.057*	-0.051*	-0.057**	-0.026	-0.026	-0.043	-0.051	-0.051	-0.056*	-0.032	-0.032	-0.045
Rothschild	-0.030	-0.032*	-0.029*	-0.029*	-0.022	-0.021	-0.027	-0.030	-0.030	-0.030	-0.021	-0.021	-0.027
Fortis	-0.043*	-0.033*	-0.030	-0.031*	-0.047*	-0.045**	-0.038	-0.033*	-0.030*	-0.031*	-0.047**	-0.047**	-0.038
HSBC Trinkaus	-0.181*	-0.121*	-0.120**	-0.126**	-0.175*	-0.181*	-0.151	-0.109*	-0.109**	-0.123*	-0.162*	-0.156**	-0.132
ING	-0.032	-0.048*	-0.053*	-0.053*	-0.022	-0.021	-0.038	-0.044	-0.044*	-0.045	-0.031	-0.031	-0.039
KBC	-0.065***	-0.043**	-0.052**	-0.054***	-0.066***	-0.066***	-0.057	-0.043**	-0.043**	-0.045**	-0.066**	-0.066**	-0.052
LB	-0.067	-0.088***	-0.081***	-0.081***	-0.052	-0.049*	-0.070	-0.074***	-0.067**	-0.067**	-0.059	-0.059	-0.065
LODH	-0.009	0.000	-0.004	-0.007	-0.002	-0.001	-0.004	0.000	0.000	-0.003	-0.004	-0.004	-0.002
Pictet	-0.093***	-0.095***	-0.065**	-0.065**	-0.089***	-0.086***	-0.082	-0.095***	-0.075***	-0.075***	-0.092**	-0.092***	-0.085
Schroder	-0.084**	-0.073***	-0.074***	-0.076***	-0.088***	-0.087***	-0.080	-0.073***	-0.073***	-0.075***	-0.088***	-0.088***	-0.079
Spängler	-0.067**	-0.069**	-0.079**	-0.084***	-0.056**	-0.058**	-0.069	-0.058*	-0.058	-0.069*	-0.056*	-0.058*	-0.060
UBAM	-0.064*	-0.059***	-0.048***	-0.049***	-0.068*	-0.065**	-0.059	-0.059***	-0.048***	-0.049***	-0.068**	-0.068*	-0.058
Uni	-0.014	-0.009	-0.019	-0.020	-0.014	-0.014	-0.015	-0.007	-0.007	-0.008	-0.014	-0.014	-0.010
Average	-0.058	-0.047	-0.046	-0.048	-0.053	-0.052	-0.051	-0.044	-0.041	-0.043	-0.053	-0.052	-0.047
Median	-0.043	-0.043	-0.048	-0.049	-0.047	-0.045	-0.043	-0.044	-0.043	-0.045	-0.047	-0.047	-0.040
Maximum	0.020	0.040	0.044	0.044	0.006	0.006	0.027	0.040	0.044	0.044	0.012	0.012	0.031
Minimum	-0.188	-0.165	-0.189	-0.191	-0.178	-0.181	-0.182	-0.156	-0.156	-0.162	-0.169	-0.166	-0.162
Positive αs (*)	1 (0)	3 (0)	2 (0)	2 (0)	2 (0)	2 (0)	2	3 (0)	3 (0)	2 (0)	1 (0)	2 (0)	2
Negative αs (*)	18 (9)	16 (12)	17 (11)	17 (12)	17 (9)	17 (10)	17	16 (10)	16 (10)	17 (10)	18 (9)	17 (9)	17
Average adjusted R^2	0.836	0.868	0.869	0.869	0.853	0.864		0.862	0.861	0.861	0.845	0.849	

(Continued)

Table 5. Continued

	SIM and MIM							Asset-class-factor models					
	SIM	MIM-1	MIM-2	MIM-3	MIM-4	MIM-5	Average	ACFM-1	ACFM-2	ACFM-3	ACFM-4	ACFM-5	Average
Panel B: Portfolios of funds													
Equally weighted	−0.058***	−0.047***	−0.046***	−0.048***	−0.053***	−0.053***	−0.051	−0.047***	−0.046***	−0.048***	−0.053***	−0.053***	−0.049
Size-weighted	−0.051***	−0.038**	−0.043**	−0.044**	−0.048***	−0.048***	−0.045	−0.038***	−0.038*	−0.040**	−0.048***	−0.048***	−0.043
Average adjusted R^2	0.959	0.951	0.951	0.951	0.962	0.961		0.950	0.949	0.949	0.961	0.960	

Panel A reports monthly αs (in percent) for the SIM, the MIM and the asset-class-factor models specified in Table 3 for each fund i. The sample period is July 2000–June 2005. The index models are given by $R'_{it} = \alpha'_i + \sum_{j=1}^{k} \beta_{ij} I'_{jt} + \varepsilon'_{jt}$, where R'_{it} and I'_{jt} denote the excess returns of the fund and the indices, respectively. The excess returns are calculated as the difference between the fund's and the indices' discrete monthly total returns and the 1-month Euribor. The model parameters are estimated via OLS. Significance tests are based on heteroscedasticity- and autocorrelation-adjusted covariance matrices according to Newey and West (1987). The asset-class-factor models are estimated by minimizing $\text{Var}(R_i - \sum_{j=1}^{k+1} \beta_{ij} I_j)$, where R_i and I_j denote the discrete monthly total returns of the fund and the indices, respectively, and the 1-month Euribor (I_{K+1}). The βs are restricted to $\sum_{j=1}^{k+1} \beta_{ij} = 1$ and $\beta_{ij} \geq 0$. The αs are given by the difference between the average fund return and the average benchmark return. Significance tests are based on 5000 simulations and a pre-test level of 50% according to Kim, White, and Stone (2005). The second and third to last row of Panel A show the number of positive and negative αs, respectively, for each model. The number in brackets gives the number of significant αs at the 10% level where the null hypothesis is $H_0 : \alpha \geq 0$. The last row of Panel A shows the average adjusted R^2 for each model. Panel B analogously shows monthly αs (in percent) and average adjusted R^2 for equally weighted and size-weighted portfolios of the funds in our sample.
*10% level. **5% level. ***1% level.

obtained by the rating-based asset-class-factor models tend to be slightly higher than the αs of the respective MIMs. In contrast, average αs of the maturity-based models remain almost unchanged. Hence, our overall findings are almost identical to the results we reported for the MIMs.

We find analog results considering portfolios of funds instead of single funds. Table 5 (Panel B) shows the results for an equally weighted and a size-weighted portfolio, respectively. Naturally, the adjusted R^2 are higher than in the single-fund case as idiosyncratic risk is diversified in the portfolios. All αs are negative and significant, which again shows that funds are not able to beat the market on average.

Summarizing our results, we can conclude that hypothesis H1 holds for most funds. This result is robust against the type of model and the model specification. However, absolute average αs are a bit smaller than average management fees. Since total costs (expense ratios) exceed management fees, this indicates that many funds are able to beat the benchmarks ex-expenses. However, on average, this out-performance is not large enough to cover the costs incurred by active fund management.

5.2 *Ranking*

While the risk-adjusted performance measure obtained from single- or multi-factor models is a 'reliable' measure when a fund is compared with a passive benchmark, α-rankings of funds have to be treated with caution. It is well known that the α is not invariant to changes in portfolio leverage with the risk-free asset. In fact, a ranking of funds based on this measure can be 'leverage biased' (Modigliani and Pogue 1974). Hence α-based rankings can be biased if the funds have differing systematic risk (e.g. due to differing cash holdings). A measure that is closely related to the α but leverage bias-free in the single-factor case is the Treynor ratio (Treynor 1966). In the following, we will apply its generalization by Hübner (2005) to the multi-factor case in order to analyze the effect of leverage bias on rankings in our data sample. The recently published leverage bias-free generalized Treynor ratio (GTR) is defined as the α of fund i per unit of premium-weighted average systematic risk, normalized by the market premium-weighted average systematic risk. Technically, it is defined by

$$GTR_i = \frac{\alpha_i}{\sum_{j=1}^{K} w_j \beta_{ij}} \sum_{j=1}^{K} w_j \beta_{mj} \text{ with } w_j = \frac{\overline{I'_j}}{\sum_{j=1}^{K} \overline{I'_j}}, \qquad (4)$$

where (again) α_i denotes the α of fund i obtained by the selected multi-index or asset-class-factor model and β_{ij} is the corresponding sensitivity of fund i to index j. β_{mj} is the sensitivity of an arbitrarily chosen benchmark portfolio m to index j. $\overline{I'_j}$ represents the average monthly excess return of index j and K the number of indices of the applied model, not including the risk-free asset class. The GTR-ranking of funds is independent of the concrete benchmark portfolio (see Hübner (2005) for details).

As a benchmark portfolio for each model, we choose an equally weighted portfolio of the included indices. For each fund and model, we calculate the GTR and rank the funds. To compare this GTR-ranking with the α-based ranking, we calculate Spearman's rank correlation coefficient between the two rankings. It varies between 0.96 and 0.99 for the MIMs and between 0.97 and 0.99 for the asset-class-factor models. This implies that a possible leverage bias of the αs does not substantially affect α-based rankings in our sample.

5.3 *Performance and fund characteristics*

In order to examine the relationship between fund performance and the fund characteristics management fee, the fund's size, its age, and its BBB exposure, we run a regression of the fund αs on the fund characteristics separately for each model and each characteristic.[13] Table 6 summarizes the results.

Based on several studies dealing with similar fund markets, we hypothesized in Section 2 that higher fees are associated with poorer performance (H2). The sign of the coefficients of the management fee (slope) is negative across all models, and, hence, in line with our hypothesis. The average slope of -0.464 is similar to the results of Maag and Zimmermann (2000) but explicitly less negative than the results reported by Blake, Elton, and Gruber (1993) and Detzler (1999). However, the relationship is not significant in our sample.

Moreover, in Section 2, we focus on how performance varies with the size of a corporate bond fund. The slope of the respective regressions is positive for each model. This sign might suggest that, in our data sample, large funds may realize economies of scale that outweigh the possible disadvantages of large mutual funds in trading in comparatively non-liquid markets. However, as the coefficient is not significant (negative or positive), a detailed analysis of the relation between performance and fund size in the European corporate bond market must be left for future research when more fund data are available.

Our next hypothesis H4 deals with the relationship between fund performance and fund age. The positive slopes are statistically significant at the 5% level which supports our hypothesis that older corporate bond funds tend to have higher αs. This relationship could be caused by a better cost structure of older funds since they can be assumed to achieve greater operating efficiency than newly established funds.

Finally, our last hypothesis H5 refers to the investment policy of the funds. We expected that funds with a higher exposure to BBB-rated bonds would have higher αs. Our first three MIMs (MIM-1 to MIM-3) and our first three asset-class-factor models (ACFM-1 to ACFM-3) estimated the (average) weights of the iBoxx € BBB Corporates index in the appropriate passive benchmark portfolios. In order to assess our hypothesis, we regress fund αs on the BBB βs in the corresponding models. All slope coefficients exhibit negative signs and, naturally, the null hypotheses of negative slopes cannot be rejected. Note that the opposite null hypothesis of positive signs can be rejected for the asset-class-factor models at the 10% level. Owing to the assumed investment restrictions, the asset-class-factor models should be more realistic when dealing with investment policy. Based on the regression results, we reject our hypothesis H5, concluding that the fund engagement in BBB bonds was not rewarded by a better, but by a poorer performance. Of course, this result is not caused by the comparatively low mean return of the iBoxx € Corporates BBB index in our sample (reported in Section 4), as this effect is already accounted for by the benchmark portfolio.

6. Summary and conclusions

This paper represents the first performance study of the 'new' segment of actively managed funds that are primarily investing in the euro-denominated investment grade corporate bond market. We followed earlier studies dealing with other bond fund markets and applied several multi-index and asset-class-factor models to measure risk-adjusted performance. Specifically, in order to take into account the particular characteristics of the market in question, we employed several rating-based and maturity-based models. All our results turned out to be robust across the different models.

Table 6. α regressed on fund characteristics.

Model	Fee Slope	Fee p-value H_0: Slope ≥ 0	Fee R^2	Asset value Slope	Asset value p-value H_0: Slope ≥ 0	Asset value R^2	Fund age Slope	Fund age p-value H_0: Slope ≤ 0	Fund age R^2	BBB exposure Slope	BBB exposure p-value H_0: Slope ≤ 0	BBB exposure R^2
SIM	−0.485	0.268	0.023	2.96E-07	0.760	0.030	6.00E-05**	0.028	0.198	–	–	–
MIM-1	−0.417	0.282	0.020	3.34E-07	0.808	0.045	5.79E-05***	0.022	0.218	−0.00055	0.825	0.051
MIM-2	−0.450	0.276	0.021	1.54E-07	0.647	0.009	5.88E-05***	0.026	0.203	−0.00061	0.830	0.054
MIM-3	−0.515	0.252	0.027	1.66E-07	0.656	0.010	6.00E-05***	0.026	0.204	−0.00051	0.781	0.036
MIM-4	−0.481	0.267	0.023	1.76E-07	0.664	0.011	5.37E-05***	0.044	0.162	–	–	–
MIM-5	−0.503	0.262	0.024	1.78E-07	0.663	0.011	5.47E-05***	0.044	0.162	–	–	–
ACFM-1	−0.439	0.259	0.025	2.88E-07	0.787	0.038	5.70E-05***	0.017	0.238	−0.00071	0.905	0.099
ACFM-2	−0.455	0.249	0.028	2.52E-07	0.759	0.030	5.63E-05***	0.017	0.237	−0.00081	0.933	0.127
ACFM-3	−0.518	0.230	0.033	2.79E-07	0.772	0.033	5.91E-05***	0.017	0.239	−0.00085	0.915	0.108
ACFM-4	−0.415	0.285	0.019	2.05E-07	0.700	0.016	5.38E-05***	0.034	0.183	–	–	–
ACFM-5	−0.423	0.276	0.021	2.04E-07	0.703	0.017	5.31E-05***	0.032	0.188	–	–	–
Average	−0.464	0.264	0.024	2.30E-07	0.720	0.023	5.68E-05	0.028	0.203	−0.00067	0.865	0.079

This table reports the results of the regression α = intercept + Slope* fund characteristic + error. We run this regression for each model and each fund characteristic separately. The abbreviations of the models correspond to the model specifications in Table 3. The monthly αs are given in Table 5. Fund characteristics are given by the management fee per month, the asset value in € million, fund age in years as of June 2005 (Table 1), and the BBB exposure measured by the respective β coefficient of the iBoxx € Corporates BBB. Significance tests are based on t-statistics.
*10% level. **5% level. ***1% level.

We found evidence that most funds under-performed relevant benchmark portfolios consisting of several indices. Across all models, there is not a single fund showing significant positive performance. These general findings for corporate bond funds are consistent with the results of earlier studies focusing on the performance of mutual funds investing in (government) bonds; for instance Blake, Elton, and Gruber (1993) for the US and Maag and Zimmermann (2000) for the German market. Additionally, the application of the GTR showed that an α-based ranking for our data sample would not substantially be affected by a possible leverage bias.

Recent studies on bond funds report that fund performance obtained from conditional models is substantially comparable to results obtained from unconditional models (Silva, Cortez, and Armada 2003, Ferson, Henry, and Kisgen 2006). It is a challenging topic for future research to analyze whether analogous conclusions hold for the type of funds we look at here. However, more research about determinants and predictability of corporate bond spreads in Europe must first be carried out.

The average under-performance of the funds in our data sample seems to be primarily due to management fees. The average size of the α (of the under-performance) is smaller than the average management fee. Since total expense ratios of the funds exceed management fees, this indicates that many fund managers would be able to beat the benchmark portfolios if gross returns were considered.

In addition to the impact of management fees, we analyzed the influence of fund age, fund size, and the BBB fraction in the funds' passive benchmark portfolios, i.e. their BBB exposure, on performance. Our analysis suggests that investors willing to invest in actively managed European corporate bond funds should select older funds with low management fees and low exposure to BBB-rated bonds.

Acknowledgements

Financial support by Konrad-Adenauer-Stiftung is gratefully acknowledged by Leif Holger Dietze. Parts of this research were done while Oliver Entrop was visiting the School of Banking and Finance, University of New South Wales. He thanks Terry Walter and the academic and administrative staff for their hospitality and support. Parts of this research were done while Marco Wilkens was visiting the Australian Graduate School of Management, University of New South Wales. He thanks Timothy Devinney and the academic and administrative staff for their hospitality and support.

We thank Feri Trust for providing data and Anette Dyroff at Feri Trust for assistance with their database. We are grateful to participations at the finance seminar at University of Hohenheim, the 18th Australasian Banking and Finance Conference 2005, Sydney, the French Finance Association International Meeting 2005, Paris, the 2006 Financial Management Association European Conference, Stockholm, the European Financial Management Association 2006 Conference, Madrid, the 4th Portuguese Finance Network International Conference 2006, Porto, and, especially, to Jonathan Fletcher, Frank K. Reilly, James D. Rosenfeld, Gilles San Filippo, and Hendrik Scholz for helpful comments and suggestions on an earlier draft of this paper. Furthermore, we thank two anonymous referees and Chris Adcock, the editor, for their helpful comments.

Notes

1. We refer to corporate bonds as both financials and non-financials.
2. To save space, we omit reporting certain details (such as the β coefficients from the regressions) and several additional analyses (such as average selection returns) we carried out. Details are available from the corresponding author upon request.
3. Many studies such as Blake, Elton, and Gruber (1993), Maag and Zimmermann (2000) and Ferson, Henry, and Kisgen (2006) report on average neutral before-cost performance.
4. Note that there is a difference between expense ratios in the studies mentioned above and the management fees we use, as the former contain, in addition to management fees, other directly chargeable operating costs that we do not have information on. However, management fees can be assumed to account for the major part of the total costs.

5. Moreover, another reason may be organizational diseconomies based on hierarchy costs (Chen et al. 2004). For a detailed analysis of all these so-called diseconomies of scale, see Perold and Salomon (1991).
6. See, e.g. Sawicki and Finn (2002) for an overview and an investigation of effects due to size and age in the smart money context.
7. For US bond mutual funds Malhotra and McLeod (1997) report an inverse, albeit not significant, effect.
8. Following Sharpe (1992), we also calculated the average selection return for each fund out-of-sample using a moving time window. As this does not change our findings, we do not report the results.
9. The indices are capitalization-weighted and rebalanced monthly. In order to be included, corporate bonds must fulfill certain criteria. For example, they have to be denominated in euros or pre-euro currencies with an outstanding amount of not less than €500 million; however, the issuer's nationality is not relevant. See International Index Company Ltd. (2004) for details.
10. It is well known that Macaulay duration has to be interpreted with caution when bonds with embedded options such as callable bonds are considered (Fabozzi 2000, 360–61), where effective duration is more suitable. However, these bonds are less common in Europe than in the US. For example, callable bonds typically represent only a minor part (about 20% in June 2006) of the Corporates BBB index as reported by International Index Company Ltd.
11. This is also supported by Wald tests of the β coefficients: in MIM-2, the coefficient of the Sovereigns index is significant at 10% level for only four funds; in MIM-3, the coefficients of the Sovereigns and the Stoxx index are jointly significant for only five funds; in MIM-5, the Stoxx index is significant for 10 funds. The latter is plausible: as the maturity-based indices are dominated by high-quality bonds, the Stoxx index can be expected to serve as a proxy for lower quality bonds (BBB). None of these coefficients are significant when portfolios of funds, described below, are considered. Analog results hold if t-tests of the coefficients are carried out.
12. None of the funds has a significantly positive α when we change the null hypothesis from $\alpha \geq 0$ to $\alpha \leq 0$. The same holds for the asset-class-factor models.
13. We also ran analogous regressions on the transformed variables log(size) and log(age). The results are qualitatively the same.

References

Blake, C.R., E.J. Elton, and M.J. Gruber. 1993. The performance of bond mutual funds. *Journal of Business* 66: 371–403.

Carhart, M.M., J.N. Carpenter, A.W. Lynch, and D.K. Musto. 2002. Mutual fund survivorship. *Review of Financial Studies* 15: 1439–63.

Chen, J., H. Hong, M. Huang, and J.D. Kubik. 2004. Does fund size erode mutual fund performance? The role of liquidity and organization. *American Economic Review* 94: 1276–302.

Collins, S., and P. Mack. 1997. The optimal amount of assets under management in the mutual fund industry. *Financial Analysts Journal* 53, no. 5: 67–73.

Cornell, B., and K. Green. 1991. The investment performance of low-grade bond funds. *Journal of Finance* 46: 29–48.

Detzler, M.L. 1999. The performance of global bond mutual funds. *Journal of Banking and Finance* 23: 1195–217.

Elton, E.J., M.J. Gruber, and C.R. Blake. 1995. Fundamental economic variables, expected returns, and bond fund performance. *Journal of Finance* 50: 1229–56.

Fabozzi, F.J. 2000. *Bond markets, analysis and strategies.* Upper Saddle River: Prentice Hall.

Ferson, W., T.R. Henry, and D.J. Kisgen. 2006. Evaluating government bond fund performance with stochastic discount factors. *Review of Financial Studies* 19: 423–55.

Gallagher, D.R., and E. Jarnecic. 2002. The performance of active Australian bond funds. *Australian Journal of Management* 27: 163–85.

Gallo, J.G., L.J. Lockwood, and P.E. Swanson. 1997. The performance of international bond funds. *International Review of Economics and Finance* 6: 17–35.

Grinblatt, M., and S. Titman. 1989. Mutual fund performance: an analysis of quarterly portfolio holdings. *Journal of Business* 62: 393–416.

Hübner, G. 2005. The generalized Treynor ratio. *Review of Finance* 9: 415–35.

International Index Company Ltd. 2004. Guide to the iBoxx € benchmark indices, Version 3.1, December 2004.

Kahn, R.N., and A. Rudd. 1995. Does historical performance predict future performance? *Financial Analysts Journal* 51, no. 6: 43–52.

Kennedy, P. 2003. *A guide to econometrics.* Malden: Blackwell.

Kim, T., H. White, and D. Stone. 2005. Asymptotic and Bayesian confidence intervals for Sharpe-style weights. *Journal of Financial Econometrics* 3: 315–43.

Maag, F., and H. Zimmermann. 2000. On benchmarks and the performance of DEM bond mutual funds. *Journal of Fixed Income* 10: 31–45.

Malhotra, D.K., and R.W. McLeod. 1997. An empirical analysis of mutual fund expenses. *Journal of Financial Research* 20: 175–90.

Merton, R.C. 1974. On the pricing of corporate debt: The risk structure of interest rates. *Journal of Finance* 29: 449–70.

Modigliani, F., and G.A. Pogue. 1974. An introduction to risk and return – II. *Financial Analysts Journal* 30, no. 3: 69–86.

Newey, W., and K. West. 1987. A simple positive semi-definite, heteroskedasticity and autocorrelation consistent covariance matrix. *Econometrica* 55: 703–8.

Perold, A.F., and R.S. Salomon. 1991. The right amount of assets under management. *Financial Analysts Journal* 47, no. 3: 31–9.

Sawicki, J., and F. Finn. 2002. Smart money and small funds. *Journal of Business Finance and Accounting* 29: 825–46.

Sharpe, W.F. 1987. An algorithm for portfolio improvement. In *Advances in mathematical programming and financial planning,* eds. K.D. Lawrence, J.B. Guerard, and G.D. Reeves, 155–70. Greenwich: JAI Press.

Sharpe, W.F. 1988. Determining a fund's effective asset mix. *Investment Management Review* November/December: 59–69.

Sharpe, W.F. 1992. Asset allocation: Management style and performance measurement. *Journal of Portfolio Management* 18: 7–19.

Silva, F., M. Cortez, and M.R. Armada. 2003. Conditioning information and European bond fund performance. *European Financial Management* 9: 201–30.

Treynor, J.L. 1966. How to rate management investment funds. *Harvard Business Review* 43: 63–75.

Index

Note:
Page numbers in **bold** type refer to figures
Page numbers in *italic* type refer to tables